BRICKTOP'S PARIS

BRICKTOP'S PARIS

African American Women in Paris between the Two World Wars

T. DENEAN SHARPLEY-WHITING

SUNY PRESS

Published by
STATE UNIVERSITY OF NEW YORK PRESS, ALBANY

© 2015 State University of New York

For information, contact
State University of New York Press, Albany, NY
www.sunypress.edu

Production, Laurie D. Searl
Marketing, Kate R. Seburyamo

Library of Congress Cataloging-in-Publication Data

Sharpley-Whiting, T. Denean.
  Bricktop's Paris : African American women in Paris between the two
World Wars / T. Denean Sharpley-Whiting.
       pages cm.
  Includes bibliographical references and index.
  ISBN 978-1-4384-5501-3 (hc : alk. paper)—978-1-4384-5500-6 (pb : alk. paper)
  ISBN 978-1-4384-5502-0 (ebook)
  1. African American women—France—Paris—History—20th century.
2. Bricktop, 1894–1984.   3. African American women—France—Paris—
Biography.   4. Women entertainers—France—Paris—Biography.
5. Nightclubs—France—History—20th century.   6. Paris (France)—Intellectual
life—20th century.   7. Americans—France—Paris—History—20th century.
8. Paris (France)—Social life and customs—20th century.   9. Montmartre
(Paris, France)—Biography.   I. Title.   II. Title: African American women in
Paris between the two World Wars.

  DC718.B56B85 2015
  305.48'8960730944361—dc23   2014010396

10 9 8 7 6 5 4 3 2 1

For Haviland

CONTENTS

ILLUSTRATIONS

ACKNOWLEDGMENTS

I'd first like to thank my editor, Beth Bouloukos, who saw my vision and believed in the trade potential of this project, as well as the editorial staff and production and marketing team at SUNY Press. I would like to acknowledge Vanderbilt University's Office of Sponsored Programs managed by the Office of the Vice Provost for Research for a summer 2007 grant that helped me mine various research leads in France. Mona Frederick and the Robert Penn Warren Center for Humanities were also instrumental in furthering my research as have been the Offices of the Provost and the Dean of the College of Arts and Science. There were many libraries, archivists, organizations, centers, and people who have assisted in the completion of this project. The staff at Beinecke Library at Yale, Moorland-Spingarn Research Center, Dean Jean Carney Smith and Fisk University Special Collections, the Schomburg Center, Maria Lopes at Rhode Island College, Danish National Archive, the various Bibliothèques nationales in France, the British Library, and the Library of Congress were especially helpful. I'd also like to thank Vivace Press, University of Missouri–St. Louis, for use of Nora Holt's musical composition, "Negro Dance."

My colleagues in African American and Diaspora Studies have been more than supportive, reading versions of the book and offering feedback. I'd like to single out in particular Victor Anderson, who understood what a sabbatical means; Houston A. Baker for his sharp mind and wit; Tiffany Patterson for her historical insights in crafting a narrative; and Alice Randall, whose command over language, long lunches and dinners, and early morning hours-long phone conversations dispensing writing advice were indispensable to this work. And I don't know what I'd do without Tara Faith Williams. I'd also like to acknowledge Karen E. Fields, who knows how to turn a phrase. In Paris 2007, you helped set the tone of this book. Bob Barsky, Holly Tucker, and Lynn Ramey in French and Italian (FRIT) have been delightful sounding boards at various stages in my writing.

The Fugitives Writing Retreat, generously supported by the College of Arts and Science Dean's Office and the AADS Research Center, made me see things I was too close to the text to see. I look forward to our annual, four-day, get-down-to-the-business-of-writing sessions. I'd also like to thank David Ikard, an amazing mind and sounding board.

I'd like to also thank Thadious Davis, a serious mentor and good friend who has always been there for me since 1991. My agent, Charlotte Sheedy, deserves a merit for understanding why I can't quit academic publishing, as does Julie Smith, my mystery-writing mentor. It was she who told me on a hot September day at the Omni in New Orleans, "Bricky has to shoot the gun, Tracy." Love to my Dad and Mom, the Sharpleys, who always delight in every one of my new projects, and my sister-cousin, Neet, the embodiment of the fearless and loyal "Changchang," who reads every one of my fictional works with glee. Love supreme to my daughter, Haviland, who appears as expensive porcelain china in this book, and my ever-supportive, fun-loving husband of twenty years, Gilman W. Whiting.

THE WOMEN

Josephine Baker
Gwendolyn Bennett
Selma Burke
Bessie Coleman
Lillian "Madame Evanti" Evans-Tibbs
Jessie Fauset
Adelaide Hall
Nora Holt
Alberta Hunter
Florence Embry Jones
Lois Mailou Jones
Nella Larsen
Florence Mills
Dorothy Peterson
Nancy Prophet
Eslanda Goode Robeson
Augusta Savage
Clara Shepard
Ada "Bricktop" Smith
Valaida Snow
Anita Thompson
A'Lelia Walker
Ethel Waters
Elisabeth Welch
Laura Wheeler Waring

Map of Bricktop's Paris

Key:

1. Josephine Baker, Casino de Paris, 15 Avenue Montaigne, 8ème arrondissement. Josephine debuts at the Théâtre des Champs-Élysées in La Revue nègre in 1924.
2. Gwendolyn Bennett, Pension Orfila, 60 Rue d'Assas, 6ème arrondissement. Her first residence upon arrival in June 1925.
3. Selma Burke, Marly-le-roi (France). Aristide Mailol's studio—sixteen miles north of Paris, or thirteen miles from Neuilly on the map. Burke studied with the master sculptor here.
4. Bessie Coleman, Société des ingénieurs civils, 19 Rue Blanche, 9ème arrondissement. The site of the 1921 Pan-African Congress in Paris, which Coleman attended.
5. Anna Julia Cooper, 5 Rue Rollin, 5ème arrondissment. Cooper's residence in 1924.
6. Lillian "Madame Evanti" Evans-Tibbs, Le Trianon, Elysée Montmartre, 80 Boulevard des Rochechouart, 9ème arrondissement. Evans-Tibbs performed here as Lakmé.
7. Jessie Fauset and Laura Wheeler, Hotel Jeanne D'Arc, 59 Rue Vaneau, 7ème arrondissement. Residence in October 1924.
8. Ida Gibbs-Hunt, The Grand Hotel, 12 Boulevard des Capucines, 9ème arrondissement. Site of the 1919 Pan-African Congress, which she helped organize with W. E. B. Du Bois.
9. Adelaide Hall, 73 Rue Jean-Baptiste Pigalle, 9ème arrondissement. La Grosse Pomme/Big Apple nightclub she opened in 1937.
10. Nora Holt, Hotel Séjour, 41 Avenue Wagram, 17ème arrondissement. Les Nuits du Prado, a nightclub where Holt performed for two weeks in October 1926.
11. Alberta Hunter, Hotel de Paris, 55 Rue Pigalle, 9ème arrondissement. Residence in August 1927 with Lottie Tyler.
12. Florence Embry-Jones, 61 Rue Blanche, 9ème arrondissement. Chez Florence nightclub.
13. Lois Mailou Jones, 9 Rue Compagne Première, 14ème arrondissement. Address of Jones's studio.
14. Nella Larsen (and Dorothy Peterson), 31 bis rue Campagne Première, 14ème arrondissement. Apartment Larsen and Peterson shared in 1931.
15. Florence Mills, Avenue Gabriel. Café des Ambassadeurs, 8ème arrondissement. Mills's *Blackbirds 1926* makes its debut in the summer café-concert venue.
16. Nancy Prophet. 147 Rue Broca, 5ème arrondissement. Prophet's studio from June 1926 to 1934. The street turns into Rue Léon-Maurice Nordmann.
17. Eslanda (Goode) Robeson, Hotel Royal, 159 Rue de Rennes, 6ème arrondissement. Residence for a few days on her first "tourist" tour of Paris in August 1925.

18. Augusta Savage. 3 Impasse de l'Astrolabe, 15ème arrondissement. One of her longer-term residences during her stay in Paris 1929.
19. Clara Shepard and Paulette, Jane, and Andrée Nardal. Clamart, six miles south of Paris, or 1.8 miles from Malakoff on the map. Site of Clamart Salon, where the idea for *The Review of the Black World* was launched.
20. Ada "Bricktop" Smith, 66 Rue Pigalle and 52 Rue Pigalle, 9ème arrondissement. Addresses of Chez Bricktop and Le Grand Duc, the most popular clubs she hosted.
21. Valaida Snow, Théatre de la Porte-Saint-Martin, 18 Boulevard Saint-Martin, 10ème arrondissement. Snow opened the operetta, *Liza*, as its star in June 1930.
22. Anita Thompson, Les Deux Magots, 6ème, 6 Boulevard Saint-Germain-des-Prés. Thompson spent hours at a time at this café writing and socializing.
23. A'Lelia Walker, Cartier, 13 Rue de la Paix, 2ème arrondissement. Walker was given a private showing at the House of Cartier.
24. Laura Wheeler (Waring), Neuilly-sur-Seine. Wheeler moved here after leaving the Hotel Jeanne D'Arc.
25. Ethel Waters (and Bricktop), 47 Avenue Trudaine, 9ème arrondissement. One of Bricktop's many apartments in Montmartre. She allowed Waters to stay here in 1929.
26. Elisabeth Welch, Le Boeuf sur le Toit, 26 Rue de Penthièvre, 8ème arrondissement. Welch was hired by Louis Moyse to sing at the cocktail and dinner hours in January 1930.

BOOK I

BRICKTOP'S PARIS

The power of place will be remarkable.

—Aristotle, *Physics*

INTRODUCTION

THE OTHER AMERICANS, 1919–1939

"Paris put my foot on the ground," declared Lois Mailou Jones in a 1996 interview in the *New York Amsterdam News*.[1] For Jones, Paris represented "freedom, [t]o be shackle free . . . released . . . from all of the pressure and stagnation which we suffered in this country. . . . France gave me my stability, and it gave me the assurance that I was talented and that I should have a successful career."[2] In Paris, she produced the famous oil-on-linen painting *Les Fétiches* (1938), now displayed at the Smithsonian. Paris was a pivotal turning point in her artistic career. She was not the first or the last black woman to express these sentiments about the City of Light. This book tells their stories in words and images.

Between the first and second World Wars, the period some call the Jazz Age, France became a place where African American women could realize personal freedom and creativity, in narrative or in performance, in clay or on canvas, in life and in love. Paris, as it appeared to them, was physically beautiful, culturally refined, inexpensive as a result of the war, and seductive with its lack of violent racial animus. "The power of place" was indeed remarkable. Places determine reality; as distinct settings, they are laden with cultural significance. Therefore, speaking, thinking, doing, simply living are never unaffected by where such activities take place.

Marita Bonner put it this way during the Harlem Renaissance: They left a place "that stifles and chokes; that cuts off and stunts."[3] They crossed the Atlantic and put their feet on the ground in another world. Before the women of Bricktop's Paris looked to France, their journey was preceded by a nineteenth-century American slave woman, simply referred to as la Négresse through the annals of time, who secured her personal freedom by stowing away on a ship that landed in France. She was the inspiration for Guy de Maupassant's short story "Boitelle" (1889), and the town, La Négresse, in the Aquitaine region of France was named in her honor oddly enough.[4]

5

Then there was late nineteenth-century African American sculptor Meta Vaux Warrick Fuller's search for a place to accommodate her artistic desires. She found a temporary home in Paris in 1899 among other aspiring artists at both the Académie Colarossi and the École des Beaux-Arts.

For a young Mary Eliza Church, who would later become the revered feminist and civil rights advocate Mary Church Terrell, Paris in 1888 kindled her ambitions to write in the manner of French women intellectuals and salonists George Sand and Mesdames de Sévigné and de Staël.[5] And in finally being allowed to "answer the call" to serve black troops in France during the last eighteen months of the Great War via their associations with the Red Cross and the Young Men's and Women's Christian Associations, Niagara movement founder Mary B. Talbert, Addie Hunton, and Kathryn Johnson present a land of unspoiled milk and sweeter honey for the Negro. Hunton and Johnson provide a hopeful recitation of French Republican ideals of freedom and equality and the dawning of France's love affair with jazz alongside an unvarnished account of American racism abroad in *Two Colored Women with the American Expeditionary Forces.* Hunton would later pursue coursework at the Université de Strasbourg. France, for its part, continued to hold out possibility and promise to African American women through nearly the first four decades of the twentieth century.

Their good fortunes in France in no way diminish their host country's incongruous relationship with its sizeable multiracial empire in Africa, Asia, the Caribbean, the Pacific, and the Indian Ocean worlds, as well as with those French blacks residing in the capital city; nor does it pardon, say, the exile to a convent at Moret of Louise Marie-Thérèse, the alleged daughter of a queen and her African dwarf servant,[6] or excuse the public parading and subsequent dissection of the South African Sarah Bartmann in the name of science. Indeed, such complexities all beg for more nuanced probing into American blackness, gender, American racism, and French exoticism and imperialism in the twentieth century.

The lure and lore of Paris was freedom, opportunity, and acceptance. While the weary and poor of Europe sailed to the New World toward Ellis Island and the Statue of Liberty, these Americans went to the Old World with its swank soirées, erudite salons and ateliers, its brasseries and cafés, and its happening jazz revues. In America, whiteness allowed the new European immigrants greater access to jobs, trade unions, and public spaces. In France, particularly in Paris, among the French and other European cosmopolitans, black Americanness had a social currency that allowed access to artistic communities and creative spaces. Though they were talented, they were also privileged as Americans and exoticized as blacks. The French fascination with American technologies and popular culture, including film, radio, and jazz introduced by African American GIs, and French Republicanism itself, embodied in the ideals of equality, liberty, and fraternity—even if imperfectly practiced—helped to further grease the wheels of social equality and freedom for African Americans in Paris.[7]

African American soldiers laid the foundation for such tolerance in France with their service abroad in World War I. Nearly two hundred thousand of them were stationed in and around cities, villages, and communes throughout the country during the war effort, interacting socially and intimately with the local populations, whose encounters with blacks were limited to popular culture, newspaper articles about the French empire in Africa and the good deeds of the civilizing mission, and racially obtuse travelogues and novels.[8]

The African American GI's conduct and countenance ran counter to the narrative of ignoble savages in need of civilizing populating French literature and popular culture and circulating in American and German war propaganda. In the aftermath of the war, the denial of black doughboys' participation in honorific military ceremonies in France and other organized discriminatory practices revealed the starkness of American racism against American citizens who had just nobly served in the Great War. American racism was then offensive to French cultural chauvinism. It enlivened that alleged legendary French arrogance. That la mère patrie dabbled in class-riddled social practices against the bunched masses of poor and working-class French citizens, which included blacks, alongside educated French black elites on the basis of color was of little consequence.

Racism American-style was different, pitiless, uncivilized, nakedly abusive; its bare-knuckled methods lacked in rhetoric and practice the paternalism of la mission civilisatrice, which, from the French perspective, possessed a surfeit of goodwill and intentions.

The relatively small population of African Americans in the city also did not inspire wholesale French xenophobia and cultural chauvinism. Most GIs had returned home, leaving mere hundreds of African American men scattered throughout the country, and only handfuls of African American men and women civilians arrived in the city in their wake post-1919. Massive French unemployment and a general concern about protecting French culture and traditions would only later inspire quotas, stringent work permits, and the reputed French surliness. The French were not colorblind; they were simply not color averse. Throw in a dash of French exoticism and paternalism and Paris had the makings of a utopia for African Americans accustomed to slipshod and occasionally murderous treatment in their home country. There's no place like home. And Paris was definitely unlike home—in a good way.

Hence, much has been made of the American expatriate experience in France during the interwar years. Ready at one's lips are such catchphrases as "the lost generation," "les années folles" (the roaring twenties), and the twilight years (1930s). Ernest Hemingway's *A Moveable Feast*, a signature American memoir of 1920s Paris, is an old standby in narrations of the delights of Paris during these years. With the exception of Josephine Baker, however, the ink dries up rather quickly regarding African American women in Paris. Of course, we have Tyler Stovall's comprehensive *Paris Noir: African Americans in the City of Light*; Theresa Leininger-Miller's finely researched *New Negro Artists in Paris: African Americans in the City of Light, 1922–1934*; William Shack's thorough anthropological study of Montmartre, jazz, and those who made the music's reception possible in France in *From Harlem to Montmartre: A Paris Jazz Story*; Michel Fabre's pioneering *From Harlem to Paris: Black American Writers in France, 1840–1980*; and Woody Allen's 2011 film *Midnight in Paris*, which mentions Chez Bricktop yet focuses briefly on an unnamed, dancing black woman—presumably Josephine Baker—once the film's characters arrive at the famous club. But no one book or film, no matter how well conceived, can do all things. So we now must digest bits of this era with a more purposeful focus on a different American invasion of France.

Importantly, as Fabre's subtitle suggests, the interwar period is only one in an ongoing saga of the black American presence in France that also included women. Even so, expatriate yarns about everybody but African American women predominate.[9] American cultural and intellectual history of this period seems riveted on maleness and whiteness.

With the exception of these aforementioned, more inclusive histories, the very phrases "American expatriate" and "American in Paris" consistently exclude African American women. David McCullough's 2011 fascinating tome on Americans in Paris a century earlier, *The Greater Journey: Americans in Paris*, fails even to include one African American woman. To my mind, Mary Church Terrell, painter Annie E. Anderson Walker, and Meta Vaux Warrick should have been likely candidates. Many of these women, whether in the nineteenth or twentieth centuries, lived in Paris for months or even years; some took up permanent residence, while others did not. And still, they are curiously jettisoned from the *grand récit* of "Americans in Paris."

Consider Ada "Bricktop" Smith, a central figure in this narrative, who opened several popular nightspots in Montmartre and stayed for many years; or cabaret performer Adelaide Hall, who starred in *Blackbirds 1929* at the Moulin Rouge and later opened the Big Apple in Montmartre, a club a few doors down from Bricktop's; and others like Laura Wheeler and Lillian Evans-Tibbs, who studied with the masters and divas in ateliers and opera houses throughout the city. Whether they lingered for many months or years at a time, or returned frequently for short stays like the singer Alberta Hunter, France during the interwar period played a singular role in the shaping of their lives as women, as a community, and as American artists, writers, and thinkers.

As soon as one looks, one finds African American women along-side the better-known white American countrymen and women during this period. Thus, for example, Ernest Hemingway's residence at 74 rue Cardinal Lemoine was no more than fifty paces away from 4 rue Rollin, where Anna Julia Cooper wrote her dissertation on slavery, France, and the Haitian Revolution. Similarly, Ada "Bricktop" Smith's nightclub in the heart of Montmartre was a haunt that F. Scott Fitzgerald, Cole Porter, T. S. Eliot, Henry Miller, and Hemingway frequented (as it turns out, Bricktop could not abide Hemingway's drink-besotted antics). If all of these Americans were present together in Paris, then our understanding of the history of Americans in Paris must accommodate not only the likes of Hemingway, Gertrude Stein, Natalie Barney, Fitzgerald, and other canonical luminaries of the "lost generation," but also their counterparts such as Nancy Elizabeth Prophet, Ada "Bricktop" Smith, Gwendolyn Bennett, Eslanda Goode Robeson, and the twenty-one other American women who are the subject of this book. In effect, the trope of the "lost generation" seems to have lost its African American women contingent.

Black women's exclusion, too, relates to access, capital, and very often leisure that combined to erect spatial boundaries on the potentially trans-formative quality of travel in their lives and in their artistry. Michel Fabre concludes plainly that "[m]any women writers of the Harlem Renaissance were unable to travel abroad."[10] That flourishing movement of black cul-tural expressivity in the United States dubbed interchangeably the Harlem Renaissance or the era of "The New Negro" coincided with the Jazz Age in Paris.

Many of the black expatriate artists, activists, writers, and performers of the era fed the insatiable negrophilic appetites of avant-garde Paris. Paris became a meeting place for the black diaspora, an epicenter of Black Inter-nationalism, as the Martinican writer Jane Nardal noted in her 1928 article "Internationalisme noir" in *La Dépêche africaine*—but only for some. African American men had their maleness, which allowed them to travel alone, unmolested. They had as well the social liberties and privileges accorded maleness despite race, which usually included better-paying jobs and the added bonuses of military service that provided access to far-flung lands like France, where, in the war's aftermath, they shepherded in the "le jazz hot" craze in Paris.

Many African American women, on the other hand, had to contend with issues of propriety, the cults of domesticity and marriage, family obli-gations, and financial precariousness. These and other issues, private and structural, would also then help to account for their marginal presence in studies of U.S. and British expatriate women writers like Morrill Cody's *The Women of Montparnasse*[11] Andrea Weiss's *Paris Was a Woman* and the accompanying film, and Shari Benstock's *Women of the Left Bank*.

White women writers of the venerable "lost generation" in France such as Djuna Barnes, Gertrude Stein, Edith Wharton, and Anaïs Nin often possessed a relative affluence and leisure that could provide the gateway to travel, self-discovery, and the mining of their craft. Many of their African American counterparts could scarcely afford, in the words of another black expatriate, James Baldwin, "the price of the ticket" to France without the assistance of white philanthropic patronage such as the Harmon, Carnegie, Guggenheim, and Rosenwald foundations and black women's leadership organizations, such as Delta Sigma Theta.

The occasion to "get lost" for longer periods of time abroad in order to find themselves was, as well, a luxury that many New Negro women writers simply could not afford. As committed race women, the struggle for social equality on American soil summoned them, forcing them to strike a balance between their creative endeavors and aspirations for the "race" at home. Additionally, American-style racism also erected its own formidable barriers when funding to subsidize study and travel abroad presented itself.

In 1923, the American Committee of Eminent American Architects, Painters, and Sculptors denied sculptor Augusta Savage a scholarship for summer study at the Palais de Fontainebleau, France, because "her presence in the school would be disagreeable to some white students and embarrassing to her."[12] And indeed, in that same year, Jessie Fauset noted in an interview with the *Paris Tribune* the travails faced by African American women in the United States and the lure of Paris.

> I like Paris because I find something here, something of integrity, which I seem to have strangely lost in my own country. It is simplest of all to say that I like to live among people and sur- roundings where I am not always conscious of "thou shall not." In order to offset criticism, the refined colored woman must not laugh too loudly, she must not stare—in general she must stiffen her self-control even though she can no longer humanly contain herself. I am colored and wish to be known as colored, but sometimes I have felt that my growth as a writer has been hampered in my own country. And so—but only temporarily—I have fled from it.[13]

Fauset presents a stark portrait of the social intricacies confronting black women in the United States behind and beyond the color line. Racism, class, and sexism have conspired to limit her development as a novelist and a woman. Because black womanhood was constantly under surveil-lance and viciously under attack as promiscuous during the antebellum and post-Reconstruction periods, women of Fauset's standing were often offered up willy-nilly as an acid test for social equality in the face of continuing discrimination and extralegal white-on-black violence. That is, they car-ried in their bodies and their souls the moral repute of the Negro race. The ever-stiffening dictates and decorum for the "refined woman of color" circumscribed her freedom and creativity to the point of a transatlantic rupture with America.

PARISIAN PASSAGEWAYS

What it was like to be an African American woman in Paris *entre deux guerres* is the subject of this study. What possibilities did Paris present to these women, more specifically for those born post-1880, who traveled there?[14] How did these women's lives and creative sensibilities realize those possibilities? While entering and exiting Paris at various moments, they were participants in the life of the black American colony and commingled with bohemian French avant-garde writers and artists like Picasso, Gide, Breton, Matisse, Bernard, Colette, Kiki, Maillol. Less the strictures of American rac-ism, they interacted socially, intellectually, and intimately with Man Ray, Hemingway, Fitzgerald, Cole Porter, male members of the predominantly white American colony. But they interacted only superficially with the white "Women of the Left Bank." In describing these women, Andrea Weiss notes,

> Although the women were of different nationalities and religions, they were all white, despite there being many influential Black American women living in Paris at the time—who were attracted to Paris precisely because they found no "colour bar" there. . . . [I]n general the encounters between black and white women did not lead to enduring friendships.[15]

Though Colette's "whiteness" has been colored in with biographer Judith Thurman's revelation of her black Martinican ancestry in *Secrets of the Flesh*, and even Josephine Baker was tempted to call her "the white Negress . . . because of her kinky hair and natural grace," Weiss's point is well taken. While religion and nationality posed no obstacles to creative alliances among white women, race, and perhaps their different experiences as American women in Paris, seems to have.

Despite the lack of a "colour bar" in Paris, deeply held beliefs about race lurked in creative and political positions. Wealthy socialite and salonist Natalie Barney would eventually support fascism. Despite Gertrude Stein's essay in *Useful Knowledge*, "Among Negroes," which mentions Paul and Eslanda Robeson, Josephine Baker, Maud de Forrest, and Ida Lewelyn, the latter three members of the cast of *La Revue nègre*, her fiction contained race-clotted characters typical of the vast majority of white writers of the era. These are but two examples.

With their intersecting lives and experiences throughout the rues, arrondissements, and quarters of Paris, from Montmartre to Montparnasse, from the Montagne de Sainte Geneviève in the Latin Quarter to Saint-Germain-des-Prés, these American women formed their own community within the community of the Negro colony with ever-changing female inhabitants primarily due to their intermittent stays in Paris. While Paris was certainly more racially hospitable, like any major city, it could also be alienating and lonely. Paris was so wonderfully Paris because the expatriate woman's desires for community and belonging could be met. As Tyler Stovall notes,

> [T]he experience of community was fundamental to the history of black Americans in the French capital. Blacks did not come to Paris as isolated individuals but generally with the encouragement and assistance of African Americans already there. Once in Paris they were able to participate in a rich community life with its own institutions, traditions, and rituals. Moreover, the creation of an expatriate black *community* played a vital role in easing the pangs of exile. Many blacks in Paris rejoiced in their escape from the United States but at the same time feared losing touch with African American culture. Informal networks enabled them to recreate a black cultural presence abroad freed from racism.[16]

Hence, the African American woman expatriate sought out not only the company of other Americans, black and white, but innovative women like themselves. From those starting points of race, gender, and nationality, the small community, by virtue of space (Paris—a city a mere six miles long and eleven miles wide) and time, also lived, ate, socialized, and worked in close proximity. Their experiences as Americans in a foreign city certainly bound them together in the City of Light, but so too did their experience as women on the threshold of something new, namely, their attempts to live differently and "do" something different.

The grande dame of cabaret culture, Ada "Bricktop" Smith was a fifteen-year resident of Paris. Bricktop served as both anchor and magnet for an expatriate community of African American women. The various eponymous clubs she opened were homes away from homes for this community of women; according to Bricktop, her club was a "combination mail-drop, bank, rehearsal hall, clubhouse—even a neighborhood bar. But it was always chic."[17] For many, such as the poet-painter Gwendolyn Bennett and portrait artist Laura Wheeler, Bricktop's was the last stop on a night out. Composer and singer Nora Holt and performance artist Florence Mills frequently dined with the saloonkeeper during their time in the city. Bricktop counseled Josephine Baker in her early days in Paris, helping her to read and write, and offered refuge to a homesick Ethel Waters who, tired of croissants and *beurre blanc*, desperately wanted a place to cook.

The ever-difficult Nancy Prophet befriended a newly arrived Augusta Savage at Pan-Africanist impresario W. E. B. Du Bois's request, while Dorothy Peterson and Nella Larsen enjoyed tea in Parisian salons and wrote countless letters to Carl Van Vechten of their travels. Many of these women had been acquainted with each other socially and professionally in Chicago and New York. They would naturally take up those bonds again in Paris. This community also included other women of the African diaspora like the British singer Mabel Mercer and Martinican salonist and editor of *La Revue du monde noir/Review of the Black World* Paulette Nardal. All of these women will have their role to play throughout this alternative vision of Paris.

As they pursued their various vocations with purpose in Paris, they all also continued to look homeward. Paris was a training ground, a field, where they could mine their dreams until mature and ripe for transport home. Many would return in the midst of the New Negro era, fully equipped to take up their roles as "pioneers" of the race in areas of art, education, letters, and civil rights. They also returned with a broader perspective. The bonds they forged with the African diaspora while in Paris and their keener appreciation of the African continent was often manifested in their art and writing. Meetings with Martinican women of letters like Nardal and the 1931 Colonial Exposition in Paris provided unique glimpses into France's complicated politics and policies on race and empire and their roles and privileges as African American women in France's colonial drama.

Using recordings, interviews, diaries, film, letters, literature, art, memoirs, autobiographies, and biographies, *Bricktop's Paris* introduces the reader to these women and the city they encountered. The study's title is certainly a nod to Bricktop. Besides Josephine Baker, she is perhaps the most well-known long-term black woman resident in Paris during the interwar era. But *Bricktop's Paris* is not a biography of Bricktop, though she is certainly deserving of one, nor is the work explicitly just about Bricktop and her interactions with the twenty-four women covered in the volume. Bricktop is a marker, a symbol of a generation lost because those comprising this generation were neither male nor white. Hence, *Bricktop's Paris* uses photographs, posters, programs, literature, art—everything it takes to invoke a lost generation. In some respects, *Bricktop's Paris* is a collage, a multilife biography over a particular period in time, an assembled portrait of black women's lives as they lived them for however long in Paris. Some women then will be accorded more space than others, walking on and off the stage at various times, for they left a richer and fuller archive to investigate and recreate.

Bricktop's Paris is a story of community, a story of migration, very often a temporary migration, and a story of recovery and reimagining. It is important to note that many black American women were not running away from something in America. Instead, some were merely reaching for something else, something different, wonderful, and new: an opportunity to perfect their language skills, to study with the masters of fine art, or the simple pursuit and experience of high culture, as was clearly the case with heiress A'Lelia Walker. For as Joan DeJean writes in The Essence of Style: How the French Invented High Fashion, Fine Food, Chic Cafés, Style, Sophistication, and Glamour:

> In the sixteenth century, the French were not thought of as the most elegant or the most sophisticated European nation. By the early nineteenth century . . . France had acquired a sort of monopoly on culture, style, luxury living, a position it has occupied ever since. At the same time, Paris had won out over all its obvious contemporary rivals—Venice, London, Amsterdam—and had become universally recognized as the place to find elegance, glamour, and even romance. Beginning in the seventeenth century, travelers were saying what novelists and filmmakers are still repeating: travel to Paris was guaranteed to add a touch of magic to every life.[18]

And why wouldn't these "other Americans," if given the opportunity, want to experience such magic?

Bricktop's Paris is divided into five chapters and includes an appendix containing one of two of the only surviving musical compositions from the prolific composer and music critic Nora Holt. The metanarrative, The Autobiography of Ada "Bricktop" Smith, or Miss Baker Regrets, follows Bricktop's Paris and is bracketed by a foreword by novelist Alice Randall. Similar to Stein's The Autobiography of Alice B. Toklas and Virginia Woolf's Orlando, and incorporating Audre Lorde's concept of biomythography, the metanarrative draws on material from Bricktop's journals, her memoir, and extant interviews and letters to create a first-person narrative wrapped in the device of a mystery set in Paris.

Chapter 1, "Les Dames, Grand and Small, of Montmartre: The Paris of Bricktop," introduces Ada Bricktop Smith Ducongé[19] along with a host of other performance artists, from the opera to the jazz club, who arrived in Paris during the interwar period. "The Gotham-Montparnasse Exchange," chapter 2, then shifts to a discussion of primarily women writers, while chapter 3, "Women of the Petit Boulevard: The Artist's Haven," delves into the lives of women artists in the city. The portrait artist Laura Wheeler is included in chapter 2 rather than chapter 3 given her close ties with Harlem Renaissance writer Jessie Fauset in both Gotham and Montparnasse. "Black Paris: Cultural Politics and Prose," chapter 4, takes up Eslanda Goode Robeson's series of articles, "Black Paris," in the U.S. literary magazine *Challenge/ New Challenge*, with a particular focus on the encounter between Eslanda Robeson and Paulette Nardal, and both women's subsequent writing on black Americans in Paris. As far as I can tell, Robeson's series represents the first articulation of the concept of "Black Paris" to an American audience. And finally, "Epilogue: Homeward Tug at a Poet's Heart—The Return," chapter 5, closes on the eve of World War II when many of the women were forced to flee the city as Hitler began his march across the continent.

ONE

LES DAMES, GRAND AND SMALL,

OF MONTMARTRE

─────────────────────────

The Paris of Bricktop

In Paris, within the last decade, one after another three colored women have risen to reign for a time as the bright particular stars of the night life of Montmartre. And all three of them have been American colored women. Princes, dukes, great artists, and kings of finance have all paid them homage (plus a very expensive cover charge) in brimming glasses of sparkling champagne lifted high in the wee hours of the morning.

—Langston Hughes, "Adelaide Hall New Star of Paris Night Life: Her 'Big Apple' Glows Over Rue Pigalle"

> Play it for the lords and ladies,
> For the dukes and counts,
> For the whores and gigolos,
> For the American millionaires,
> And the school teachers
> Out for a spree.
> Play it
> Jazz band!

—Langston Hughes, "To a Negro Jazz Band in a Parisian Cabaret," *The Crisis*

"The last night I saw the Paris of Bricktop. . . . it was pouring down rain. The car drove through the dimly lit streets at a snail's pace, and I looked out at the city I loved and wondered when I would see it again."

—Ada "Bricktop" Smith Ducongé

On her last night in Paris, October 26, 1939, on the eve of World War II, those were Ada Smith Ducongé's parting words. Gazing at the *hôtels particuliers*, illuminated architectural marvels, and the twinkling lights of the grand boulevards, she said goodbye to the city that she had called home for over fifteen years, "the Paris of Bricktop." The Paris she had found upon her arrival was certainly different in spirit from the Paris she was leaving behind.

With the signing of the Armistice in Compiègne, France, on November 11, 1918, the Allies declared victory over Germany. The Negro jazz bands, led by the likes of James Reese Europe, Noble Sissle, and others, as arms of various colored infantries, played throughout the streets of cities in France to celebrate. While newspaper headlines from New York to Paris celebrated the signing, the mood of the citizens of the great republic of France was antinationalism of any sort and antiwar. The success of Abel Gance's 1919 silent film *J'accuse*, which captured the suffering of World War I, highlighted the blight the Great War had left on the French psyche. In the immediate aftermath of the war, real wages had stagnated and disease, mortality, and poverty were widespread in the rural areas. With a high male mortality rate due to war and illness, widows and single women entered the workforce in droves. Influenced largely by Coco Chanel, cloche hats, cigarettes, cropped hair, and shorter skirts became a signature style among newly independent, working French women. The French lost over three hundred thousand soldiers at the battle at Verdun. Fertility rates were now at a low; and the sale of contraception was prohibited in 1920, while Mother's Day was inaugurated to celebrate mothers of large families as part of national anti–low birth rate efforts.

Despite the hardship and poverty, culture thrived. Paris was a magnet for foreign laborers in search of work and French peasants whose agrarian lifestyle was disrupted by the war. In search of all manner of diversion, the French sought out café concerts, the theater, and movies houses. With protectionist measures in place for the film industry, French cinema began rebuilding, experiencing a golden era with the popularity of colonial films and comedies. Art and literature flourished, and intellectuals gathered in coffee houses to debate Dadaism and surrealism and Marcel Proust. France once again became the destination for foreign writers and artists—its openness to creativity and resistance to censorship making it a haven. On Sunday afternoons, the parks—from Luxembourg to the Bois de Boulogne—were filled with flaneurs and couples. The crazy years of the 1920s morphed into the twilight years of the 1930s and a global recession, eventually giving way to the bleakness of impending war and the occupation of France.

But Bricktop had arrived just when Paris and the French were opening their arms to embrace all and sundry distractions. She left as she had arrived—on an ocean liner and flat broke. As the poet laureate of the

Negro race, Langston Hughes, noted in 1937, "She made several fortunes, so they say, and lost them, or spent them. Or maybe gave them away, the godness [*sic*] of her heart being almost a legend in Montmartre."[1] Bricktop had sailed to Paris on the Cunard line's *America*, docking May 11, 1924. She was twenty-nine. She left on the *Washington* in October 1939. She was forty-five years old. Her journey from a small town named after a Baptist preacher in Greenbrier County, West Virginia, to Europe's cultural capital was a circuitous one.

Born on August 14, 1894, in Alderson, "West-by-God-Virginia," as she affectionately referred to the state of her birth, Ada Beatrice Queen Victoria Louise Virginia Smith was christened with five middle names so that her parents, Thomas and Harriet "Hattie" Elizabeth Smith (*née* Thompson), would avoid offending the neighbors who all wanted to name the Smiths' fifth and last child. Ada, Etta, Ethel, and Robert were the Smiths' surviving four children; and like most black families, their complexions ran the gamut of the color spectrum.[2]

Harriet Thompson was born into slavery in 1861, two years before Lincoln issued the Emancipation Proclamation. A lithe woman with blue-gray eyes and blondish hair, Hattie and her dark-brown-skinned husband Thomas passed on complexions and hair color ranging from high yellow with red freckles and red-gold hair (Ada) to rich nut brown with a head of deep, dark waves (her older brother Robert). Ada's eldest sister by eleven years, Etta, was called Blonzetta because of her blond hair and light eyes.

A barber by trade, Thomas Smith comfortably supported his family of six on wages and tips from his exclusively white clientele in Alderson; Hattie stayed at home and doted on the children like any respectable, middle-class wife of the post-Reconstruction era. Thomas Smith's trade conferred on him social respect and financial independence in the segregated town of Alderson.

He had joined a profession whose history of black male participants dates back to colonial America. As Douglas W. Bristol writes in *Knights of the Razor: Black Barbers in Slavery and Freedom*, it was also a profession that "illustrated the tensions at the heart of race relations." Bristol continues,

> With a flick of the wrist, nineteenth-century black barbers could have slit the throats of the white men they shaved. . . . [T]hey used their trade to navigate the forbidding terrain of a racist country. . . . They consolidated their hold over the trade in the early Republic by exploiting the stigma that white men increasingly associated with personal service. . . . Even though other skilled trades excluded black men during the antebellum period, black barbers competed against white barbers for white customers,

and they won, dominating the upscale tonsorial market serving affluent white men. . . . Barbering grew out of the courts of European society, lending the trade positive connotations that black men appropriated for their own purposes. Rather than seeing themselves as despised menials occupying a marginal economic niche, black barbers conceived of themselves as heirs to a tradition that made them men of the world. . . . Their achievements in business, however, represented only a means to an end, for they sought to establish a basis for a black middle-class identity.[3]

Through the upscale tonsorial trade, Thomas Smith was able to lift his family out of the maelstrom of slavery's legacy to most Southern blacks—sharecropping—and into the middle class. His association with white male elites also afforded the Smith household some protections from the rabblerousing element of whites who saw the family's ascension as a threat to white economic security and indicative of black uppitiness. Alderson was a peaceable town where each racial group heeded the exigencies of the color line. However, by the time Ada was four years old, the semblance of black middle-class life that her father and mother had achieved in Alderson was disrupted when Thomas Smith died suddenly of a series of strokes in 1898.

At thirty-seven years old, the young widow Hattie sought to start life anew with the assistance of a relative who was passing as white in Chicago, Illinois. Working first as a domestic for affluent white families, Hattie settled the family at 171 East Chicago Avenue. Hattie Smith eventually moved on to running her own rooming house in a tumbledown, working-class section on Chicago's Southside made up of migrating blacks and immigrant whites looking for cheap housing. Located at 3237 State Street, the rooming house was in the thick of Chicago's burgeoning Black Belt and its vice district with gambling houses, prostitution, and saloons in abundance. As Bricktop remembers:

> Crime was no stranger to State Street, or to anyone who lived on it. People got into knife fights there. . . . Thinking back, I realize that a lot of the fights started in the saloons. . . . Saloons were a part of our everyday life. . . . I knew the back doors of most of the nearby saloons, but I wasn't interested in them. It was what went on behind the swinging doors up front that fascinated me.[4]

Hattie's entrepreneurial undertaking afforded her the opportunity to again stay at home with her four children; the move from 171 East Chicago Avenue to State Street also exposed the young, wiry Ada to the entertainment culture in the saloons and the front stage of the theater, namely the Pekin Theatre owned by black powerbroker and gambler Robert Mott.

Chicago at the turn of the century had its fair share of theaters with marquee-name stars as well as raucous saloons with backrooms where entertainers and working girls plied their trade. The Pekin Theatre, "The Temple of Music," was the only black-managed and operated playhouse in the city. Mott had passed time in Paris and was greatly impressed by the performances at the Café Chantants music hall during his 1901 visit.[5] He opened the Pekin in 1905. Once Ada took in one of its matinees, she "became stagestruck" and "more interested in the Pekin Theatre than the State Street saloons."[6]

A natural dancer and enthusiastic singer, at the age of sixteen, Ada Smith began traveling with blackface minstrel troupes and playing in vaudeville houses throughout predominantly white Southern towns in Illinois and in bordering states. The repertoire of crowd-pleasing songs included the popular "Coon! Coon! Coon!":

> Coon! Coon! Coon!
> I wish my color would fade.
> Coon! Coon! Coon!
> I'd like a different shade.
> Coon! Coon! Coon!
> Morning, night and noon.
> I wish I was a white man
> 'Stead of a Coon! Coon! Coon!

Written by Gene Jefferson, the song was a hit for white vaudeville and blackface performer Lew Dockstader in 1901. That black performers would incorporate the popular song in their lineup to the delight of their audiences signaled a very low barometer in American race relations.

Ada continued working the black entertaining circuits through the Theater Owners Booking Association (TOBA), also known during that era as Tough on Black Asses. She crisscrossed the country as part of the Oma Crosby Trio, landed for a while at boxer Jack Johnson's Chicago cabaret Café de Champion, moved onward to California where she sang and danced with Jelly Roll Morton, trekked to New York and back to Chicago where at the Panama Café she formed the Panama Trio with Cora Green and Florence Mills.

Along the way, she adopted the name "Adah," believing the "h" added a bit of theatrical flourish only to have her mother send her a letter admonishing her with the correct the spelling. She continued to use the spelling in various correspondences throughout her years in Paris.[7] A chance encounter with the portly Barron Wilkins, owner of the Harlem club Barron's Exclusive at 7th Avenue and 134th Street, led to her taking the name Bricktop in 1911. When Wilkins spotted the underage young woman in his club, he asked her her name and then told her he would call her Bricktop because of her red-gold mane. Hattie Smith again objected. An Irish prostitute who resided in Chicago went by that moniker because she, too, had red-gold hair. Years later, Mrs. Hattie Smith's ire was further piqued when the French called her daughter "Madame" Bricktop, an ignoble merging in her mind of the Chicago prostitute and a brothel madame.[8]

When Ada Smith returned to New York in 1922 to work at Barron's Exclusive Club with its "only light-bright Negroes need apply" and "white and famous black clientele only welcomed here" policies, the high-toned Smith had fully embraced the one-name moniker "Bricktop" and fancied herself a hostess and performance artist. It was the Prohibition era and she was twenty-eight years old. Her stint at Barron's was rapidly followed by her headlining debut at the equally race and color conscious Connie's Inn. But by 1924, a telegram from Paris sent by the American expatriate and manager of the Le Grand Duc cabaret in Montmartre, Eugene Bullard, requested her presence in the City of Light; at least this is Bricktop's version of her life-changing journey to Paris.

Eugene Jacques Bullard was born in Columbus, Georgia. As a youth he stowed away on a ship heading to Scotland, working his way through the United Kingdom as a journeyman boxer. He ended up in Paris, joining the French Foreign Legion during World War I as a pilot. At the war's conclusion, he received various military distinctions for his service in his adopted country. He remained in Paris where he excelled at managing nightclubs.

In the memoir *Bricktop*, the saloonkeeper recalled the events that led up to her voyage to Paris:

> At the time, there weren't more than eight or ten Negro enter-
> tainers in all of Paris. . . . There was exactly one female Negro
> entertainer. She was Palmer Jones's wife and her name was
> Florence. She was a sharp-dressing little girl, very haughty, and
> she'd been so popular at a place called Le Grand Duc that she
> was leaving to headline at a new place down the street.
>
> Florence's leaving gave Gene Bullard . . . the unwelcome
> problem of having to replace her. Florence's husband, Palmer
> Jones, had a suggestion. "Why don't you send to New York?
> There's a little girl over there called Bricktop. She don't have no
> great big voice or anything like that, but she has the damndest
> personality, and she can dance. She'll be a big success here." So
> they cabled Sammy Richardson, who was in New York at the time

and asked him to find me and make me an offer. Sammy tracked me down in Washington [DC] and followed me there. . . . There was nothing left to do but accept.[9]

As with the fabled tale of utter disappointment surrounding her arrival at Le Grand Duc, whereby she cried upon entering the tiny cabaret, the "how" of the decision to come to Paris in the first place has become part of Bricktop lore, repeated time and time again in oral histories and newspaper accounts of her life. Bricktop assures us that her rendezvous in Paris was by invitation. It was like an unexpected beckoning.

Nonetheless, fellow Chicagoan, longtime Bricktop friend, and renowned blues singer Alberta "Bert" Hunter, who would later venture to Paris, throws freezing cold water on Bricktop's story of a fortuitous confluence of events. In *Alberta Hunter: A Celebration in Blues*, an authorized posthumously published biography, cowriters Frank C. Taylor and Gerald Cook relate after an interview with one of Hunter's closest friends, Harry Watkins:

> And one could miss golden opportunities by not being in New York. That was the case with an offer to go to Paris. It happened while Alberta was out of town. Gene Bullard, manager of a little bistro in Paris called Le Grand Duc, at 52 Rue Pigalle, tried to get a singer from New York to replace Florence Embry. . . . Bricktop, in her autobiography . . . says Bullard sent for her.
>
> Alberta had her own version of the event, which she learned of several years later. She personally wouldn't tell Bricktop but expected Harry Watkins to do so. He would talk about it only after Alberta's death. Even then he looked heavenward and said, "Now, don't you all hit me." According to him, Kid Coles (a black American Harry believes was Florence's husband) sent the telegram for Bullard to Alberta c/o Eva Blanche, a former chorus girl who served meals around the clock to black entertainers in the large dining room of her Harlem apartment and held messages and mail for them when they were on the road. Bricktop picked up the telegram for Alberta, saying she was going to deliver it, read it instead and then took off immediately for Paris. As Harry said, "In those days you had to survive. You got a job wherever you could, however you could."[10]

The conflicting accounts add more color to the notoriously rancorous and competitive but close relationship between Brick and Bert. The friendship began while they performed at the Panama Club in Chicago. Hunter, a native of Memphis who ran away to Chicago as a young teen, worked the crowds of gritty, blues-seeking club revelers. Ada, along with Florence Mills and Cora Green, tweeted and danced as the Panama Trio to a more restrained audience on another floor of the club.

Did Bricktop's admitted "restless[ness]"[11] in New York and career ambitions collide with the auspicious arrival of a cablegram from Paris requesting another singer? That Sammy Richardson, a saxophonist, not a pianist as Bricktop describes him, happened to be in New York from Paris and had been tasked with tracking down Bricktop in Washington is also plausible. Many black entertainers worked the New York circuit in the winter months and Europe during the spring and summer tourist season. Richardson was playing at the Accacius Club in Paris in the summer of 1923 with renowned singer and banjoist Opal Cooper.[12] By Easter 1924, he could very well have made his way stateside.

The details as told by Harry Watkins, though, lend some credence to Alberta's account. Kid Coles, a musician, was indeed in Paris at the time and could have sent the telegram for Bullard to Alberta in care of Eva Blanche in New York. Watkins was also an acquaintance of Bricktop's. Together they participated in a series of interviews with Delilah Jackson about their lives as entertainers in the 1920s through the 1950s.[13] According to Hunter's biographers, before her departure from Paris, Florence Embry Jones informed Alberta about Bricktop's cable-grabbing skullduggery.[14] The original cablegram no longer exists; however, Eugene Bullard provides the last word on the Le Grand Duc affair in a letter from Paris to the *Chicago Defender* on April 4, 1925:

> Miss Ada Smith, Bricktop entertainer is still at the Grand Duke at 52 Rue Pigalle singing as before. There has been no change in her employer. I, Gene Bullard, am no longer at the Grand Duke. When I left August 2, 1924, Bricktop remained with my previous partner as a singer and entertainer, as was understood when I engaged her from America to work for me.[15]

Though she would later employ him at her own club, Bullard and Bricky had a perfectly stormy relationship as well due to his quick temper and foul mouth. Bullard's eminence as a club manager and talent scout was waning by this time just as Bricktop's reputation was beginning to burnish. He had written the letter to the *Defender* to establish two points: that Bricktop, whom the paper covered with regularity, was not the manager of Le Grand Duc but an employee; she had been erroneously reported as running the nightclub, much to Bullard's irritation. The second point of clarification related, of course, to Bullard's being the party primarily responsible for her growing success since he had initially extended the invitation

ILLUSTRATION 1.1. Panama Trio, 1916, Cora Green, Florence Mills, and Ada Smith.
Courtesy of Manuscript, Archives, and Rare Book Library, Emory University.

ILLUSTRATION 1.2. Bricktop, Paris, Le Grand Duc, 1925. Courtesy of Schomburg Center for Research on Black Culture, New York Public Library, Astor, Lenox, Tilden Foundations.

to her. Bullard's letter sheds some light on the intrigue surrounding the alleged "purloined" telegram; this incident would represent one in a series of clashing narratives of Paris offered up by Bert and Brick. And generally, Brick would be on the receiving end of Bert's pointed criticisms thanks to Florence Jones's pot-stirring.

The coveted spot at Le Grand Duc had been vacated by Jones. In his homage to the three American colored queens of Montmartre, Langston Hughes writes,

> [P]etite Florence Embry, lovely vision in brown, was the reigning queen of Montmartre after midnight. Today, even after her death, "Chez Florence" is still a fashionable club. And the memory of the very pretty, very reserved little brownskin woman who paid attention only to royalty or to people with a great deal of money, still lingers in the minds of international nightlifers.[16]

A native of Bridgeport, Connecticut, Florence Embry was born in 1892; she was married to pianist Palmer Jones, not Kid Coles, whom Harry Watkins thought may have been her husband.[17] She left Le Grand Duc to perform at a club/restaurant owned by Louis Mitchell. Mitchell was a musician who had worked at the Casino de Paris. Along with his band, Mitchell's Jazz Kings, Mitchell purportedly assembled the first recording of jazz in Paris in 1922 for Pathé, the French cinema and production company.[18] That recording included the iconic ditty "Ain't We Got Fun."

Embry Jones was known to be difficult but nonetheless riveting in her performances. And so much so that Mitchell renamed the club Chez Florence instead of Mitchell's. Jones also merited a short article, "Chez Florence," in *Time* magazine in 1927, where she is described as follows:

> Ivory-white [teeth], lipstick-red, and a suave, tawny brown are the colors of Florence Jones. These were colors good enough for smart, expatriate Americans of both hemispheres. . . . The fact that this handsome Negress . . . keeps the smartest *boîte de nuit* in Paris, was evident again last week, when His Royal Highness, 27-year-old Prince Henry of Britain, strolled into Chez Florence, atop Montmartre, at 3 a. m., with a highly unofficial entourage.[19]

Embry Jones's status as the only "Negress" in Montmartre with the "smartest" nightclub in Paris would be slowly upended first with the entrance of Bricky, then Josie, and concluding with Bert by 1927.

The less than fairytale-like confection of Bricktop's arrival in Paris has been recounted, too, multiple times, or at least the highlights of it: her utter dismay at the 52 rue Pigalle's Lilliputian cabaret and her encounter with a busboy by the name of Langston Hughes who offered her some food as comfort upon witnessing her teary outburst. In between those details are many unpromising others that would have seemed to signal that Paris was not the glamorous cure for her New York *ennui* but a colossal mistake.

May 11, 1924, was gray and windy. Between seasickness from the eleven-day transoceanic journey, the loss of her purse containing her life savings totaling twenty-five to thirty dollars, and an opening night to an empty club, Bricktop's first week in Paris ended with an emergency hospitalization for an appendectomy.

Over the course of two nights nonetheless, Bullard introduced her to Paris nightlife and the handful of Negroes in Paris, who could be found, for the most part, either performing or eating after-hours in the clubs and restaurants along rue Fontaine, rue de la Trinité, rue Pigalle, and rue des Martyrs, the beating heart of Black Montmartre. Bricktop lived in a succession of apartments in the area. Her first was at 36 rue Pigalle; by 1929, she had settled for a few years at 47 rue Trudaine, then moved on to 35 rue Victor Massé in 1935.

The northern part of Paris, Montmartre, or La Butte or the hill, rises above the Paris cityscape. Situated in the eighteenth arrondissement on the Right Back, just above the lively quarter, sits the Sacre Coeur Basilica at its summit. From its lofty perch, the late-nineteenth-century monument has been a witness to the many vices and artistic transformations of the district. As a quasi-outpost of Paris, the hill attracted artists, thespians, bohemians, and those in search of more decadent offerings. While Pablo Picasso lived for a while on La Butte in a colony of artists, Toulouse-Lautrec's Moulin Rouge series of posters featuring French cancan dancers Jane Avril and La Goulue captured the irrepressible spirit of Montmartre. The trickling in of the black expatriate community added a rare and flavorful gloss to the district's distinction. An almost melodically written twenty-four-page account by British writer Henry Hurford Janes describes Bricktop's Montmartre and the invasion of jazz on the hill:

> The second invasion of Montmartre was already underway, and little Harlem was springing up next to little Russia. Negro bands were gaining a fanatical following, and Paul Colin's witty black posters showing only white teeth, white eyes and shiny trombones drew people up the Butte to see drummers throw their sticks in the air and beat six drums at once. Trombones blared, saxophones wailed and the bands jerked up and down in fascinating rhythms. No one quite knew where the men and music had come from, but they pushed into Bricktops [*sic*] and Florence and Mitchell's

and came away crazed with jazz. . . . Jazz was the coming thing, a compulsive beat that still hadn't found its dance.[20]

Overrun with prostitutes, gangsters, and conmen of all stripes and nationality, Montmartre had also made room for a little Harlem thanks to the Negro jazz bands. And Hurford Janes's passage describes Bricktop's change in luck post-spring 1925. For after an uneventful spring, a chance visit to Le Grand Duc by John Dean, husband of vaudeville and silent film actress Fannie Ward, significantly changed the hostess's circumstances. Though she had been able to earn a comfortable living on the few stragglers who dropped into Le Duc, the Dean-Ward discovery of her unique performing charms bolstered Bricktop's verve. Tired of Florence Jones's antics at Chez Florence, who would "condescend to their table" for hefty sums of cash, Dean and Ward steered their friends and business to Le Grand Duc, where the "pleasingly plump, freckled-face, reddish-haired young lady who sang well and danced a little . . . treated everybody so hospitably."[21]

Fannie Ward believed Jones had "got excited," that she "need[ed] a lesson." "She's too spoiled,"[22] the actress concluded. Bricktop benefited then from a nifty coming together of white American arrogance and American Negro hubris. That is, part of Jones's international standing in Paris was her elegant uppitiness, which ran directly counter to white American ideas about a black woman's place in social hierarchies. They may have been in Paris where American dictates about race, class, and gender loosened, but these barriers were not altogether abandoned. Ward aimed to bring Florence Jones down a peg through her financial connivance or at the very least show her her place as the entertaining "help" in the hospitality industry. Ward's maneuverings and Bricktop's celebrity windfall were certainly not lost on Jones that spring 1925 and were undoubtedly still stinging by the time Alberta Hunter arrived in Paris in 1927.

Settled with a small but devoted clientele, Bricktop also began sending correspondences to the *Chicago Defender*. As part of their entertainment section, her hometown black newspaper had been following the chanteuse as early as 1916 when she danced and sang on the Chicago club circuit to her engagements out west in Los Angeles. Bricktop's move to Paris was meant to inspire; it was proudly held up to readers in a kind of "look at how our hometown girl made good." While she certainly delighted in talking up her modest success, she also used her correspondences to inform potential travelers in search of the much-ballyhooed racial and financial nirvana in Paris about the realities on the ground in post–World War I France. Bricktop was earnest in her assessment, writing, "I receive so many letters from different bands and entertainers inquiring about jobs over here. Please let them know through your columns that of the thousands of cabarets in Paris but [sic] very few use American entertainment. Unless one is booked through contract it is foolish for them to come. If they are booked in advance, however, the pay is good and sure."[23]

Her counsel was certainly in keeping with the dismal situation in Paris described by Langston Hughes in a letter to Countee Cullen in March 1924, several weeks after his arrival:

Dear Countee,

I am in Paris. I had a disagreement on the ship, left and came to Paris purely on my nerve, as I knew no one here and I had less than nine dollars in my pocket when I arrived. For a week I came as near starvation as I ever want to be, but I got to know Paris, as I tramped from one end to the other looking for a job. And at last I found one and then another one and yet another!

I have fallen into the very whirling heart of Parisian night-life—Montmartre where topsy-turvy no one gets up before seven or eight in the evening, breakfast at nine and nothing starts before midnight. Montmartre of the Moulin Rouge, Le Rat Mort and the famous night clubs and cabarets! I've just had tea over in the Latin Quarter with three of the most charming English colored girls! Claude McKay just left here for the South. Smith is in Brussels and Roland Hayes is coming.

I myself go to work at eleven pm and finish at nine in the morning. I'm working at the "Grand Duc" where the culinary staff and the entertainers are American Negroes. One of the owners is colored too. The jazz-band starts playing at one and we're still serving champagne long after day-light. I'm vastly amused.

But about France! Kid, stay in Harlem! The French are the most franc-loving, sou-clutching, hard-faced, hard worked, cold and half-starved set of people I've ever seen in life. Heat-unknown. Hot water—water—what is it? You can pay for a smile here. Nothing, absolutely nothing is given away. You even pay for water in a restaurant on the use of the toilette. And do they like Americans of any color? They do not!! Paris—old and ugly and dirty. Style, class? You see more well-dressed people in a New York subway station in five seconds than I've seen in all my three weeks in Paris. Little old New York for me! But the colored people here are fine. There are lots of us.[24]

And by May 1924, Hughes was still sounding the "stay in America" alarm. This time to Harold Jackman:

Stay home! Europe is the last place in the world to come looking for a job, and unless you've got a dollar for every day you expect to stay here, don't come. Jobs in Paris are like needles in hay-stacks for everybody, and especially English-speaking foreigners. The city is over-run with Spaniards and Italians who work for nothing, literally nothing. And all French wages are low enough anyway. I've never in my life seen so many English and Americans, colored and white, male and female, broke and without a place to sleep as I have seen here. Yet if you'd give them a ticket home tomorrow, I doubt if ten would leave Paris. Not even hunger drives them away. The colored jazz bands and performers are about the only ones doing really well here. The rest of us, with a dozen or so exceptions, merely get along.[25]

As Hughes relates, chronic unemployment, onerous work permit restrictions, a readily available cheap immigrant labor source, and virtual poverty were not enough to make Americans, colored and white, flee Paris. Paris was still a cultural haven, an incomparable brew of cosmopolitanism and freedom that America couldn't match on any day. And Bricktop had found a place for herself in it and was doing fairly well. But it was the Montparnasse and Saint-Germain crowd of artists and writers' discovery of her at Le Grand Duc however that sealed her status as the Queen of Nightclubs in the Jazz Age.

F. Scott Fitzgerald described this era of jazz in France in his *Echoes of the Jazz Age* as "an age of miracles, [. . .] an age of art, [. . .] an age of excess, and [. . .] an age of satire"; it was also F. Scott Fitzgerald who famously stated that his "greatest claim to fame is that [he] discovered Bricktop before Cole Porter."[26] Indeed, in the short story "Babylon Revisited," published in 1931 in the February 21st edition of the *Saturday Evening Post*, Fitzgerald's dissipated protagonist, Charles J. Wales, describes endless nights into the wee morning hours and countless dollars spent, "large enough to pay a month's rent"[27] at Le Grand Duc with Bricktop.

Charlie Wales returns to Paris—Babylon—after a lengthy absence that includes a stay in a sanitarium. Like the United States, which is still reeling from the stock market crash in 1929 and the Depression that followed, Paris appears sullen, having been virtually emptied of its American expatriate community. Headlines in the United States announced the continued downward spiral of global markets: "Market Continues Unsettled—Government Obligations Decline Sharply. MOST GROUPS LESS ACTIVE Foreign Loans Slightly Easier, With German International 5 s Off 2 1/8 Points," while the Sunday edition of *Le Figaro* detailed the failures of a commission on unemployment.[28]

No longer in its heyday, from Fitzgerald's (via Wales) jaundiced-eye perspective, it had an Old World feel rather than the New World cheap and exotic exuberance imported by Americans who were now down-at-the-heels:

> He was not really disappointed to find Paris was so empty. But the stillness in the Ritz bar was strange and portentous. It was not an American bar anymore—he felt polite in it, and not as if he owned it. It had gone back into France. . . . He was curious to see Paris by night with clearer and more judicious eyes than those of other days. He bought a *strapontin* for the Casino and watched Josephine Baker go through her chocolate arabesques.
>
> After an hour he left and strolled toward Montmartre, up the Rue Pigalle into the Place Blanche. The rain had stopped and there were a few people in evening clothes disembarking from taxis in front of cabarets, and *cocottes* prowling singly or in pairs, and many Negroes. He passed a lighted door from which issued music, and stopped with the sense of familiarity; it was Bricktop's, where he had parted with so many hours and so much money.
>
> Zelli's was closed, the bleak and sinister cheap hotels surrounding it were dark; up in the Rue Blanche there was more light and a local, colloquial French crowd. . . .
>
> So much for the effort and ingenuity of Montmartre. All the catering to vice and waste was on an utterly childish scale, and he suddenly realized the meaning of the word "dissipate."[29]

Like Ernest Hemingway before him, Fitzgerald had practically declared Montmartre washed up and the era of jazz dead in 1931. Whatever filial bonds Fitzgerald may have felt for Negroes as fellow Americans in Paris, and certainly Bricktop felt a near-motherly tenderness for the writer, whatever bonding they all may have had over jazz in his frequently sloshed exits from Le Grand Duc, by the time he wrote *The Great Gatsby* with its Negrophobic pronouncements, all bets were off.

Bricktop soldiers on nonetheless. By 1926, she had added saloonkeeper to her list of trades with the opening and just as rapid closing of Music Box on rue Pigalle. And by December 1929, she had added the title Mrs. to her name, as in Mrs. Peter Ducongé. By 1931, while everyone around her is closing shop and hightailing it back to the United States or other, more hospitable places, she imprudently, as time would tell, opens a larger club at 66 rue Pigalle and purchases a home in Bougival, a hamlet that impressionist painters made famous, feats remarkably few Americans, black or white, were able to do. There in Bougival she set up a tranquil idyll away from the bustle and hustle of Paris.

The dance the Charleston was her entrée, though, into Cole Porter's rarefied world in the 1920s. As she remembers, "I have to give the Charleston the credit it deserves for launching me on my career as a saloon-keeper. . . . It caught on and I caught on, Cole Porter standing right there behind me and never leaving me until I became Bricktop, the one and only."[30] She gives her first Charleston lesson to Porter on the first Monday of May 1926.[31] A July 4, 1926, telegram from Porter to Bricky from his hideaway in Venice, Italy, attests to the popularity of her private dance lessons: "All fixed for you to give lesson [a]t Excelsior Twice Week Let Me Know Date of Arrival Advise Auguste Will Engage Room."[32]

"They came to Bricktop's and I went wherever they paid me to come,"[33] she wrote in notes for her memoir. Porter and his wife, Linda Lee, invited Bricktop to entertain at 13 rue Monsieur, their luxurious apartment in Paris's seventh arrondissement and at their rented palazzo, Rezzonico, in Venice, and she went gladly; in exchange Bricktop greased the wheels for Cole Porter's entry into Paris's nightlife. Porter biographer William McBrien notes, "Along with Elsa Maxwell, three black entertainers contributed to Porter's social success in the 1920's: Bricktop, Josephine Baker, and Leslie Hutchison."[34] Leslie "Hutch" Hutchison, as he was called, was a native of the island of Grenada. Unlike Paul Robeson, who may have heeded Bricktop's advice regarding the damage a divorce and interracial marriage with an Englishwoman would wreak on his career,[35] the highly accomplished piano player and cabaret performer plunged headlong into an affair with Edwina Mountbatten, a member of the British royal family. It ruined him professionally.

Porter and Bricktop indeed formed a mutually beneficial social relationship that included the composer's spending lavish amounts of money to keep

ILLUSTRATION 1.3. Invitation to the Opening of Chez Bricktop at 66 rue Pigalle. Courtesy of Yale Collection of American Literature, Beinecke Rare Book and Manuscript Library, Yale University.

the saloonkeeper in style and her various clubs in vogue and thus in business. Adding to Bricktop's social capital as fashionable was designer Elsa Schiaparelli. The saloonkeeper's success and ballooning bank account also allowed her to indulge a fondness for Cartier. She purchased two diamond rings for tidy sums from the original rue de la Paix boutique in 1928 and 1929.[36]

The friendship did not last however. Though he did host a welcoming party for her initial return to New York, sought her out at her Rome club in 1960, and she would eventually record "Miss Otis Regrets" for the composer, Bricktop's cachet was not portable. Upon her return to New York in the 1960s, she repeatedly attempted to contact Porter, who refused to see her or answer her many calls.[37] And Porter, too, known to be gracious but equally persnickety, may have realized that the social barriers crossed in Europe did not apply in America. It was a classic: "What happens in Europe stays in Europe."

As she was "beginning to consider Paris [her] home,"[38] Bricktop continued her ascent as hostess extraordinaire, moving from Le Grand Duc to Music Box and on to a succession of Chez Bricktop clubs. The last of these latter business undertakings involved a seven-year partnership with the black British-American singer Mabel Mercer, who had begun her career in vaudeville and the music halls in England. According to Mercer biographer James Haskins, Mercer, who spoke infrequently of her youthful years, was born February 3, 1900, in Staffordshire, England, to a white British vaudeville mother who went by the stage name Mabel Lablanche and a black American musician father with the last name Mercer.

She had been abandoned by both parents and pawned off on her maternal grandmother, who in turn sent her to a convent boarding school called Blakely. Upon completion of her studies at age fourteen, Mercer joined her extended family's traveling vaudeville act, the Romany Five.[39] She arrived in Paris in 1920 with the John Payne and Roseman trio, a troupe that sang Negro spirituals. Mercer began singing at the Le Grand Duc in the immediate aftermath of Florence Embry Jones's departure for Chez Florence. Her inability to mimic the style of jazz that was the craze in Paris and her angelic soprano voice left much to be desired in the jazz-crazed twenties. Bricktop eventually replaced Mercer at Le Duc in May 1924. She continued to do pickup work in revues, even performing at Chez Florence once Embry Jones departed permanently for the United States.

Bricktop found Mabel elegant. She believed the singer, with her clipped British accent, would bring an element of heightened refinement to her establishment. And Chez Bricktop was all about refinement and class. It was through Bricktop's sheer will and Cole Porter's melodic tunes that Mabel Mercer became a cabaret star in Paris. Her presence at Bricktop's helped solidify the club's stature.

With Porter's money, Schiaparelli's clothing, and Mercer's to-the-manor-born veneer, Chez Bricktop rose to the very top of expatriates' and tourists' list of places to be seen. Bricktop attributed her success to "my being able to take strangers from all different parts of the world and make a party. In Paris, Mexico, Rome and wherever I was I am a party. I do know I am a presence."[40]

In his Paris memoir with supplementary chapters by Kay Boyle, *Being Geniuses Together: A Binocular View of Paris in the '20s*, American writer Robert McAlmon, who often frequented Bricktop's, describes the savoir faire of the hostess and the cabaret's ambience in a lengthy passage:

> At the same time Brick's night club was having a good deal of success, and while she sang and danced now and then, she generally sat at her cashier's desk keeping accounts, while at the same time observing every action that went on in the cabaret. If ever a person possessed perfect co-ordination of faculties and reflexes, Brick is that person. She is large and firm-fleshed, and although she "lays down the law" while singing her songs, she thinks more of her dancing than her singing. It's a great show to watch her skipping about the floor while rendering "Bon-Bon-Buddie, the Chocolate Drop," or Cole Porter's latest witty

ILLUSTRATION 1.4. Chez Bricktop with Ada "Bricktop" Smith, Mabel Mercer, and guests, 1932. Courtesy of Manuscript, Archives, and Rare Book Library, Emory University.

song. She has singing feet, and she puts across her songs with intelligence and wit.

When . . . I arrived there the place was crowded. One drunken Frenchmen wanted to get away without paying his bill. At another table a French actress in her cups was giving her boyfriend hell and throwing champagne into his face. In the back room several Negroes were having an argument. Brick sat at the cashier's desk keeping things in order. With a wisecrack she halted the actress in her temper, cajolingly made the Frenchmen pay his bill, and all the while she was adding up accounts, calling out to the orchestra to play this or that requested number. Indicating to the waiters that this or that table needed services; and when asked, she began to sing, "Love for Sale," while still adding up accounts. Halfway through the song there was a commotion in the back room where the argument was taking place, which meant that the colored boys had now come to blows. Brick skipped down from her stool, glided across the room, still singing. She jerked aside the curtain and stopped singing long enough to say, "Hey you guys, get out in the street if you want to fight. This ain't that kind of joint!" Then she continued the song, having missing but two phrases, and was at her desk again adding accounts.

The quarrelsome lads quieted down, for Brick's admonition had been altogether understanding. She herself liked to drink, and liked an argument, and those of her race understood this. Her reproof had been good-natured, and it somehow suggested the possibility of jokes later, when most of the cash customers would be gone.[41]

McAlmon captures the atmospherics at the nightclub and the diffuse talents of its owner. A consummate multi-taskmaster, in her diary between notations on Florence Mills's arrival in Paris with the revue *Blackbirds*, Charleston lessons for Cole Porter or Lady Mendl, Bricktop enters tabulations for bottles of champagne sold.[42] She did in fact "like to drink," enjoying more than an occasional flute of champagne, which she attributed to the loss of her svelte figure. And so much so that by the late 1930s, she began tracking her consumption: "stopped drink" and "no drink 15 days."[43]

While jazz ruled in the streets of Black Montmartre on the hill during *les années folles*, at the site of the gardens of the Élysée Montmartre at 80 Boulevard de Rochechouart, down a few paces from the hill, and at rue Saint-François de Paule in Nice, a different sound could be heard. Lillian Evans-Tibbs, whose stage name was Madame Evanti, was singing operatic

ILLUSTRATION 1.5. Lillian "Madame Evanti" Evans-Tibbs as Lakmé, Paris, 1927.
Courtesy of Center for Black Music Research Library and Archives, Chicago, Illinois.

arias at the Trianon in Paris and at Nice's *belle époque* Opera House. In Nice, she performed the role of Lakmé in French composer Clément Philibert Léo Delibes's 1883 opera of the same name.[44] *Lakmé* draws its inspiration from nineteenth-century French travel writer Pierre Loti's autobiographical novel, *Rarahu ou le Mariage de Loti. Rarahu or the Marriage of Loti* is standard Loti exoticist fare: a far-flung locale (Tahiti), a French military officer who eventually chooses honor and duty to country over love, and a native woman who falls in love with the foreigner only to kill herself when that love is not reciprocated. Delibes's opera changes the locale to India since French tastes ran more toward Orientalism. The officer is British and the native woman is of Hindu origin. Lakmé is derived from the Sanskrit Lakshmi, the Hindu goddess of prosperity and beauty.

Born in Washington, DC, in 1890 into a prominent middle-class family, Annie Wilson Lillian Evans pursued a degree in music at Howard University. She married Roy Tibbs, a music professor at the university. A coloratura soprano, she sought out France for increased opportunities to perform in the opera since American racism barred her from many roles. She departed from New York on June 21, 1924, on the SS *Homeric* in the company of portrait artist Laura Wheeler.[45] With Wheeler, she settled at 59 rue Vaneau in Saint-Germain at the Hotel Jeanne d'Arc, within walking distance of the Eiffel Tower and Les Invalides, the resting place of the emperor Napoleon Bonaparte. In Paris, Lillian began her dramatic transformation into a diva, starting with the adoption of a stage name.

She combined her surname and married name into the more theatrical-sounding "Evanti," becoming professionally known as "Madame Evanti" at the suggestion of Harlem Renaissance writer and *Crisis* editor Jessie Fauset, who had arrived in Paris in September:

> Jessie Fauset joined Laura, Helen and me at a party. I wanted
> my name changed to a more euphonious-sounding one as an
> artist. So with pencil in hand, I wrote down "Evans," my maiden
> name, and "Tibbs," my husband's name. I came up with Tivani.
> But Jessie Fauset, a master of words, crossed that out and wrote
> Evanti instead. . . . [W]e uncorked a bottle of champagne, and
> I have been Evanti ever since.[46]

During her eight-month-long hiatus from America to work on her novel, Jessie Fauset met up with several "charming people, indeed, 3 of 4 friends here" in Paris, including "Mrs. Tibbs (Evanti)."[47] Madame Evanti would become the first black American woman to perform with an organized European opera company. She studied under Gabrielle Ritter-Ciampi, the lyric soprano best known for her role as Violetta in Verdi's *Traviata*, which was inspired by Alexandre Dumas-fils's (the son of the renowned writer of *The Three Musketeers* and *The Count of Monte Cristo*) 1852 novel, *La Dame aux Camélias*. By 1927, Lillian was performing the title role of Lakmé in Paris's Trianon in Montmartre, a café-concert theater that originally hosted music hall stars on the cabaret circuit like La Goulue and Mistinguett before it morphed for a time into an opera house.

In the prologue to her unfinished memoirs, "Where My Caravan Has Rested: Autobiography of International Concert and Opera Soprano Lillian Evanti," Evans-Tibbs writes:

> Come with me and join my caravan to visit great world opera houses. . . . Gypsies carried their talents as musicians, dancers, soothsayers and smithies to different parts of the world. In this manner I carried my talents through storm and sunshine. . . . There were two counts against me—I was an American of color and I had very little money. . . . Bursting with desire for action, determined to surmount vicissitudes, I was eager to do my best and a little better to achieve a new high in the cultural and artistic development of my race. Thank you la belle France for my debut in Grand Opera. France offered Libert[é], Equalit[é], Fraternit[é]. . . . I was free![48]

An old Gypsy song, "Where My Caravan Has Rested," inspired the title of Evans-Tibbs's chronicle. In the few pages she completed of this autobiography, she'd written at least two, she expresses a sentiment that many interwar-period African American women held once they arrived in France: "I was free!" Free of racial discrimination, the social constraints of puritan womanhood, and undeterred by monetary issues, the diva sought professional opportunities in the storied land of France, where liberty, equality, and fraternity seemed to rule the day in theory and practice. As fair in complexion and well educated as Evans-Tibbs was, she was unable to pole vault over the class and racial mountains in opera. Opera was high art and culture, considered the purview of the wealthy and white, none of which Evans-Tibbs could lay claim to in the United States despite her considerable talent. Like Jessie Fauset, Lillian Evans-Tibbs pursued a transatlantic rupture with America in order grow as an artist.

SHUFFLING ALONG LACLEDE'S LANDING
WITH MANY LOVES: JO BAKER

Nothing could have prepared Paris for the *tumulte noir* that arrived with Carolyn Dudley Reagan on the SS *Berengaria* in September. The much-anticipated all-black musical extravaganza *La Revue nègre* took Paris by storm in the fall of 1925 when it debuted at the Théâtre des Champs-Élysées. A premarketing blitz was launched in the Paris newspapers. Even the center-right *Le Figaro* announced the troupe's arrival at the Paris music hall: "*La Revue nègre*. 25 Negroes arrived who have done the rounds in New York. Costumes, décor, Negro music. Wonderful Jazz. For the first time in Paris."[49]

Among the troupe was Josephine Baker. Freda Josephine McDonald was born on the third of June 1906 in St. Louis, Missouri; the Cinderella rags-to-riches rise of Josephine Baker and the formation of her utopian community of Rainbow Children have filled scores of ghost-written autobiographies as well as critical biographies and scholarly articles. Even her younger sister, Margarette Martin, began writing a collaborative posthumous memoir with British biographer Henry Hurford Janes in February 1977, "The True Life of Josephine," on the woman she affectionately called "Tumpy."[50]

In short, after a childhood of mind-numbing poverty and illiteracy in slums near Laclede's Landing on the banks of the Mississippi River, Baker began performing in blackface vaudeville and, in due course, found herself in Noble Sissle and Eubie Blakes's productions *Shuffle Along* and *Chocolate Dandies* in New York, and finally as a chorine at the Plantation Club in Harlem, where the irascible singer-actress Ethel Waters headlined.

Unlike other black American women who went solo to Paris in search of opportunity or a creative community, Baker went as part of a troupe. Certainly, her many memoirs discuss the meaning of France, and Paris in particular, to black Americans: the freedom and equality offered there but not in America. And once in Paris, she contributed to the castle-in-the-sky tale: "Everyone seemed to be bursting with life. And most surprising of all, I saw couples *kissing* in the streets. In America, you went to jail for that. It was true—this *was* a free country. France was a wonderful place!"[51] Again, Henry Hurford Janes, who had also worked closely with Baker toward the end of her life and career to craft a memoir, offers a rich guide to Paris in the 1920s and Baker and the troupe's arrival by channeling the entertainer's remembrances of things past:

> The troupe came up dressed to kill on the last day, all colour and glad rags, the screaming oranges and purple of a Harlem summer. No one had bothered to tell them it would be cold and raining in Cherbourg. From the deck they could see small tramways, low houses, tiny boats—a city in miniature, and hopes began to shrink. They trailed down the docks like a group of wet parrots and shivered towards the barriers, already regretting the comforts of the Berengaria. The luggage that had looked so fine the week before gave off the damning shine of cheap leather and

cardboard in the watery light. The American customs men had pawed through everything, turned their luggage inside out, but here they were waved through peremptorily [*sic*]. . . . Rien à déclarer. When they got to the station the first thing they noticed was that all the porters were white, and there was a special group waiting to take their things. Spirits lifted right away, and they swaggered out to the train stepping high.

The porters had been paid in advance, but when Josephine's trunk rolled up she tried to give the man a big tip, 50 cents. He refused with a sneer and the money went back and forth, push and shove. She couldn't understand a word he was saying, but knew that tone of voice. *I won't take no nigger money.* Miss Rudgin came running up, laughing at Josephine's big eyes. He wanted francs, that was all. Some of the girls sniggered when they heard about it because Josephine was always trying to be grand, but she laughed louder than any of them. What a joke, it was the colour of her money that had given offence—not her skin.[52]

Much like Bricktop's arrival, Baker's and the troupe's first impressions were dampened by the weather and the sight of a city in miniature. The unmolested passage through French customs and the novel sight of white porters attending to black passengers immediately altered their perceptions of France. Used to third-class treatment even when willing to pay top-shelf prices, Baker seemed ready to lump the French in with the Americans when a porter refuses her tip. All is well we are assured by the narrative's end, as France lives up to its colorblind reputation as does Josephine with her pretensions. Reflecting in hindsight to her would-be biographer, France's social equality was only as shocking as its sexual liberalism. In America, black women were corseted, policed—and policed one another and themselves. In Paris, freedom was creative, social, and sexual. And no one made greater use of the latter in Paris than Josephine Baker.

Josephine Baker did more than temporarily flee the corset, she shredded it only to stitch its shorn pieces back together with the help of her Sicilian lover, taskmaster, and Svengali Guiseppe "Pepito" Abatino in her pursuit of professional respectability and a refined, ladylike elegance post her banana-and-pink-boaed performances. Such reinvention was entirely permissible for an African American ingénue in France.

But before this latter much-sought-after transformation came the *danse sauvage*, her going native for the French natives and iconoclast Americans in *La Revue nègre*. She enthralled F. Scott Fitzgerald with her "chocolate arabesque," and Janet Flanner, the American correspondent in Paris for *The*

ILLUSTRATION 1.6. Josephine Baker undated, seated at piano, Paris. Courtesy of Yale Collection of American Literature, Beinecke Rare Book and Manuscript Library, Yale University.

New Yorker magazine, describes the reactions to Baker's debut "fifty years later" in the introduction to *Paris Was Yesterday*. Flanner calls herself a "dullard" and her writing "timid" in her first attempts to write about Baker and *La Revue*.[53] She rewrites in hindsight:

> As a matter of fact, it [*La Revue nègre*] was so incomparably novel in French public pleasures, that its star, hitherto unknown, named Josephine Baker, remains to me now like a still fresh vision, sensual, exciting and isolated in my memory today, almost fifty years later. So here follows what I should have written then about her appearance, as a belated tribute.
>
> She made her entry entirely nude except for a pink flamingo feather between her limbs; she was being carried upside down and doing the split on the shoulder of a black giant. . . . She was an unforgettable female ebony statue. A scream of salutation spread through the theater.[54]

André Daven, director of the Théâtre des Champs Élysées, also shares reactions to the revue's opening night:

> Opening night was unforgettable. At midnight Parisian café society *invaded* the theater, shoving aside the security guards. Because of advance reviews in the press, the air was crackling with tension. . . . At last the curtain rose. . . . Now it was Josephine whose presence filled the stage, bringing with her a glimpse of another world. As she danced, quivering with intensity, the entire room felt the raw force of her passion, the excitement of her rhythm. She was eroticism personified.[55]

Both Flanner and Daven detail the sensational hunger Baker's debut caused in Paris. It was a hunger matched only by Baker's own for fame and fortune. By 1927, she was starring in *Folies du jour* where the banana belt is born with Paul Derval. And by 1928, she launches a world tour with the assistance of her manager/lover Pepito Abatino.

On the way up in those early days in Paris, Josephine Baker's star status allowed her to move from the shared digs with the other cast members to the Hotel Fournet on the Right Bank of Paris. Her penchant for extravagance, one that would also lead to her financial undoing in later years, forced her return to shared accommodations in Montmartre. It was here that she encountered Bricktop, whose reputation in Montmartre was beginning to gel.[56]

Except in the last chapter of the Baker/Bouillon autobiography, *Josephine*, where both Josie and Brick appeared at Carnegie Hall, Bricktop seems unworthy of any sustained mention in any of Baker's memoirs and post-humously published autobiographies: "When the curtain rose on opening night, revealing a portly matron, some of the spectators must have thought it was Josephine. In fact, the performer was seventy-eight year old Brick-top. . . . By 1924, she had conquered Paris and gone on to share the late twenties with Josephine."[57] Where the Baker autobiography is cryptic as to their relationship, Bricktop's 1983 memoir and cache of letters is voluminous on the subject of their complicated friendship:

> [S]he was still a kid, and she was one of the most vulnerable stars I've ever met. At the time, Negro female entertainers were still a rarity in Paris. Naturally, Josephine and I got together. She was only about seventeen years old. She brought out the mother instinct in me.
>
> She hadn't had much schooling. She could hardly write her name and suddenly everyone wanted her autograph. I said, "Baby, get a stamp." I talked her into writing her name in the clearest and best script she could manage, and having it made into a rubber stamp. That saved her a lot of embarrassment.
>
> She didn't know how to take care of nice things. . . . I became her big sister. She'd come into Le Grand Duc and ask me about everything. She'd say, "Bricky, tell me what to do." She wouldn't go around the corner without asking my advice.
>
> A big sister doesn't get far when she gives advice about men, however, and when Josephine needed advice most, I couldn't do much good.[58]

It was precisely Bricktop's counsel about Pepito Abatino that led to her years-long estrangement from Baker. In Paris, there were as many gigolos and would-be-counts as there were nightclubs. After an intense and romantic courtship, Baker was won over by Count Pepito Abatino. From Bricktop's perspective, Pepito had about as much royal blood as she had, and she began calling him "no-account Count." She was possibly right on that score, for at one point during his exclusive management of Josie's career, Pepito received fifty percent of her income and had unlimited power of attorney to negotiate on her behalf.[59]

Pepito was born in Calatifimi, a province of Palermo on November 10, 1898. Fluent in French and Italian, he allegedly received a gentleman's education, which included some military service. He was second lieutenant in the Alpine Corps of the Italian Armed Forces in World War I. After the war, he held an appointment in the Department of Widows and Orphans in the Office of War Pensions in the Italian Ministry of Finance in Rome.[60]

He met Josephine in the fall of 1926 during a visit with a cousin who lived in Paris, Vincenzo Zito, a painter and caricaturist. Pepito was twenty-seven; Josie, twenty.

They exchanged a series of letters in French before he moved permanently to Paris to be with her. Josephine was smitten and had taken to purchasing expensive jewelry and such for him, which had the effect of irritating Bricktop. Josephine had also developed a very close attachment to Pepito's family, particularly his older sister, Christina Abatino Scoto, and his mother, Maria Di Bassa Molé, continuing correspondences for over a forty-year period and, at one point, even leaving Christina Scoto all powers to manage her estate, Château des Milandes, during her absence in 1947.[61]

There has been some speculation about both Bricktop's and Josephine's sexuality and whether their relationship was more than platonic and sisterly. Baker's adopted son, Jean-Claude, is the primary source of this conjecture. Jean-Claude Baker participated in a series of interviews with Bricktop about Josephine Baker and Paris during his mother's heyday.[62] Neither interviewee

ILLUSTRATION 1.7. Château des Milandes, Castelnaud-la-Chapelle, France. Josephine Baker's estate in the Dordogne region of France. Courtesy of Yale Collection of American Literature, Beinecke Rare Book and Manuscript Library.

mentions a romantic relationship between them. And Jean-Claude Baker's revelations of sexual intimacy between the two are offered up only after Bricktop's death in 1984.

And yet, Bricktop's interference with Pepito's and Josephine's budding relationship lends some credence to such speculations. Moreover, Josephine Baker's personal letters reveal an intense relationship with an unnamed woman in her later years—who was not Bricktop.[63] And some scholars have suggested a one-night stand between Frida Kahlo and Baker during the Mexican artist's time in Paris.

In the community of black women in Paris in the interwar years, lesbian relationships and bisexuality were common despite the beards of marriage. Alberta Hunter married and never consummated her relationship with her husband while she continued a long and at times tumultuous relationship with Lottie Tyler, the niece of actor Bert Williams. Ethel Waters married three times, and yet her fights with her lesbian lovers were legion, causing embarrassment for the likes of Hunter who believed that such relationships should be carried out clandestinely and respectfully. Baker, representing a grab-bag of French male sexual fantasy and later a symbol of elegance, respectability, and a civil rights stalwart, never addressed the rumors swirling around her sexual predilections.

And for her part, Bricktop, who married Peter Ducongé on December 29, 1929, a jazz saxophonist originally from New Orleans, appears unequivocal on the matter:

> I had plenty of opportunities for friendships—with men and women. I had some romantic involvements, and I could have had romantic involvements with women, but I never liked women. . . . Even meeting a bunch of other women for lunch wasn't my disposition.
>
> I also kept my private life private. My clients didn't know who my lovers were. It wasn't any of their business. . . . I was doing plenty in those days. It was always with men, and always with one at a time, of course, but in those early Paris years I had a lot of men—a whole passel of men—and I did it up and down alleys, in taxi cabs, in the bed, out of the bed, all around the bed. I slept with white men and black men.[64]

Bricktop's no nonsense candor about her sexual history runs counter to Jean-Claude Baker's narrative. But, of course, being honest about risqué heterosexual behavior in a risqué era is very different from Bricktop's own understanding of the prohibitions against public lesbianism then *and* when she was coauthoring her memoirs. Indeed, her admitted skill at secretiveness and discretion would seem to have abetted such liaisons. On Gay Paris, she notes, "As I've said, everybody was fooling around with everybody else. There was homosexuality, but it was pretty discreet."[65] Whether the fallout between Josie and Bricky was due to sexual jealousy or overzealous sisterly concern as rumors mounted that Pepito, an extraordinary business manager for Baker to be sure, had further convinced Josephine to place all her assets in his name,[6] thus leading to some legal wrangling with his family after his death in 1936, the two legends eventually mended fences.

On Friday, March 17, 1948, Bricktop writes her sister, Blonzetta, from her Mexico City Bricktop club. She discusses the weather and then goes on to mention that Josephine had visited: "Josephine Baker from Paris had big success here. She's back in Paris and I had a letter from her today. She wants me to come over to bring her mother and sister who live in St. Louis Mo so they can live over there with her but we think there is going to be another war . . ."[67]

The friendship between Josie and Bricky as well as Baker's success in Paris might never have been had the socialite Caroline Dudley Reagan had her way. The entrepreneurial Reagan wanted Florence Mills, one-third of Brick-

ILLUSTRATION 1.8. Bricktop and Josephine Baker at Bricktop's in Mexico City, undated. Courtesy of Manuscript, Archives, and Rare Book Library, Emory University.

top's Panama Trio from Chicago, at the top of the bill. She had offered the nymph-like Mills the starring role in *La Revue nègre*. Mills was previously committed. A mezzo soprano, Mills had a string of music hall revues under her belt in New York. She began with Noble Sissle and Eubie Blake's mega-hit *Shuffle Along*, which also featured Baker and *Imitation of Life* star Fredi Washington. Her stated salary on August 4, 1921, was $100 ($1300 today); but by September 5, 1921, scribbled in the margin of her contract in Noble Sissle's hand, her salary was raised to $125 per week.[68] Unable to meet the salary demands of the rising celebrity, she signed on with Lew Leslie's *Plantation Revue* and *Dixie to Broadway*. Leslie raised her salary to $200 ($2600 today) per week for a five-week, seven-performance engagement, beginning February 2, 1922.[69] Leslie booked Mills for the C. B. Cochran 1923 London musical *Dover Street to Dixie*. Of Mills's *Shuffle Along* performance, Claude McKay, Harlem Renaissance novelist, journalist, and author of the inspirational poem "If We Must Die," wrote at length in his autobiography, *A Long Way from Home*:

> Happy Harlem had come to Broadway in a titillating musical piece called *Shuffle Along*. . . . And there was Florence Mills. Florence Mills was so effortless in her perfect mimicry and elfin brown voice that the Negro impresarios were not even aware that they possessed in her a priceless goldstar. For they had given her a secondary role in the revue. Never had I seen a colored actress whose artistry was as fetching as Florence Mills's. After the show I went backstage to see her. I said: "You're the star of the show." No, she said, the stars are Lottie Gee and someone else whose name I don't remember. I said, "You're the star for me, and I'm going to say so in my review." She laughed deliciously.
>
> I thought I'd feature *Shuffle Along* in the *The Liberator*. . . . [T]hat issue of *The Liberator* was a sensation among the theatrical set of Harlem.
>
> Florence Mills ran away with the show, mimicking and kicking her marvelous way right over the heads of all the cast . . . until she was transformed into a glorious star.[70]

Claude McKay was so taken with Mills that he also engaged her to perform on behalf of the Liberator Publishing Company to "sing three songs between midnight and 2 A M March 10, 1922, at the New Star Casino 107th St and Lexington Ave."[71] Under the direction of Lew Leslie, Mills's career soared, with the capstone experience of the international *Blackbirds 1926*, a revue that also featured Mabel Mercer in the London chorus. While Leslie rummaged around in "Welcome Back to the Good Old Days" plantation-themed productions, he was intent on making Florence Mills an international star, a black showgirl phenomenon to rival the white showgirls of the Ziegfeld Follies.

That every aspiring black female chanteuse from Harlem to Broadway in 1920s black entertainment hoped to emulate Mills's successes would be an understatement. Both Josephine Baker and Ethel Waters during their time at the Plantation Club together understood that, in the words of Waters, "the world loves a winner."[72] And Florence Mills was the declared winner, the new "It" girl, all the way up to Harlem and back down to Broadway. Indeed, the song that many today associate with Josephine Baker, "I'm a Little Blackbird," was a signature song of Mills's repertoire from her 1925 *Dixie to Broadway* show. When she finally sang it in Paris to rave reviews and rapt audiences at the theater-restaurant club Les Ambassadeurs, she had to learn the French version phonetically, writing:

> Jer swee ung waso nwar
> Kee shairsh o fong du see el l'waso blu
> Mong kerr, cooleur du swar

> Je suis un oiseau noir
> Qui cherche au fond du ciel l'oiseau bleue
> Mon coeur, couleur du soir.[73]

Mills's climb to the top of the music hall industry had some assistance from Bricktop early in her career. Staying at the same rooming house in Chicago, Bricktop urged Isadore Levine, owner of the Panama Club, to allow Mills to join the trio. When Mills arrived in New York in search of work, she again sought out Bricktop at Barron's Exclusive, where the affable Bricky asked the owner to hire Mills. According to Bill Egan's biography of Florence Mills, the greatest assist from Bricky came when she "used her friendship with Harriet Sissle [Noble Sissle's wife] to press Florence's claim" for a part in *Shuffle Along*.[74] Mills would repay Bricky for her years of loyalty by sending her money to assist her with some legal entanglements in Berlin in the summer of 1927. In August 1921 in New York, Noble Sissle eventually relented and a new star was born in black theater.

Born Florence Winfrey on January 25, 1896, per her passport, though a District of Columbia health officer lists her date of birth as January 15, 1896, at 503 D Street N. W. Washington, DC,[75] the tiny, sweet-voiced Mills took the stage name Mills in honor of the attending physician, R. N. Mills, at her birth.[76] By the time she arrived in Paris in 1926 with The Blackbirds, or Les Oiseaux Noirs,[77] she had garnered the attention of *Vogue* and *Vanity Fair*, earning a photographic spread in the February 1925 issue of the latter, and Paul Colin would sketch a lithograph of her that many

ILLUSTRATION 1.9. Florence Mills, undated. Courtesy of Yale Collection of American Literature, Beinecke Rare Book and Manuscript Library, Yale University.

continue to identify as "Man with Hat."[78] The *Vanity Fair* coverage was a first for any black entertainer, including the venerable Paul Robeson, who would not be featured until 1933.

Like Baker, Mills arrived in Paris on the *France* with a troupe in May 1926. This is perhaps where any real similarities with Baker stop. Bricktop is the first from the Black Montmartre set to welcome her to the city with a typo-riddled telegram, "Welcome to Paris may Non [You] and Noer [Your] Company Have the Success of your Life Pal Brick."[79] Unlike Baker, Mills was already a star in her country of birth in her own right. She was able to skip the "Naked at the Feast" antics that made Josephine a star in France. That her presence in Paris in 1926 overshadowed her *Shuffle Along* former cast mate was due in part to the fickleness of the Parisian public, Mills's newness on the Paris revue scene, and her uncompromising talent.

The French went agog over Mills and Les Oiseaux Noirs, which opened at the chic Les Ambassadeurs on the avenue Gabriel, adjacent to the Champs-Élysées toward the Place de la Concorde. Her voice was declared "full of charm and expression,"[80] and she was crowned "the queen of jazz dance."[81] Comparisons between Flo and Jo were inevitable in the French press. Baker had been in France not quite a year. But her place in the hearts, minds, and libidinal French fantasies was firmly secure. The French preferred their ideas of blacks as childlike, exotic, and sexual. Mills was thin, small, and birdlike with round saucer-like eyes; and she was way too demure for the role of sex siren or exotic savage. Indeed, it would be Mills's refinement and her vocal stylistics that Baker would try on for size when she began to shed the French corset of exoticism, much to the chagrin of her Parisian audiences.[82] Paris burnished Mill's star brighter; she had not arrived, however, in the City of Light hoping to repeat what the French had done for Baker professionally. She enjoyed Paris, liked France and the French, and greatly appreciated the success that every star needs for the next big venture. But she had no intentions of staying. Paris did nonetheless provide a ready-made community for her to escape to after the grind of the theater, a Harlem in Montmartre.

Once in the City of Light, she and her husband, U.S. Kid Thompson, met up with Bricktop. Bricktop had been in Paris two years. By July 1926, she had opened and closed the club Music Box, and reassumed her position as hostess at Le Grand Duc. She dined with "Flo" and "Kid" frequently during that summer in Paris.[83] And on a few occasions, those dinners involved the composer, music critic, and singer Nora Holt.[84]

A native of Kansas and daughter of the Reverend Calvin N. Douglas, Holt was born Lena Douglas in 1885 in Kansas City. She graduated with a degree in music from Western University in Quindaro, Kansas, and later pursued a master's degree from the Chicago Musical College, earning her the distinction of being the first African American woman to have done so in 1918. Douglas's move to Chicago allowed her to flourish as a music critic for the *Chicago Defender* and cofounder of the National Association of Negro Musicians in 1919. With her marriage to George Holt, a wealthy saloonkeeper who had left her a sizable inheritance at his death,[85] she changed her first name to Nora in 1916 and took his last name. In 1931, she studied voice at the American Conservatory of Music in Fontainebleau, France.[86]

Her talents have been interestingly overshadowed by her five marriages to men of some means, a series of very messy public divorces, and her friendship with Harlem Renaissance patron Carl Van Vechten upon her move to New York. Van Vechten's portrait of the seductress Lasca Sartoris fresh from Paris in *Nigger Heaven* is a full-blown tribute to Holt wherein the narrator waxes on about the siren:

> [T]he most striking woman . . . like a cocotte of the golden era! . . . She had beauty, wit and money. She was rich and successful and happy. She had won. Problems didn't bother her. She had found what she wanted by wanting what she could get, and then always demanding more, more, until now the world poured gifts into her bewitching lap . . . so vibrant a personality . . . and golden brown.[87]

Holt relished the send-up. Something of an iconoclast, Holt began her friendship with both Bricktop and Mills in Chicago and continued the relationships in New York. She set sail for Paris on a Saturday in May 1926 on the *SS France* in room 617. Prior to her arrival in Paris, she was known as Nora Holt Ray, signaling yet another marriage and this time to the wealthy Joseph L. Ray, the personal secretary to millionaire financier Charles M. Schwab in July 1923. She proclaimed the acrimonious divorce nineteen months later with its back-and-forth recriminations "a flimsy suit . . . I can beat it hands down, but did not want the annoyance. However, the publicity should be of value."[88]

By October 1926, she had dropped the name Ray for her debut at the Les Nuits du Prado in Paris. Having dyed her hair blond, Holt writes cynically to Van Vechten of the French: "These French are too excitable to be stable. . . . The little music hall "Prado" goes on well. It is quite chic, no dancing and only French people. Imagine them liking me and they don't know a word I am singing or what it's all about. The real truth is, I'm selling my hair and personality. So far so good. I am not greatly enthused. It's a lark for me you know."[89]

ILLUSTRATION 1.10. Nora Holt. Courtesy of Yale Collection of American Literature, Beinecke Rare Book and Manuscript Library, Yale University.

Though she strikes a derisive tone about the French, Holt is nonetheless taken with the Paris she found in the late fall of 1926:

> What an experience I am all excited about it. The French people—I find insincere and wary and too poor to live. But Paris—Everything that happens in the world happens here also. I spread my pallette [sic] and cast its many colours.
>
> The women are all alike mourner gait and dress and the men are *impasaible* [sic] and one hears eternally the cry of poverty. I soon pick it up myself. To all beggars, I remark, "Je suis très pauvre" with the saddest expression I know. In wonderment they pass on . . . I like most to walk in the Bois Sunday morning at 11. Such a parade! And *tous le soir* [sic], I walk from the Arche [sic] de Triomphe to Cleopatra's Needle about 2 miles in 50 minutes. An hour of rest, then to work. Am in awfully good health and when I return to dear old NY will be ready for a Charleston marathon. Am sending my photo tomorrow. Don't be alarmed. It's me *a verité* [sic]. *Moi.* It's just how like I look now and I don't go to the Fannie Ward's Fountain of Youth shop. I only pass there every night when I walk down the Champs-Élysées.
>
> Miss Stein wrote me . . . that she would be home in a few weeks. She remarked—Carl has been writing me about a Nora Ray. You write me Nora Holt. Well, "Rose is a Rose is ——."[90]

In a throwaway comment about the actress Fannie Ward's botched facelift, Holt nonetheless understands her role in the Parisian economy of desire. And like many Americans unable to penetrate the interior lives of the citizens in their temporarily adopted host country, Holt nevertheless adores Paris for its possibilities. Her rainbow of opportunities is made possible because of her black American femaleness; in selling her hair (which she had dyed blond) and personality (a black American female foreignness that the French found irresistible), she became the quintessence of exotic, feminine beauty as imagined by the French—an indeed rare combination of youthful blond, African American womanliness.

With her femme fatale reputation preceding her at every turn, Nora receives a cablegram asking if she would "consider starring in an important Negro Revue" by none other than Carolyn Dudley Reagan. Dudley Reagan explains that it was she who "took Revue Negre to Paris."[91] Having had no idea who Carolyn Dudley Reagan of "60 West 12th Street"[92] in New York is, Nora seeks Van Vechten's counsel on the matter, as she heads for a season-long booking in Monte Carlo set to open on January 13. It appears that Dudley Reagan was on the hunt for another revue. Baker had moved on to the Casino de Paris, sparking a dispute with the entrepreneur over the starlet's contractual obligations. Mills was naturally unavailable again, reprising *Blackbirds 1926* in London.

Dudley Reagan found herself much in the same spot in 1926 as she had been in 1925, casting about for the perfect female lead. In 1926, Nora Holt appeared on her radar. In 1925, with Mills committed, she turned initially to Ethel Waters before striking gold with Baker. Reluctant to travel, Ethel Waters had asked for a hefty fee for the *Revue nègre* booking. Waters recalls:

> I . . . [was] asked to go to Europe and appear in Paris. I said I preferred to see America first. So I asked for five hundred dollars a week, which was like asking those French for all their Chateaubriand steak and world-famous fried potatoes. They do not part happily with a buck, those French, and five hundred dollars a week! *Sacrebleu!*
>
> Josephine, who didn't want so much, [went] to France. Josephine ended up with a chateau, an Italian count, and all Paris at her feet permanently. Again, *sacrebleu!*[93]

Waters, born October 31, 1896, in Chester, Pennsylvania, did eventually arrive in Paris four years later in 1929. Once there, she made it to the hill where the growing black American colony gathered. She wrote of various encounters there with Florence Embry Jones and the triple-threat dancer, singer, and trumpet player Valaida Snow, who would later have guest appearances in two French films, *L'Alibi* (1937) and *Pièges* (1939), and play dates at the Paris Coliseum in 1938 with French jazz great Django Reinhardt. Such were her trumpet-playing skills that she was often compared to Louis Armstrong, even sometimes called "Little Louis Armstrong." Known for her flamboyance and tendency to parse the truth, Snow married three times and was fond of traveling in "an orchid-colored Mercedes-Benz, dressed in an orchid suit, her pet monkey rigged out in an orchid jacket and cap, with her chauffer in orchid as well."[94] She spent nearly fourteen years abroad, touring the world, from the Far East to Eastern Europe. When work proved scarce in one place, her talents would take her to another.

Her beginnings ran through Chattanooga, Tennessee. Born on June 2, in 1904, or 1900, 1903, 1909,[95] Snow arrived in Paris in 1929, setting up residence like so many other female performance artists in Montmartre. She made her debut at the Embassy nightclub on the Champs-Élysées in October of that year.[96] She partied and dined with Bricktop and toured Paris oftentimes in the company of Alberta Hunter and her soon-to-be professional nemesis, Ethel Waters.

ILLUSTRATION 1.11. Ethel Waters, undated. Courtesy of Yale Collection of American Literature, Beinecke Rare Book and Manuscript Library.

On Waters's few-months sojourn in Paris, the city's culinary delights failed to satisfy her Southern palate. In stepped Bricktop to offer up a home away from home in Paris:

> I remember Ethel Waters's first trip to Paris. She was the talk of the town, but she took me aside and confided, "Brick, I'm starving to death." It wasn't a matter of money, but of food. Right in the middle of Paris, with all those fabulous restaurants, Ethel was starving for some real American food, so I let her move into my place for about three weeks and she cooked collard greens to her heart's content. Ethel was never one to stay or to drink. I was able to turn Paris for her from a nightmare into a place where she could really enjoy herself in her own way.[97]

While the broader Montmartre community provided a space that most resembled Harlem, Bricktop offered a private space and, more to the point, a domestic one—the kitchen—in order to facilitate Waters's adjustment in Paris. Brick's apartment at 47 rue Trudaine in Montmartre felt like home.

Though Waters remembers dancing in Paris "quite a bit" with bantamweight champion Panama Al Brown in Paris, being compared to "Josephine" when she did go out at night, which must have felt bizarrely like trading places since the two had traded fierce barbs and dirty looks after Baker stood in for Ethel at the Plantation Club because of a "pondful of frogs in her throat,"[98] and meeting up with Florence Embry Jones, who had actually left Paris by then, Bricktop's generosity is not repaid in the thespian's 1951 autobiography, *His Eye Is on the Sparrow.* Otherwise Waters's time in Paris is very sketchy except for the pages upon pages devoted to her discussing her foray into motherhood with her "adopted" daughter Algretta and secondhand recollections from those who interacted with her such as cabaret singer Elisabeth Welch and Bricktop during her stay in the city.

New York born and bred, London expatriate Welch was born Elisabeth Margaret Welsh in 1904. Later changing her name to Welch, "Lis," as she was called, was very clear that she was not from the Harlem set, that she lived on 63rd Street.[99] Nonetheless she found her way to Harlem and later on to Paris as part of Leslie's *Blackbirds 1929*, where she describes her days as "absolutely splendid" and found the city "completely relaxed, compared to America."[100] During her time in Paris, Welch had even served as an occasional correspondent for the *New York Amsterdam News*, reporting on the ceremonies honoring fallen American soldiers in France.[101]

Of Waters, Welch recalls, "She was adorable. . . . a marvelous singer, had a lovely face and she had fun. She didn't like everybody, especially girl singers."[102] Josephine Baker, Billie Holiday, Lena Horne, and later Valaida

ILLUSTRATION 1.12. Valaida Snow, undated. Courtesy of Manuscript, Archives, and Rare Book Library, Emory University.

Snow, particularly after producer Lew Leslie built *Rhapsody in Black* around the trumpet player, had all incurred Waters's wrath and fury. Even Alberta Hunter remembered how "Ethel gave me a bad time. . . . She treated me like a dog. Fine artist, but oh, she was so mean."[103]

Though Waters states that Florence Embry Jones was "becoming rich and famous with her Chez Florence,"[104] by 1929, Bricktop had eclipsed Embry Jones to become the reigning queen of the jazz cabaret in Montmartre, which would have been ample motivation for her telling the more reserved Alberta Hunter that Bricktop pocketed Bullard's "Come to Paris" cablegram. Louis Mitchell, due to his own fondness for spirits and gambling, had been forced to relinquish interest in Chez Florence. Bricktop sought his advice about opening the short-lived club, Music Box. Together, they opened Music Box in a house-turned-brothel that had been formerly occupied by one of the Van Gogh sisters and was right across the street from the original Chez Florence. Later, another longstanding and perennially popular Chez Florence opened but without Embry Jones as the headlining act. Jones and her husband departed for the United States in November 1927, leaving Alberta Hunter to take her place in the cabaret, and by 1932, Embry Jones was dead. Indeed, Elisabeth Welch sang at the new Chez Florence many a night, replacing Mabel Mercer who had moved on to Chez Bricktop.

Welch's memories and memoirs give insight into Bricktop's omnipresence in Montmartre, which may have set off Waters's well-documented insecurities, but also into how that presence was a beacon for other black women, particularly performers: "All the greats went to Bricktop's and she was a wonderful hostess. When I visited Bricktop's she would invite me to do a 'turn.' It was expected if you went to her club and were known to be a cabaret artist. Let's face it, we liked being asked."[105] It may be that Waters decided to remember Florence Embry Jones and her Chez Florence because it allowed her to reminisce about how Embry Jones paid for private singing lessons so that she could "study my style" back in Harlem.[106] That Waters could be ornery and was known to have serious bouts of professional jealousy perhaps translated into her omitting from her memoirs the three-week respite provided by Bricktop.

And though Waters didn't write of Bricktop during her time in Paris in *His Eye Is on the Sparrow*, she certainly wrote of her to "her Nordic Savior," Carl Van Vechten, on October 9, 1929: "The reason I'm still in Paris living out in the country not at Brick's is because I'm under a doctor's care who is curing my throat for that wart which had grown on my left vocal cord."[107] Waters had journeyed to Paris to rest her strained vocal cords. Once there, she sought the medical help of a specialist, who eventually sliced the growth off the vocal cord.

ILLUSTRATION 1.13. Elisabeth Welch, 1935. Courtesy of National Portrait Gallery, London, United Kingdom.

Of Waters's condition, Bricktop in turn wrote to Van Vechten four days earlier: "Ethel is getting along fine with her throat[.] [S]he is living out in the country at Mitchell's home. I think she will open in London sometime in November if her throat is all right."[108] What is evidently clear is that the fluid community of black women forming in and around Paris's Montmartre quarter, while close knit and supportive, did not escape those human frailties of ambition, jealousy, and pettiness.

"HEAVEN ON EARTH FOR THE NEGRO . . . WOMAN": ON BEAUTY AND LETTERS FROM PARIS

The flow of black female entertainers, seeking in many ways to replicate the successes of Bricktop, Baker, and Mills, continued from America to France. On August 5, 1927, Memphis, Tennessee, native Alberta Hunter decided to take her talents abroad. Sailing on the *De Grasse* liner, Hunter arrived in Paris with Lottie Tyler at her side. She was thirty-two years old. The two headed directly to Montmartre, taking a room at the Hotel de Paris at 55 rue Pigalle after a short stay with friends at 35 rue Victor-Massé, the same building occupied by Bricktop. After doing the requisite turn at Bricktop's, Hunter frequently sang at Chez Florence and later Fred Payne's bar before she left to sing in Nice, Monaco, and other parts of the continent, and even appeared at the Casino de Paris.[109] Despite the raunchiness of some of her more bluesy ballads, Hunter could sing upbeat cabaret music with equal verve, and she personally insisted on comporting herself along the dictates of black female respectability under which Jessie Fauset chaffed in America but to which others, including Bricktop, also laid claim in Europe—at least publicly.

Social decorum represents another area of contrasting self-representations between Bert and Brick in Paris. With both women in such close proximity in Montmartre, they recommenced their complicated friendship of personal feuding, mutual respect and caring, and caterwauling jealousy. They dined together, sang together, and clubbed together. But Bricktop's "always keep it classy" mantra and self-imposed shunning of foul language is challenged by Alberta Hunter's detailed recollections of the demure but spunky saloonkeeper "clacking around Pigalle by day in her copper shoes and housecoat, shouting raucously from the street up to the windows of friends, 'Hey you bitches, whatcha doing?' and 'Kiss my ass,' if someone like Alberta didn't respond."[110]

Hunter might have very well caught her friend during one of her notorious therapeutic walks for bad nerves. Bricktop had suffered from a nervous breakdown after a few years in Paris. Mere weeks before the stock market crash that immediately sent the American economy into turmoil, Bricktop had her own crash. In October 1929, she writes the bon vivant

Carl Van Vechten about her mother's visit to Paris, Ethel Waters's throat malady, the sensation Nora (Holt) Ray was making in London, and her own fragile psychological and physical condition asking him to "[p]lease excuse bad writing as I have or am just getting over a nervous spell. . . . I sure went through hell for a few days. [T]he doctor has ordered me to take a rest so I am opening a place in Cannes in January."[111] Her French doctors insisted that her breakdown was due to her accommodating nature in her business practices; she had allowed her frustrations to bottle up. The cure was a sort of scream therapy in which it was recommended that she march up and down Montmartre's streets saying all the things she would never, ever say. As Bricktop remembers it:

> I had a nervous breakdown. . . . I broke down because I was working too hard, trying to please too many people. . . . I was jittery, bad-tempered, depressed. I went to a doctor, who said I was suffering from repressed nerves, that I was holding myself in. It came from saying yes to everybody for so many hours each day. "You've got something inside that you have to let out," he said. . . . "Start saying 'No, go to hell.'" "I don't swear," I said. Then he gave me some really good advice. "When it's raining, walk in the rain and just scream out loud whatever you feel." Well it rains a lot in Paris, especially in the mornings, and it was in the mornings after a night of running Bricktop's that I'd go out. . . . I'd be screaming very nicely and my face would be all wet and the rain streaming down over my cheeks, and I'd feel much better. . . . I'd watch the window shutters open, the concierges come out and start sweeping the sidewalks, the flower and fruit vendors opening their stalls. They didn't pay any attention to the crazy little woman walking along screaming at the top of her voice. The people of Montmartre understood and never complained. Once in a while a stranger would hear me and inquire of one of the gendarmes, and he'd answer, "Oh, that's just Madame Bricktop getting rid of her nerves."[112]

Bert had to have known about Brick's bout with nerves, but given her lingering hurt about the pilfered Paris cablegram, and then another suspicion that Brick pinched a second invitation meant for Alberta in 1935 to perform in Budapest, not to mention Bert's probable jealousy concerning Bricktop's subsequent successes at her expense, she dispensed little compassion in Brick's favor and instead opted for caricature, even going as far as saying that Bricktop "dyed her hair orange."[113]

The second charge launched by Alberta against Bricktop in 1935 concerned an invitation to perform in Budapest—one of Bricktop's favorite cities given a few romantic entanglements she fondly pursued there. Allegedly, Brick nicked an invitation meant for Alberta during her guesting at Fred Payne's Bar. The client had only heard about Bert and thus equipped with a full description, upon meeting the "light-skinned, freckle-faced Bricktop . . . shouted, 'You get on the next train and go back because you're not the nigger I sent for.' "[114] That Brick or Bert, who raved about Europe's lack of a color bar, would have agreed to work for any proprietor who brazenly used such language is questionable. In playing the dozens, it appears that Alberta reached for hyperbole to drive home a point about Bricktop's penchant for mischief as well as to make plain the demand for Alberta's very own unique brand of talent in Europe.

Despite these setbacks, real or perceived, Alberta Hunter did achieve considerable success once she arrived in Paris, and this despite the fact that she constantly ran up against criticisms of her particular kind of beauty, so much so that Hunter had taken to referring to herself as ugly.[115] Accolades describing her extraordinary talent, allure, and grace were pockmarked with "buts" and "despites" with respect to her beauty quotient. Some went so far as to say she was "mannish," "didn't even have good tits," "her ugliness was fascinating," and she lacked sex appeal.[116] Oddly, these critics were not the Europeans who welcomed her with open arms but fellow black American entertainers, who, simultaneously dumbfounded and perplexed by Hunter's magnetism and success as an international talent, adhered to a color and beauty hierarchy reinforced by American show business practices and gendered racialism.

Alberta's browner, less aquiline features and less voluptuous figure were immediately discounted in an era of showbiz America where fairer, shapely black women fared better. Hunter's beauty quotient was comparable to Josephine Baker's, who had also been cast aside as "too dark and too skinny" to be a Broadway or uptown headliner; what both lacked, for want of a better word, in rigid aesthetics of black American feminine beauty, they made up for with talent and charisma. Clearly attractive, Hunter played "nicety" with her audiences, a combination of nice and nasty.[117] She'd be coy, sensual, sexy, but not outright nasty, as if in deliberate contrast to the sexually laden double entendres of her blues music. Songs like "Two-Fisted, Double Jointed Man" and "Organ Grinder" were suggestive, naughty, oozing with eroticism even when delivered by the upright Hunter. She wore slinky couture dresses, but there were no accompanying wild hip gyrations, uncontrollable bumping, grinding, and shimmying to fill in the listener's imagination. It was all in the delivery.

ILLUSTRATION 1.14. Alberta Hunter, Paris 1929. Courtesy of Schomburg Center for Research in Black Culture, New York Public Library, Astor, Lenox, Tilden Foundations.

Like Bricktop before her, Hunter began a series of "Letters from Paris" with the *Chicago Defender*, *New York Amsterdam News*, and *Pittsburgh Courier*. In France, she hurdled over the obstacles of race, color, and feminine beauty. In her first missive from Paris, she writes of the beautiful architecture, the "most spectacular" cabarets, her outings with Fredi Washington and Florence Mills, and "Mr. and Mrs. Jones (meaning Florence and Palmer Jones)," having "the smartest cabaret" that "cater[s] to royalty and the ultra smart people of Europe," and more importantly the lack of racial animus:

> I am just beginning to gain consciousness. I pictured everything quite beautiful, but not so beautiful as they are. I do not know when I will be home. I am mad about the freedom of Paris. Color means nothing over here. If anything they treat the colored people better. . . . The white Americans look positively silly over here. They do their utmost to start trouble—to start the color question—but to no avail. To begin with, the French people do not like them. I am only praying no colored person will ever cause the French people to dislike us; as Paris, in fact, all of France, is a heaven on earth for the Negro man or woman.[118]

Even as Hunter eventually concludes that American cabaret is light years ahead of that of France, which "depend[s] solely upon nudity, which has a tendency to get on one's nerves," there is nothing quite like Paris.

Alberta hop-scotches across Europe, as far as Turkey and Egypt, visiting some twenty-five countries over thirteen years; yet, she always ended up back in France. The work permit laws were less restrictive. But France also drew her in because of her reception in the country. Though she would fall in love with Copenhagen, France was her oyster. She writes in another letter about her dazzling reception on the Cote d'Azur in Nice:

> The people applauded, stamped, yelled bravos, and I did encore after encore. I did the "Black Bottom" in my own humble way, but to them it was great. I came here for one week, have been asked to stay three months. . . . This is a very beautiful city and it is quite like Paris. You would be very proud if you could see . . . how I am received.[119]

With descriptions such as "heaven on earth" and "being mad about the freedom of Paris," Alberta helped contribute to the land-of-milk-and-honey lore of France in her letters. Like most performers who occasionally served as foreign correspondents abroad to the cash-strapped black press in America, Hunter speaks only of her successes, the ups, and rarely the downs in her reminisces. She occasionally tsk-tsked the bad behavior of certain black entertainers whom she claimed made it difficult for others. Though she never named names, Valaida Snow's would have been on the tip of her tongue just as it had been on the pen tips of writers for the *Chicago Defender* and *Pittsburgh Courier* in February 1938. Snow had skipped out on a hotel bill in Montmartre, leaving drug paraphernalia, and as recompense did a small bid in a Paris hoosegow.[120] For Hunter, the lows in France came only with the collapse of the economy in which working conditions became increasingly tough. Scandinavia was a boon, but she did warn Americans off Germany as Nazism began to rear its head. On a stopover in Germany on her way to Denmark, children on Hamburg's streets had treated her to a round of "Nigger, nigger, nigger."[121]

She returned to the United States in 1930 whereupon seeing the "Statue of Liberty brought tears to her eyes instead of joy."[122] Opportunities to perform were few and far between. She complained bitterly,

> So far as I am concerned . . . I would be willing to stay in Europe always. I was treated kindly everywhere and my work was heartily appreciated. . . . Here in America . . . my reception has been different. . . . They [American audiences] do not want refinement and finesse in a Negro performer. All they want is niggerism, a whole lot of foot-stamping and shouting.[123]

But Alberta couldn't stay forever in Europe as she had to attend to her mother, Miss Laura. As soon as she was able, she immediately booked return passage to Europe with a first stop in France in May 1933.

Alberta continued the back and forth to Europe, mentoring along the way another rising star who went from Harlem to Montmartre, Adelaide Hall. Stuck on the other side of the pond, Alberta wanted out just as the U.S. State Department issued a warning to Americans in Europe to leave the continent for safer harbors. Oblivious to the imminent dangers abroad because of the seeming magnitude of the ones she faced at home, Alberta writes the passport division to request a renewal for travel to Europe on May 1, 1940:

> I am a colored American girl but have been to Europe for about fourteen years. I have been in twenty-five different countries, having sung in each. . . . Will you please let me go back to Europe where I am accepted as a fine artist and where my color is not a *curse*? [Hunter's emphasis]. I speak, read and write

French fluently. I sing in French, Danish, Italian, Viennese. I sing any type of songs but the classics still I cannot get work in my own country. They say I'm too refine [*sic*]. . . . I do not want anyone to give me anything. I am too proud for that but I am turned down because of my "*race*" [Hunter's emphasis]. I have my passport and my English visa is still good in fact it will be for another month.[124]

With "regrets" and after "careful and sympathetic consideration," the request was denied. Alberta Hunter is asked to turn over passport number 708. She would tour with the United Service Organizations, but her days as a headliner in Europe were over until her resurrection in the 1980s.

DIGA DIGA DOING IN MONTMARTRE'S BIG APPLE

"Florence is gone, Bricktop is with the British. A new colorful girl swings out from Montmartre's midnight throne! Everybody Suzy-Q in homage to Miss Adelaide Hall!"

—Langston Hughes, "Adelaide Hall New Star of Paris Night Life"

Born in Brooklyn, New York, on October 20, 1901, Adelaide Louise Hall's birth was not registered at City Hall. Her undocumented beginnings are in sharp contrast to the amount of ink used to track her day-to-day activities as an acclaimed theater performer. Hall never achieved the kind of notoriety that conferred on her a one-name moniker, like Josephine or Bricktop. She was Miss Hall. But the fame of "the chocolate brown, young, vivacious and good to look upon on"[125] Adelaide did pique the jealousy of both women when she set up shop in their backyard of Paris. She had however shared the stage as a chorine with Josephine in *Shuffle Along*. The two had an uneasy friendship due to Jo's aloofness that moved into the realm of professional rivalry for a time in Paris, before eventually settling on something like close companions in the late 1930s following Pepito Abatino's death and the end of World War II.

In 1925, Hall had her first tour abroad in Budapest, Stockholm, Vienna, Zurich, and Berlin with the musical *Chocolate Kiddies*. It was the first black revue of its scale and size to arrive on the European continent in May 1925, months before Dudley's *La Revue nègre*. The SS *Arabic* anchored in the port city of Hamburg, Germany, where the revue's cast was quickly dispatched to Berlin. According to Hall biographer Iain Cameron Williams, Hall found the city of Berlin full of contradictions. . . . Noble yet feeble, frivolous yet staid, cautious yet wild . . . Adelaide couldn't help but find Berlin incredibly exciting. It wasn't just the expanse of culture on offer that she found so interesting, it was the liberated feel of its people. She discovered a side to herself she never knew existed. . . . Her journey of self-discovery through the wild temptations of Berlin's nightlife was an exercise in restraint.[126]

Williams describes a Hall at odds with her notions of self-respect and restraint and the openness of Berlin. It was a balance that many black American women had to negotiate once in Europe when confronted with much more liberal ideas about sex and sexuality, vice, and drugs. Berlin was even a jolt to the senses for the well-schooled Bricktop:

Berlin . . . I loved that city. It was a circus. Compared to it, Montmartre, even at two o'clock, was a sleepy little town. . . . At night the sounds of music and singing and laughing made a steady, joyful din, and there were so many lights that you could hardly see the sky. Anything went in Berlin, and I mean anything. All the dope-taking and homosexuality that was done in a light-hearted sort of way in Paris was serious business in Berlin. Some people said it was depraved, but I think it was just a way to forget the humiliating war defeat, to block out what you couldn't help seeing when the sun came up in the morning.[127]

This was Berlin before Adolf Hitler. Like other postwar economies in search of better times, Germany experienced its version of *les années folles* despite the animosities that lingered after the Treaty of Versailles of 1919. For the megalomaniacal leader of the Third Reich, this was the Berlin that needed to be remade, chastened. And jazz and all those Negros who had come along with it would become practically *verboten* in the German Fatherland with Hitler's officially becoming chancellor in 1934.

Hall's breakthrough debut, though, came when Lew Leslie tapped her to be Florence Mills's successor in *Blackbirds 1928*. Mills had died unexpectedly in 1927 in New York due to complications relating to pelvic tuberculosis. Decked out in skimpy shorts, bare legs and midriff, and a plume of feathers emerging from her backside, Hall was at once sensual and elegant, her dancing evocative yet superb, and her duet with Bill Bojangles Robinson left audiences begging for encores. At her debut, the audience requested seven encores of "Diga Diga Do," and the newspapers heralded the coming of Broadway's newest black female star. She created such a stir that debates raged in black newspapers that questioned whether her dance compromised Negro womanhood or released women from imposed social constraints.

ILLUSTRATION 1.15. Adelaide Hall, undated. Courtesy of Yale Collection of American Literature, Beinecke Rare Book and Manuscript Library, Yale University.

In the end, it didn't matter what the newspapers debated. *Blackbirds 1928* had been a runaway success; and on Friday, May 24, 1929, Adelaide Hall was bound for Paris on the SS *Ile de France* where the production opened at the Moulin Rouge. With her neatly parted, short, tapered hair and a spit curl in the front, Addie welcomed Paris with open arms. And it greeted her back with a four-story high illuminated likeness of her in the skimpy "Diga Diga Do" costume towering over the entrance of the Moulin Rouge. "If Berlin had liberated Adelaide, then Paris," according to Williams, "reaffirmed her belief in humanity and threw open the doors to her heart."[128]

Settling at the Hotel Mont Joli on 8 rue Fromentin, Hall proceeded to triumph over Paris. The star-attended opening night included Mistinguett. As was typical of the French fascination with places *ailleurs*, Addie's rendition of "Diga Diga Do" for *Blackbirds 1929* took place in a jungle in Polynesia. She garnered a sitting with the artist Paul Colin, whose posters of Josephine and *La Revue nègre*, and Mills as the star of *Blackbirds 1926*, contributed to the frenzy surrounding those revues' openings in Paris in October 1925 and May 1926, respectively. Hall, unlike Baker, refused to pose nude, so the posters, while in trademark Colin style—exaggerated lips and smiles—were less risqué. The cast ended its evenings at Bricktop's. Here she reconnected with her mentor Alberta Hunter, whose counsels she had sought before marrying her Trinidadian beau Bert Hicks.

Adelaide Hall had become the toast of Paris, inciting the curiosity of its other resident Black Venus, Josephine Baker. Baker attended the production days after its opening.[129] Unlike Hall, and Florence Mills's before her, Josephine Baker had yet to conquer America, so Hall's arrival on French soil to much fanfare served only to twist the knife.

Hall toured with *Blackbirds 1929* for two years. But by 1934, she had returned to Paris where she was promptly thrown a party at Bricktop's. She and her husband moved to an apartment on rue Lepic in Montmartre. In 1936, Bricktop and Hall sent a jointly written postcard to Van Vechten that was if nothing else illustrative of their closeness. Hall informs Van Vechten that she is "singing at the Monte Cristo Bar and also playing Biarritz Casino," while Bricktop asks, "[H]ow are you?" and then tells him she is "working on my 10th whiskey."[130] Singing with much success for her supper across Europe, Hall and her husband opened the nightclub Big Apple on 73 rue Pigalle in December 1937.

Like all the clubs in Montmartre, Big Apple initially struggled. But its competition was completely laid to waste after a few months. Bricktop, as Langston Hughes remarked, had moved on to London, becoming a sort of itinerant entertainer marketing her brand of hostessing in 1937. Unlike Hall and Hunter, Bricky was also a profligate spender and loaner. Her generosity contributed to her undoing in the later years in Paris. From August to October 1938 alone, she loaned Gene Bullard close to 2,500 francs.[131] Forced to sell her country estate in Bougival in order to stay financially solvent, Bricky had even cabled Cole Porter from Biarritz as early as 1936 about her employment prospects in America to which he promptly replied on Waldorf Astoria letterhead:

Dear Bricktop:

Things may be bad in Paris but they are much worse here. Harlem is totally dead and even when the Autumn [*sic*] comes there will only be one colored show in town, and this the Cotton Club moved downtown to 48th Street. So I think you are very unwise contemplating coming to America and advise strongly against it. If, however, you are hard up later on, let me know and I will gather together a few sheckles and send them over to you.[132]

Even her hometown paper reported on her downward spiral. Edgar Wiggins, the ubiquitous *Chicago Defender* correspondent abroad in the 1930s, posted in his "Across the Pond" column and in a series of other articles Bricktop's professional obituary and Addie's triumphal rise, stating:

Adelaide Hall is the big name today in the Paris nightclub circle. Her place of joy and amusement the Big Apple is the mecca for all pleasure seekers. Maybe it's only a coincidence, nevertheless, the fact remains that since the opening of her club on Dec. 11 last, "Bricktop," one time queen of all Parisian night clubs, departed for London.[133]

Bricky's reign as the Queen of Montmartre nightlife had run its course; the younger, deeper-pocketed "Queen of Parisian Nightlife," Adelaide Hall, had replaced her. Rather than stay and face the humiliation of her fall, she promptly decamped to London. Mabel remained in Paris, occasionally performing at Big Apple with Addie. As if switching roles, Addie, too, would exchange Paris for a more lucrative offer in London in 1938. And Bricktop would find herself at the helm of Big Apple.

By August 1938, Bricky was back in Paris and desperate for paid work. Her own club was done except for the shingle announcing its closing. In November 1938, Chez Bricktop shuttered its doors for good at 66 rue Pigalle. Hall's Big Apple was now in disarray, with a lawsuit pending between Hall and Hetty Flacks, her principal financial partner in the cabaret, because of Addie's performance commitments in London. Flacks was in need of a regular hostess replacement. Hetty Flacks and her husband Louis Swirn saw an opportunity and promptly approached Brick, cutting ties altogether with Hall. Despite her business failings, Bricktop was still a grand hostess. She and Mabel resumed their hostessing and singing dual roles. A series of calamities, namely, the death of her mother, Hattie Smith, and her bitterness over her reversal of fortunes, led to her own avowal to "never return to said club."[134] The Bricktop-Flacks-Swirn partnership became rancorous.

Swirn, who maintained to the *Chicago Defender* that she had "messed them all up," hurled accusations of mismanagement at Bricktop.[135]

Like the passing of the "great good years" of Paris, Big Apple closed its doors a little over a year after its opening. Flacks had brought in singer Una Mae Carlyle to replace Bricktop, but she was no Bricky, Addie, or even Mabel.

TWO

THE GOTHAM-MONTPARNASSE EXCHANGE

On April afternoons I say,
"Mama, I'd like to skate today."
She thinks I'll play out in the street
With Maude and Harold Jones and Pete,—

Sometimes I skate in Switzerland,
With ice-clad hills on every hand;
Sometimes I'm off in Russia far,—
(They still talk there about the czar!)
I'm never *here*, you understand!

I skate in Greenland; Norway, too,
And skim its fjords of icy blue.
When I get back my mother calls,
"Come in before the dampness falls!"
She'd wonder if she really knew!

—Jessie Fauset, "Adventures on Roller Skates,"
The Brownie's Book, May 1920

As Montmartre continued to sizzle with the influx of jazzmen and women, Montparnasse and Saint-Germain hummed along as well, initiating writers and artists of all stripes to its café culture and salons. When Jessie Fauset, doyenne of the Harlem Renaissance, arrived in September 1924, Bricktop was still settling in as a hostess at Le Grand Duc. The saloonkeeper's glory days were still way ahead of her, as Chez Florence ruled La Butte among the smart set. Fauset may have surely stopped by Le Grand Duc when she did a round of tours of "some of the cafes at Montmartre" and always accompanied by "a friend" who would "take me and protect."[1] She had planned to "see

73

some others" after her brief sojourn to Nice and Carcassonne.[2] Mindful of the hill's reputation for vice, drinking, and carousing as high art, even more mindful of her place as a single, middle-class African American woman despite the freedoms of France, Fauset was decidedly against soliciting the peripatetic Claude McKay as an escort to "such places. He is a better artist than a man I imagine."[3]

As editor of *The Brownie's Book*, a monthly children's magazine launched by W. E. B. Du Bois, Jessie Fauset endeavored to rouse her young readers' imaginations with tales of other worlds, places, and people, to instill in them and their parents a sense of wonder about the world and the rewards of travel. "Adventures on Roller Skates" captures the mind's expansive ability to travel in place as the body moves effortlessly on roller skates. The travel is both physical and metaphysical. And the destinations are faraway and thrilling, with icy hills, blue fjords, and the dreamy allusion to the legend of Anastasia Romanov and the era of Russian czars.

The exquisite cover art—hand-drawn, water-colored brown children, flowering borders, and spring maypole dances—was done by the artist Laura Wheeler. The short stories, poetry, and fairytales contained within *The Brownie's Book* pages wholly reflected Fauset's imaginative prowess, particularly as it spilled over into the writing of middle-class African American women's lives. Two thematic and imaginative drivers of *The Brownie's Book*, the fairytale and travel, greatly informed Fauset's adult novels, particularly her second and most successful work, *Plum Bun: A Novel without Moral*, which would be published in 1928.

With the financial collapse of *The Brownie's Book* in 1921, and the publication to middling reviews in 1924 of her first novel, *There Is Confusion*, about love, hope, and marriage in the maelstrom of American racism and colorism,[4] Fauset deliberately and romantically focused her sights on Paris for inspiration. Where America constantly ensnarled romantic love in its racial anxieties in both novels, Paris is held out as a place where it may flourish freely. Certainly her letters to those already abroad in the City of Light and even those she wrote once she arrived herself in 1924 would seem to support this point of view of Paris as a site of inspiration, freedom, and romance. That Fauset wrote poetry that leaned more toward French romanticism also colored her views of France and Paris, in particular.

In writing to Langston Hughes in May 1924, she knew of the younger poet's misery, and fleeting distaste for the French and the Paris rain, yet she cheers him on, not the least bit swayed from her near starry-eyed wistfulness about Paris:

> Are you having a wonderful time or do you still have a nostalgia
> for the Hudson? The first time I was in Paris I was a very young

ILLUSTRATION 2.1. Jessie Fauset. Courtesy of the Library of Congress, Washington, DC.

girl, but I was suffering from confusion worse than death, so I did not enjoy myself as I should. I cannot think of anything lovelier than being young, healthy, a poet and in Paris. Not even comparative poverty could destroy that satisfaction. Be happy if you possibly can for just this combination of circumstance never can happen again.[5]

For all of his grumblings, Hughes never completely swore off Paris. He frequently made pit stops there when zigzagging through Europe. For her part, Fauset was gearing up for the trip of a lifetime in 1924, one that would finally allow her to take full advantage of the city's offerings, having, as she had, "enough money to manage on and no restraints."[6]

Between her first trip to Paris as a "very young girl" and this antici-
pated one, Jessie Fauset had made another significant but short trip to the
city in 1921. She was part of the National Association for the Advancement of Colored People (NAACP) delegation to the Pan-African Congress, along with the association's editor and founder of *The Crisis* magazine,
W. E. B. Du Bois. Du Bois was an organizer of the Pan-African Congress.
The Congress took place in London, Brussels, and Paris. Speaking less than
passable French, according to Du Bois biographer David Levering Lewis, Du
Bois depended greatly on Fauset's near-native French skills. Fauset however
did not attend the 1919 Congress in Paris. She had only just begun her
work at *The Crisis* under Du Bois. Her romantic ideas about the city were
most certainly aroused at the 1921 Congress. For, if she and Du Bois had
not been lovers before, they were so by the time they arrived in Paris in
1921. Though very married, Du Bois was known to pluck his lovers from
the most able and intelligent women of the Negro race.[7] Hence, at that
1919 conference, he had leaned heavily instead on his former paramour,
the highly educated and socially adept wife of diplomat William H. Hunt,
Ida Gibbs Hunt, who resided in France.[8]

Fauset wrote up her impressions in two subsequent articles for *The
Crisis* in November and December 1921: "Impressions of the Second Pan-
African Congress" and "What Europe Thought of the Pan-African Congress." Fauset also noted the attendance of various black diasporic luminaries
at the conference such as the internationally recognized African American
expatriate painter Henry Ossawa Tanner and Haitian minister to France
Dantès Bellegarde. Over one thousand people attended the meetings, including the aviator and pilot Bessie Coleman.[9]

Fascinated with air shows and barnstorming, the part Cherokee and
African American Coleman was born in Atlanta, Texas, on January 26,
1892. She moved to Chicago in 1915. Coleman was denied flight training in
the United States because she was an African American woman. While her
more famous white counterpart Amelia Earhart pursued expensive flight lessons in 1921, Coleman left the country in November 1920 with the financial
backing of African American newspaper magnate Robert Sengstacke Abbott
to enroll at the Caudron Brothers' School of Aviation in Le Crotoy, France.
Born to slave parents in Saint Simon's Island, Georgia, or thereabouts, the
self-made millionaire Abbott was the publisher of one of the most widely
circulated black newspapers in America, the *Chicago Defender*.

With his support, Coleman was able to fine-tune her repertoire in
France. She received her international aviation license from the Fédération
Aéronautique Internationale in June 1921. She returned again to France
then Amsterdam and Germany for more training in the winter of 1922.
Denied the opportunity to train as a pilot because of racism and sexism,

ILLUSTRATION 2.2. Bessie Coleman, undated. Courtesy of National Air and Space Museum Archives, Smithsonian Institution.

Coleman hoped to start a flight school of her own for aspiring black and female pilots in the United States.

In between her training sessions outside Paris in 1921, she attended the Pan-African Congress held in Paris. Celebrated as "Queen Bess" in the pages of the *Chicago Defender* and the *New York Times*, she had both moxie and notoriety. Though Fauset did not note the "Brown-Skinned Lady Bird's" presence in her who's-who list of attendees in her first "Impressions of the Second Pan-African Congress," she did include Coleman in the December 1921 "What Europe Thought of the Pan-African Congress" by way of a citation from the journal *Paris Humanité*:

> How can we consider inferior to white men these orators with their clear thought and their ready words; these audiences at once calm and attentive; these delegates, men and women representing strong organizations of tens, yes hundreds and thousands of members; that charming young woman who was the first colored aviatrix of America?[10]

The French newspaper in this case is very clear about Coleman's place in American history, even if Fauset, in initially failing to mention Coleman in her November 1921 "Impressions," and even Ida Gibbs Hunt—who was also present—was not. In this instance, Coleman becomes a useful example, for Fauset, to challenge whites on the question of black inferiority.

ILLUSTRATION 2.3. Bessie Coleman's pilot's license, 1921. Courtesy of National Air and Space Museum Archives, Smithsonian Institution.

Nonetheless, in Fauset's recitation to Hughes about Paris, the allusion to her very first trip to Paris strikes a fascinating chord in that it provides a small window onto Fauset's interior life, one that she guarded carefully, and the persona that she attempted to cultivate and project in a world where younger writers constantly orbited around her and concerns about marriageability were ever present.

Jessie Redmon Fauset was born in the predominantly black small town of Fredericksville, New Jersey, on April 27, 1882. Her family moved to Philadelphia while she was still quite young. By 1914, the date of her first trip to Paris, she would have been a woman of thirty-two years old, not a "very young girl" . . . "suffering from a confusion worse than death." Whatever unsettled Fauset in Paris in 1914 she never disclosed. Perhaps it was loneliness or the march of the Great War in Europe that was in the offing during her stay; but what is evidently clear, as Fauset literary biographer Carolyn Wedin Sylvander notes, Jessie Fauset was not above shaving years off her age when convenient.[11]

Perhaps taking to heart the maxims offered up by Oscar Wilde in A Woman of No Importance, Act II (1893): "One should never trust a woman who tells one her real age. A woman who would do that would tell anything," and in Oliver Goldsmith's She Stoops to Conquer, Act III (1773): "Oh, sir, I must not tell you my age; they say women and music should never be dated," Fauset's 1928 Harmon Foundation Award application indicated she was born in 1891. She would thus have been forty-two years old in 1924 when her first novel, which helped put the idea of a Harlem Renaissance on sure footing, was published.

Though Langston Hughes credited Jessie Fauset as the "mid-wife" to the Harlem Renaissance, the metaphor may have chafed an obviously age-sensitive, unmarried, and late-to-the-novel-publishing-world Fauset. Surrounded as she was by the youthful perspicacity of Countee Cullen, Arna Bontemps, and Hughes, and despite the fact that many of the other writers associated with the era, like Zora Neale Hurston and Claude McKay, were thirty-somethings or just at its threshold, as was the case with the venerable Jean Toomer, Jessie Fauset, through various tactics, resisted being characterized as crusty. She may have been a gatekeeper in her capacity as editor for the literary section of The Crisis, but she would not, by her own assent, be passé or old guard.

Author of four adult novels, Fauset's corpus though is often dismissed as lighthearted fare because of its reliance on melodrama and the structure and arc of romance and fairytale novels, as well as its concern with middle-class values and morals. And yet, it is precisely the romance and fairytale thematics that allowed for a discussion of modern themes such as sexuality, race-mixing, color, passing, racism, and class. As literary scholars Thadious

Davis, Ann duCille, Deborah McDowell, and Cheryl Wall have noted, the
ease with which Jessie Fauset has been cast aside in this regard also belies
how radical her literary imagination was for the era.[12] That is, Fauset imagined African American women as part of the fairytale world rather than
outside of it, a realm that had certainly been denied them in the mainstream
literature of the genre. Forever grounded in the real as opposed to the "once
upon a time, far, far away" from any place we can place, Fauset wrote black
women into the fairytale with its happy endings in a real place that seemed
mythical, for it was where color, race, and gender would not be obstacles
to creative pursuits, and love could thrive without the "thou shall nots" of
American racism and African American middle-class constraints she spoke
of in her 1924 interview with the *Paris Tribune*. Fauset was not naïve about
French xenophobia and nationalism, however, particularly in the South of
France and in the more provincial countryside as opposed to cosmopolitan
Paris; she tackled such issues directly in her correspondences as well as in
her last novel published in 1933, *Comedy: American Style*. However, in
1924–1925, Paris became a strategic plot device.

Paris was that fairytale-like real place; it was the place where Fauset
lived for eight months and wrote parts of the novel *Plum Bun* during 1924
and 1925. In many respects, Angela Murray, *Plum Bun*'s protagonist, retraces
the author's own route to Paris: Philadelphia to New York to Paris. Initially,
Murray "saw her life rounding out like a fairytale" among New York's avant-
garde set and with the loutish, wealthy white Lothario, Roger Fielding, only
to discover that "New York . . . had two visages. . . . With its flattering
possibilities it could elevate to the seventh heaven, or lower to the depths
of hell with its crushing negations."[13] And so she flees to Paris, like Fauset,
"but only temporarily," to grow as an artist.[14]

Fauset structures this coming of age novel (*bildungsroman*) around a
nursery rhyme. The rhyme suggests the protagonist's naïveté about the com-
merce, the picking and choosing, the courtship and desire, involved in the
marriage marketplace that is part and parcel of the "And they lived happily
ever after" thread of the fairytale. Indeed, as Deborah McDowell writes,
the nursery rhyme "To Market, to Market" denotes "the tension between
expectation and fulfillment":[15]

> To market, to market, to buy a fat pig,
> Home again, home again, dancing a jig;
> To market, to market, to buy a fat hog;
> Home again, home again, jiggety-jog;
> To market, to market, to buy a plum bun,
> Home again, home again, market is done.

Despite the protagonist's loss of sexual innocence to Roger Fielding and her misunderstanding of the marketplace of marriage and sex, Fauset's fairytale nonetheless completes itself by the novel's conclusion. The "happily ever after" is in the making with the delivery of the prince, the struggling African American artist Anthony Cross, to the doorstep of Angela Murray's Paris apartment.

The novel's denouement, where Paris becomes a sought-after place for artistic freedom, a fairytale land of opportunity for the battered and bruised by U.S. racism and colorism, is highly consonant with Fauset's own ideas about Paris that emerged before and over the course of her eight-month stay in Paris in her correspondences.

Her imagination takes flight even before her arrival in another letter to Langston Hughes:

> How glad I am you are in Paris. Do stay. Or if you are planning to come, do plan to return shortly. I myself am crossing in October to stay at least 8 months, probably 10. . . . I'll probably never get abroad again for any length of time. . . . I wish you'd stay in Paris for another year, working and later studying. I wish you'd meet me in October at Le Havre and get me back to Paris, (at my expense, *bien entendu*). I don't mind the ocean trip but I shall hate like everything finding my train and getting my luggage arranged.
>
> Probably we'll both be studying, you and I, but we can take a part of our lives to explore Paris and really get to know it. You can take me to all the dangerous places and I can take you to all the beautiful ones. There are heavenly spots in the Bois and the environs of Paris where countless poets and writers have written long before our time.[16]

Fauset envisions a Paris that is tantalizingly dangerous and aesthetically beautiful. With Langston Hughes as her companion, guide, and protector of her propriety, she could fully pursue a bohemian writer's life. Hughes would act as both chaperone and shield, safeguarding her status as a proper black woman yet acting as an "open sesame" to places a black, middle-class woman dare not venture alone.

By the time she arrives in Paris on September 7, 1924, Hughes has left the city for other adventures. Fauset's long-term residence in Paris is at the Hotel Jeanne D'Arc at 59 rue Vaneau in the well-heeled seventh arrondissement. Like Hughes, her initial romantic notions about Paris are cut short. "Well I am in Paris—have been here for a month and a day—like the refrain in an old fashioned poem. Curiously enough this time Paris struck me as it seems to have struck you at first, as not wonderful," only to change her assessment mid-letter, "But Today the charm of the city is growing on me again. It is sunny, though not especially warm day and the distances are magnificent, the buildings beautiful and Paris is the Paris of my first love."[17]

Moving back and forth between high highs and low spirits due to occasional boredom and loneliness, French "chauvinis[m]" and "too col[d] rationalis[m],"[18] Fauset sounds much like her heroine whose sense of wonder seems to ebb and flow with the change of seasons in Paris:

> Paris at first charmed and wooed her. For a while it seemed her old sense of joy in living for living's sake had returned to her. . . . She rode delightfully in the motorbuses on and on to the unknown, unpredictable terminus; she followed the winding Seine; crossing and re-crossing the bridges each with its distinctive characteristics.
>
> Back of the Panthéon, near the church of St. Généviève she discovered a Russian restaurant where strange and exotic dishes were served . . . she had never felt so lonely in her life. For the first time in her adventuresome existence. . . . Then this passed too with summer, she found herself by the end of September engrossed in her work. . . .
>
> With the coming fall the sense of adventure left her. Paris, so beautiful in the summer, so gay with thronging thousands, its hosts bent on pleasure, took on another garb in the sullen greyness of late autumn. Once or twice, in periods of utter loneliness or boredom, she let her mind dwell on her curiously thwarted and twisted life.[19]

While late autumn's "sullen greyness" forces the artist to reflect on her failed grab at the plum bun, Fauset writes to the dashing friend of just about every Harlem Renaissance writer, Harold Jackman, that winter's "[g]rey sky, grey walls, grey mists. . . . like a grey blanket soft and thick and woolly over everything"[20] are monotonous. Despite the ups and downs of the seasons that Fauset comes to accept almost philosophically as "a good thing to know that like everywhere is just *life* [Fauset's emphasis] with only an occasional high spirit," she is "having an unusual period of freedom composed of all sorts of phases of liberty such as I have not before in my life."[21]

She would continue to sound that note in a letter to philanthropist Arthur Spingarn and his wife:

It is the first time since I was seventeen that I have been comparatively free of fetters. As it is I have been a little too much bound down for I've been studying, writing articles, and also working on a book. But it has been beautiful to be for once outside the pull of routine duties. And then too I've had some taste of truly cosmopolitan life such as I should never have met with in America. Not even in New York.[22]

She settles herself in the company of the artist Laura Wheeler and Lillian Evans-Tibbs with whom she wanders through the rues and *allées* of Paris. The larger communities of both Montparnasse and Montmartre, made up of black and white Americans, beckoned her as well.

Freed from the conventions of race, gender, and class in Paris to pursue the life of the mind at salons, teas, and cafés, Fauset's experiences in these milieus among Americans of different shades and stripes was unlike anything she had ever experienced—even in the great cosmopolitan city of New York. The teas are not the formal social ones that she had herself hosted in New York but intellectual gatherings without the ceremony and fuss, the pomp of canapés handled in glove-handed circumstances:

I've met a lot of Americans over here, writers, etc. who have been most exceedingly kind. They give teas, not social ones, and they meet in cafés to drink apéritifs (perfectly harmless things) somewhere between 4:30 to 6:00, and to discuss, —well the world at large. And believe me I sit with them whenever I'm invited. I never see such life as this in America it is worth,—oh so much![23]

Fauset's unparalleled freedom is still self-regulated. She is clear to blunt the mention of *apéritifs* and her presumed imbibing of them as "perfectly harmless things."

Unlike so many other Americans, Fauset's fluency in French also allowed her to move even more freely in Paris and among French intellectuals. She met and conversed with the French black writer René Maran. Born in Martinique and raised in French Guiana, Maran was the author of the Prix de Goncourt–winning novel *Batouala*. Educated in Bordeaux, Maran, like his father, joined the French colonial service in French Equatorial Africa. His experiences in the military services informed the novel's representations of Africa and Africans. Fauset was an admirer. She had written a full-throated endorsement of his work for *The Crisis*; however, she did not much care for the black Frenchman in the flesh: "I've also met Maran who I didn't find charming—whatever may be said of American whites, there is no question that American Negroes are the best there are."[24]

Despite her renewed love affair with Paris, Fauset was nonplussed by what she perceived as French chauvinism. Whereas she had been ready before to leave white out of the equation in terms of "best" Americans, her disappointment about the French even leads her to embrace her compatriots: "Americans, black or white, are nicer than any other people in the world. I used to love the French but this time they leave me cold. The war has spoiled them poor things. I've been lucky enough to run into a group of writers whom I knew in New York."[25]

In France, Fauset interacted with white Americans willing to consort with Negroes in ways not seen even in Harlem. Paris helped facilitate these relations to such an extent that Fauset absolves her fellow Americans of their complicity with the forces that led to her rupture with America in the first place and "hindered her growth as a writer." Fauset hoists up a paradoxical aphorism: A Paris without the French. The imagined racial utopia of Paris, enabled by a more superficially tolerant France, the presence of a sizable enough black American colony that helped to evoke a sense of familiarity—home—a forward-thinking gaggle of white Americans, and "the sense of freedom! So that one doesn't have to dread shortness of funds etc, it is just heaven. Particularly for one of us,"[26] allows Fauset to live a charmed life replete with rose-tinted *lunettes*: "[M]y life has been—to me—charming. It is lovely just being oneself and not bickering about color or prejudice. I think strangely enough that's why my book progresses slowly so slowly because I'm away from the pressure."[27]

Frenchmen and women were behaving badly due to their hard-knock life post World War I and a "driving fear of poverty."[28] Known the world over for their pessimism, the bruising aftermath of the war understandably heightened their bleak worldview. And white Americans in Paris, on the other hand, were behaving differently. In writing to Langston Hughes of the matter, who left Paris on a late-night train for Italy, it is clear that Fauset would have been counted among those Americans who wouldn't have left Paris, despite the "franc-loving, sou-clutching, hard-faced, hard worked, cold and half-starved"[29] French, as Hughes had described them.

And, of course, she did not. She stays on for four more months, traveling and planning upon her return to Paris to revisit the hill where the black colony gathered so she could dance.[30]

Fauset laments that her productivity is bogged down by a freedom to create decoupled from racial animus. Still, she is quite productive, churning out articles for *The Crisis*—"Yarrow Revisited" (January 1925) about her Paris, then and now; the self-explanatory "This Way to the Flea Market" (February 1925); and "The Enigma of the Sorbonne" (March 1925)—taking classes at the Sorbonne and the Alliance Française as well as private French tutoring, and writing a novel initially titled "Marker" that would become the lauded *Plum Bun*. It is this freedom that allows her to imagine a thwarted but recovered "happily ever after" tale of an African American woman artist named Angela Murray who, freighted by race in the United States, escapes to France to pursue instruction at the "Academy," to "immerse herself in the art" and "atmosphere of the Louvre and Luxembourg galleries" in order to fulfill her "one ambition . . . to become an acknowledged, a significant painter of portraits."[31]

While Angela Murray's "adventuresome existence" seemingly paralleled Fauset's own, Fauset might have also drawn inspiration from her friend and travel companion in Europe and Africa, the very fair-skinned portrait artist Laura Wheeler. Like Fauset, Wheeler was a Philadelphian. Though her French *carte d'identité* issued in November 1924 lists her date of birth as May 25, 1889,[32] Laura Wheeler was born May 16, 1887, in Hartford, Connecticut, to a solidly middle-class, educated, and musically inclined family. Her father, Robert Foster Wheeler, received a degree in theology from Howard University. He became pastor of the Talcott Congregational Church. Laura's grandfather had also been minister at Talcott during the Civil War. Her mother, Mary Freeman Wheeler, was musically and artistically gifted.[33]

It was her parents who introduced her to art and music and helped to sustain her interest:

> I remember being taken to the art galleries in Hartford many times, and I suppose my delight in them was not only because of the outing it gave me but perhaps I had a love for the paintings—the color, the beauty of the galleries. I noticed particularly, I recall, the portraits. I often drew them at home. In fact, I can not remember the time that I did not have a great thrill with my paints and pencils. My father always provided us with these and seemed to enjoy watching us draw and paint. Sometimes both father and mother would draw with us. We thought them great artists, and I do believe they each had some sort of talent, my mother particularly. Several of her drawings were framed in my grandmother's home.[34]

Wheeler moved to Philadelphia to pursue studies in illustration and portraiture at the Pennsylvania Academy of the Fine Arts. She eventually received the A. William Emlen Cresson Memorial Travel Scholarship, which allowed her to study art at the "great galleries" in Europe for three months in 1914.[35] Other Cresson recipients included nineteenth-century American impressionist painter Mary Cassatt, another Philadelphia native, who had also been a student at the Pennsylvania Academy of the Fine Arts. Cassatt spent much of her adult life in France and was a close associate of the French impressionist Edgar Degas.[36] Laura's time in Paris was disrupted by the outbreak of World War I. She would though over the course of the next 15 years return twice more to Paris.

Upon returning to the United States, she eventually assumed a teaching position with the historically black Cheyney Training School for Teachers,[37] twenty-five miles west of Philadelphia. At Cheyney, she taught art and music. Wheeler also established a longstanding association with *The Crisis* as an illustrator, regularly doing cover art for the journal. Besides *The Brownie's Book*, she often illustrated Fauset's short stories and nonfiction essays inside *The Crisis*'s pages. With extended family obligations, Laura was never able to focus exclusively on her art. Illustrating was not especially lucrative, so teaching became her focus. In a letter to William Harmon of the Harmon Foundation, she explains: "Although I have had painting as the great aim in my life, I have needed always to be sure of a regular income because of certain responsibilities. I have taught, therefore, most of all of my time and have had little chance to devote to painting after my schooling."[38]

In June 1924, through earnest savings and hard work, Laura Wheeler sailed to Paris on the SS *Homeric*. She remained for over a year to pursue the study of painting at Académie de la Grande Chaumière.[39] One of her travel companions to Paris was Lillian Evans-Tibbs. Wheeler was able to work with the master Louis-Maurice Boutet de Monvel. Boutet de Monvel, originally from Orléans, France, and trained at the École des Beaux-Arts, was an academic painter and watercolorist best known for his illustrations in children's books.

At the Académie, according to art critic James Porter in a Howard University retrospective on Wheeler's work in 1949, Wheeler learned more about light, atmosphere, and color.[40] Artistically, she found a fountainhead of like-minded and supportive artists in Henry Ossawa Tanner and Gwendolyn Bennett, with whom she could "talk of this and that, principally, of artists and how they suffer in Paris,"[41] and her Académie colleagues and masters. She boarded at the Hotel Jeanne d'Arc before moving out to the suburb of Neuilly-sur-Seine. This period for Wheeler was "my only period of uninterrupted life as an artist with an environment and associates that were a constant stimulus and inspiration. My savings, however, would not allow me to continue this life indefinitely."[42]

She and Fauset would eventually travel onward off the grid to North Africa. Fauset submitted the article "Algeria the White" to *The Crisis*, accompanied by Wheeler's illustrations. But before she sailed homeward, Laura Wheeler toured the South of France. Like Van Gogh, Gauguin, Cezanne, and Pissarro before her, she was drawn to the light for which the region was known. On the way south, she stopped along the Cote d'Or, the Golden Coast, in Semur, France, where she painted her only landscape painting from this period, *The Houses at Semur, France* (1925), which seems to have evoked the style of her French mentor, Boutet de Monvel, with its attention to color and light.[43] Known for its wines and the steep sloop of limestone from which the region takes its name, the Golden Coast is located in Burgundy—to the southeast of Paris, between Chablis and Beaune—the region's wine capital. Verdant and temperate in climate, the picturesque town of Semur is medieval and hilly, rising as it does from the banks of the River Armançon. The gorge, ramparts, citadel, narrow cobbled streets, and stone houses refract a pinkish hue, which are natural feasts for the artist's eyes. Laura's were no exception.

By 1925, she and Fauset were stateside. The skills she had developed in Paris set the stage for her winning the Harmon Gold Award in Fine Arts in 1927. She returned to Paris once more in 1929 as Mrs. Laura Wheeler Waring and in the company of her husband, Walter E. Waring. On this shorter, two-month sojourn in France, she turned south again—and this time to the mountainous Pyrenees in the southwest where she painted *Saint-Jean-Pied-de-Port (French Pyrénées)* (1929) and *Farm in the Pyrénées, France*

ILLUSTRATION 2.4. Laura Wheeler Waring, undated. Courtesy of Moorland-Spingarn Research Center, Howard University.

(1929). Her work would also be exhibited at the Galerie du Luxembourg on the Boulevard Saint-Germain-des-Prés. As with submission and acceptance to Paris art salons, the prestige of a gallery exhibit for Laura in Paris would translate well at home in the United States.[44] And like other African American women artists who traveled to France during this period, much of Laura's work in France is unrecoverable but for the Howard University Exhibition Catalog. Laura Wheeler Waring would later be commissioned by the Harmon Foundation to paint portraits of prominent African Americans. Her friends, Jessie Redmond Fauset and Lillian Evans-Tibbs, were among her sitters.

Fauset exited Paris in the spring of 1925. When Jessie departed on June 15 for Cherbourg, France, the summer of 1925 saw the arrival of Gwendolyn Bennett as the new Paris companion for Laura. Bennett's literary and artistic pursuits would have been quite well known to Fauset as well in her capacity as *The Crisis's* literary editor. The two were also correspondents during Bennett's stay in Paris.[45] Two of her poems, "Nocturne" and "To Usward," were published in the magazine's pages, and one of her drawings, *Pipes of Pan*, inspired by Greek mythology with its satyrs and nymphs and the heralding of spring, was featured on the cover of the March 1924 issue of the chronicle.

"To Usward" was dedicated to Fauset upon the publication of her first novel, *There Is Confusion*.

> If any have a song to sing
> That's different from the rest,
> Oh let them sing. . . .
> We claim no part with racial dearth;
> We want to sing the songs of birth!

Bennett recited the poem at the Manhattan Civic on March 21, 1924, before an audience comprised of the future leading lights of the black literary world. It was conceptualized as a book-launch event for Fauset. But it became so much more. Organized by Charles S. Johnson, the editor of the National Urban League's *Opportunity* magazine, Bennett shared the poet's platform with Countee Cullen; and the event, which brought together black writers and white editors, patrons, and publishers, is often cited as marking the official start of the Harlem Renaissance.

"To Usward" trumpets the coming, the birth, of the New Negro with their different songs that needed a hearing. The notes struck by this New Negro in the areas of letters, art, and music were varied and plentiful. The Negro race was moving up, onward, bending toward the self, *to usward*, as reflected in their race-themed artistic and academic pursuits.

Bennett was part of a tight-knit group of authors and artists that included Wallace Thurman, Augusta Savage, Aaron Douglass, Langston

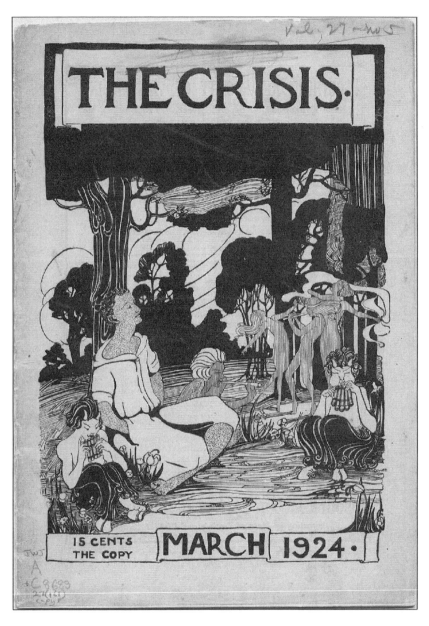

ILLUSTRATION 2.5. Gwendolyn Bennett, *Pipes of Pan* cover art for *The Crisis*, 1924. Courtesy of Yale Collection of American Literature, Beinecke Rare Book and Manuscript Library, Yale University.

Hughes, Zora Neale Hurston, Countee Cullen, and Claude McKay, with whom she exchanged correspondences as he was already abroad. Despite the reach of the Black Renaissance's tentacles across America into other cities like Chicago and Washington, DC, Harlem acted as a nerve center. And in that nerve center, there were schisms that emerged along generational lines. Younger writers backed up against an old guard that primarily included W. E. B. Du Bois and Alain Locke. Pure literary aesthetics, art for art's sake versus art for racial uplift and propaganda, were positioned as the site of the literary fault lines, though ego, a desire for recognition and displacement that teetered on the verge of a "young eating the old" ethos was detectable as well.

A literary salon, The Dark Tower, named after Countee Cullen's poem, was established in 1926 to accommodate the younger generation at 136th Street and Edgecombe Avenue on a floor of the townhouse owned by A'Lelia Walker, "[t]he joy goddess of Harlem's 1920s," as dubbed by Langston Hughes. As vivacious and statuesque as the ermine-coat draped character Adora Boniface—drawn from her persona in Carl Van Vechten's *Nigger Heaven*—Walker, born Lelia McWilliams on June 6, 1885, in Mississippi, was the only daughter of hair and skin-care magnate Madam C. J. Walker.[46]

A campy novel of questionable literary merit and dubious taste, Van Vechten attempted to capture Walker's spirit in Adora and her place among the black intellectual and artistic classes of New York:

> Frowned upon in many quarters, not actually accepted intimately in others—not accepted in any sense of the word, of course, by the old and exclusive Brooklyn set—Adora nevertheless was a figure not to be ignored. She was too rich, too important, too influential, for that. To be sure, she had never been conspicuous for benefactions to her race. On the other hand, she could be counted on for occasional splurges when a hospital was in need of an endowment or when a riot in some city demanded a call for a defence [*sic*] fund. Also she was undeniably warm-hearted, amusing, in her outspoken way, and even beautiful, in a queenly African manner that set her apart from the other beauties of her race whose loveliness was more frequently of a Latin than Ethiopian character.[47]

The occasional splurge and the society into which A'Lelia Walker chose to enter were artistic. Fashioning herself as a patron, Walker stated, "Having no talent or gift, but a love and keen appreciation for art, the Dark Tower was my contribution."[48]

ILLUSTRATION 2.6. A'Lelia Walker, undated. Yale Collection of American Literature, Beinecke Rare Book and Manuscript Library, Yale University.

Like her mother, Walker had a certain affinity for Frenchness. Madam C. J. Walker took the name Madam certainly in defiance of racial protocols of the era, forcing whites to refer to her respectfully as Madam when asked her name, but she also recognized the idea of luxury, style, and sophistication associated with Frenchness, more specifically Paris, as she thought about how to market her beauty products. In the biography of her great-great-grandmother, *On Her Own Ground: The Life and Times of Madam C. J. Walker*, A'Lelia Bundles confirms that when the young woman from Louisiana, Sarah Breedlove, renamed herself and mapped out her business strategy, she consciously chose the name Madam, folding it into a marketing strategy; she knew her customers would associate Madam/*Madame* with Paris, the capital of fashion and beauty.[49]

For the younger Walker, the salon too had its origins in French traditions, in the art of intellectual exchange. While Madam C. J. Walker desired to go to Paris to attend the 1919 Pan-African Congress but was blocked by the U.S. State Department, her daughter, A'Lelia, would make it to the city in 1921 as part of a cultural tour that included Europe, Africa, and the Middle East.

She arrived in Paris on the *SS Paris*, the same ship as the French prime minister Aristide Briand. Briand had attended a conference in Washington, DC, with President Warren G. Harding and the leaders of countries involved in the Great War. On the agenda were not only peace but also German reparations and strategic American interventions in the Pacific.

Aristide Briand became known as the "Pilgrim of Peace." The Kellogg-Briand Pact, or the Pact of Paris, of 1928, an outgrowth of the discussions held at the 1921 Washington, DC, conference, was a hallmark of Briand's pacifist inclinations. With that pact, also bearing the name of U.S. secretary of state Frank B. Kellogg, sixty-two nations agreed that war should not be the recourse to solving international disputes.[50] Briand returned to Paris on the *Paris*. His departure and arrival were covered in the French dailies. A'Lelia Walker's arrival was also mentioned in the French press, though she objected to being referred to as a "negresse" in one of the newspapers (*L'Intransigeant*). She went so far as to craft a letter to the editor.[51]

A decidedly right-wing mouthpiece, *L'Intransigeant*, under the editorial management of Léon Bailby, was also no stranger to anti-Semitism, highlighted in its obtuse commentaries during the Alfred Dreyfus espionage case and subsequent military cover-up. As A'Lelia was neither a headliner at a major cabaret nor a celebrated woman of art or letters, the presence of a wealthy African American socialite in Paris, as unusual as it was in 1921, particularly one with Walker's proclivities for excess and extravagances, would not have been found especially newsworthy in Paris; but her coincidental arrival on the same ship as the prime minister, whose every move in America and return voyage was reported obsessively and with alacrity would have been.[52] As a businesswoman on a mostly leisure tour of Paris, Walker did the standard tourist fare of shopping, lunching, and site-seeing before heading south to Monaco.

Like her mother, A'Lelia Walker, in briefly becoming a salonnière, tapped into American associations of high culture and art and letters with Frenchness. She not only joined an esteemed list of French intellectual women going as far back as the Enlightenment,[53] but her trip to Paris further added the veneer of cosmopolitanism and authenticity to the endeavor.

Unfortunately, the Dark Tower folded in 1927. Walker's attempt to monetize the salon led to the exclusion of the men and women of arts and culture for whom it was conceived; they could neither afford the pricey hors d'oeuvres on offer nor the cover charge. In its place came Niggeratti Manor at Wallace Thurman's studio apartment in Greenwich Village. Thurman borrowed the term "niggeratti" from Zora Neale Hurston, who was also part of the "new" New Negro movement. This group formed an editorial collective and produced the one-issue journal *Fire!!*. Other collaborators included Hughes, Aaron Douglass, Richard Bruce Nugent, Cullen, and Gwendolyn Bennett.

Wally Thurman took the title of managing editor. In an attempt to leave their mark in black letters and on the Black Renaissance and, most importantly, outside of the established journals like *The Crisis* and *Opportunity*, the young writers opted to create their own journal, a modernist take on the Negro experience that would set ablaze the literary world, upend stodgy conventions, and spit at middle-class values and notions of respectability. Rather than launch a public internecine battle, the old guard ignored the upstarts. Privately, they railed in abhorrence. In letters to Charlotte Osgood Mason, the white female patron to many of the writers of the New Negro movement who preferred to be called "Godmother," Locke fulminated that the young writers were in the wilderness, had lost their way, and in the process had sold out the literary movement. The group, as far as Locke was concerned, catered to the baser instincts of whites and their thoughts about blacks, mimicking in style and characterizations of black life white decadence.[54]

With Thurman at the helm, Locke and Du Bois believed the group had, like Icarus, flown to close to Van Vechten's corrupting sun. The reception, criticisms, and literary aftereffects of *Nigger Heaven* had kept its author on tenterhooks, and so much so that as late as 1931 he was writing to Nella Larsen in Spain for assurance about the book's qualities.[55] In the pages of A. Philip Randolph's *The Messenger*, the contrarian George Schuyler channels Van Vechten's anxieties as well as those of the old guard of the Black Renaissance in a parody written in verse in his column "Shafts and Darts: A Page of Calumny and Satire":

The Curse of My Aching Heart
By Carl Von Vickton
A very touching love lyric dedicated to
The New Negro Artists

I've made you what you are today,
Yet I'm dissatisfied.
I've boosted you until 'twas said,
No one so glibly lied.
Now book men print your puerile trash;
Your jongleurs dine à la carte.
Though your vogue's nearly through,
To think I boosted you—
That's the curse of my aching heart.[56]

Some members of the avant-garde of the Black Renaissance were flame-throwers, while others strived to explore the complexity of black life, and that included sexuality, color, class, and gender. Among race leaders and literary critics, scintillation and shock were this brand of New Negro's sole contributions. And Thurman's "Cordelia The Crude, A Harlem Sketch" and Richard Bruce Nugent's "Smoke, Lilies, & Jade" qualified, for them, as utter tripe, with characters that were not fully drawn but were mere raced types.

Gwendolyn Bennett escaped such criticism. Her contribution of the short story "Wedding Day," with its Paris backdrop and themes of racial prejudice and interracial relations, conformed to the aesthetic dictates of the avant-garde class only to the extent that her characters were from the working class; but their location in Paris—even if it was the tumbledown Montmartre district—and her ability to recreate it immediately lent a cosmopolitan spin to her work.

Bennett walked a fine line between *Fire's!!* new black literary vanguard and the old guard she still depended on for publication and support. After all, *Opportunity* and *The Crisis* had provided her a literary platform. As subscriptions faltered, the financial hardships involved in managing a journal set in. Interests among its *afire* vanguard waned. *Fire!!*'s survival dimmed. Even with Hurston and Hughes's help, Thurman, who had shouldered the bulk of the responsibility, complained to Hughes, "If I don't hear from Gwenny [*sic*] . . . I, well, shall want to cast [her] from our presence. Gwenny has not even obtained a subs, or sent in a patron's name, yet she will strut most grandly when pointed out as one of the *Fire* editors."[57]

Producing more poetry than fiction, though she never published a collection of her poems, Bennett ventured once more into literary fiction with a second short story published in 1927 in Charles S. Johnson's anthology,

Ebony and Topaz. Again drawing on Paris, both short stories are melancholy portraits of black soldiers turned jazzmen in Paris. Bennett, like most African Americans who had made their way to Montmartre, was clearly attuned to the dissipation of the black jazzman's life during *les années folles.* Fast money spent on fast women, alcohol, and drugs usually led to an ending reminiscent of the one described in F. Scott Fitzgerald's short story "Babylon Revisited."

But it is unrequited love, love crushed under the weight of racism and ambition, at the center of both Bennett's Parisian stories, that reveals the rather sensitive and sentimental sides of the jazzmen. Predating Fitzgerald's jaundiced rendering of goodtime Montmartre, Bennett's men are undone, blindsided by love. Jenks Barnett of "Tokens" slowly wastes away from tuberculosis in Merlin Hospital after "Tollie Saunders with her golden voice and lush laughter" had come and gone just "before the pinch of poverty came." He spends his days looking out onto the Seine, hacking until overcome by a "paroxysm of pain."[58]

Paul Watson, the steely protagonist of "Wedding Day," eerily recalls the rough-around-the-edges club manager, boxer, and expatriate Eugene Bullard, who welcomed Bricktop to Paris in 1924 and who too had arrived "in the days before colored jazz bands were the style in Paris,"[59] a reference Bennett makes twice in the span of one paragraph. Watson is a boxer—though not as polished as the legendary Joe Gans. Here, Bennett is doing a bit of recuperative history with an allusion to the barely remembered, particularly in the wake of Jack Johnson, lightweight boxing champion Joe Gans. Gans, a native of Baltimore, had also opened a black and tan club called the Goldfield Hotel in Baltimore in 1907 where Eubie Blake made his debut at the piano.[60]

Watson makes his way across the Atlantic; with the arrival of the colored bands, he takes up the banjo. Irrepressible in his disdain for "American white folks," the solitary and seemingly untouched by the underbelly of Montmartre and its easy women Watson falls hard for Mary, a white American woman of easy virtue who "wasn't the marrying kind." "[F]orget[ting] all [he] ever said about hatin' white folks," once that "gang of golden hair and blue eyes rub[bed] up close to [him],"[61] Paul plunges headlong in love, falling just as rapidly "from his place as bronze God to almost less than dust" among the other jazzmen in his Montmartre crew.

On the day of their planned nuptials, Mary decides she "just couldn't go through with it," that is, marrying "a colored man."[62] But Bennett doesn't tell the reader straight off. The denouement is ostensibly revealed amid the most mundane of details—the shrill whistle of the subway, musings about a first-class ticket purchased for a second-class car, and a flashback to a trouncing he gave a white American in Paris. Clambering onto the train, it is precisely that flashback where Paul Watson remembers he'd have a "hell of time in America where black is black" that the immediate past-present is recalled, that he "got ahold" of the "thought . . . bumping around in his head."[63] Bennett leaves our antihero dazed, shell-shocked, on the Paris subway with an overpriced ticket for a second-class car, a metaphor for the woman who had just dumped him, and mud on his suit.

In contrast to the charging forward optimism of "To Usward," Bennett's Paris stories are studies in loneliness, solitariness, romantic melancholia. Despite her own very full life in Paris, as revealed in the diary she kept during her time in the city, Bennett, like her jazzmen, experienced the freedoms of Paris and yet its blues, for she would vacillate between idylls of sheer delight in the simplicities of life, only to contemplate whether "all people who are twenty-three and have loved are this melancholy."[64] And she was in love—with "Gene," who was back in New York. Bennett alternates between a Rousseau-like solitary flaneur in the more pastoral surroundings of a pension in the leafy countryside of the village of Pontoise, a suburb northwest of Paris, and a Baudelairean flaneur in the streets of Paris suffering varying degrees of ennui, loneliness, and romantic enchantment with everything from the Saint Sulpice church, the Seine, and Luxembourg Gardens. On a drive through Paris, she writes:

> There was never a more beautiful city than Paris. . . . there couldn't be! On every hand are works of art and beautiful vistas. . . . one has the impression of looking through at fairy-tale worlds as one sees gorgeous buildings, arches and towers rising from among mounds of trees from afar. And there are flowers, too, in Paris—or just billions of them.[65]

Like her characters, the multitalented Gwennie, as she called herself and was called, was prone to an artist's sensitivities. And as it was for Jessie Fauset, Paris is a fairytale world.

Born July 8, 1902, in Giddings, Texas, Gwendolyn Bennetta Bennett arrived in Harlem, New York, by way of Brooklyn in 1921. Her roving, underground days were now behind her. In a fit of spite, her father, Joshua Bennett, had kidnapped her as a child from her mother when Maime Bennett was awarded custody after their divorce. As a woman, aspiring artist, and student of fine arts at Columbia University and the Pratt Institute, she could now live openly.[66] With the help of a $1,000 foreign scholarship from the graduate chapter of the black women's Greek-letter organization, Delta Sigma Theta,[67] she was able to take a leave of absence from her position in the fine arts department at Howard University to pursue, as she wrote in a letter to Langston Hughes, "the road . . . less traveled" in June 1925.[68] Bennett was right. There were very few African American women, let alone artists and writers, in Paris in 1925.

ILLUSTRATION 2.7. Gwendolyn Bennett, Columbia University, summer 1924. Courtesy of Yale Collection of American Literature, Beinecke Rare Book and Manuscript Library, Yale University.

She took a room at the Hotel Orfila at 60 rue d'Assas, which she described as "neither bohemian or dirty."[69] She then moved on to the "beautiful" and "quaint village"[70] of Pontoise, a commune some seventeen miles from Paris, before resettling in Paris for six months at a "very very cheap and very clean"[71] pension on 13 Carrefour de l'Odeon.

Given the number of prestigious art academies in the city, she had yet to choose one, telling her friend Langston Hughes, "I haven't yet decided what school I shall attend. It is quite difficult to decide . . . Gwendolyn Sinclair doesn't seem to think much about the Academic Julienne [sic]. I really don't know whose advice to take."[72] The Académie Julian, like the Académie Colarossi, was the first on nearly everyone's list and lips primarily because of its popularity with American art students abroad. But one particular attraction for a young woman with Bennett's race pride would have been the Julian's connection to artist Henry Ossawa Tanner.

Tanner was born in Pittsburgh. He studied under Thomas Eakin at the Pennsylvania Academy of the Fine Arts. Finding opportunities foreclosed to him because of his race in the United States, he left for Paris in 1891 intending to stay for only a short time before settling in Rome. Taken with the city, he made it his permanent home. Tanner was the only African American at the Académie Julian. He found it as hospitable as he found the city. He worked closely with French master painters Jean Paul Laurens and Jean Joseph Benjamin-Constant. In 1893 and 1894, he painted his two most recognized African American themed classic works: *The Banjo Lesson* and *The Thankful Poor*.[73]

Eventually Bennett sampled from the lot, taking classes at the Académies Julian, de la Grande Chaumière, and Colarossi, and the École du Panthéon. Founded by Rodolphe Julian in 1868, the Académie Julian readily accepted and trained women as compared to the conservative École des Beaux Arts, which did not begin accepting women until 1897. The Colarossi offered classes in life drawing and life sculpting. The Swiss painter Martha Stettler established the Grande Chaumière, with fees lower than even those of the Académie Julian, in 1904. Both academies occupied the same street, numbers 10 and 14, respectively, rue de la Grande Chaumière, on the Left Bank in the sixth arrondissement of Montparnasse. The Colarossi also had the distinction of having welcomed Meta Vaux Warrick Fuller in 1899.

The Montparnasse district, anchored by the grand Boulevard Montparnasse and running along the crossroads between the rue de Rennes and Boulevard Raspail, and sweeping up the Luxembourg Gardens and the small cross streets, was known for its cafes and bars like Le Dôme and La Rotonde and the myriad studios for cheap rent to artists and writers tucked away in areas like the Carrefour Vavin. At each of these ateliers and écoles, Bennett was able to pursue her craft in some fashion. She painted, sketched, and submitted poetry and cover art to literary magazines back in Harlem

during her year in Paris. One morning spent at la Grande Chaumiére produced a "nude in oil," a first for the artist. "Much in the morning's work,"
she writes, "to discourage me. Art is loving!"[74] But she also realizes that
"Paris has been a revelation . . . so far as modern work is concerned. Our
American modernists are about a thousand years behind the Europeans."[75]

Seesawing between homesickness and awe, she relates to Countee
Cullen:

> My first impressions were of extreme loneliness and intense
> home-sickness. . . . this and incessant rain. My second impres-
> sions were of hometies, stirred by my American friends who
> were visiting Europe this summer. And now . . . through the
> hazy veil of memories I see that Paris is a very beautiful city
> and that people here are basicly [sic] different from those I have
> always known. I feel that I shall like being here bye and bye.[76]

And she did. Her longing for "hometies" was met by an active social life:
tea at Shakespeare and Company, a meeting with James Joyce and Henri Matisse, time spent with Richard Wright, Gertrude Stein, and Ernest
Hemingway, while keeping regular company with Essie and Paul Robeson
in early November. She had Thanksgiving dinner with Sylvia Beach and
fell in with fellow student artist, Laura Wheeler, who had moved to Neuilly
after Fauset's departure.

And when Bennett's longing for "hometies" and "homethoughts" lingered too long, she made her way to Montmartre where a sense of home
could be sufficiently nursed in the familiarity Bricktop provided:

> Then at 4:15 A.M. to dear old "Bricktop's" . . . and Lottie Gee
> sings for Brick her hit from "Shuffle Along"—"I'm Just Wild
> About Harry." Her voice is not what it might have been and she
> had too much champaign [sic] but still there was something very
> personal and dear about her singing it and we colored folks just
> applauded like mad. "Brick" singing as well as ever her hits—
> "Insufficient Sweetie" and "I'm In Love Again."[77]

Lottie Gee, who had been Eubie Blake's mistress, had defected from her
leading role in the *Chocolate Kiddies* revue after an eight-week, sold-out run
in Berlin, Germany. The up-and-coming starlet Adelaide Hall took her place
as lead. Down in her cups because of Blake's unwillingness to leave his wife
of twenty-eight years, she decamped to Paris, and more specifically to Montmartre, for a good cry on Bricky's shoulders. As slushy as her performance
may have been, for Bennett, it reinforced a sense of community among the
"colored folks." Such was the force of Bricktop's personality that many, even

Bennett, referred to Le Grand Duc as Bricktop's. The sense of community, preciousness of the moment that only other African Americans would have appreciated, was perhaps heightened by the fact that the clientele of Le Grand Duc and later at Chez Bricktop, while integrated, was predominantly white—European and American.

Bennett eventually found a studio in January 1926, after seven months. Content with the space at rue de la Tour d'Auvergne on the outskirts of Montmartre and convinced that she would now be able to "do some real work,"[78] Paris, for all of its rain, inspired the artist-poet: "Just think of being able to see Carot's palette and hat and Delacroix's brush and pipe. I felt fired with a new purpose to do and learn."[79]

Her enthusiasm was dampened only by money: "Money is so necessary to make a place for beauty. Today when I so want to live and learn I am filled with sorrow to feel that money keeps me from so much."[80] The fellowship funds were slow to arrive. She confided in Essie Robeson who had been in Paris during the month of August about her "financial condition." Essie suggested that she request an additional "two hundred dollars to the original one thousand dollars."[81] From London, her friend, and Langston Hughes's former sweetheart, Anne Marie Coussey, expressed sympathy for her "tight squeeze," while Opportunity editor Charles Johnson "took the liberty of trying to trace" a $100 check she had not as yet received. He also found a seller for the batiks she hoped to create in Paris in order to earn extra monies.[82]

Gwendolyn Bennett returned to New York in June 1926, and to her teaching post in fine arts at Howard University. Unlike other African American women artists who entered Paris art salons, she preferred a "homecoming exhibition"[83] for her work. Besides her poetry and short stories, she created a pithy travel guide in typescript pages. It is not clear if the pages were meant to be addressed to a personal friend as there is no signature, addressee, or even date. Whether Bennett had intentions of publishing her miniguide in one of the literary magazines for which she wrote or the "you" in the pages were addressed to a friend, the Bennett travel guide is unusual for the form and detail that travelers to Paris could expect to find in the more popular Galignani's Messenger and Paris travel books used by English-speaking visitors to France. It is worth quoting at length.

In listing the hotels in which she and others stayed, she offered tips on the views ("Luxembourg Gardens" at Hotel Orfila), cleanliness, private baths, and whether the rate was meal inclusive; she also reviewed "the very comfortable" looking Hotel Jeanne D'Arc at 59 rue Vaneau—"where Jessie Fauset and Laura Wheeler stayed for ever so long." She noted that the hotel was pricier than what she was "accustomed to pay[ing] but not so much as New York hotels." She also recommended a moderately priced accommodation at 5 rue Corneille.[84]

She continued:

Because I want you to get the most out of this trip I am going
to copy a part bodily [sic] from a letter Rayford Logan sent me
before I sailed:

> The rue de la Paix, Avenue del [sic] Opera, Rue de
> Rivoli, Rue Royale, Place Vendome and Rue de Cas-
> tiglione are very high priced.
>   There is a hotel at no. 1 Rue de Vaugirard
> (I think it is the Hotel Trianon). You might go there.
> Whatever you do, do not take a room in Montmartre.
>   Until you are settled eat in Prix Fixe restau-
> rant, rather than one a la carte [sic]. There are quite a
> few along the Boulevard Saint Michel. The Café du
> Dome Boulevard Montparnasse is the artists hangout
> on the left bank. Beware of adventurers and adven-
> turesses. Do not go to call on any one who is not
> recommended. Don't display a lot of money or tell
> anyone where your bank is.
>   Give ten per cent on the bill for a tip but
> never give less than 50 centimes tip in a first class
> restaurant.[85]

A Washington, DC, native, Rayford Logan served in the First Great War.
After facing down discrimination in the armed services, he threw his lot in
with France, staying on for five years after the war. Fluent in French, Logan
was also instrumental to Du Bois's efforts with the Pan-African Congresses,
following the 1919 Congress. A graduate of Williams College and Harvard
University, Logan was a member of President Franklin D. Roosevelt's "Black
Cabinet." He was resolute in his counsels to the president on black participation in the military services.[86]

Logan had already returned to the United States by the time Gwendolyn Bennett embarked on her trip abroad. His practical advice provides
a concise assist to Bennett's narrative. He maps out Paris by quarters and
reputation. Montparnasse is for the artists. Montmartre, with its high-ener-
gy nightlife, is seedy by day and night. The first and second arrondissements, home to Cartier, the Ritz-Carlton, Galignani's, and Café Angelina,
by contrast, are pricey. Bennett followed his advice scrupulously—even
eating at the occasional prix fixe restaurant. She concluded her guide by
recommending bookshops (Shakespeare and Company, naturally) and inexpensive restaurants.

With her return from France, Gwennie's expanded credentials as a result of her travel abroad allowed her to resume a burgeoning role as a *porte-parole* of the New Negro movement with the 1926 debut of the column "The Ebony Flute" in *Opportunity*. In July 1926, she published the first of her Paris trilogy of short literary fiction and a poem, "Lines Written at the Grave of Alexandre Dumas," in the pages of the magazine. A lyric poem, Bennett's "Lines" ring with solemn tones of death but equally joy and a desire to wake the genius from death's slumber:

> Oh, stir the lucid waters of thy sleep
> And coin for me a tale
> Of happy loves and gems and joyous limbs
> And hearts where love is sweet!

Bennett's feting of Dumas is not random but rather filial. Across time and space, immersed in the recuperative, internationalist tendencies of the New Negro era, Bennett planted a diasporic flag at Dumas's grave. Frenchmen though he was, Dumas may have cottoned to this reclaiming, evident in a riposte he delivered to white Frenchmen skewering him about his colorful background: "Mon père était un mulâtre, mon grand-père était un nègre et mon arrière grand-père un singe. Vous voyez, Monsieur: ma famille commence où la vôtre finit" (My father was mulatto, my grandfather was a Negro, my great-grandfather a monkey. You see, Sir: my family begins where yours ends).[87]

In bringing Dumas home (to America), placing him within the field of a black literary diaspora, and consecrating his place as one of France's most vivid storytellers, the twenty-three-year-old Gwennie Bennett was a good seventy-six years ahead of the French Republic in offering such laurels. For in a postcard of the Panthéon and a statue of Jean-Jacques Rousseau sent to Countee Cullen, Bennett is thrilled to be among the "tombs" of "Victor Hugo, Voltaire, Rousseau, Zola, etc, to know that that you are close to the ashes of such great people." And yet, the tomb of the author of *The Count of Monte Cristo* and *The Three Musketeers* was noticeably absent. In 1925, he was interred at Villers-Cotterêts in the Picardy, France—the place of his birth. It was only on the bicentennial of his birth in 2002 that Alexandre Dumas's remains were moved to the Panthéon.

My trip over was smooth. . . . I looked like a dark skinned maiden when I arrived. Nella and I were almost moved to kiss each other—which has only happened twice in our lives, you know.

—Dorothy Peterson to Carl Van Vechten, July 19, 1931

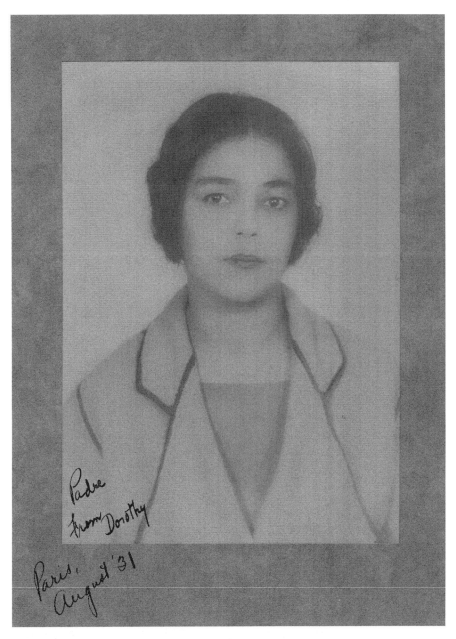

ILLUSTRATION 2.8. Dorothy Peterson, August 1931. Courtesy of Yale Collection of American Literature, Beinecke Rare Book and Manuscript Library, Yale University.

So wrote Dorothy Peterson in July 1931 of her arrival in France. The recipient of her correspondence was none other than the ubiquitous—in terms of his role in the lives of Negro artists, intellectuals, and writers—Carl Van Vechten. This was not Peterson's first trip to Paris. Indeed, she had ventured on another transatlantic voyage on the SS *Aquitania*, which docked in Cherbourg, France. She stayed at the Hotel Trianon Palace on 1 bis and 3 rue de Vaugirard, which lies between the Latin Quarter and Saint-Germain. The street is the longest in Paris, running through the sixth and fifteenth arrondissements, and the hotel housed Richard Wright during his first visit to Paris. During Peterson's August 1927 visit, she made her way to the Fontainebleau Institute, where the spiritual leader George Ivanovitch Gurdjieff held forth and Peterson's paramour, Jean Toomer, author of the high-modernist Harlem Renaissance novel *Cane* and an avid follower of Gurdjieff, could be found.

Born in Armenia in either 1866 or 1877, when the country was part of the Russian Empire, Gurdjieff was, depending on whom one asked, an itinerant spiritualist, a guru, a sexist, serial philanderer, or a self-help hustler on the order of the hustlers and hucksters vividly described in African American expatriate writer Chester Himes's *A Rage in Harlem*. Gurdjieff trekked throughout the former Russian Empire and Western Europe before settling south of Paris in Fontainebleau-Avon where he set up his Institute for the Harmonious Development of Man. There he taught his principles of self-help, spirituality, and self-awareness under the rubric "Fourth Way." He also made his way to New York in 1925, raising substantial funds for his quixotic philosophy of life.[88]

But Peterson's visit to Paris in 1931 was as companion and confidant to writer Nella Larsen. Accomplished in her own right, Dorothy Randolph Peterson was born June 21, 1897. She grew up between Venezuela, Puerto Rico, and New York as a consequence of her father's various government appointments. A high school teacher, Peterson spoke fluent Spanish, had theatrical aspirations culminating in a turn in the Broadway production *The Green Pastures*, and the serious contemplation of leaving teaching full-time for the stage in 1929; she had also supported the Harlem Renaissance/New Negro movements financially and via literary salons at her Brooklyn apartment.[89]

She arrived in Paris to a jubilant Larsen. Following the critical successes of her novels *Quicksand* and *Passing*, Larsen had won a Guggenheim Fellowship to work on a third novel. She decided to travel to Europe for multiple reasons—to write her third novel, to escape her troubled domestic situation, and to put behind her the charges of plagiarism regarding her short story "Sanctuary." "Sanctuary" was, by all accounts, in some ways derivative of British writer Sheila Kaye-Smith's 1919 short story "Mrs. Adis: A Tragedy in One Act"; but a more interesting tale is that "Mrs. Adis" may have well been a palimpsest of a story written by the canonized French bishop Saint François de Sales.[90]

Nella Larsen was born Nellie Walker in Chicago, Illinois, on April 13, 1891, to a Danish mother and West Indian father. No stranger to Europe as she had passed some of her youth and teenage years with relatives in Denmark,[91] the Guggenheim again opened the door to travel. Larsen stopped first in Lisbon before settling in Palma de Mallorca in Spain's Balearic Islands. Larsen had been rather "forlorn,"[92] in her own words, during her last weeks in Spain. Her husband, the respected physicist and Fisk University professor Elmer Imes, continued his involvement with Ethel Gilbert, a white female coworker at the university, and a flirtation of her own did not yield much. To boot, the "amusing people" comprising the English-speaking expat community had "gone, and really I've never been so lonely in my life."[93]

She was finishing up her novel but found it was not a good read. Europe was meant to be a new beginning; away from the weight of her professional fall from grace and her messy domestic situation, she expected to marshal productively her creativity. As Thadious Davis contends, "Larsen turned forcefully to expending her creative energy on a more lasting representation of her female self. At the apogee of her life as a writer, she understood her writing to be her best form of control of her identity and understood the depth of her commitment to literary work."[94] Spain did not deliver her from life's doldrums.

She had hoped Paris would. And indeed it did. Larsen's arrival in Paris in early May coincided with the May 6th opening of the Paris Colonial Exposition of 1931. She was lucky to find a room at the Hotel Rovaro, 44 rue Brunel in the seventeenth arrondissement. The hotel was walking distance to the Arc de Triomphe and Place Charles De Gaulle.

L'Exposition coloniale internationale de Paris, or the Paris Colonial Exposition, ran from May 6, 1931 to November 15, 1931. Its intentions were to educate rather than to entertain the French public and tourists about the colonial world in the aftermath of the scramble for Africa at the Berlin Conference. For the architect of the Colonial Exposition, Maréchal Hubert Lyautey, it was an important display of French military muscle and metropolitan benevolence that also threw into sharp contrast the savage and the civilizer. Though other colonial powers participated, the primary goal of Lyautey's vision was for the public to come to the Bois de Vincennes in the outskirts of Paris for a tour around the world *en un jour* in order to witness *la plus grande France* and the accomplishments of *la mission civilisatrice*. And they did. In droves.

The Exposition was structured like an open-air natural history museum with its villages populated by *les indigènes*, displays of rare cultural artifacts,

ILLUSTRATION 2.9. Nella Larsen. Courtesy of Yale Collection of American Literature, Beinecke Rare Book and Manuscript Library, Yale University.

and large-scale dioramas. With over 33 million visitors, the Paris Colonial Exposition was a financial and propagandistic success, dwarfing the four thousand or so visitors who passed through the surrealists' mounted Counter-Colonial Exposition.[95]

But for all of its claims to scientific and ethnographic verisimilitude, fanfare, and profits, Nella Larsen received the Paris Colonial Exposition unenthusiastically. The city was nonetheless even more than usual teeming with tourists and activities. Her social life picked up as it had in Spain before the departure of "the amusing people." Between teas and lunches during her first week, Larsen was also being shown "Nigger Heaven" (Montmartre), which included a stop at Bricktop's. Brick was not there, and Larsen, with her admitted peculiar mind, found the fabled nightspot "pretty dull. An off-night perhaps."[96]

Though Larsen professed boredom, Paris was anything but boring with days filled with touring and nights of dinners and concerts. She would even take up with Harold Jackman in Paris, though he had expressly avoided her in New York after the plagiarism charges emerged. She had secured an apartment in the heart of Montparnasse at 31 bis rue Campagne Première by the time Dorothy Peterson arrived. Bracketed by the Boulevard Montparnasse in the sixth arrondissement, the street ran along toward the Boulevard Raspail in the fourteenth arrondissement.

The apartment was situated in the fourteenth and closer to Raspail; it belonged to abstract expressionist artist Paul Burlin. Peterson was quite taken with it, its environs, and the French shop girls, describing the scenes from her window as

> perfectly marvelous and from the high studio window, we look down the Boulevard Edgar Quinet with its five lovely trees. We have . . . a view altho [sic] at present it is quite cluttered with French servant girls off for Sunday afternoon with their lovers, who with one hand clutch[ing] their funny little hats always a size too small and with the hand grab[bing] the girl by the neck as tho [sic] she were going to take her first chance and run away.[97]

The Paris whirlwind of activities continued for the two with nights spent in Montmartre, cocktail parties, and luncheons. Larsen would spend five months in Paris. The number of Americans, black and white, in her orbit gave the city a feeling of home. Certainly, Dorothy Peterson noted the extensive network of American contacts they had tapped into in Paris, remarking that her first week was "really like old home week."[98]

Peterson and Larsen continued on from Paris to Spain where Peterson contemplated permanent expatriation. Paris had not fueled Larsen's literary imagination as it had Fauset's and Bennett's. Rather, the city offered her freedom and fun, an escape from the painful and slow disintegration of her marriage and career as a novelist that would come with her return to America.

∾

> There are a couple of stories, current in the Latin Quarter now that I'm sure will interest you. One is fiction. The other as true as historical record in the Bibliotheque National [sic] can make it.
>
> —Anita Thompson, "A Story from Paris," 1929

The fictional tale was the one the aspiring writer Anita Thompson chose to tell the readers of *Flash*, a West Coast news and literary magazine founded in 1928 by the African American journalist Fay Jackson. A friend of Dorothy Peterson, Larsen thought Thompson "rather pretty."[99] To the clucking novelist's disappointment, Thompson was palling around Paris and later Tangiers with the wayward Claude McKay. In a letter to her mother, Thompson makes plain her relationship with McKay and her travels to Morocco: "Don't think that it is scandalous; he is a fairy. And he ain't got no use for nothing my color no how . . . even if I were a boy. HA!"[100]

Born March 28, 1901, in Chicago, Illinois, Thompson's family relocated to Los Angeles in 1906. She grew up in a stable, middle-class family that was financially supportive of her quixotic, if flighty ambitions that also involved travel to New York. Open to new experiences and not afraid to seek them out, her first sexual experience was a thrilling one with a female acquaintance; intercourse with a clumsy male bordered on violation. Anita Thompson went to Paris because she could; it was fashionable, and she hoped to come back the better for it. An aspiring model, actress, painter, and writer, she traveled to Paris with ambitions to accomplish something in 1928. A reproving letter from her father about her precarious finances and dependency on the family's financial support encouraged her to return home. Undeterred, she remained hopeful as ever. She stayed for twelve years. She moved within the various black and white expatriate colonies, cultivating friendships with the likes of Man Ray, Arthur Wheeler, Claude McKay, Countee Cullen.[101]

While in Paris, Thompson crafted "A Story from Paris" for *Flash*. Using the epistolary form to deliver her story, Anita assumes a familiarity with the readership by addressing the story-letter to "My dear Godchild 'Flash.'" After recounting the existence of two tales—one fact, one fiction—floating around the Latin Quarter, she continues:

ILLUSTRATION 2.10. Anita Thompson, Paris, 1928. Courtesy of Moorland-Spingarn Research Center, Howard University.

This week I shall tell you the fanciful one but, very soon, you must hear the other for it is about a famous French Queen and her African lover and their daughter. It is a very beautiful story.

But now for the tale of a chateau in the mountains above the rolling fields of the Vosge country.[102]

Thompson's fictional tale mixes mystery, murder, and madness as it centers on a country chateau, a hunting party, an escaped lunatic, and the murder of the chateau's concierge. What is even more interesting than the word-of-mouth fictional tale is her passing reference to the "historical" one involving ostensibly Queen Marie-Thérèse, Louis XIV's royal consort, and her Dahomean page at the court, Nabo, also known as Augustin, according to noted French historian Jean-Christian Petitfils.

The debate about an affair between Nabo/Augustin and the Queen, and their supposed offspring began in eighteenth-century France. Even the Jamaican-born, autodidact, historian, and correspondent for various African American newspapers J. A. Rogers entered the fray in 1941 with the self-published volume *Sex and Race: Negro-Caucasian Mixing in All Ages and All Lands, Volume I: The Old World*. It appears though that Anita Thompson beat him to publication with the mention of the affair in her 1929 short story in *Flash*.

African children, slaves, and dwarfs were fashionable in European courts as was their presence in court portraitures. Africans were symbols of social prestige, successful empire building, and power, and countermarks in emerging ideas about European whiteness and identity. As Thompson's "the beautiful story" went, the queen had a child by her elfin page Nabo/Augustin in 1664. He was allegedly disappeared from the royal court shortly after these events to the Bastille, where he became, for some, the famed Man in the Iron Mask. The child, publicly announced as dead shortly after her birth, survived but was spirited off and raised outside of Versailles.

In 1695 at a convent in Moret, near Fontainebleau, a thirty-year-old black woman named Louise Marie-Thérèse took the veil.[103] Thirty years after the death of Queen Marie-Thérèse, Louise Marie-Thérèse claimed to have had royal parentage. With a name derived from both the king and his royal consort's, Louise Marie-Thérèse also received a royal pension. That there is a portrait of Louise Marie-Thérèse, also known as the Black Nun of Moret, painted around the same time by the same artist used by the royal court, and hanging in the Bibliothèque Sainte Geneviève in the Latin Quarter, or the "Bibliotheque National," as Anita writes, adds the sheen of truth to the centuries'-old handed-down tale. The portrait, per Anita, makes the "story" "as true as historical record . . . can make it." What had been considered mere gossip-mongering looking to create a royal scandal in the eighteenth century, in the hands of black writers in the twentieth century *La Religieuse noire de Moret* saga takes on the aura of the romantic legend of the Grand Duchess of Russia Anastasia Romanov, with the Latin adage *mater semper certa est/pater semper incertus est*, simply translated as "Mama's Baby, Papa's Maybe."

The seventeenth- and eighteenth-century sources of the Nabo/Augustin–Marie-Thérèse affair are not especially numerous, but some are questionable. Enlightenment philosopher Voltaire, who had also bizarrely argued through firsthand knowledge that the blood of Africans was the same color as their skin and that the Man in the Iron Mask was the illegitimate brother of King Louis XIV, dabbled in rekindling the story. Not a witness to the birth as he was born well after, Voltaire claimed to have visited Louise Marie-Thérèse at the convent near Fontainebleau. He concluded that the king not the queen was her biological father and, thus, the source of her royal patrimony.[104] The memoirs of the king's mistress, Madame de la Marquise de Montespan, also not a witness to the birth, stoked the rumor with the following:

> The Queen being pregnant, public prayers were offered up for her according to custom, and her Majesty was forever saying: "My pregnancy this time is different from preceding ones. I am a prey to nausea and strange whims; I have never felt like this before. If, for propriety's sake, I did not restrain myself, I should now dearly like to be turning somersaults on the carpet, like little Osmin. He eats green fruit and raw game; that is what I should like to do, too. I should like to—"
>
> "Oh, madame, you frighten us!" exclaimed the King. "Don't let all those whimsies trouble you further, or you will give birth to some monstrosity, some freak of nature." His Majesty was a true prophet. The Queen was delivered of a fine little girl, black as ink from head to foot. They did not tell her this at once, fearing a catastrophe, but persuaded her to go to sleep, saying that the child had been taken away to be christened.
>
> The physicians met in one room, the bishops and chaplains in another. One prelate was opposed to baptising the infant; another only agreed to this upon certain conditions. The majority decided that it should be baptised without the name of father or mother, and such suppression was unanimously advocated.
>
> The little thing, despite its swarthy hue, was most beautifully made; its features bore none of those marks peculiar to people of colour.
>
> It was sent away to the Gisors district to be suckled as a negro's daughter, and the Gazette de France contained an

announcement to the effect that the royal infant had died, after
having been baptised by the chaplains.

[This daughter of the Queen lived, and was obliged to enter
a Benedictine nunnery at Moret. Her portrait is to be seen in
the Sainte Genevieve Library of Henri IV.'s College, where it
hangs in the winter saloon.—EDITOR'S NOTE.]

The little African was sent away, as may well be imagined; and the Queen admitted that, one day soon after she was
pregnant, he had hidden himself behind a piece of furniture and
suddenly jumped out upon her to give her a fright. In this he
was but too successful.

The Court ladies no longer dared come near the Queen
attended by their little blackamoors. These, however, they kept
for a while longer, as if they were mere nick-nacks or ornaments; in Paris they were still to be seen in public. But the
ladies' husbands at last got wind of the tale, when all the little
negroes disappeared.[105]

The veracity of the memoir is dubious, as it was not written by Montespan but ghosted some 150 years later. Augustin is transformed into Osmin,
and the "swarthy hue[d]," "beautifully made" child's dark skin is attributed
to the queen's being frightened by the Lilliputian Negro's childish game
of hide-and-leap-out-from-behind-a-piece-of-furniture. The consequence of
which was that "little negroes" were no longer fashionable at the court as
"nick-nacks or ornaments."

The queen's propriety is never in question. Rather, blackness and those
deemed blackamoors or Negros represented a range of tangled ideas and
symbols in the European mind in the Age of Enlightenment and onward,
from evil and infamy to magical powers and hypersexuality. A penetrating look as opposed to penetration itself transforms a white child already
conceived in its mother's womb into one as "black as ink from head
to foot."

One of the more plausible sources on the "black royal daughter back
from the dead" intrigue is the king's cousin, La Grande Mademoiselle, or
the Duchesse Anne-Marie-Louise d'Orléans de Montpensier. While not present at the birth, her cousin and the king's brother, Philippe I, the Duke of
Orléans, who was, provided her an account. In her *Memoirs of la Grande
Mademoiselle: Duchesse de Montpensier*, she wrote: "[L]a fille, ressembloit un
petit maure . . . qui étoit fort joli, qui étoit toujours avec la reine"/"The
girl resembled a little handsome Moor, who was always with the queen."[106]

In her biography, *Marie-Thérèse d'Autriche: Epouse de Louis XIV*, Joëlle
Chevé relates that the devout Marie-Thérèse did in fact give birth prema-

turely to a daughter named Marie-Anne of France in November 16, 1664. The queen herself was also terribly ill and had received her last rites during the birth, though she survived. Louis XIV announced the death of his daughter on December 26, 1664, to all of Europe. The child evidently had troubled breathing and manifested a complexion that appeared violet and bluish. None of the attending physicians noted anything else about the child's physical appearance. Two years before, the queen had given birth to a daughter who had lived only six weeks. Indeed, between 1661 and 1672, the queen gave birth to six children: four died in infancy, one at five years of age, and only one, Louis Grand Dauphin, survived to adulthood. As was customary, Chevé offers, the birth of royal children was public with the king himself in attendance. Moreover, the princess's body was publicly displayed in the chapel of the Louvre on December 30.[107] The public viewing ceremony was, for naysayers, a ruse whereby the child's body was switched in a conspiracy to protect the royals from scandal.

In all likelihood, the Nun of Moret's royal parentage would have been paternal. Indeed, Louise Marie-Thérèse supposedly claimed the king was her father. The Sun King had numerous mistresses and frequented with regularity the brothels of Paris. He was known for his generosity toward his illegitimate children. He would marry them off within branches of the royal family, legitimize others by bestowing "de Bourbon," the royal surname, as well as provide pensions and dowries. A black one, though, would have required the added step of sequester and the convent primarily to prevent reproduction and hence the propagation of French royal blood via an African lineage. With her flair for drama, romantic inclinations, and wry humor, Anita Thompson would have been intrigued by this tale as she searched for subjects to further her writer's ambitions.

By 1930, she had found a topic and a patron to support those ambitions in the wealthy American expatriate Arthur Wheeler. Wheeler was also a financial supporter of Man Ray and encouraged the avant-garde photographer's film career. It was no doubt Thompson's friendship with Man Ray that helped secure her Wheeler's patronage. Of her budding writing career, "grâce à un Americain [sic],"[108] she boasted that she wrote

> everyday like a trooper . . . in a little room high up over the palaces and river and the great Place de la Concorde. . . . Wheeler pays my rent, the typewriter, etc, etc. He and his wife are from New York. Needless to add that they are rich and patrons of art. They give me 3,000 francs a month until the book is finished without any strings, that is if it is never published . . . tant pis . . . if it is, I owe them nothing. . . . P.S. For God's sake please don't give any chance of publicity to my work here. Or

to any of my ambitions. If it falls thru there'll be no niggers to shut up. You know how it is.[109]

Thompson's book, "Mocking-Bird," a family history, did in fact fail to find a publishing house despite her many Left Bank connections. And her desire to keep her writing life a secret faltered as well. Nella Larsen had already passed on this tidbit to Carl Van Vechten in May 1931.

In the opening pages of her unpublished[110] memoirs, variously titled *The Tan Experience, American Cocktail: The Tan Experience, American Cocktail,* and *Caramel: Autobiography of a Drop of Burned Sugar,* Anita Thompson looked back wistfully on her Paris years:

> The mind wanders to pleasanter times. Paris in the 30s. Montparnasse and St. Germain des Pres [sic], where the artists and writers flocked in never-ending numbers. I was an asteroid then, in orbit about the brilliant stars: Breton, Derain, Matisse, Picasso, Brancusi, Max Ernst, James Joyce, Hemingway, Carlos Williams. Perhaps, I thought, some of their genius would rub off on me. Perhaps a word of encouragement.[111]

She was more than a very fair-skinned, pretty hanger-on in a world of intellectual and artistic celebrity. Anita became fluent in French and studied at the École du Louvre and the Sorbonne. She read avidly and debated many of the heady ideas sweeping through Paris. What Paris could not spark with respect to any writerly gifts, it did spur in terms of her intellectual zeal.

Anita continued leading a bohemian life in Paris, flirting with surrealism and traveling throughout Europe and North Africa, spending eighteen months in Morocco and six months in Tunisia. When she settled back into Paris after these adventures, she came face to face with the crisis that had been smoldering just beneath the gay times in Paris. While Americans who remained abroad "played on," in the words of Bricktop, economies collapsed and old wounds opened, unleashing with them the return of nationalism, xenophobia, and the coming of the Second Great War.

THREE

WOMEN OF THE PETIT BOULEVARD

The Artist's Haven

"When I arrived in Paris, African art was just the thing. All the galleries and museums were featuring African sculptures, African designs, and I sketch, sketched everything."

—Lois Mailou Jones, from an interview with Catherine Bernard,
quoted in the preface, "1937–1938: Lois Mailou Jones,"
Tritobia Hayes Benjamin, ed., *The Life and Art of Lois Mailou Jones*

By the time Lois Mailou Jones and Selma Hortense Burke arrived in Paris in 1937 and 1938, respectively, the exclusive, by virtue of its size rather than snobbery, haven of creativity and connections that had developed in Paris among African American women artists was fast disappearing. Jones, who was born on November 3, 1905, was a native of Boston. She attended both the School of the Museum of Fine Arts and the Boston Normal Art School in Boston, graduating in 1927 before going on to pursue advanced studies at the Designers School of Boston. Upon graduating and finding very little recognition for her work, she nominated herself for a Harmon Foundation Award at the age of twenty-three in 1928, and again in 1929 and 1930, presumably to study abroad.[1] The William E. Harmon Awards for Distinguished Achievement among Negroes were established in 1926 in eight categories. Founded by the real estate magnate William E. Harmon with the encouragement of Alain Locke, the awards helped to bolster and sustain the Harlem Renaissance with its support of fledgling artists.

Counseled by the sculptor Meta Vaux Warrick Fuller to study abroad during her summers as a teenager at Oak Bluffs on Martha's Vineyard, Jones remembered:

I should say that practically every summer of my childhood my
mother took me and my brother to Martha's Vineyard Island,
where we spent our summer vacations. . . . It was there that I
first began to paint. . . . it was there that I met Meta Warrick
Fuller. Meta Fuller told me this on the beach one day: "Lois, you
know, if you want to be successful in your career you're going
to have to go abroad." (We had been talking about my career
because I was just about to graduate from the Museum School.)
Meta related that she had gone to Paris. She had even studied
with Rodin. You see, the establishment in this country was not
ready to accept us. It's the case in the history of our art. Look
what happened to Henry O. Tanner. He couldn't make it in this
country; he had to go abroad. The same thing happened to Hale
Woodruff. He went to France. And there were many others. This
country wasn't interested in exhibiting our work or allowing us
any of the opportunities that the white artists enjoyed. I made
up my mind at that moment that I would go to Paris.[2]

Unable to secure an award, Jones turned south to Sedalia, North Carolina.
She taught art at the Palmer Memorial Institute before landing in the art
department faculty at Howard University in September 1930. It was not
until 1937, with a sabbatical and the assistance of a General Education
Board fellowship, that she was finally able to study abroad.

She sailed in September 1937 on the SS *Normandie le Havre*. She was
welcomed in Paris by Louis Achilles, a fellow professor at Howard University
and cousin to Martinican journalist Paulette Nardal. Jones rented a studio
in Montparnasse, at 23 rue Campagne Première, in close proximity to the
Académie Julian.[3] While in France, she completed nearly forty paintings
during her nine months of study at the Julian. She entered several oil paintings in salons, including a watercolor, *Pecheurs sur la Seine* (1937), at the
Septième Exposition des Beaux-Arts et Arts Décoratifs in Ville d'Asnières,
France, and *La Cuisine dans l'Atelier de l'Artiste* (1938) at the Société des
Artistes Français. Asnières was a small village to the northwest of Paris on
the Seine River. Postimpressionist painters like Georges Seurat and Van
Gogh were drawn to the commune's landscape. Jones painted still lifes and
landscapes. Her use of color, light, brush strokes, and palette knife in these
works reveal the early influences of impressionism and postimpressionism.[4]

Like the sculptor Augusta Savage before her, Jones also captures a
Martinican woman in art—this time on canvas. Jones's Martinican woman
is dressed in the creole style of the island with a colorful headdress. One
wonders if *Jeanne, Martiniquaise* (1938) (*Jane, Martinican Woman*) was in
homage to Louis Achilles's cousin and Paulette Nardal's sister, Jane Nardal,

ILLUSTRATION 3.1. Lois Mailou Jones on a boat to Paris, France, 1937. Courtesy of Moorland-Spingarn Research Center, Howard University.

ILLUSTRATION 3.2. Lois Mailou Jones painting on the banks of the Seine, undated. Courtesy of Moorland-Spingarn Research Center, Howard University.

or a nod to Charles Baudelaire's Martinican mistress made famous as Black Venus in his *Les Fleurs du mal*.

While the old masters influenced Jones, so too did Africa as the art transported from the French colonial outposts on the continent continued to be positioned front and center following the Colonial Exposition in Paris in 1931. Still in the throes of negrophilia, helped along by the aftereffects of the 1931 Exposition, for many artists like Jones, Picasso, and Modigliani, Paris became the gateway to Africa. This now-opened gateway led to the creation of Lois Jones's highly original oil-on-linen *Les Fétiches* (1938) as well as her *African Bathers* (1937). With its African mask and fetish symbols, rhythmic and spiritual inflections, *Les Fétiches* was a break from her impressionist and postimpressionist-influenced works. She desired to stay in Paris for another year to continue mining this new art, but the request for an extension of her sabbatical from Howard was denied.

Though their paths did not cross in Paris in 1938 when she arrived, Selma Burke and Lois Jones were close friends with the latter mindfully collecting newspaper articles and ephemera on the former and welcoming her at her home in Washington, DC, during a weeklong cultural festival hosted by Howard University's College of Fine Arts.[5] Burke, born on December 31, 1900, had made her way to Paris from New York by way of her hometown of Mooresville, North Carolina.[6] Educated at the Nannie Burroughs School for Girls, where girls were encouraged to become ladies by wearing "your silk-ribbed stockings, patent leather Mary Janes and gloves," Burke insisted, "I wanted to be a lady but also an artist."[7] Discouraged from pursuing art for a more practical career by her family, Selma took up nursing instead.

She arrived in New York in 1928 as a private nurse, at the tail end of the official Harlem Renaissance, and a year before the collapse of the American stock market and the onset of the Great Depression. She soon took up with the artistic New York crowd that included Claude McKay. Of her relationship with the writer, she offered in a 1975 interview with Jacqueline Trescott of the *Washington Post*:

> I used to eat at Dick Heweys's and one night a man in a great coat and a cap came in. And Dick said, "I can't give you another dinner on credit Claude. I asked if it was McKay and said, "Make that dinner for two. . . .
>
> McKay had just returned from Europe and was practically penniless. "He told me his plight. His landlady had locked him out and he had been sleeping on the subway for a couple of days. He was absolutely filthy. So I took him home, washed his clothes.[8]

She set up house with the moody McKay at 63rd Street and 10th Avenue. Though Burke maintained the two were married, a New York marriage

ILLUSTRATION 3.3. Lois Mailou Jones, *Les Fétiches*, 1938. Courtesy of Smithsonian American Art Museum. Museum purchase made possible by Mrs. Norvin H. Green, Dr. R. Harlan, and Francis Musgrave.

license has yet to materialize. Even Trescott notes, "Though she recalls the smallest detail of what she was wearing or who was at what party, Burke doesn't remember the dates she and McKay were married or divorced."[9] Bohemian though she may have been in the artistic sense, Burke was clearly attuned to issues of propriety in an era where living together unmarried was not yet fashionable.

The Burke-McKay "marriage" was difficult. Selma's desire to become a sculptor did not wane. She pursued coursework in sculpture at Columbia University in 1936–1937 as well as worked with Augusta Savage's Works Progress Administration–assisted Harlem Community Art Center (HCAC) as a teacher of sculpture. The WPA was a massive public works initiative that assisted unemployed workers during the Great Depression; it was part of President Franklin Delano Roosevelt's New Deal. Many artists of all stripes found themselves in the category of unemployed and unemployable. Art had become a luxury not a necessity even for those with discretionary income. Savage, a sculptor who had spent two years abroad and was in 1934 the first African American inductee to the National Association of Women Painters and Sculptors, established the Harlem Community Art Center as a way to develop artists in the black community despite precarious economic times. She employed Gwendolyn Bennett and Selma Burke with the assistance of the WPA to teach HCAC workshops.

With the support of a Julius Rosenwald fellowship and a Hans Böhler Award for study in France and Austria, Selma eventually left New York and McKay behind to pursue art in Paris and Vienna in 1938 and 1939. In Paris, Burke sought out the neoclassical sculptor Aristide Maillol, who had moved his apartment and studio to Marly-le-Roi, a suburb outside of Paris. Maillol had started out a painter and admirer of Paul Gauguin. He moved to tapestries before finally picking up sculpture, as his eyesight became greatly impaired by the tediousness required in the making of tapestry. Trained at the École des Beaux-Arts, by the time Selma arrived in Paris, Maillol's work focused on large-scale classical female nudes cast in bronze.[10]

The mood in Paris in the late-1930s was glum. Never having fully recovered from World War I, the global economic insecurity all at once engulfed France. Other European economies imploded and old antagonisms were revived, as Hitler was on the move annexing countries to Germany's east and encroaching on borderlands to its west. American millionaires who had long enjoyed Paris at the expense of a deflated franc found their fortunes reversed. The exodus from the City of Light was as quick as it was considerable in number. The Ritz was no longer the roost of Cole Porter or Ernest Hemingway, and Le Dôme Café was no longer chock-a-block with American tourists and expatriates, advised, as they had been, to come home.

ILLUSTRATION 3.4. Selma Burke fellowship application photograph, ca. 1936–1937. Courtesy of Julius Rosenwald Archives, Fisk University.

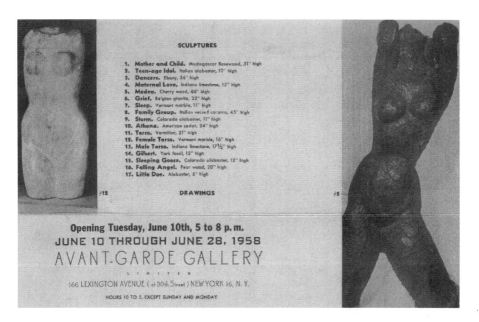

SCULPTURES

1. **Mother and Child.** Madagascar Rosewood, 31" high
2. **Teen-age Idol.** Italian alabaster, 13" high
3. **Dancers.** Ebony, 36" high
4. **Maternal Love.** Indiana limestone, 15" high
5. **Medea.** Cherry wood, 60" high
6. **Grief.** Belgian granite, 32" high
7. **Sleep.** Vermont marble, 11" high
8. **Family Group.** Italian veined cararra, 45" high
9. **Storm.** Colorado alabaster, 11" high
10. **Athena.** American cedar, 24" high
11. **Torso.** Vermilion, 21" high
12. **Female Torso.** Vermont marble, 16" high
13. **Male Torso.** Indiana limestone, 17½" high
14. **Gilbert.** York fossil, 12" high
15. **Sleeping Goose.** Colorado alabaster, 12" high
16. **Falling Angel.** Pear wood, 20" high
17. **Little Doe.** Alabaster, 6" high

DRAWINGS

Opening Tuesday, June 10th, 5 to 8 p.m.
JUNE 10 THROUGH JUNE 28, 1958
AVANT-GARDE GALLERY
L I M I T E D
166 LEXINGTON AVENUE (at 30th Street) NEW YORK 16, N. Y.
HOURS 10 TO 5, EXCEPT SUNDAY AND MONDAY

ILLUSTRATION 3.5. Selma Burke Avant-Garde Gallery Brochure, Courtesy of Yale Collection of American Literature, Beinecke Rare Book and Manuscript Library, Yale University.

Not one to follow the crowd, Bricktop remained. She struggled to open Chez Bricktop during the season, but by 1937, she flitted from club to club in cities throughout Europe and London "to keep looking for a way to pay [her] rent and buy some food."[11] A 1934 headline in the *Chicago Defender* announced her dire straits: "'Bricktop,' Café Owner, Is Broke." Bricktop in her own optimistic and flip way tells her hometown newspaper, "As long as I wear a dress, my chances are as good as any."[12] Artists, though, were accustomed to creating in even the most impoverished of circumstances since few had their gifts recompensed during their lifetimes. While the ranks of black women artists in Paris continued to thin to threads, the draw of Paris as an artist's haven persisted.

Those black women artists who landed at the ports of Le Havre or Cherbourg throughout the crazy years of the 1920s and the twilight years of the 1930s, bound for Paris via a nearly four-hour train ride, in many ways, resembled the community of artists Vincent Van Gogh sought to forge in the late nineteenth century—except they were "Women of the Petit Boulevard." These women arrived with a boundless energy and desire to create and transform the art world abroad and at home. Paris was a place of new possibilities that allowed artistic exploration, a blending of the Old World (Africa and Europe) with New World imperatives. Their art could be moored to the tenets of racial propaganda, or unmoored such that a flea market or a Romanesque profile begged for the painter's brush and the sculptor's chisel. Paris appeared full of options and choices. Only financial resources limited freedom. That was different. And the city allowed them and their art to be different as well.

VAN GOGH'S "PAINTERS OF THE PETIT BOULEVARD" AND WOMEN OF THE PETIT BOULEVARD

In 1886, Vincent Van Gogh arrived in Paris. And as with those African American women artists, the fate of place was remarkable. In Paris's Montmartre district, the site of Bricktop's triumphant rise, Van Gogh was transformed artistically from a painter who used a dark somber palette to one whose use of complementary colors and broad brushstrokes became the hallmarks of his best works. As opposed to the more established and appreciated artists of the day—Monet, Degas, and Pissarro—Van Gogh imagined that he, Paul Gauguin, Paul Signac, Emile Bernard, and Toulouse-Lautrec, among others, whose artistic approaches were vastly different, "stood on the threshold of a new art. They were the "'horses pulling the carriage'—in other words, the pioneers of the art of the future."[13] Their works were not accepted as yet on the more established grand boulevards of Paris or in the chic galleries throughout Paris. Marginalized figures on the art scene, they worked along in Paris's narrow streets in small studios, exhibited in cafés and entered salons, hoping to bend the arc of art history in their favor. Such was the path that African American women artists also traveled in the first four decades of the twentieth century. Success in Paris could provide needed accolades and awards at home.

Paris's longest-term artist-in-residence was sculptor Nancy Elizabeth Prophet. She arrived in August 1922 on the SS *La France*. The diary she kept during her twelve years abroad reveals a woman who was easily enervated, secretive, reclusive, and ambitious. Born in Rhode Island in March 1890 as Nancy Elizabeth Proffitt, she appears to have immediately started down a path of reinvention upon her arrival in Paris with the name change to Prophet. The reinvention also included putting an ocean between her and a worrisome husband, Francis Ford; she would later beckon him to come to Paris "out of pure weakness. [T]his was a very stupid mistake on my part, he being a good man but completely helpless, without ambition, without hope, character, personality and of a fearful nature."[14]

ILLUSTRATION 3.6. Nancy Elizabeth Prophet on a boat to Paris, 1922. Courtesy of Nancy Elizabeth Prophet Collection, James P. Adams Library, Rhode Island College.

Ford attended Brown University in 1906 and 1907. His class photo
and biography in *Liber Brunensis* mentions his affinity for the institution of
marriage:

> Ford, born in 1881, prepared for college at the Hope Street High
> School and entered Brown with the class of 1906. He was, how-
> ever, quick to see the error of his ways and later allied himself
> with '07. The greater part of his time here has been spent with
> the Mathematics Department, but he has come to know the
> entire faculty pretty thoroughly. . . . He also confesses to having
> a firm belief in matrimony, for says he, "I've been married, and
> know all about it."[15]

Nine years separated Prophet and Ford. They married in January 1915, a
first marriage for Prophet, the second for Ford, since the marriage mentioned in Brown's yearbook is in the past tense. Prophet was twenty-four;
Ford was thirty-three. Prophet graduated from the Rhode Island School of
Design in 1918; Ford never took the degree at Brown University. By April
1929, Prophet raises enough funds to send "the man I married" back to
America.[16] Free of her husband, Prophet could pursue her work in the way
that she loved best—in solitude and quiet. She worked prodigiously, actively
exhibiting her work in various salons, Salon d'Automne, August Salon, and
the Salon des Artistes Français.[17]

She had arrived in Paris in 1922 rather dispirited and physically run
down, "having worked so hard to earn the money to get here. What with
the worry and disgust with the kind of work I was obliged to do, being in
America. I was bitter and hurt."[18] She never totted up the menial jobs she
was obliged to take in order to support her Paris sojourn. She did however
take to her bed for two months at her studio at 36 avenue de Châtillon
in Montparnasse before eventually enrolling at the École des Beaux-Arts
in Saint-Germain.

There she studied with the sculptor Victor Joseph Jean Ambroise Segoffin. Born in Toulouse, Segoffin was also educated at the École des Beaux-
Arts. He was an admirer of Auguste Rodin, who oddly had been denied
entrance to the *grand école* in sculpture. In 1920, Segoffin was appointed
head of the women's sculpture atelier at the École. Prophet studied with
the master for two years until his death in 1925. Under his tutelage, she
was able to cut a "bust in wood" in 1923 that "was accepted in the Salon
d'Automne"[19] in 1924.

The titles of Prophet's works reflect the artist's temperament. Borrow-
ing from neoclassical to modern forms and themes and African American
traditions, the Paris sculptures and bas-reliefs titled *Silence, Poise, Discontent,*

ILLUSTRATION 3.7. *Prayer*, Nancy Elizabeth Prophet. Courtesy of Nancy Elizabeth Prophet Collection, John P. Adams Library, Rhode Island College.

Volonté (*Will*), which in a fit of insecurity about its quality she smashes,[20] *Peace, Youth, Violence, Bitter Laughter*, and *Poverty*, or *Prayer* represent studies in character and states of mind—the full range of emotions and worries that Prophet gives voice to in her diary.

For Prophet, silence and solitude are "beautiful," her dire poverty and bouts of starvation, from which she prays for deliverance, test her resolve, her will to work, and leave her discontented, dispirited—bitter. Yet, she perseveres:

> How swiftly the happy days slip by. It's only the unhappy ones that linger. . . . Days of laughter and days of tears. . . . Days of plenty, and then days of want. Poverty, detestable poverty how you trail behind me ever screeching out your presence. . . . Going without eating is common . . . so frequent that it neither interests nor frightens me. Poverty, weary not yourself in trying to humiliate me. . . . Poverty your grace I accept your challenge.[21]

Paris was cheap. Prophet was a woman of meager means. She had chosen a costly "medium of expression," she knew, as she wrote in an eloquent letter addressed to actress Louise Brooks in June 1927, asking for understanding and patronage:

> [B]ut this thing money or the lack of it is too crushing. . . . I must continue to work. People like my things and if they like them shall I not someday be able to take care of myself? I want to, I expect that of myself, shall respect myself more when I can, but at this moment I seem not to be able to and I am sad, almost ashamed to ask. Sculpture is an expensive medium, I know, but I have not chosen my medium of expression, it has chosen me.[22]

Brook's secretary secured funding from the Student's Fund of Boston. The organization sponsored Prophet for two years at thirty dollars a month. "It stopped," Prophet lamented, "as suddenly as it began at the end of that time without warning."[23]

The miserable poverty, squalid housing, malnutrition from prolonged periods of starvation, and a hospitalization at the American Hospital in Paris where she was thought a "drug addict" given her debilitated physical condition did not dampen the artist's enthusiasm for France or lessen her determination to remain in Paris. In a letter to W. E. B. Du Bois, a lifelong advocate, ally, and mutual Francophile, Prophet writes, "Beautiful Paris! and Wonderful France! . . . It is the only well poised nation of the day. . . . It is a Nation Elite."[24]

Nor did those privations endear America, and Harlem—an epicenter of black cultural expressivity—to her. Returning to the United States twice, once in October 1929 and in May 1932 to sell her work, Prophet writes:

> Harlem, night where there is no light
> Transition
> From Paris to the sordid filth of Harlem[25]

Inspirational and dynamic to many, Harlem offers no such cultural or artistic light to slake Prophet's sensibilities. The borough had certainly fallen on hard times during the Great Depression. Paris is an aperture. Harlem is a blank darkness whose nights blanket over brightly lit stars. For Prophet, "beauty is conceived in paradise but found in the depths of hell." Paris was paradisiacal in its beauty, notwithstanding her own hellish material circumstances; it was in the "midst of burning hell," a physical state of wretched penury, that she conceived her "beauties of paradise."[26]

Harlem's association with black creativity may have also obscured its charms for Prophet. By turns, temperamental and taciturn, the African American and Narragansett Indian–descended Prophet[27] was understandably prickly about being identified exclusively as a Negro. She resisted being hemmed in by the calls from W. E. B. Du Bois and Alain Locke for Negro-themed art by "artists of the race," even as she nibbled around the edges of the energy associated with the New Negro/Black Renaissance movements while in Paris with the works *Head of a Negro*, *Head of Ebony*, and *Congolais*.[28]

In a correspondence with Du Bois where she translates a review of her work, "Elizabeth Prophet American Artist, Sculptor of Temperament," in *L'Art Contemporaine*, Prophet initially writes: "Elizabeth Prophet is a sculptor of race, one feels it in everything, in her work, in her firmness of her will, in her independence. One has called her one of the most expressive sculptors of her country, and of her time. This is easily possible." She insists, in writing Du Bois, that "race" is not "racial" but rather means "breed," "origin," "ancestry," "generation."[29] She draws, and not necessarily inaccurately in terms of French use, on its universal meaning of humanity, humankind. Yet in an effort to secure funding from the Harmon Foundation, for which she received the Exhibition Prize for Fine Arts in 1929 and the Otto H. Kahn Prize awarded by the Harmon in 1930, Prophet sent this same translation, quibbling only over the word "nerveuse" when she writes:

> I am going to ask you too to allow me to translate a word which
> the French critics always use when speaking of my things for I
> should like to send you articles from time to time. The word

(nerveuse) style which is translated, brawny, lusty, powerful. It is the word névrose which corresponds to the English nervous and there is none of this in my things. There is entirely the contrary, an absolute quiet and calm. . . . I pray you will not find me impertinent.[30]

With Du Bois, Prophet expressly desires to avoid being pinned down as a Negro artist, though it is precisely as a Negro sculptor that she is able to apply for support to the Harmon. Since she provided the French and English translation for the foundation, she is quite concerned about interpretations of her work as schizophrenic or neurotic. And given Prophet's outsized temperament, the slippage between "nerveuse" and "névrose" might have been too close to the mark.

Her racial fealty and naïveté do seem to kick in again with Du Bois with the arrival of the Colonial Exposition: "[I]n regards to the Colonial Exposition . . . it is a very wonderful thing that the French government has done. Very instructive . . . Africans with scull [sic] development that is unusual among the average European. . . . Heads of thought and reflection, types of great beauty and dignity of carriage."[31] For Prophet, Paris too was the gateway to Africa. At the Exposition the brutalities of French colonialism in Africa, documented in André Gide's *Voyage au Congo* and later in Ousmane Sembene's *Les bouts des bois de Dieu*, were replaced with Africans in sanitized pavilions in native dress working quietly and happily on some "primitive" artifacts.[32] Prophet's enthusiasm for the Colonial Exposition translated more than likely into the androgynous head in wood, *Congolais* (1931).

Recluse that she was, Prophet could also be irregularly useful to African American women newcomers when they arrived in the City of Light. Preferring to hold herself at a distance, she was still known among fellow women artists-in-residence such as Gwendolyn Bennett (1925–1926), Laura Wheeler (1924–1925), and Augusta Savage (1929–1931). It was due to Du Bois's nudging via a telegram that Prophet befriended the latter sculptor: "Augusta Savage colored woman sculptor arrives for study on LA France about September Six [sic]. Would appreciate advice and guidance."[33]

I made an application to the committee in the regular way without thinking it necessary to mention my race. . . . Democracy is a strange thing. My brother was good enough to be accepted in one of the regiments that saw service in France during the war, but it seems his sister is not good enough to be a guest of the country for which he fought.

—"Color Line Drawn by Americans,"
New York Amsterdam News, April 25, 1923

Augusta Savage offered the preceding plainly by way of a response to the firestorm that followed the rejection of her application to pursue summer study at Fontainebleau, France, by a committee comprised of seven, white, eminent American architects, painters, and sculptors. Savage was denied admissions because she was a "Negress,"[34] the headlines blared. From the *New York Times* to the *New York World* to the *Negro World*, some version of the lead, "the color line in art," ran for months.

Novelist Jessie Fauset further immortalized the woman at the center of the controversy in her novel *Plum Bun* as Miss Rachel Powell, an art student at Cooper Union of "sensitive dignity," "ambition," "chilly pride," and "remoteness," "who lent her belongings, borrowed nothing, and spoke only when she was spoken to":

> The young lady had one secret aspiration; to win or earn enough money to go to France, and then after that, she said with sudden ardor, "anything can happen." To this end she had worked, saved, scraped, gone without pleasures and clothes. "And then it gives me a chance to show America that one of us can stick; that we have some idea above the ordinary humdrum of existence." Studying at Fontainebleau would have undoubtedly changed Miss Powell's attitude toward life forever.[35]

Like Savage, Rachel Powell too is denied the prestigious Fontainebleau fellowship, for as a "young colored woman knowing conditions in America" she has no right to "thrust her company on a group of people with whom she could have nothing in common with except for art."[36]

Unlike the reserved Rachel Powell whose public humiliation was suffered with a quiet dignity and determination, Augusta Savage publicly challenged the injustice:

> I wanted to go so badly that I worked night and day and bought new clothes so that I would look all right. I was much surprised when they told me I was a little too dark. I am the only colored girl in my class at Cooper Union and the others look on me as though I were a freak. If I accomplish anything that is worthwhile they pat me on the back as though I were a little child. . . . It is difficult for us to get ahead, but I have worked hard to do it.
>
> I am going to fight for as long as I can; not for my own sake now, but for colored girls in the future. If our race quits now, Fontainebleau will probably never be open to us.[37]

Savage wanted the chance to develop herself as an artist; she knew all roads eventually led through Europe, particularly Paris, toward that end. Even Du

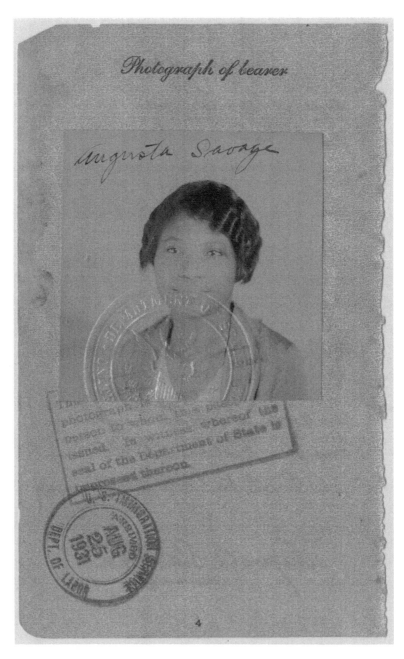

ILLUSTRATION 3.8. Augusta Savage, 1931 passport. Courtesy of Schomburg Center for Research on Black Culture, New York Public Library, Astor, Lenox, Tilden Foundations.

Bois had written her so. She had come from Florida to New York to pursue formal studies in sculpting. She finally arrived in Paris in September 1929.

∽

Augusta Christine Fells Savage was born in 1892 at Green Cove Springs, Florida, though she lists 1901 as her date of birth on her passport. As a child, she began sculpting with clay soil. By the age of twenty-three, she was a widow, had become a mother, married a second time and then divorced James Savage and moved to West Palm Beach, Florida; she had also held the first exhibit of her sculptures at the Palm Beach County Fair.[38]

When her plans to make portrait busts of wealthy African Americans in Jacksonville, Florida, did not pan out, Savage made her way to New York in 1921, where she promptly enrolled in Cooper Union for the Advancement of Science and Art. Founded by philanthropist and abolitionist Peter Cooper in 1859, the school had no color bar. Savage excelled at her studies, completing four years of coursework in three. As in Jacksonville, Savage hoped to make busts of New York's African American elite in order to support herself.[39] In 1922, she sculpted a bust of United Negro Improvement Association (UNIA) founder Marcus Garvey and began submitting poetry to the organization's journal, The Negro World.

Savage also did readings and exhibitions of her sculpture at the Harlem branch of the New York Public Library. Here she made the acquaintance of Ernestine Rose, a white librarian, who would also serve as a reference for her 1927 application to the Harmon Foundation. In the letter of reference, Rose made sure to mention the disservice the Fontainebleau committee had rendered Savage: "Miss Savage studied sculpture at Cooper Union. . . . The only alleged reason for refusing her a scholarship to study in the school of art at Fontainebleau . . . was her color."[42]

Prior to the Fontainebleau brouhaha, Savage had had a near year-long flirtation with Garvey's organization. She was a striver, adventurous, and eager for self-improvement. Her work ethic and values dovetailed with UNIA ideas about black self-improvement and independence; yet, her determination to succeed as an artist and the vertical move from Florida to New York toward accomplishing those ends had been firmly established before 1922.

With its emphasis on Negro pride, Black Nationalism, autonomy and self-rule in Africa, which eventually led to a massive mobilization of black Americans in support of a "Back to Africa" movement, the UNIA and the charismatic Garvey found themselves at odds and often pitted against the other "race leader" of the era, Crisis editor W. E. B. Du Bois and the multiracial NAACP. Both men had stepped in to fill the ostensible leadership void left by none other than the Wizard of Tuskegee, Booker T. Washington,

who had died in 1915 and had during his time on earth deeply opposed Du
Bois's more radical approaches to social equality.

Fiercely critical of one another's aspirations for the Negro race in
America and in the world, Garvey found Du Bois, "an unfortunate mulatto
who bewails every day the drop of Negro blood in his veins. . . . That is
why he likes to dance with white people and dine with them and sometimes
sleep with them,"[41] while Du Bois described Garvey in the pages of *The
Crisis* as "a little, fat black man; ugly, but with intelligent eyes and a big
head"[42] who "is, without doubt," the most dangerous enemy of the Negro
race in America and in the world. He is either a lunatic or a traitor."[43] As
an artist only in need of advocacy and patronage, Savage had no trouble
balancing Du Bois's Talented Tenth ideas of race leadership and Garvey's
self-improvement ideologies. She walked the line between these two titans
and eventually sculpted a bust of Du Bois in 1923, which was donated to
the 135th Street branch of the New York Public Library. And in 1923, she
married Garveyite Robert Poston, secretary general for the UNIA, who
would die tragically less than a year after their marriage on a return voyage
from Liberia.

Liberia held a particular storied history with respect to African American migration. As the ranks of free blacks swelled in the United States,
proposals for emigration to Africa began as early as the colonial period,
continuing on into the 1800s by abolitionists, free blacks, slaveholders, and
those who feared racial amalgamation and socializing of any kind between
the races, and others who proclaimed irremediable black inferiority. With
varying objectives and aims, from Thomas Jefferson to Martin Delany to the
American Colonization Society and Abraham Lincoln, colonizing Liberia for
African American repatriation to Africa was proposed. In 1847, Americo-
Liberians declared Liberia a sovereign nation. Robert Poston's 1923 voyage
to Liberia as part of a UNIA delegation was to continue talks with the
Liberian government about black resettlement in the country; it was part
of Garvey's broader vision—a "Back to Africa" movement.[44]

The reproachable decision by the American committee and the
groundswell of support that it had mobilized on behalf of Augusta Savage
opened the artist's social circle even wider. Like-minded artists and writers
such as rising poet and W. E. B. Du Bois's future son-in-law Countee Cullen,
Gwendolyn Bennett, Langston Hughes, Bruce Nugent, Wallace Thurman,
Zora Neal Hurston, Jessie Fauset, and Laura Wheeler befriended her. And
as he had for Nancy Prophet, Du Bois tried to drum up financial support
to assist Savage with her plans to study abroad.

An opportunity to study in Rome at the Royal Academy of Fine Arts
presented itself with Du Bois's aid in the form of a patron from the Italian-
American Society, Countess Irene Di Robilant. Though Di Robilant offered

to cover tuition and expenses for materials when in Rome, Savage lacked the funds to travel and live abroad.[45] She was finally able to secure funding from the Julius Rosenwald Fund due to the tireless efforts and enthusiastic support of Eugene Kinckle Jones, executive secretary of the National Urban League, and George Robert Arthur, author of *Life on the Negro Frontier*. Arthur was charged with overseeing the "welfare" of Negroes as it related to the Rosenwald Fund's mission.[46]

In her application, Savage requested funding in the amount of $5,760 for two years with the qualifier that she "would be willing to make any sacrifice and get along with less, if necessary."[47] The fund allocated $3,600, or $1,800 per year. Additional funds were raised on her behalf by community organizations and neighbors. Over the course of the two years she spent in Europe, Arthur gave Savage advice about the importance of Negro-themed art. He proved a critical liaison for Savage to the Rosenwald Fund. Not so for Nancy Prophet, whom he curtly turned down for monies with one sentence written in January 1930: "We regret that we cannot help Miss Elizabeth Prophet in the matter of a scholarship at the present time."[48]

Sears, Roebuck and Company magnate Julius Rosenwald established the Rosenwald Fund in 1917. Being Jewish, he claimed a particular "sympathy for the victims of discrimination. Having experienced the indignity of anti-Semitism, he felt compassion for those who suffered from racism":[49]

> I am interested in the Negro people because I am also interested in the white people. Negroes are one-tenth of our population. If we promote better citizenship among the Negroes not only are they improved, but our entire citizenship is benefitted. . . . I also belong to a race that suffers and has suffered for centuries. . . . You would also probably be surprised to know that there are . . . clubs in the city of Chicago, representing what you might call the best type of citizenship . . . that would not admit a Jew.[50]

Influenced by Booker T. Washington's autobiography, *Up from Slavery*, Rosenwald's philosophy on charitable giving lined up with the self-help philosophies espoused by Washington. So much so that Julius Rosenwald lent his financial support to Washington's educational causes for the Negro. With funding in place, Savage selected Paris as her European base. In the run-up to her departure for Paris, Savage remarked on her resolve in the face of obstacles: "I guess I was just a little pigheaded and did not want to consider myself licked."[51] In Paris, she would find a ready-made community of African Americans.

Du Bois provided Savage a series of contacts and letters of introduction:

> Mrs. Prophet is your best bet. She can give you a great deal of favorable information and guidance, but has the artistic temperament and she is planning to leave Paris for America soon. Write her just as soon as you arrive. Do not call without an appointment. She usually gets so absorbed in her work that she won't open her door to any visitor. Yolande is sure that Countee will meet you. In case there is any hitch, I would advise your going to the Hotel Trianon, 22 Avenue de Maine. You can communicate with Countee there. I am enclosing a letter of introduction to Mr. Tanner.[52]

Prophet in turn, urged Du Bois, "not to expect too much of me for I myself am facing a great undertaking. I have neither friends nor money to aid me. I am very weary."[53] Unlike Savage, Prophet had arrived in Paris friendless and with less than half of what Savage had received her first year from the Rosenwald Fund. Savage followed Du Bois's counsels, though she had missed Countee:

> [A]t the station. . . . I took a taxi up to the Trianon. . . . The people remembered your family and the garçon recognized your stationary. Having lost the address of Countee, I got in touch with Mr. J. A. Rogers and he helped me to find this place, which is not so expensive as the Trianon but quite comfortable although it is; it is not suitable for a sculptor's studio, so Countee and Mrs. Prophet are on the lookout for a real studio for me.[54]

With the help of Joel Augustus Rogers, Savage settled in briefly at 50 rue des Écoles, a few steps from the University of Paris, Sorbonne, in the Latin Quarter. Rogers, an émigré from Jamaica to the United States' metropolises of New York and Chicago, was a self-trained journalist and author. He wrote for numerous newspapers and journals, such as the *Pittsburgh Courier*, *The Crisis*, *Opportunity*, and the *New York Amsterdam News*. He frequently acted as a correspondent in Paris, writing articles and letters on the comings and goings of American Negroes in Europe.

Savage had contacted Prophet, who had initially rebuffed the overture, only to assist her in finding a suitable place to live at 3 Impasse de l'Astrolabe. Two years older than Savage, Prophet found the younger woman "very sweet,"[55] while Savage informed Du Bois that they became "quite good friends."[56] Savage later assumed a studio at 36 avenue de Châtillon, the first studio Prophet occupied in Paris when she arrived in 1922.

Savage found a "wonderful master"[57] in Félix Benneteau-Desgrois, who allowed her to work in his studio at 5 rue de Bagneux, a street which ran between rue Cherche Midi and ended at rue Vaugirard in the sixth arrondissement. Benneteau-Desgrois, a native Parisian born in the twentieth arrondissement, had been a professor of sculpture at the Académie de la Grande Chaumière. He found Savage conscientious and artistically "very gifted."[58] They worked together until the spring 1930 when Savage decided to begin "working in a style quite different."

Encouraged by George Arthur's "words of brotherly advice"[59] to "continue to work primarily with negro models . . . to develop something original, born out of a deep spirituality which you, as a Negro woman, must feel in depicting modern Negro subjects,"[60] she tries her hand at "develop[ing] an original technique," which she explains is "African in feeling but quite modern in design; but whatever else might be said it *is* [Savage's emphasis] original."

In Paris, Savage experimented with modern subjects and themes while drawing inspiration from ancient myths and legends. Her *Divinité nègre*, completed around 1930,[61] represents a modern design imbued at once with an African feel and a spirituality drawn from the femininity that Arthur supposed Savage to feel as a "Negro woman" artist when composing her works.

The *Divinité nègre*, a small figurine, featured a deity with four heads, four raised arms lifting a globe, and whose four crossed legs on the pedestal form a star. The four-sided figure is seated with her legs crossed, similar to the Hindu goddess Lakshmi, goddess of wealth and good fortune, and wife of Vishnu. Lakshmi is often represented with four arms and seated on a lotus flower. The opera *Lakmé*, whose titular character's name is derived from Lakshmi, starred the coloratura soprano Lillian "Madame Evanti" Evans-Tibbs in 1925 in Nice. The opera was a perennial favorite in Paris where Madame Evanti reprised the role in 1927. The opera reached its thousandth performance in early May 1931.[62] Evans-Tibbs, Fauset, and Wheeler toured Paris together and well before Savage's arrival in 1929. Savage nonetheless interacted with the three women in New York prior to her departure for Paris at the 135th Street Library in Harlem and socially. Just as the Harlem circle would have known of her as a result of the Fontainebleau controversy, she certainly would have known about Evans-Tibbs turn as Lakmé. Whatever Savage's inspirations—the first African American woman to perform as a Hindu deity in a French opera, the opera's enduring popularity in Paris, a flirtation with Eastern religion and philosophy with an African twist, or nineteenth-century French sculptor Jean-Baptiste Carpeaux's *Les Quatre Parties du monde soutenant la sphére céleste* (The Four Parts of the World Supporting the Celestial Sphere) with its four women, one of whom is African with a broken chain at her foot, representing the four parts of the world in the Luxembourg Gardens Fountain—less than a mile down Rue Vaugirard from her apartment at 3 Impasse de l'Astrolabe, Savage's *Negro Deity* was very different from anything she had composed to date.

While Benneteau-Desgrois had suggested in his progress report of November 1, 1929, that she would be accepted in the May 1930 Salon des Artistes Français, Savage was instead accepted in the 1930 Salon d'Automne[63] and at the 1931 Société des Artistes Français and the Salon du Printemps at the Grand Palais.[64] In reporting her progress to her funders, Savage enclosed "a clipping of an article which appeared in the leading negro [sic] paper a few weeks ago."[65] The journalist who wrote the article was the Martinican Paulette Nardal; the newspaper was *La Dépêche africaine*.

"A Black Woman Sculptor" ("Une femme sculpteur noire") appeared in the August–September 1930 issue of the newspaper. *La Dépêche africaine*, the journalistic arm of the Comité de defense des interest de la race noire (CDIRN), was published in Paris in 1928. Its editor was Maurice Satineau, originally from the island of Guadeloupe in the French West Indies. The journal's board was multiracial and its ideological leanings appealed to those who trumpeted the "good" in the colonial mission in Africa and hence assimilation to French ideals even as the various articles published therein suggested reforms to perfect the colonial enterprise. Finally, the journal argued for diasporic connections between "Negroes of Africa, Madagascar, the Antilles, and America."

Just how Savage, despite the march of myriad black women artists across the pond to Paris, ended up featured in its pages owes as much to timing—*La Dépêche africaine*'s date of publication—as it does to the author René Maran. Maran was involved in a series of multiracial organizations with interests in colonial reform and black social conditions. He cofounded the newspaper *Les Continents*, hosted a salon where visitors to the city of Paris—like Fauset, Savage, Bennett, and others—commingled with French Antilleans, Africans, and white French and American members of the literati, glitterati, artistic community, and intelligentsia. Nardal made Savage's acquaintance at the salon of René Maran. The other tenuous connection between Nardal and Augusta Savage was Marcus Garvey. Agents for the government maintained that *La Dépêche africaine* received funding from Garvey's organization.[66] And it was because of its varying criticisms of the French colonial project and shades of Garveyism in its articles and editorials that the journal came under the scrutiny of the French police in November, mere months after its February 1928 debut.

The political intrigue surrounding *La Dépêche africaine* aside, Paulette Nardal's article begins, "Among our artists of color, we have heretofore musicians, dancers, singers, painters (for the most part Americans). Do our compatriots realize that for a year now Miss Augusta Savage, the first black woman sculptor, has been residing in Paris?"[67] Of course, Nancy Prophet had been in the city for eight years. Savage obviously did not choose to correct Nardal. And given Prophet's reclusive nature and prickly temperament, she might not have cut so easy-going a figure as Savage, "a thin young woman with an extraordinarily soft voice and of a simplicity that is immediately pleasant."[68] Nardal's admiration bubbles on the page, as she says Savage embodies, "in the full sense of the word, a 'self-made woman.' "[69] She goes on to recount Savage's rise from Florida, from the sordid tale of American racism and Fontainebleau to her arrival in Paris on a fellowship. Nardal notes that Savage has executed a number of busts and heads using white models, but that she was stunned to hear that "black models refused to pose for her. Could it be the effect of a prejudice even more absurd among the blacks than whites?"[70] Could it have been just as easily the barrier of language? Or that Savage was also a woman artist? Savage was nonetheless able to overcome this obstacle, as she created a series of works that featured black models, *Tête de jeune fille*, *The Amazon*, *The Call*, which George Arthur found intriguing, and the androgynous *Martiniquaise* [*Martinican woman*] or *Head of Boy*. While finding Savage's *Green Apples* (1928) sculpture in bronze amusing, Nardal concludes by paying particular tribute to Savage's *Divinité nègre*[71] and the Amazon series. These works she believes represent Savage's obsession with history and an originality premised on racial and feminine sensibilities.

As Savage's time in Paris wound down, she desperately sought more funds to stay on. She had, as she explained in a May 1931 letter to Edwin Embree, president of the Rosenwald Fund,

> [P]lanned to govern myself accordingly, but after my success at the Salon d'Automne last year, I was advised to try for the Salon Printemps this year which I did. I am enclosing the receipts for two pieces which were accepted and are now on exhibition at the Grand Palais. . . .
>
> Now the matter is this. I cannot have my work back until the fifteenth of July and as I spent all of my money to have my entries cast in bronze—one has a better chance if the work is in bronze or marble—I have no funds left with which to finish my other work or to pack and ship my finished work to America. Would it be an imposition on my part if I asked for an extension of my fellowship until September? Perhaps you will think that I acted unwisely, but I assure you that the chance of having work accepted by the Salon is more than an artist can resist.[72]

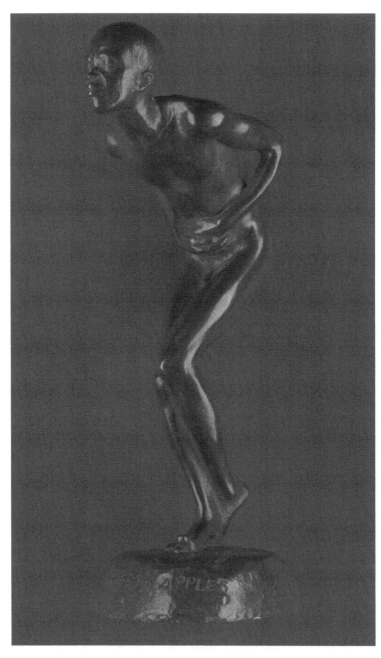

ILLUSTRATION 3.9. *Green Apples*, Augusta Savage, 1928. Courtesy of Yale Collection of American Literature, Beinecke Rare Book and Manuscript Library, Yale University.

Embree relented. George Arthur provided Savage with an additional $750 to carry her through the summer. Insulated from the deprivation and poverty experienced by Prophet in Paris thanks largely to community efforts, the Rosenwald Fund, and the Carnegie Corporation, Savage had the freedom to mine her art. Sculpting; experimenting with different techniques, styles, and models; visiting museums, galleries, and exhibitions throughout Europe became a full-time preoccupation instead of spare time activities.

She disembarked in New York on August 25, 1931, on the *Ile de France* with hopes of returning to Paris the following spring.[73] She found in Paris that "[o]f course, the French hate the American whites, but there is little evidence that this hostility extends to the Negro."[74] In a follow-up report about the benefits she received from the fellowship and her study in Europe, Savage wrote:

> One of the greatest benefits I received from studying in Europe . . . was the first-hand encounter with the sources of art (The opportunity to visit the galleries where world famous works of art are on view). Another benefit . . . was the opportunity to study wood-carving and sculpture in the free manner in which it is taught in European schools as contrasted to the more formal, conventional type of training I had rec'd [*sic*] in America.[75]

In a testament to her newfound freedom in a place where the American Negro is spared the hostility of racial animus, Savage cast a small-scale female figure in bronze called *La Citadelle—Freedom*. With her arm extended upward and one foot on tiptoe, the woman appears to beckon the viewer. She is the citadel, the refuge, freedom. Paris.

FOUR

BLACK PARIS

Cultural Politics and Prose

By the time Eslanda "Essie" Goode Robeson embarked on a series of interviews that would appear in the literary magazine *Challenge*, the revolving
door to Paris for African American women had been open seventeen years.
She had already walked through that door in 1925, seven years before she
conducted the interviews and eleven years before they were published.

Born Eslanda Cardozo Goode in 1896 in Washington, DC, she grew
up between New York and Chicago, eventually attending the University of
Illinois, Urbana-Champaign and Columbia University. Wired it seemed for
the sciences, she worked in histology at New York's Presbyterian Hospital
with an eye toward medicine. By 1921, she had married a charming, ath-
letic, and accomplished student attending Columbia University Law School,
Paul Robeson.[1]

Living in New York as the Harlem Renaissance flourished proved an
exciting time in the young Robesons' marriage. As Paul Robeson's acting
career began its lift off under Essie's skillful eye as manager of both his personal and professional life, the couple had a calendar chock full of parties
and dinners with Manhattan and Harlem elites. They met Jessie Fauset,
James Weldon Johnson, Roland Hayes, and patron and confidant to many of
the era's leading black writers and artists Carl Van Vechten.[2] By 1924, Paul
Robeson's talents and Essie's smarts eventually took the couple beyond New
York. During the mid-1920s and early 1930s, the Robesons resided mostly
between the United States and the United Kingdom.

With long stays in London, Eslanda Robeson began to pursue studies in
psychology, archaeology, and anthropology at the University College at London,[3] as her interests in Africa began to grow. She consulted with the only

ILLUSTRATION 4.1. Eslanda Goode Robeson, undated. Courtesy of Yale Collection of American Literature, Beinecke Rare Book and Manuscript Library, Yale University.

other black woman anthropologist among her Harlem associates, Zora Neale Hurston, about her studies and possible classes with the renowned anthropologist at the London School of Economics, Bronislaw Kasper Malinowski. Hurston responded with support and enthusiasm: "What you tell me about your studies is thrilling. . . . You are realizing everyday how silly our 'leaders' sound—talknig [sic] what they dont [sic] know."[4] After a series of failed attempts at publishing plays and novels, Essie put her ethnographic training to good use by documenting the presence of the African diaspora in Paris in a two-part series that appeared in the pages of *Challenge* in 1936.

    Challenge was founded in 1934. Its editor was the energetic Dorothy West. A New England native from Boston, Massachusetts, West had moved to Harlem in 1926. Here, she met and collaborated with various notable writers, artists, and activists associated with the New Negro movement. She participated in writing contests sponsored by *The Crisis* and *Opportunity* magazines. Her short story "The Typewriter" had tied for second place with a submission by Zora Neale Hurston at *Opportunity*'s Second Annual Literary Awards dinner.[5] West also served on the editorial board of the short-lived *Harlem: A Forum*, a Wallace Thurman–founded literary magazine. Thurman, of *The Blacker the Berry* notoriety, was brilliant but mercurial; he was also the creative force behind the one-issue magazine *Fire!!*. *Fire!!*'s abbreviated run was laid at Thurman's doorstep. He was accused of fiscal mismanagement and all-around irresponsibility. The prospect of another Thurman-led literary endeavor left many of Gotham's black residents lukewarm.

    In private correspondences, Dorothy Peterson, a financial contributor to *Fire!!*, expressed her uncertainty:

> A new magazine of Negro descent is about to be launched on its uncertain career and i[t] is to be hoped that it will have a longer life than "Fire" even tho [sic] the editor is the same. The new magazine is to be called *Harlem: a Forum*, and on the editorial board are Wallace Thurman, Richard Bruce, Aaron Douglass, Dorothy West and Scholley Alexander. My connection with it is very strange. Both Bruce and Scholley came down to talk to me about it without mentioning Wallace's name and it was agreed that I was to do a theatrical page for them every month. Then the idea that Scholley was the editor and they were looking for a business manager. Suddenly I received a letter from Thurman telling me how glad he was to be to have my cooperation etc, etc and on the letterhead his name as editor. So you see they are still putting things over on your poor friend.[6]

Peterson's apprehension sums up the general sentiment about *Harlem* with Thurman at the editorial helm. She had pursued Thurman and his collective for a return of her funds to no avail and was hence dismayed to discover that this new journal, for which she was asked to contribute labor rather than monies, was another Thurman vehicle. Within short order, *Harlem* collapsed from a lack of enthusiasm and funds.[7] Upon her return from the Soviet Union, Dorothy West filled the journalistic void left by *Harlem* with *Challenge*.

The road to Essie Robeson's contributions in *Challenge* began with her introduction to Paris in August 1925, while still residing in London. This five-day trip was, more importantly, without her husband. She ventured to the city via a boat to Dieppe, France, and then a train ride into Paris with longtime friend Bert McGhee. In those five days, the women did their version of tourist Paris, "[I]n short all that young Americans do here when they go to Paris: We have been to the theater every night . . . seen the Folies Bergeres [sic] . . . went to Casino de Paris & found the show terrible. . . . Visited the Louvre, gardens and up and down the Seine in a boat, taxied all over Paris and rode in a fiacre."[8] At 90 cents a night, she thought the Hotel Royale was "very lovely—big room, bed, hot running water and cold in lovely basin in room" with French windows that "open unto balconies which are directly above rue de Rennes."[9] In short order, Essie visited with "Gwenny [sic] Bennett," took in an "only fair" show at the Moulin Rouge,[10] switched hotels, and purchased a paperback copy of James Joyce's *Ulysses* in English at the rue de la Paix for Paul. For the last two days of her stay in Paris, she moved to Hotel Minerva. It was only upon her return to London that she discovered that the Hotel Royale, at bustling 159 rue de Rennes in the heart of Montparnasse, was "a whorehouse."[11] Perhaps the rock-bottom cost, which Essie noted with an exclamation point in her diary, demanded more scrutiny.

After the hectic and disappointing five-week run of *The Emperor Jones*, and two weeks of nonstop socializing in London, both Robesons arrived in Paris in November 1925 on their way south for a respite.[12] With young poet Gwennie Bennett in tow, they did a round of teas and visits with members of the venerable "lost generation," from Gertrude Stein to Sylvia Beach to Hemingway.

They also managed to take in two performances of the Josephine Baker–led *La Revue nègre*, which Essie found just "rotten."[13] Finding Baker's showmanship initially amazing, then monotonous and crass, and her voice a mere screech above the orchestra, Essie also did not spare Baker's costar, Maud de Forrest, in her colorful *entre nous*—between us—review of *La Revue* to Carl Van Vechten. She remarked that the "de Forrest girl hasn't even a note in her voice."[14] Parisians, on the other hand, were "mad about it."[15] Enamored with the wild stylings of the Charleston, the jazzy theatrics of the production, and Baker's brown, semi-nude body, Robeson was clearly attuned to the negrophilia sweeping through Paris when she wrote: "[T]hey sit breathless to watch it all. They seem to adore the music and the color and the crudity of it all."[16] *La Revue nègre* launched Baker's long career in France.

Paris was still in the throes of the irreverent *années folles* in 1925, and the Negro was very much in vogue. Black Americans continued to arrive in the city that seemed to smile on them. News of Baker's rousing success, Bricktop's steady climb in Montmartre, and descriptions of Paris as an artist and writer's haven beckoned the adventurous. With the French franc at record lows to the dollar, the cost of the transatlantic ticket was less than $100.

While Paris on this second visit proved exhilarating, the Robesons turned south to Villefranche-sur-Mer, a port town on the French Riviera, for six weeks. They again briefly stopped over in Paris on the return trip to London.[17] With jaunts to Paris over the next few years, Eslanda Robeson returned for a longer stay by herself in June 1932—and for less auspicious reasons.

The Robesons' marriage had over the years proved inconvenient with regards to monogamy. Indeed, Essie seems to have negotiated with herself over her husband's numerous dalliances; hurt though she may have been, as long as these affairs were not flagrantly disrespectful, public, and seemed to pose no threat to the marital union, the household hummed along nicely. Moreover, Essie appears to have engaged in an affair or two when it became clear that Paul had abandoned the marital bed and had no intentions of returning to it exclusively.[18] The biggest threat to the bargain though came with Paul's torrid affair with Yolande Jackson, an aspiring British dilettante *cum* actress from a family of some means. He asked Eslanda for a divorce. Paul had in fact directed Essie to secure evidence of his infidelity from the reluctant proprietor of the Hotel Lancaster in Paris in late April–early May 1932 in order to expedite divorce proceedings.

With what seemed to be the imminent demise of her marriage, Essie busied herself with writing. The material for *Challenge* was gathered during the June 1932 trip to Paris. She arrived in Paris on the third of June. She was promptly welcomed at the station by her old acquaintance Kojo Tovalou Houénou (sometimes spelled Touvalou; he would also occasionally drop Houénou),[19] the African intellectual, activist, situational Marcus Garvey acolyte, and self-styled prince from the former French Dahomey (Republic of Benin).[20] Houénou was ubiquitous in political, intellectual, and good-times circles in Paris and New York. Essie had initially exchanged niceties with him at a party hosted by author and NAACP national secretary Walter White in New York.

Paris was full to the brim with posers and imposters from far-off lands claiming royal lineage. Josephine Baker's "no-account" Count Guiseppe

"Pepito" Abatino was, for members of Paris's black colony, the shiniest exam-ple. Whatever Houénou's royal bona fides, he represented, in the French parlance of the time, an *évolué*, an African assimilated to French values and education. Houénou was born Marc Tovalou Quénum in Porto-Novo. He arrived in France in 1900 with his father, Joseph Tovalou Quénum, a well-established African businessman with an impregnable allegiance and affinity for metropolitan France and all things French. He left Marc in France to pursue studies in Bordeaux. Houénou served in the Great War and was eventually granted French citizenship, a rarity for colonized Africans.[21]

Houénou was thus strategic in deploying his Garveyite leanings. He was *French French* understandably when the colonial authorities leaned on him and his various affiliates and affiliations, among them, the newspaper *Les Continents* that he had cofounded with René Maran. Hence, when he delivered an address to Garveyites in New York in 1924 that was published in *Les Continents* as "Paris coeur de la race noire" ("Paris, heart of the black race"), he struck a tone more like the vintage Du Bois of the 1919 Pan-African Congress on the question of French racial tolerance when he stated: "France is the only country that does not have race prejudice, but struggles for its disappearance."[22] Yet, he covertly continued to nurture a relation-ship—financially, politically, and ideologically—with Garvey's United Negro Improvement Association (UNIA). Houénou's flirtations with Garveyism rested on the demand for self rule in Africa rather than a wholesale pan-Black sensibility.

Polished and well connected, the French African and René Maran were instrumental in introducing Essie to members of the larger African diasporic community, whom she briefly profiles in the first of the two-part series in *Challenge*. Her growing interest in Africa manifested itself most plainly in this series, as Houénou, his family history, and an abbreviated history of the various kingdoms in Dahomey, were the foci of the January 1936 article, "Black Paris." The Kingdom of Porto-Novo, where Houénou was born, had been a slave-trading port established by the Portuguese. In the scramble for Africa, and the more specific rivalry with the British for colonial domination along the continent's Atlantic coast, the French justi-fied their incursions into Africa as a "civilizing mission." Porto-Novo became part of French Dahomey in 1883.

While W. E. B. Du Bois initially published "The American Negro in Paris" in the *American Monthly Review of Reviews* in 1900, gave the speech "Negro at Paris," and penned both "Vive la France" in 1919 and an opinion piece titled "Black France"[23] in the pages of *The Crisis*, Eslanda Robeson appears to have been the first to put a name to the phenomenon that was happening on the ground in the City of Light among the African diaspora with the term "Black Paris." Her two-part series captured the transnational, multilingual, and creative cosmopolitan ethos of the African diaspora in Paris.

Essie begins "Black Paris," part 1, by tapping into the reader's imagination of what Paris in June looks, tastes, and feels like: "Paris in June. What a glamourous [sic] vision those three words conjure up in the minds of those who have been, and those who have longed to go to Paris."[24] She continues with a vivid description of the cityscape and its abundant offerings: "Sacre coeur in the sunlight, in the moonlight. Notre Dame. Bookstalls on the banks of the Seine. . . . Marvellous [sic] food. Luxurious expensive fashionable hotels; tiny little inexpensive hotels tucked away in convenient corners. Restaurants and cafes to fit every purse."[25] Paris offers a bounty that would both soothe and revitalize the most troubled of minds. Essie, though, arrives at the crucial question that informs the quasi-historical and ethnographic essay: "In such a setting, who would think of Negroes? Not even Negroes themselves. And yet Negroes form a definite part of Parisian life, and play an important role in the political, educational, intellectual, literary and theatrical life of Paris, in the ordinary every-day life, and in the night life."[26] She then rolls out the varied cast of Negro characters with a part to play in the rhythms of Parisian life, from the Afro-Algerian dancer-actor Benglia to René Maran to Gratien Candace and Paulette Nardal, who had not only written short stories and profile pieces for the pan-Black newspaper La Dépêche africaine in the 1920s on black women artists in Paris such as Augusta Savage and singers such as Roland Hayes, she also wrote an essay in the one-issue journal L'Etudiant noir (The Black Student), where Aimé Césaire and Léopold Senghor of the incipient Negritude movement published their first essays on questions of race and identity.

Paulette Nardal was the focus of "Black Paris," part 2, which was published in the June 1936 issue of Challenge. Born October 12, 1896, in François, Martinique, Nardal was educated at the Colonial College for Girls in Martinique. Studying English in the British West Indies, she arrived in Paris to continue her studies at the Sorbonne. Fluent in English, she assiduously studied the trends in African American literature and wrote her thesis on Harriet Beecher Stowe's Uncle Tom's Cabin. She and her sisters, Jeanne, or Jane as she preferred to be called, born in 1902 in Lamentin, Martinique, and Andrée, established a salon at the apartment they shared in the Paris suburb of Clamart. The Nardal sisters; novelist Louis Jean Finot; Dr. Léo Sajous, a Haitian scholar who had originally proposed the idea for a bilingual journal; and Clara W. Shepard, an African American educator who wrote for, coedited, and translated the bilingual journal, launched the monthly La Revue du monde noir/The Review of the Black World in October 1931.[27]

Essie Robeson met Paulette Nardal and Clara Shepard by happenstance. Set to interview René Maran, whom she found "shy, scholarly, and

charming, frank, honest, sincere, idealistic, all for the race," she was introduced to the "handsome, queenly"[28] Martinican and her American counterpart at his apartment. Essie made a later appointment to interview both
women at Nardal's residence in Clamart. She met up with Shepard and
together they took the Paris-Montparnasse line to reach the suburb. At
nearly six miles southwest of the center of Paris and with cheaper rents,
Clamart in 1932 was a sleepy commune bisected by a forest and famous for
its peas. In *bas Clamart*, near the historical center where Nardal lived, Essie
was given back issues of *The Review* and also subscribed. When Robeson
interviewed Nardal in June 1932, *The Review* had published its last issue
in April 1932; the French Colonial Ministry withdrew financial support
because the venture was deemed more political than cultural.[29] It may be
that Nardal and Shepard believed they could somehow revive the journal
with other funding. Given the flatlined state of both the French and American economies, the goal was more wishful thinking than reality.

Clara W. Shepard, the only African American on the journal's founding board, left a not negligible imprint on the landscape of Black Internationalism and letters. Originally from Philadelphia, Shepard was in Paris to
study French second-language acquisition. She had taught French at Tuskegee Normal and Industrial Institute in the 1920s. In the journal's second
issue, Shepard fetes the legendary Booker T. Washington and the fiftieth year
anniversary of the educational institution he founded in 1881, writing for
her bilingual audience a brief history of American education and the Negro:

> For fifty years Tuskegee . . . has exerted a distinctive influence
> upon the educational development of the United-States [*sic*]. In
> 1881, industrial education was unheard of in the United-States;
> to-day [*sic*] Booker T. Washington's precept has so revolutionized
> educational principles that thousands of instructors are hasten-
> ing to prepare themselves to meet the new criterion. . . . White
> America has at least realized the futility of an Academic education
> for the masses; as a panacea for this ill, she has eagerly accepted
> industrial education. . . . Barely after the close of the Civil War, it
> was imperative that at least superficially, Negro education should
> train its youth for occupations markedly inferior to those sought
> by her Nordic contemporaries. Philanthropists who would not
> have given a penny toward the dissemination of a liberal educa-
> tion for the Negro, willingly contributed thousands toward his
> industrial education. But the founder's broader view saw in the
> closely correlated training of the mind and hand the economic
> salvation of the Negro. For him, economic security depended
> not upon a few highly cultured gentlemen, but upon the masses
> trained to satisfy their demands by force of their skilled labor.[30]

Shepard demonstrates the complexity of Washington's vision of education and his wiliness at securing white philanthropy for ends that went counter to the desire to keep the Negro tied to the land. For Washington, according to Shepard, the hand and the mind went hand-in-hand. This twinning was essential for black uplift. Interestingly, Paulette Nardal would pick up on these ideas of industrial education, which included "Home Economics," for the downtrodden masses when she returned to Martinique. She proposed such measures to her female middle-class readership as a way of dealing with the widespread poverty and illiteracy among young women and girls from Martinique's poor and working classes in the pages of the journal she founded in 1945 in Fort-de-France, La Femme dans la Cité/Woman in the City.

Shepard follows up the article with the February 1932 "Les Noirs américains et les langues étrangères," where she demonstrated in practice how Tuskegee blended industrial education with the liberal arts. She argued in historical terms that the Negro American exhibited a predisposition for foreign-language acquisition. For Shepard, black Americans' creativity and adaptability was evidence of their acquisitive nature; but more important, through studying French, the American Negro could be introduced to "French-speaking Negroes," opening up their worldview and spurring a desire to understand the "world progress of the Negro."[31] Language study for Shepard offered a window onto the African diaspora. This window in turn could allow for comparative analyses of the black condition globally and strategic alliances.

Essie "found both [women] interesting."[32] The second article in the Challenge series, though, focused exclusively on Nardal. Essie details the Martinican's family history; the color, class, and racial caste conflicts in Martinique exacerbated by French colonialism; and sex and class politics in France.[33] "Black Paris" also offers the only firsthand account of the history of the founding of La Revue du monde noir. Finding Nardal perhaps a broader canvas on which to draw a compelling story, "Black Paris," part 1, where Houénou was featured, folded other African, West Indian, and African American men and women of music, art, and belles lettres into the rich brew that collectively formed the "Black Paris" essays: Kobina Sekyi, a Cape Coast (Ghana) lawyer who worked in London but also spent time in Paris; composer and violinist Clarence Cameron White; artist Aaron Douglas; "café au lait queen of entertainers"[34] Josephine Baker, who Essie had privately "run down"[35] a mere seven years before. And Bricktop:

> There is "Bricktop," otherwise Adah Smith du Conge, light skinned red haired Negro business woman who defied cabaret tradition in MontMartre [sic], whose night club in Pigalle is the rendezvous for world celebrities, and who is favourite entertainer and instructress of royal princes and society queens in the intricate art of the Negro dance step.[36]

Incorrectly spelling Bricktop's birth name "Adah" instead of "Ada," Essie interestingly though spelled the saloonkeeper's first name in just the way Bricktop occasionally signed herself—to the chagrin of her mother. "Adah" was also the name of the character Essie played in the 1930 feature-length silent film *Borderline*.[37] Visiting the club in Montmartre on several occasions, where she had the opportunity to interview Mabel Mercer; watch U.S. Kid Thompson, the late Florence Mills's husband, dance; and take in Cole Porter's previewing of the song "Mr. and Mrs. Fitch" accompanied by Bricktop, Brick and Essie became "kindred souls"[38] in June 1932.

Bricktop was known for her generosity and discretion, and Essie Robeson was in dire need of a confidant. Given the upheaval in her personal life, the life Bricktop had created in Paris and at her estate in Bougival seemed positively idyllic to Essie. She was especially taken with Bougival's pastoral environs, the camaraderie on display at Bricktop's garden parties, and the domestic bliss exhibited by Mr. and Mrs. Ducongé:

> At Bricktop's—the house was lovely. She has the most beautiful garden, flower[s] and kitchen. The roses climbed over everything—luscious, full blown, fragrant, gorgeous peonies; other flowers in profusion, carnations, etc. Rows upon rows of lettuce, etc., apples growing as I have never seen them . . . in hedges, and Brick says the fruit is large and luscious. . . . Pears too!
>
> And Peter's (her husband) great pride—the chickens. They collect eggs every night, and the new chicks were so soft, and velvety. Brick's mother adores every foot of the place—every flower, every chicken, etc. There was a wholesome atmosphere about the place . . . they all enjoyed it so much . . . so healthy, free and open. Louis Cole—he is training to be Brick's assistant—and he has the top floor of her house. He and Peter and one or two other men discussing tennis, practicing, etc. They love it all—so open, healthy, wholesome, and splendid for them.
>
> We had a marvelous dinner—chicken, string beans, gravy, potatoes, salad, strawberry pie, and real lemonade, with ice. [. . .] After dinner, Brick I strolled down the country lanes, and talked. She told me all about herself, and I told her all about my novel "Black Progress." We are as thick as thieves. I think she really liked me, and certainly, I liked her. She is a regular fellow—clean, strong, friendly, and no nonsense.[39]

Bricktop shows Eslanda Robeson the other side of Black Paris in a hamlet twelve miles outside of the glamour, political maneuverings, and cultural undertakings of the city and the nightlights of Montmartre. This Black Paris is serene, familial, nurturing, hale and hearty.

The enthusiasm Essie conjures in the private thoughts of her diary and even in the opening pages of the first "Black Paris" article was palpable and quantifiable. Paris felt like real freedom to her, a gambol in the midst of chaos, when she recounts her visit two months later:

> I was in Paris for a month beginning the end of May. Although I have been six or seven times, this was like the first time I actually enjoyed myself there, and really liked the town. Nothing has ever been wrong with Paris, but a great deal has been wrong with me. But I'm getting myself all cleared up now, and arranging my life. Its [sic] grand fun. To be free, and young enough still to use that freedom.[40]

Continuing to come to terms with Paul's request for a divorce, Paris was a much-needed tonic for Essie. She had originally come to the city to seek out evidence that would crater her marriage along with her secret hopes and efforts to rebuild it. Paris in June became something more. Having tried her hand at novel writing and playwriting, Paris's *joie de vivre* and vibrant African diasporic community teased Essie's senses and provided her with material to launch what would become a rather prolific career in journalism.[41]

FIVE

EPILOGUE:

"HOMEWARD TUG AT A POET'S HEART"

The Return

In a lengthy letter to Harold Jackman, Gwennie Bennett wrote of her upcoming return to New York in the summer of 1926 as a "homeward tug at a poet's heart." Love was calling her homeward, but so was the desire to show what she had learned in "fairytale" Paris. Jessie Fauset had come and gone the year before. After a productive eight months abroad, a new fallout with Du Bois now forced her to contemplate a return to the teaching profession, though she believed her experiences were infinitely more suitable for something in the publishing industry among the editorial ranks. And Nella and Dorothy had arrived when France was attempting to slough off the foreboding tremors of the U.S. economic meltdown and flex its empire-building muscle by mounting the Colonial Exposition of 1931. They were gone five months later. Nella eventually headed south to join her husband at Nashville's Fisk University. That prospect was as unhappy as the charade of the marriage, while Dorothy returned to teaching and her dramaturgical aspirations with the Harlem Experimental Theatre. Aviator Bessie Coleman fell tragically to her death from a Curtiss JN-4 "Jenny" plane in Jacksonville, Florida, in April 1926, never realizing her dreams of a flight school.

The twilight years of the 1930s dimmed to complete darkness when Germany launched its September Campaign in Poland in 1939. With the French rejection of Germany's peace plan in October, war was inevitable. African Americans' prospects of earning a decent living in Paris had already begun to whither and dry up by 1935; and the feast that had been Paris was, by late 1938, the picked-over remains of an era.

Rat pâté did not appear on menus as it had previously during the Franco-Prussian war and the 1882 Paris Bourse crash, but food rationing began in earnest in 1939. The State Department had warned all U.S. citizens abroad that the party was over. It was time to come home. Most Americans promptly exited. Others scattered to various corners of the European continent. Some were stranded, unable to raise their fare for passage home.

Those artists whose time abroad was verily circumscribed by family obligations, philanthropic support, and institutional commitments had cleared out of the city well before the Fall of France in June 1940. Howard University recalled Lois Jones home to attend to her teaching duties; Augusta Savage was unable to raise the fare for a planned return to Paris. The funds and funding sources had dried up for Gwennie, Nancy, and Selma, while Laura Wheeler had become a married woman and professional artist armed with a Harmon Foundation medal and commission to paint Negro portraits that would eventually end up in the National Portrait Gallery. Her travel companion Lillian Evans-Tibbs launched a global tour of Europe and South America, retired from the national stage for twelve years in Washington, DC, to attend to her difficult marriage and raise a son, before eventually joining the National Negro Opera Company.

Most of the writers had departed while there were good times still to be had. Clara Shepard resumed teaching at Tuskegee for the fall term in 1932, shortly after the collapse of *La Revue du monde noir*. Essie Robeson returned first to London where she continued her studies in anthropology; traveled to Africa in 1936, one of the first of her three trips; and when war proved a foregone conclusion, the Robesons relocated to Harlem. Only Anita Thompson lingered. She joined the Société des Blessés Militaire and the Red Cross in Dinard, France. But by July 1940, she too arrived stateside on the *Manhattan*. Some performers though, unlike Nora Holt, who had traded Europe for a star turn at Bolito King Casper Holstein's Saratoga Club in May 1930 and became a music teacher in Los Angeles by 1937, found it harder to say goodbye.[1]

Alberta, who seemed to apply to leave the United States for Europe every six months after her return to the less hospitable America, had a contract to perform in Copenhagen in May 1940. She was duly informed by the State Department, "It is impossible to grant you a validation of your passport to enable you to travel to Europe at this time."[2] Jo Baker drove by car to her chateau in Dordogne, Les Milandes; from here and during her tours as an entertainer for the troops she assisted La Résistance française. Addie fled to London, just as the bombs began to rain down on Paris, joining Lis Welch, who had already made London her permanent home base in 1933 after a show-stopping performance in *Nymph Errant*. And Valaida Snow hightailed it out of Paris for Northern Europe, first to Holland then

Denmark. Addicted to oxycodone, which she received illegally during her two-year stay in Denmark, she continued to perform.

Detained in Copenhagen for her own protection in March 1942, Valaida had been caught with a sizable quantity of stolen silverware and crystal; and with a reputation as a drug addict, she was, according to biographer Mark Miller,

> increasingly at risk in occupied Denmark since the United States had entered the war in December 1941; her new vulnerability as enemy alien was further complicated by her race and her profession, as well as her notoriety as a drug addict and, apparently, thief—the last two of which corresponded all too well with the Nazi view of jazz, and those who would play it, as morally degenerate.[3]

She was in Danish custody for ten weeks. Seven of those weeks were spent at Vestre Faengsel, a prison, and three in a medical facility,[4] where she was treated as a result of her addiction. She departed in late May 1942 on the refugee liner SS *Gripsholm* out of Gothenburg, Sweden, bound for New Jersey. Upon her arrival in June, she explained her gaunt frame in economically truthful Valaida fashion: "What could you expect of one who has lived more or less on a rationed boiled potato diet for the past six months."[5]

∾

The *Chicago Defender* and *New York Amsterdam News* ran the headlines, "European War Clouds Cause Big Slump in Paris Night Life" and "Menaced by European War Rumbles,"[6] as Bricktop reluctantly scrambled to acquire funds to leave her adopted home of over fifteen years. She wrote her sister Blonzetta in Chicago urgently requesting monies on October 1, 1939:

> [O]n receiving this letter cable me at once to the American Express $300 . . . leave hear [sic] at once & on the last safe boat I can catch sailing around 15th or 16 October. Now I told you in my letter I would only ask if necessarily so. You will receive this amount the 10th or 11 Oct so please cable money at once to American Express payable in dollar travelers checks. Don't fail me please.[7]

Blonzetta, a real estate whiz, did not fail her younger sister. She had become accustomed to boosting Ada's income over the last few years, as cablegrams were wired from Paris or wherever Ada may have been stranded to Chicago.

Ada gathered those nominal funds along with the monies given her by the Duchess of Windsor, Wallis Simpson, and Lady Mendl, Elsie de Wolfe, leaving the "Paris of Bricktop" in late October. In some respects, she arrived in New York as she had left: cash-strapped, but unlike her auspicious arrival in Paris, with no prospects for work. For the experience of Paris though, Ada "Bricktop" Smith Ducongé was yet all the richer.

APPENDIX

"NEGRO DANCE," OPUS 25, NO. 1
NORA DOUGLAS HOLT

Negro Dance
op. 25, No. 1

NORA DOUGLAS HOLT
Edited by Helen Walker-Hill

"Negro Dance," Opus 25, No. 1, Nora Douglas Holt

BOOK II

THE AUTOBIOGRAPHY OF ADA "BRICKTOP" SMITH, *OR* MISS BAKER REGRETS

GAINED IN TRANSLATION?

Alice Randall

The Lost Generation lost its black women. Tracy Sharpley-Whiting found them. She's found the streets and neighborhoods where they lived, worked, and visited. She's found their boat tickets and telegraphs home for money, their menus and their men, but, more importantly, she's found their paintings and their pages, she's found their bent notes and their lyrics, she's found their hours in the studio and café conversations that lead to particular paintings and pages. And she returns them to us with the precision of an academic who enjoys her time in archives.

What she has shown us in the pages previous to this are the things she can prove.

You are about to undertake a border crossing. You are leaving the worlds of academic writing about an era and entering the world of fiction. And not just any world of fiction: you are entering a particular neighborhood, genre fiction, and a very specific block in that neighborhood. Sharpley-Whiting has written a murder mystery set in Paris starring Bricktop with supporting appearances by Langston Hughes, Anaïs Nin, Henry and June Miller, Gertrude Stein, Alice Toklas, and, most notably, Josephine Baker, as we have not seen her before, and her "No-Account Count."

These texts, *Bricktop's Paris* and *The Autobiography of Ada "Bricktop" Smith, or Miss Baker Regrets*, talk across to each other in significant ways that invite the reader to do as Sharpley-Whiting does, to employ the power of rigorous scrutiny even as she acknowledges the limits of scrutiny.

We never have all the facts, particularly when we are examining less-documented lives and parts of lives: the interior and imaginative lives of black women in Paris, lives that often went unseen, facts that go missing, and facts that are present but may mislead.

By constructing, by this double mimesis, by attempting to capture Bricktop's Paris from two apparently contradictory means, Sharpley-Whiting creates a high, wide door into a little-known world. By writing a memoir of a circle of friends connected by artistic ambition and ethnicity, she captures the nuance and detail of their travels and actions, the known facts of their lives. But by writing the novel, Sharpley-Whiting has found a way to undo the erasure of these black women from their time in the salons and the saloons of Paris, from the imaginative life of the American nation.

Readers with a taste for Fitzgerald's and Hemingway's Paris-based fiction and Stein's Paris-based nonfiction will find Sharpley-Whiting's Paris texts to be of particular interest. Her work raises many questions about how and why these authors, and so many white American authors, sought to whitewash the Paris they knew: the Paris where they would have engaged intelligent black women intelligently or where they chose not to engage intelligent black women intelligently—or at least chose not to write about it if they did.

Sharpley-Whiting writes about it. Both *Bricktop's Paris* and *The Autobiography of Ada "Bricktop" Smith* are delicious and refreshing engagements with American black women boldly crossing boundaries with significant purposes.

By yoking together this particular work of nonfiction and this particular work of fiction, Sharpley-Whiting has proved herself to be another such bold and significant boundary crosser.

The title of the novel, *The Autobiography of . . .* , reminds us of an earlier boundary-crossing work from that place and time, Gertrude Stein's *Autobiography of Alice B. Toklas*, the 1933 potboiler that allowed Gertrude and Alice to live in a bit more splendor.

We reimagine the past daily. The public past and the private past. Even as we read the facts of a literary memoir, biography, or autobiography, we are imagining, we are filling in the blanks. By coupling a nonfiction account of the period with a work of fiction from the period, Sharpley-Whiting raises important new questions about the limits of fact and the possibilities of fiction illuminating, not blurring, the boundaries between the two approaches.

When she reimagines Bricktop's Paris, she does so openly. When she documents Bricktop's Paris, she does so rigorously. Side-by-side the two very different narratives create a clear awareness of the significance of atmosphere to the individual and to the group, the complexity of the secular ineffable, the weight of what cannot be absolutely known but may be engaged through informed and informing speculation.

But her nonfiction doesn't stoop to speculation. She leaves her fiction to dance with it.

This is the heart of the genius of this project for me. To scrutinize these women objectively is to honor them, but it is also to objectify them one more time, to make free with them, where freedom has not been invited. No disrespect is intended, but a grievance occurs. By closing with this layer of fiction, Sharpley-Whiting acknowledges that there is more to these women than we can know—though we want to know all. They retain essential elements of their selves and their unknowable mystery. At the same time, by the audacious imagining of their inner lives, even in the quick, bold strokes of a murder mystery, she allows her imagination to be in conversation with their imaginations. She offers back what the women were offering; she reciprocates.

The women offer art, works of art of their own. Sharpley-Whiting offers back, almost as the price of writing about them, a work of art of her own. It is an innovative act of intellectual generosity.

That so many of the women worked in the world of pop culture makes it more appropriate that the art Sharpley-Whiting chooses to create and hang her top hat on is a page-turning, smut-slinging, slut-boasting mystery I like to imagine Bricktop might have picked up in the middle of a cold night.

But that is not all this novel, sly as its heroine, is. It is more.

Like Jessie Fauset, who according to Sharpley-Whiting, "wrote black women into the fairytale with its happy endings in a real place that seemed mythical, for it was where color, race, and gender would not be obstacles to creative pursuits, and love could thrive without the 'thou shall nots' of American racism and African American middle-class constraints she spoke of in her 1924 interview with the *Paris Tribune*," Sharpley-Whiting writes black women back into the story of justice by writing a murder mystery with Bricktop as its ethical center.

And similar to the way the poet Gwendolyn Bennett writes a travel guide, this bagatelle of fiction is also a travel guide sweeping the reader to another time and place, Bricktop's Paris, or through the streets of twenty-first-century Paris looking for these particular brown ghosts from the twentieth.

But more significantly, Sharpley-Whiting is able to use the novel to delve into a complex interrogation of the concept of possession from a specifically black and feminine perspective. She explores possession of an image; delight of self-possession and the delight of self-exhibition even as her twinned-engagement of fiction and nonfiction emphasizes the refusal of her subjects to be contained—and her unwillingness to wish to contain them. Each text becomes an alternative to the other, providing for the subjects of her fiction and nonfiction a territory of escape from the lie that they can be fully known without being fully engaged.

She begins *The Autobiography of Ada "Bricktop" Smith* with a long, overlooked, and under-read nineteenth-century quotation from Anna Julia Cooper: "Only the Black woman can say when and where I enter . . . then and there the whole *Negro race enters with me.*"—Anna Julia Cooper, 1886.

This present moment, "when and where I enter," is pregnant. It contains within the body of one specific and individual woman other women, men, and children.

Cooper asserts that "the whole Negro race enters with me." How? In her body? In her history? In her being? In her assertion?

What is lost and what is gained when the individual personal gesture, the entry into a room or place, is understood as an embodiment of complex, creative, collaboration, not as the act of a single person?

Over and over, Sharpley-Whiting captures women in the act of defying race-representation even as they seek to define and redefine race representation. Sharpley-Whiting captures women seeking the respite of escape from the racism they know and shares the Paris spaces black women discovered and made, across an ocean, where their race was a blessing. She shares the places where race, for these specific individuals in these specific moments, disappeared.

Sharpley-Whiting gets us to notice how much America lost in the absence of these women. As the women come to understand themselves differently in Paris, they also come to understand America differently. In Paris they understand, they are the wealth of the nation.

Josie Baker and Bricktop. Where do they take us in this novel? What is the world they are entering? *Bricktop's Paris*, yes! But ultimately these pages of Sharpley-Whiting's nonfiction and fiction tell us as much if not more about the land Bricktop and her fellow brown-and-bound-for-Paris travelers left as it does about Paris. And so Josie and Bricktop, with Sharpley-Whiting's help, take us to a far clearer understanding of America.

"The word 'translation' comes, etymologically, from the Latin for 'bearing across.' Having been borne across the world, we are translated men. It is normally supposed that something always gets lost in translation; I cling, obstinately, to the notion that something can also be gained," writes Salman Rushdie in *Imaginary Homelands: Essays and Criticism, 1981–1991*.

And what of translated women? This is the question asked and answered by both the text of T. Denean Sharpley-Whiting's novel, *The Autobiography of Ada "Bricktop" Smith*, or *Miss Baker Regrets*, and by her nonfiction, sociocultural, literary history *Bricktop's Paris*.

Ultimately the novel and the history are examinations of what we gain dragging our brown, black, and beige asses back across the ocean.

Bricktop and Josephine Baker, as well as Lois Mailou Jones and Selma Burke (to name just a few of the many black women in Paris between World

Wars I and II that people Sharpley-Whiting's pages), are women who have lost something, perhaps in a previous translation, and they are traveling, translating again with ambition—but as Sharpley-Whiting carefully parses, it is not an ambition to find what has been lost but to find something new, new and eclipsingly significant: an internal self that resonates with pleasure and power to external political realities.

These women do not travel to turn back the clock, or deny the past, they travel to claim a present more tightly braided to the future than the past. And to do this they seek a new place to be rather than, to call out and on Gertrude Stein, a new "be" to place.

PREFACE

HISTORY'S MARGINALIA,

AUTOFICTIONAL MYSTERIES,

AND A FONDNESS FOR MATTERS FRENCH

T. Denean Sharpley-Whiting

It was at my grandmother's white Formica kitchen table that I first learned about France and Josephine Baker. It was winter in St. Louis, and my paternal grandmother and great-grand were going through the morning ritual of coffee drinking and reminiscences as if they hadn't just sat at that table the morning and night before, as if they didn't live together. I was treated to homemade hot chocolate with buttery toast for dipping. My grandmother preferred to toast the bread in the oven, loading it down with pats of butter. Room temperature butter didn't slather on quite as well on bread toasted in the newfangled toaster oven, she complained with a "Well sir." It ripped. It tore. Left crumbs. Plus, it was never buttery enough. Since she wasn't a cursing kind of woman, this, and "Darn your time," were her go-to expressions of frustration, though "Well sir" could serve other purposes—joy, amazement—if it was punctuated by her matchless chortle. I didn't especially care for the softer white side of the oven-toasted bread. But I was dipping it anyway and it *was* buttery and well before I cared about cholesterol or fat.

Between calling out names of relatives I didn't know from Independence, Missouri, and loud talk about fooling white folks by "passing" at certain de facto segregated St. Louis establishments, and more humorously "passing" my browner, curly headed father off as Spanish at some of these places, my grandmothers started talking up France. Passing was their way of challenging "place-ism." The site of the 1857 *Dred Scott* court decision that declared blacks were not citizens of the United States and therefore had no claims to freedom, St. Louis had never been an easy place. For them, their place was any and everywhere their abled bodies and imaginations could take them. They didn't have to look far for France; it was everywhere in the city, from its name in honor of King Louis of France and its founding by Pierre Laclède and Auguste Chouteau. Like New Orleans, of which my great-grand was verily fond, it, too, had belonged to France, flying the *Tricolore* in 1800 until the Louisiana Purchase. Neither had visited the Old World, but I didn't know that at nine years old. They talked about France as if they had. Their talk was mesmerizing. They told me about Josephine Baker and how France loved colored people. They had never called themselves Negro or black as long as I had known them. France was for them both a testament to French righteousness and American obsolescence. All of this talk was well before Baker got her bronze star on Delmar Boulevard in the Loop of University City in St. Louis.

The memory of that talk stayed with me. By the time I reached middle school, I was placed in Spanish class. The very next day, I was directed to the French class. I went to visit my grandmother that evening with the French textbook clutched in my hands. I still remember "Monsieur Jean-Claude, Monsieur Jean-Claude" being summoned to "*le téléphone*" by his landlady. All the girls in class tried to imitate the mellifluous inflections of Jacqueline, his *petite-amie*. We sounded like a twangy claw-and-cackle club. By then, my great-grand had passed. My grandmother reached for the book and smiled. She smiled even more after I had studied abroad in France, particularly when I presented her with hand-stitched doilies and a tablecloth from Paris. From that second day of middle school on, I had fallen for France and all things French. And it was all my grandmothers' doing.

Because of them I became intrigued, and admittedly more critical with the assistance of Fanon, Freud, and Léon-François Hoffman, as I studied questions of race, gender, representation, and sexuality, mostly in eighteenth- and nineteenth-century France. French intellectual history and the Age of Enlightenment, Rousseau's social contract, the rise of anthropology, Diderot's Tahitian maidens in *Le Supplément au voyage de Bougainville*, Baudelaire's odes to his Martinican mistress, Balzac's realism, Zola's naturalism, and Gauguin's postimpressionism all fascinated me. It was Josephine Baker, though, who prodded me into the twentieth century. She brought me to Bricktop—who most resembled my paternal grandmother with her fair skin and red hair—but acted more like my feisty maternal grandmother from Mississippi. Through Bricky and Josie, I found the collection of women I hoped to reassemble and reimagine as a community in Paris.

These women, forty in all, have been with me since the birth of my daughter in February 2002. I carried Haviland all the time. Everywhere. I carried her all the way to Europe for the first time of many times to come at the age of fifteen months. I wished she had taken her first steps in Paris. Instead, she first stood up for a good long while in a bed and breakfast in the quaint town of Bruges and toddled unassisted and confidently across the floor of a small hotel in Amsterdam my husband and I christened the boom-boom room because of its interesting choice of paint color. We put *Rick Steves* in permanent time-out after that. Once in Paris, Haviland pattered up and down the streets of Montmartre, Saint-Germain, the Latin Quarter, and Montparnasse. She danced unexpectedly on the steps of Versailles to some whimsical sonata while the fountains gushed water in time. I kissed her on those steps, following the example of Prince in his ditty "Girls and Boys." Our days were long ones, and Paris was experiencing an unusual heat wave that summer of 2003. We did every walking tour imaginable, in print and online, and crosschecked street addresses against biographies. As a preteen, Haviland browsed wall hangings at the Amistad Center in New Orleans, while I combed through letters between Countee Cullen and Langston Hughes; she read quietly on the floor of the Fisk Special Collections Library with a bribe of Hattie B's Hot Chicken for lunch. After a visit to Josephine Baker's Les Milandes in Dordogne, she, too, wanted a chateau and a *Croix de Guerre*. She settled for three framed photos of Baker on a wall in her room in Nashville. She and I and the women of *Bricktop's Paris* have been together for a very long time, on six continents and in dozens of libraries, museums, and archives.

Initially, I imagined doing a Paris version of J. A. Rogers's sweeping *Sex and Race*, culling together women from the *ancien régime* (the Black Nun of Moret) to the twenty-first century (Nicolle Rochelle). But the project became unwieldy. By 2010, I had winnowed my list of forty down to twenty-five. I also narrowed the frame to the interwar period; the era represented a youthful one filled with possibility and promise and unprecedented travel abroad en masse for African Americans. I wanted an anchor for this community of women. And so I turned to Ada Bricktop Smith. Like Josephine Baker, she had been able to create a brand with longevity in Paris. But unlike Baker, Bricktop prided herself on her accessibility even at the height of her popularity. She cultivated a dependable, down-home, and discrete woman-friend persona that was a magnet for the rich and not so flush.

In reassembling these lives into the narrative *Bricktop's Paris*, I found a treasure trove of materials at Emory University's MARBL and Stanford University's Eugene Lerner Collection on Bricktop and Josephine, respectively. Despite the Baker brand, reinforced through her memoirs, in her private letters to Pepito Abatino and his family members, one sees a very vulnerable yet ambitious, highly inventive, and, dare I say, improvisational Josephine. We also witness, in her own hand, the evolution of her literacy in English and French. This, for me, was especially touching.

Though she had collaborated with James Haskins on a memoir, Bricktop was still busily writing notes as if she had planned to publish more in her own hand. The brilliance of the Bricktop-Haskins memoir is that you can clearly hear her voice. It seems she had more she wanted to say. As I began piecing together letters, diaries, oral history interviews, and invitations, I also wanted this incredibly vivacious, no nonsense woman to say more. In the end, this desire for more led me to autobiographical fiction. The truth of the matter is Bricktop felt too much like kin—fictive kin—for me to just leave her and her story be. Josephine Baker had inspired me to work through the layers of French exoticism and colonial *Sturm und Drang* as a graduate student and younger professor; Bricktop had become my mid-career academic muse.

I turned to Phillippe Sollers's theories on autobiographical fiction, Louis Aragon's concept of *mentir-vrai*, where I played the game (*jeu*) with the first-person narrator (*je*), and Audre Lorde's biomythography for grounding. I then reread Gertrude Stein's autobiography of her lover, Alice Toklas, and Virginia Woolf's *Orlando*. And finally I plumbed Ernest Gaines's *The Autobiography of Miss Jane Pittman* and Toni Morrison's *Beloved* and *What Moves at the Margin* for their creativity. I was interested in the ways that literature and history were in conversation in these latter texts, how the works bridged the two disciplines, even as they took certain liberties with the historical record, exploring as they did what moved at the margins of history. I, too, wanted to explore figures at the margins of history and literary subjects. Autobiographical fiction would allow me to capture Bricktop's voice, to rewrite her story from her notes and ephemera, as well as her world, to expand and expound upon this alternative story of Paris without being wholly freighted by the archive, the primacy of evidence.

As I searched for a specific literary vehicle for Bricktop redux, I turned to the genre of the mystery. An avid reader of Edgar Allan Poe since girlhood, as an adult, I leaned more toward the *noir* of Walter Mosley and Paula Woods's police procedurals as well as the classical tendencies in Stephen Carter's academic murder mystery, *The Emperor of Ocean Park*. Mysteries have their own structure. Setting and character development are critical, and plot pacing even more so. I required a genre of fiction that demanded action. Bricktop was a woman of action as was Josephine. It is Josephine who sets Bricktop off on her quest. Baker as a mystery herself animates Bricktop. Unlike historical nonfiction, fiction also allowed me to complicate Josephine the icon using the traces in the archive. I did not want to recreate heroic Josephine, Rainbow-Tribe-mother Josephine, civil-rights-icon Josephine, or exotic, plumed Josephine, but the vulnerable Josephine that Bricktop knew and wrote and spoke about, the selfish, youthful, ambitious, and even desperate-for-a-second act Josephine Baker by 1931. This might trouble Baker fans. And that is precisely what I sought to do, trouble the icon.

When I completed the autofictional mystery *The Autobiography of Ada "Bricktop" Smith, or Miss Baker Regrets*, I resisted separating it from the nonfiction. The volumes indeed spoke to one another, it seemed to me, across the disciplines; they informed each other: the one (the multilife nonfiction) needling me to write the other (the autofictional mystery). And so I decided to present to the reader two volumes drawn from the same archive toward similar ends: a view into the Paris of Bricktop.

THE AUTOBIOGRAPHY OF

ADA "BRICKTOP" SMITH,

OR MISS BAKER REGRETS

Ada "Bricktop" Smith and
T. Denean Sharpley-Whiting

"Only the Black woman can say when and where I enter . . . then and there the whole *Negro race enters with me*."

—Anna Julia Cooper, 1886

GANGSTER'S PARADISE

I.

Paris, 1931

My glossy red curls bounced wildly about my head as I jerked up hard at the sound of the Frenchman's melodic voice.

"*Mon petit oiseau*, my little bird." He gestured grandly. The air kisses from his cupid's-bow mouth blew to each side of my cheeks. He took up the seat beside me at the club's long, ebony bar. The French language made even a threat sound inviting. The words were sweet even. But the tall, reedy man in the dark bespoke suit and made-to-measure black shoes was rotten.

"Back so soon?" I casually turned the ciphering book that was in front of me to a blank page.

"I like to keep watch on, how do you say, ummm?" His mouth was making sounds like he tasted something dear. The saliva swished about inside. "Future investments."

I stiffened. When he grinned, he revealed perfectly white straight teeth. I glanced at his clean-shaven face and well-manicured hands—a dainty diamond be-ringed a misshapen pinkie finger on his left hand. The flesh was pulpy and discolored white and bright pink. It reminded me of a pale worm. The Frenchman was a local gangster called the Baron.

This was his second visit to Chez Bricktop. And, as he had the first time last Friday morning, he came alone. The menacing air of who stood behind him—hard-up coppers on the take and underworld crime bosses— was enough to make business owners quake and fold quickly in MoMart. That's short for Montmartre. The Baron was in the protection and prostitu- tion rackets. I was the last holdout. I wasn't innocent enough to be crippled with fear of organized crime. I cut my teeth in Chicago's saloons; and in Harlem, I sang and danced for my supper in clubs overrun with ruthless men with funny names. Paris in 1931 was no different, teeming as it was with gangsters, American, French, Italian, Russian.

I was turning over a pretty penny and had been for the last five years despite the lean times brought on by the market crash of 1929. The mob was now trying to crash my party. I had built Chez Bricktop one customer at a time. I poured everything I had into my club. I was like a proud and protective mother with her child—prepared to fight to the death before I'd willingly turn her over to any man, woman, or the mob.

"I'm afraid you've caught us at a bad time." I smoothed my hands over my Quattrocento blue Jeanne Lanvin dress. I traced my fingers along the crystal appliqués that dotted up and down the slit of the dress until I could feel the comfort of the steel peacemaker at my thigh. Sufficiently distracted, the Baron's tongue flicked out over his girlish pink lips; he really was a pretty man who easily appreciated pretty women. Like most men of his culture and country. His gray-blue eyes followed every one of those touches, as if I had performed a fully clothed cocotte ablution.

"We're not open for another hour or else I'd offer you a drink," I said drily. I rose to go, closing my ciphering book. He snorted. Then a glass exploded. He had shot a bottle of whiskey near where I was sitting at the bar. Liquor was expensive in Paris and my dress even more so. I sat there calmly, as the brown liquid ran down the dark wood, splashing onto my dress and then doing a steady trickle onto the floor. A full ten seconds passed. The air filled with nothing but our calculating smiles and hard stares. Our eye colors matched in nearly every way except his were matte and cold. His black revolver gleamed from the bar top where he had offhandedly placed it. The barrel, though, was deliberately pointed in my direction. That's when Changchang—my full-time assistant, part-time cook, and niece by love rather than blood—came out from the kitchen with a knife, ready for cutting.

She aimed the knife at the bar where the Baron sat smugly. The blade caught his sleeve, anchoring the delicate dark fabric and him to the polished wood. "I think you meant to pay for that bottle of whiskey." She smiled sweetly. The Baron tugged his jacket sleeve hard, dislodging the knife. It made a light clinking sound as its blade flipped and bounced off the bar onto the floor. A few newly loosened threads of material rose from the sleeve. He returned her smile, while reaching inside his jacket. Changchang moved her hand into the large front pockets of her cooking apron. She pulled out a saw and razor blade knife, prepping for another assault. A flash of light from the steel blade and tang twinkled with each smack against her lean, opened hand.

The Baron lifted from his interior pocket a brown, thin, animal-skinned billfold. He placed a couple of hundred francs on the bar top—enough to purchase a good week's worth of whiskey. Changchang had that effect on people. She was much taller than me. In her bare feet, she was at least five foot eight. A deep honey brown, and not at all hard on anybody's eyes.

"Clyde," I called to the back for our clean-up man. "I need you to get a towel to soak up this whiskey." I was pointing at the floor but still smiling at the Baron.

"As you can see, I can protect myself fairly well. I don't need your services."

"It is not a question of need, *mon petit oiseau*." He snatched up his gun and hat. A slip of blonde hair had escaped from under the brim of the charcoal-gray Trilby hat. The Baron stood, defiantly surveying the club once more. I could hear the tapping of his shoes on the custom-made glass floor and then a swoosh from the black patent leather curtains I had installed at the club's main exit-entrance. His feet continued to strike briskly on the stairs that led out onto rue Pigalle.

"He'll be back."

"And we'll be ready, Aunt Ada." Changchang said this as she side-stepped Clyde to scoop up the bird's beak knife from floor.

I nodded. In the meantime, I had a club to open and a dress to change.

BEGIN THE BEGUINE

II.

I swore I was through with Josie Baker after she'd cut the fool and turned her back on our kind of people over a man. For a year we'd been as close as sisters, until that fateful day when Guiseppe Pepito Abatino—or the No-Account Count as I preferred to call him—tore Josie right out of my life. And that selfish thing walked out on our friendship without even looking back.

Four years later, she showed up at Bricktop's, right out of the blue. Slinking into my club with her lean brown arms outstretched, right in the middle of my debut performance of a song Cole Porter had written for me, she ignored the fact that I was on stage.

She called out, "Bricky, Bricky!"

I felt my heart being yanked right out of my body, but I didn't let it show. I just let my fingers do a wave as I leaned against the piano and carefully sucked in my gut. Though my girdle contained most of my expanding waistline, I was no longer the svelte woman who blew into Paris on the *America* ocean liner in May 1924. It was now February 1931, and I was a curvy woman with a great pair of gams who could still out-Charleston and Black Bottom the best of them.

Who knows why I felt I had to impress Josephine Baker. I didn't want her to think I'd slid downhill since our days at Le Grand Duc, where I'd been a hostess and singer. I gathered a bit of my sparkling blue dress to show off my dancing legs and caressed the last few lines of my lynching ballad:

They strung her upon the old willow across the way

"Nice, Jonny. Real nice," I sang out to the piano player as his thin brown fingers stroked the keys. And then a small commotion offstage caught my attention. Even when I was performing, I was still the owner of Bricktop's, and I didn't put up with foolishness at my club. I called out to a cluster of musicians who waited to take my place on the stage. "You boys need to keep that racket down before I get Changchang on you."

"Send her on back. I ain't scared," one of the musicians yelled, loud enough for the packed house out front to hear.

There was a ripple of laughter from the crowd. I smiled at my patrons and motioned for Josie to take a seat, humming the next few bars before I crooned softly.

Miss Otis regrets, she's unable to lunch today.

The crowd was up clapping and shouting, "Sing it, Brick." I never had much of a singing voice but my timing and pitch were perfect. "Bluesy" is how my new husband Peter described it. And he was a lifelong jazz man, so he knew what he was talking about.

"Take that, Josie, with your chirpy 'J'ai Deux Amours,' " I murmured as I hustled offstage. I needed a glass of champagne.

Josie met me at the bar, tricked out in the latest Paris finery and wearing a toothy smile that reminded me of those damn Paul Colin drawings of her that were all over Paris. Oh, she was fetching. The Bakerfix pomade was holding her fingered waves in place just so, though I personally never liked that gummy stuff.

"Hi, doll," I said all sugary as I took my seat at the bar. "What brings you to Bricktop's?" I wanted to add, *after four long years, you selfish thing.* But my Mama raised me better than to be rude to my guests—especially in my own home. And that's what Bricktop's was.

Josie leaned on the bar. "I see the talking-singing-and-running-the-club-from-the-stage routine is still part of your repertoire." Her strained smile looked more like a grimace.

"Why mess up a good thing?" I tossed back.

"I am surprised, though, that you're letting Jonny Dumont play here again."

Josie had no right nosing around in my business, but I knew she was just making small talk, working her way up to explaining what on earth she was doing in my club, so I played along. "I was in a pinch. Leroy's had a bad cold going on two days now. Jonny arrived on time; he's playing like old times and he ain't shaking at all."

"That's because he's probably high on something."

I deliberately turned away from her at the bar. I felt bad about Jonny and his habit. He was a wasted talent. He reminded me of Mr. Clovis back on State Street in Chicago. When we moved to Chicago from Alderson, West-by-God-Virginia, after Daddy died of a stroke, Mama took to running a rooming house for long-term boarders so she could be home for us children. It was a three-story, red brick job. We occupied the first floor, while the boarders lived on the others, entering and exiting through a back entrance and stairs.

Mr. Clovis rented a room on the top floor. He was a sweet man who bought us soda pops on his way home from work. He played piano at the Shimmy Shack in the vice district. I was just a girl of nine, so soda and candy were the surest way to my heart.

Mama didn't allow cook-top stoves in the rooms. She didn't want anyone burning down the house in the middle of night. So she did the cooking for the whole house, including Sunday dinners. She had us four kids to cook for, so making breakfast and dinner for six more didn't matter much. We were like a big family.

Mr. Clovis would shake like a leaf in the mornings before he had a cup of coffee. Whatever he was doing, he was doing it at the club because Mama didn't allow any drugs or other monkey business at her rooming house. But she saw Mr. Clovis needed help. She made the coffee extra strong with lots of sugar. It worked for awhile, but Mr. Clovis couldn't shake the habit. He had missed his weekly rent for going on two months. Mama would talk to him real soft about it. He'd ask for another chance, but when he got paid on Friday, he'd go straight to the dope house.

I came home from school one day and there was no soda pop in the icebox. Mama explained to me that if she had to choose between seeing me smile about a soda pop or having a roof over my head, then the pop would lose every time. She'd cut her loses and turned Mr. Clovis out. Miss Lula, a teacher, took his room. That's where I was at with Jonny now. I had replaced him with Leroy about three months ago. I needed him now. I wouldn't need him once Leroy recovered from his cold. But I didn't want to discuss any of this with Josie.

"Bricky, can we go somewhere and talk?" I could feel the urgency in Josie's voice, and her eyes kept darting sideways like she was afraid someone was watching.

"We can talk here," I snapped. I had no intention of leaving my own club and circling the block with Josephine Baker. She had made her bed with Pepito, and that was that. Years ago, I'd chalked up her impulsive actions to her youth. And tonight that desperate look in her eyes was reminding me of how young she'd been back then. But Josie was no longer the naïve and vulnerable girl I had met when she'd first arrived in Paris. The Josie I saw tonight was world-wise, ambitious, and fickle. And I was now Mrs. Ada Beatrice Queen Victoria Louise Virginia "Bricktop" Smith Ducongé, a thirty-six-year-old newlywed and owner of a Parisian cabaret. We were both way past the delicious dreams of young womanhood. We were living our dreams now.

"I was thinking of somewhere private. Like your office."

"This is my office." I tapped my polished fingernail on the bar counter, drawing her attention to my accounting books and my glass of champagne. Sure, I had a real office in the back, but I hardly used it when the club was open. And I didn't want to invite Josie into it.

Something was digging into my thigh. As I shifted on my barstool, my dress parted to reveal "Mister Speaker," the pistol that I always kept tucked snuggly into my garter. When he spoke, everybody up in Bricktop's listened.

"You still carrying around that peashooter for protection?"

"Humph. It was Mister Speaker, as I recall, who kept that crazy Spanish flamenco dancer from chopping you up like chitlins over her no good two-timing boyfriend."

"I wasn't hardly even studying him," Josie said, and we both smiled, recalling the time I'd threatened to pistol-whip that wild-eyed woman.

I quickly froze that friendly look right off my face, because Josie hadn't earned it. "She thought you were. And he did, too."

"She even gave you that butcher knife she was swinging around," Josie heehawed.

"That's right," I said, fighting to keep my face serious. "Because I talked to her like I was her mama. I told that there was no man worth fighting over, and I was going to beat her with Mister Speaker to prove it."

"I wasn't trouble all the time, Brick. Besides, you owe some of your happiness to me. Who dragged you over to Parisi's bar over on rue Fontaine to hear Leon Abbey's band, remember? I'm the one who introduced you to Peter Ducongé."

A flood of warmth rushed to my chest as I thought about my Peter and his saxophone. Josie had made my happily-ever-after possible. But that didn't excuse everything that followed. Josie was an expert at seduction. She could get you tipsy just by talking to you in her sweet St. Louis drawl. I could feel her trying to move us back in time, back to our former coziness, and it sobered me right up. I said, "What you want, Josie? Why are you here?"

"I need your help," she said, her eyes filling up. "You know I wouldn't bother you otherwise. Bricky, the police . . ." And now the full waterworks were coming down and my customers were starting to notice. I jumped up from the barstool and yanked her gangly, couture-dressed behind up with me. "Come on back then," I grunted, leading her toward my private office and dreading whatever it was that she'd come to tell me. Already I could smell big trouble.

Between the French gangster that had just left my club no more than two hours ago and the corrupt cops on his payroll surely to come, I'd be getting it from both sides soon enough. I didn't need Josie bringing no more mess to my door, and that included the straight-and-narrow po-lice.

My policy was to avoid trouble whenever possible and to face it head-on when it came straight at me. So I would hear what Josie had to say, offer what advice I could, and then get her out of my club and good riddance.

As we headed down the corridor, Josie lost all self-control. She was blubbering and shaking something fierce, squeezing my arm for support.

"Bricky, I've made such a mess of things. Please don't tell me no."

"Get ahold of yourself and tell me what's wrong," I said, peeling her off my arm.

We burst into the back office where Changchang sat at my desk with a tub of soapy water and a cottony white cloth, surrounded by boning and filet knives. Her elegant fingers were wrapped around the rosewood knife handle. She sat upright when I opened the door and her long dark curls did a lean-to, giving her a peek-a-boo hairstyle.

I said, "Changchang, this is—"

"I know who she is, Aunt Ada. That's Miss Josephine Baker. Pleased to meet you, Ma'am." Changchang said this like she collected Josephine Baker memorabilia. She had met royalty, film and singing stars at Chez Bricktop, but there was no Negro woman star to rival Josephine. She was proud of her. I knew that wouldn't last but a minute.

Nodding to acknowledge Changchang, Josie pulled at her kiss curls and wiped her tear-streaked face with her hands to look presentable. "I can't talk here. Not in front of her. She's just a young girl. Please excuse us, Chingching."

"Changchang, Ma'am." She put down the knife and helped Josie into a chair. Josie studied Changchang's tall slender frame and almond eyes with suspicion.

"Changchang's okay, Josie. I trust her because I helped raise her. I've known her since she was twelve, from back in Harlem. Know her people real well. You probably do, too. Bing Li's Chop Suey and Chinese Laundry uptown."

Changchang's father had come over from China in 1905, right when the U.S. government was escalating their crackdown on Chinese immigration. The Yellow Peril they called it. He had been working in Chinatown for the associations doing pick-up jobs when he up and decided he could make a better living catering to Negroes in Harlem with a hand-laundry and restaurant.

He selected two common and easy to remember colored names: Jones and Johnson. And then Mr. Johnson Jones had married gangly Tina LeBon from Martinique, the niece of Madame Stephanie St. Clair, queen of the Harlem numbers racket. And this exotic couple had produced Changchang, a remarkable young woman who had become a part of my family.

Josie was not impressed. "She's all of what? Nineteen? I just . . . I don't know, Bricky."

"Changchang stays," I said, plopping into my comfy wingback chair. "Now tell me why we're here. I have customers out front who expect to see Bricktop."

Josie looked from me to Changchang, calculating her risks and the return. She must've been feeling desperate because she stopped putting up a fuss. "A woman was murdered," she said. "A reporter called Pippa Nelson."

"I read about it in today's *Paris Tribune*," I said. "What about her?"

"She did freelance work with Janet Flanner at *The New Yorker*. Janet introduced me to her at one of Natalie's salons."

"Salons? Humph. Is that what Nat calls them now? So you been going to Natalie Barney's Sapphic socials where everybody talks about high-brow things as foreplay to *in flagrante delicto*? Oh, Josie." I leaned back in my chair, wishing I'd thought to bring a glass of champagne with me.

"I said I messed up good this time, Bricky. The police came to talk to me this afternoon because . . ."

"Let me guess: You two were lovers."

Stony silence from Josie.

"But if you didn't kill her, what difference does it make?"

"Of course I didn't kill her," Josie said defiantly. "And it ain't so much that I had to talk to the police. I denied the affair. You know how things are here, Bricky. No one openly frowns on these relationships as long as they stay private. But there are pictures of me and Pippa together, and other pictures of me at Natalie's—doin' things, you know." She glanced nervously at Changchang who was hanging on every word. "If the police get their hands on those pictures, they may think I had something to do with her murder because I already lied to them about me and Pippa."

Changchang spoke up. "What did they ask and what exactly did you tell the police, Miss Josie?"

There was a long pause. Josie's mouth was open but no words came out. All you could hear was the faint swish-swash of soapy water as Changchang retrieved another knife to wipe down. Josie decided to ignore Changchang, picking up right where she had left off.

"Pepito is working to get me an offer to do an opera at the Théâtre Marigny. He's talking to studios about two new films for me. I been asked to represent the French colonies at the upcoming Paris Colonial Exposition in May."

"Josie, answer Changchang's question. What did they ask and what did you tell them? I can't help you if you don't level with me."

Josie glared at the door like it was calling out to her. "I didn't ask for her help," she said, nodding towards Changchang. "I asked for yours. They had Pippa's appointment book. They wanted to know why we were meeting so frequently. I told them that she was a reporter doing a story on Americans in Paris and I met with her for interviews and a photography session to accompany the story. I figured that would explain any pictures they might have found of me in her apartment. I said she was a nice young woman and I couldn't imagine why anyone would want to hurt her. That seemed to satisfy them fine." She had delivered this entire monologue to the wall and door, refusing to look at either Changchang or me.

Orgies, of which there were plenty in Paris; murder, naked photographs, and now, more French films. I hadn't cared for the last one Josie had made in 1928. I was fairly certain I wouldn't care to see two more. As I said, Josie always did bring out the Big Mama in me, and Big Mama did not approve. I couldn't help asking, "Why did you take those pictures, Jo?"

"Pippa and I were having fun. We all do crazy things sometimes, Brick. Don't judge me. But I swear I didn't know about those group pictures until Pippa told me before she was killed. I loved her, Brick. And she loved me."

I, too, had done some crazy things in my time, chief among them, letting a girlfriend from my Chicago neighborhood talk me into getting a gold tooth. It was a sign of prestige in our ramshackle part of the city. To this day, I can't stand that tooth sitting on the left side of my mouth. I've learned to hide it when I smile for pictures, which gives me a kind of lopsided look.

"Umm hmm. So you're saying you and Pippa posed for some pictures together at her apartment, but someone took the group pictures without your knowledge at Natalie's? Why didn't Pippa just give you the damn pictures then if she loved you so much?"

"That's what I'm saying! She was going to—last night. We were supposed to meet at her place after my show. She never answered the telephone when I called from the Casino de Paris to confirm our rendezvous. Whoever killed her slapped her around, broke her neck, and then shot her. Her apartment was ransacked. I'm not lying, Bricky. It's in all the newspapers. Read them again if you don't believe me. Somebody has those pictures. I need them. I need you to find them."

So here it was—the reason for Josie's visit. She needed me to get back some dirty pictures. I could feel the wheels in my head spinning. Josie had completely abandoned our friendship and now she was trying to involve me in a tawdry affair with some hen hussy whom she claimed to have loved. I sucked my teeth. *Why should I give a wooden nickel about her? She never even came by to say hello to Mama when she was visiting Paris.*

"I know what you're thinking, Brick. But we're family. We fuss, cuss, and fight but we make up eventually." Josie's voice softened. "I'll never forget that it was you who helped me learn to read and write. You'd take my hand, show me how to hold a pencil, and trace the letters and then sound out the words."

"I'm sorry Miss Josie," Changchang interrupted the reminiscence, "but your idea of family is sure different from mine. You don't run out on your family and then sashay back when you get in trouble. Where I'm from, we call that having no home training." Changchang calmly moved the white cloth over a blade and neatly placed it in the leather slot of a knife pouch.

Josie glared hot at her.

Proud of my almost-niece, I suppressed an "Umm hmm," followed by an "Ain't it the truth." Changchang had been looking after me in her own way since her arrival in Paris. She might look like a child, but she was the best wingman a woman could ask for, and unlike Josie, her loyalty would never be in question.

Josie sensed that she had lost some ground so she pleaded her case. "If I've been selfish, it's only because I had to look out for myself. You know the cards I was dealt—being poor, skinny, and a colored girl too scared to death to go back to where I came from. I've had to make sure that there's always something in it for Jo."

It was true that Josie had it hard. Growing up raggedy in a scratched-out shack near the banks of the Mississippi River in St. Louis, there had been little room for home training. She was self-made. At six years old, she was put to work as a domestic and beaten by the trashy white woman who employed her. By fourteen, she had married and run off with a traveling show. In Harlem, she was told she was too dark, too skinny, and too thin-voiced to ever become a star. She was relegated to the chorus, despite her talents. Life had not been fair to Josephine Baker.

When Josie saw that my tough resolve was cracking, she pressed it further. "You have connections, Brick," she said. "Eyes and ears everywhere. People tell you things they wouldn't tell their mothers, wives, husbands, or lovers; they trust you. You've got a million little secrets locked in that head of yours, Bricky. Some of them mine. I need those pictures—not just for me, but for every one of us Negroes here in Paris." Her dark, heavily made-up eyes were wide and bright now.

"How so?," I asked

I got an "Umm hmm" from the Changchang choir.

"What if the American newspapers get a whiff of this? If I go down—and you know they will delight in taking my uppity colored ass down—it's on all our nappy heads." She pursed her bright red lips. "Folks back home been writing up stories in the *New York Amsterdam News*, the *Afro-American*, the *Defender*, not to mention my hometown paper, the *Argus*, about how well we *all* doing in Paris; they're going to suffer for it. It's a crying shame because we've all worked so hard. The white press will go to town. We may be free in France but not in America where our families live. Thanks to those pictures, we'll all be painted as fools, plain ridiculed. I can't stand the thought of it. And you know murder will be on menu because I lied to the police. I don't want to be a debit to the race, Bricky. I just can't be. My mama will never be able live it down back in St. Louis."

She took a breath to let her words sink in.

They were having their intended effect. Changchang had stopped wiping down knife blades and looked up. I had to steady myself by standing up and adjusting my girdle, which suddenly felt too tight. My first thoughts were ugly ones. Leave it to Josie to muck up the paradise we Negroes had created in Paris. I wanted to beat her like she had stolen something from me, because that's what those pictures of her doing God-knows-what with a bevy of white women were going to do: steal my happiness. My Paris.

Josie spoke the truth. What one Negro did in Alabama had rever-berations as far as San Francisco. It made you hate to read the papers sometimes. We three sat down in that back office thinking long and hard about how it was such an inconvenience to be a colored woman in America; how America reached over the Atlantic and back. Josephine Baker was an international star, a beacon of hope and possibility. Her fall would be a hard tumble down. And her skirt tails were long enough for us all to get tangled up in.

Changchang fixed her almond eyes on me. "You can't trust her as far as you can throw her from a handstand position, Aunt Ada. But you can't say no to her either. There's too much at stake."

Josie honored Changchang with a tearful nod and turned her gaze to me. "You've danced to this music before, Brick. In 1927."

"You're talking about Robeson and Hutch? I didn't care much for those compositions either," I chuckled, soft and sad.

Again, Josie knew just which tune to play. It was true, I had found myself in the role of "keeper of the race" on other occasions. It usually involved counseling Negro men hell bent on destroying their careers by divorcing their wives and marrying white Englishwomen in London. This had happened with Paul Robeson, the magnificent singer and actor, and Leslie Hutchison, a promising piano player. Robeson's agent had explained to me that the biggest colored star in the world would be ruined profession-ally, and that his dangerous liaison could start race riots and a new round of lynchings in America. He said it would be even worse than when Jack Johnson beat the daylights out of James Jeffries in 1910.

"It's no different now, Brick," said Josie, almost triumphantly. She saw from the look in my eyes that I was going to help.

I bowed my head in defeat. Changchang was right—I couldn't walk away from this.

I didn't relish having the role of race leader foisted on me, but this wasn't about choice. I was the most successful, self-made colored business-woman in Europe. I represented the race abroad; even those who didn't care for the saloon business had to admit I ran a respectable shop and was therefore a credit to the race. And I owed it to the race to do everything in my power to prevent our collective humiliation.

Josie rose from her seat to pick up her coat and we left Changchang in the office to finish putting away the cutlery. We walked back down the corridor to the bar in silence, and I handed Jo a white handkerchief, a symbol of our truce, to dab her eyes and face. "I'll try to get your damn fool pictures back," I told her.

But it wasn't for Josie. It was for the race. For Negro womanhood. I was feeling pretty full of my own importance in that moment. But you know it didn't last too long.

LOOKING FOR LANGSTON

III.

As soon as Josie left, I did a round of meet-and-greet out front, to keep my customers happy. Oh, you should've seen my club in its heyday. Bricktop's was beautiful. We had fine banquettes covered in plush black velvet, lacquered tables lit by heavy, crystal-covered candle ornaments, glass-paneled floors, and artistically hung crystal chandeliers and wall sconces. There were only about fourteen tables. It was an intimate club with a sizable stage for entertainers and dancing on the glass floors. I didn't allow crowding at the bar. Once everyone had a seat, latecomers had to wait outside until a banquette or barstool opened up.

Things were running like clockwork out front, so I ducked into the kitchen for a word with Changchang.

She looked up from her cooking to throw me one of her half-smiles. "So how will you find those pictures?"

"Haven't a clue, but I do know where to start. Like Josie said, I know a lot of people."

"What's the story with her husband?" Changchang asked.

"He's not her husband. He's her man and her manager and he never cared for the nickname I gave him: No-Account Count. He claimed to be to the manor born, but we all knew he was a gigolo. Josie told him what I said—that he was a Sicilian leech and she'd be a fool to put half her money and property in his name. That's when he dragged her and her pet leopard Chiquita out of MoMart, all the way to Montparnasse and the Champs Élysées districts. But that wasn't far enough, so he moved them just out of the city to Beau Chêne, their fancy estate.

"If only you could have been in Paris when she first opened Chez Josephine in 1926 in Montmartre. It was a hole in the wall as far as size; but that just made it more intimate and exclusive. It was hard to get in, and the food was expensive. The place stayed packed anyway. Everyone felt they could touch a star. Of course, Pepito hoped to rival Chez Bricktop. But we're still here and Chez Josephine is long gone. Josie used to dress so elegantly every evening, and she serenaded her guests with that Florence Mills song, "I'm a Little Blackbird." At Chez Josephine's it was all class and pizzazz; she left that uncouth banana dancing and eye rolling at the door of the Casino de Paris.

"But that No-Account Count decided that her star would rise faster in Montparnasse and among the Champs-Élysées and Parc Monceau elite. I've seen the two of them at La Coupole, that grand café on the Boulevard Montparnasse, but never stopped to say hello. I knew I wasn't welcome. He's kept her far, far away from our mostly colored crowd. Truth be told, he's done alright by *La Bakair*, turning her into a star and all. And maybe this is just the beginning. Unless, of course, those blasted pictures and a charge of murder ruin her career and take the rest of us down, too."

Changchang watched me gather my coat and a copy of the latest *Paris Tribune*. "Can I come along?"

"Not this time," I told her. "I need you here, at Bricktop's. Wish me luck, baby. I'm off to find me a poet."

I slipped out into the cold, rainy night and into a taxi.

✺

I first met Langston Hughes on the very day I arrived in Paris and landed on the doorstep of 52 rue Pigalle. He was a dishwasher and busboy at Le Grand Duc. When he saw me burst into tears at the puny size of the Duc, he comforted me with a steaming bowl of tender chicken and dumplings. I was used to the grandeur of Barron's Exclusive Club in Harlem. Le Grand Duc was a dump by comparison. But I came to realize it was no more than I deserved.

You see, I had intercepted a wire Gene Bullard sent to Connie's Inn in Harlem, asking for a girl to come over to Paris to sing at Le Grand Duc. I had been looking to shake things up in my life; jobs were getting harder to come by for us singers and dancers, no matter how high-toned we were. We were all competing for a few spots. The jazzmen traveling back and forth across the Atlantic said the living was easier in Paris. Best of all, it was free of race prejudice. I dreamed about eating, drinking, and socializing wherever and with whomever I chose.

But Mr. Bullard hadn't asked for just any girl to come to Paris. He'd asked for Alberta Hunter. I was sure that Alberta's voice would eventually take her all over the world. I was the one who really needed help, and so I took it. And I was right about Alberta. She's had quite a career. Later, I tried to make up for my misbehavior by having her sing at Bricktop's. I always wondered if she'd ever discovered the truth; but if she did, she never confronted me with it.

When my taxi pulled up in front of Le Dôme, I paid the driver and scurried through the hard rain, straight into the café's vestibule. I prayed that my guess would be right—that this was where I'd find Langston tonight. I'd heard that he was back in Paris after a seven-year absence and revisiting his old haunts. If he wasn't here, I'd have to keep searching, and the rain showed no hint of letting up.

Even from his regular Harlem perch, Lang was wise to the pulse of things in Paris. For years, he'd maintained close connections in both cities, since colored folks were always traveling to and from Europe. They kept him apprised of the latest gossip. I couldn't risk asking just anyone what I needed to know. Paris was too small and our close-knit, black-and-white American colony was even smaller. I didn't want to set tongues wagging, but Langston was discreet. I called him the Vault. And it was lucky for me that he happened to be in Paris at the moment.

Looking around at the half-empty café, I could see that Le Dôme had seen better days. Some of the regulars had moved on to the café society in Saint-Germain-des-Prés. Le Dôme had lost much of its cachet among American tourists and expatriates as a result of the recent stock market crash. Starting in 1929, waves of expats whose U.S. investments had evaporated began high-tailing it back home to a depressed America. Those of us who stayed in Paris had weighed the options and concluded we were better off in France than in Lynch Law America.

My heart leaped when I spotted Langston deep in the bowels of the café, sitting alone in a booth. His expression was serious and thoughtful. My old friend had a pen in one hand, and his elbow was resting on a writing tablet. A glass of mulled wine sat within easy reach. I could see the steam rising from the glass swirling into the air.

I sailed across the room and gave him a quick peck on the cheek. "Hey, Lang!"

"Brick!" He stood up to give me a long hug. "However did you find me?"

"I heard you were in town and remembered that this was one of your favorite haunts."

Langston slipped me a good-natured wink. "What did you have in mind? Aren't you a married woman now? I figured I missed my chance, unless you tell me it was meant to be."

Lang had always been a flirt. He was a brilliant, beautiful man. We all wanted him. But I would have bet a dime to a dollar that Lang preferred the company of the less fair sex. And, of course, I was just crazy about my Peter. Suddenly remembering that my husband would be back that very weekend from his latest jazz tour made me want to grin like a fool. But this was no time to get all dreamy. I sat across from Lang and got straight down to business.

"I need some information in a bad way."

"About what?"

"This." I took out my rain-spattered copy of the *Paris Tribune* and slid it across the table, tapping my finger on the photo of a striking woman who stared back at both of us. Her porcelain skin was pale against the gauze of dark hair. Even on rough newsprint you could tell that her skin shone. This was a calculation, a statement on how she wanted to be perceived. The contrast made her appear innocent and angelic. Her eyes looked like they were dancing with mirth. Pippa Nelson had clearly been a vivacious woman.

"Yes," he sighed. "I read about it this morning. Terrible shame. She was from a working-class family back in Chicago. A real scrapper, that one. She would come up to Harlem sometimes with the Dutchman. She also dealt in spades. I've read some of her articles in a little monthly out of New York. I can't recall the name of the review. Janet Flanner was her mentor. Looks like she ran into some rough trade this time."

"So she liked running with gangsters and spades to boot? A free spirit."

Lang shook his head. "No fear that one. She was ambitious, too. She liked to scuffle with the newsboys for the juiciest stories."

"Did you know that she was one of Josie's lovers?"

His ears appeared to wiggle at that revelation. "Now, that I didn't know. Got right passed me. Do tell."

"Seems they fell in love. Met through Flanner over at Natalie Barney's place. The police questioned Josie about her."

"What did she tell them?"

"Some claptrap about an Americans in Paris story."

"Pippa was working on a story with that angle. She interviewed me for it."

"Did the police contact you as well?"

"No. But I've been in New York. Brick, what's your interest in Pippa's murder?"

I shrugged my shoulders and tried to act nonchalant. "Josie and Pippa and a gaggle of white women had an orgy and did some porno at Natalie's. Photographs were taken. Pippa was supposed to meet Josie the night she was murdered to give the pictures to her. And they've gone missing."

"And now, when those photos turn up, Josie will be run down as a debauched murderess and we will all be left exposed as sexual reprobates giving license to more rapes, lynching, and public smear campaigns, if they aren't recovered."

"You got it." *And much quicker than I had.*

Lang opened his jacket and pulled out a neatly rolled cigarette. I drank but I never smoked, so he didn't bother to offer me one. "This isn't good, Brick. Not for any of us colored folks at home or abroad. How could Josephine be so careless?"

He hadn't really meant for me to answer that question. "You got an address for Pippa? The paper doesn't say where she lived."

Lang took out a small black book and flipped the pages. "Rue Fleurus. 19. Near Stein and Toklas."

"Can you put your contacts to use in New York? Find out if she was working on some other stories? I suspect the Americans in Paris might have been a cover. Maybe she was digging into things better left buried."

He nodded, and I could feel that his mood had suddenly darkened. Was it because I'd mentioned New York? I'd heard he was in a funk after his fallout with Zora Neale Hurston over the play *Mule Bone*. I felt bad for the poet laureate of our race. He and Zora had been close, sharing literary tastes and even the same white benefactor, Charlotte Osgood Mason. Some called her Godmother. I wondered who would be left standing in this battle between literary titans, and who would enjoy Mason's patronage in its aftermath.

Langston cleared his throat. "Brick, you're trying to get those pictures back and take them out of circulation, right?"

I nodded.

"So why do you need to go prying into what stories Pippa was working on? The pictures of her and Josie won't have anything to do with her other stories, right? I just hate to see you getting into something that could be dangerous."

"Lang, I want to focus on the pictures. But it can't hurt to have a bigger picture of Pippa—who she was close to and what she was working on. How else am I going to find those photographs? Maybe the people who killed her took them by mistake and wouldn't mind giving them back."

He began massaging his temples like he was trying to get the jump on a migraine. "Brick, I really wish I could stay to help you with this, but I'm off to Haiti day after tomorrow. I hate the idea of you getting mixed up in a murder. Does your husband know what you're up to?"

I almost slapped my friend upside the head. "I'm a grown woman and a respected business owner," I told him. "You think I can't handle myself? Besides, I've got Changchang to back me up."

That made Lang smile. He'd heard about my almost-niece. "I'm glad you've got Tina Le Bon and Johnson Jones's girl here with you. I hear Miss Changchang is a tall, cool drink of water and quite surgical with knives. Slicing up stick-up kids and junkies in Harlem that were foolish enough to shake her down for her parent's delivery money was good preparation. Who would have thought you would need those skills in Paris, France?"

"Too true," I said. "So you'll get me what I asked for?"

"Who could say no to you, Brick?"

"Good. Then I'm heading over to Natalie's salon. See? Nothing to worry about, I'll be surrounded by women."

"You planning to join her Temple of Friendship?" He threw me a mischievous smile, alluding to the towering stone structure in Natalie's courtyard garden that was apparently the setting of much naughty behavior. "You damn near white and bright enough to cross her gilded threshold. That Miss Anne don't much deal in coal. She hosts the Women's Academy on Fridays."

"So I've heard," I told him. "Which means that I've got to get." I started to leave the table but something drew me back. "Lang . . . Why Haiti?"

Langston shrugged. "I thought it was the Old World I needed to repair to, but I'm heading to the Caribbean to do some soul searching. Figure out my next moves as a writer. In case you hadn't heard, Harlem is no longer in vogue. I pronounced it dead over a year ago along with the taste for all things Negro. There was no way Harlem could have survived the crash intact. But it sure was a nice ten-year run. Haiti was the world's first Negro Republic. There's a great writer there: Jacques Roumain. Walter White gave me a letter of introduction." The oracle of Harlem stroked his jacket pocket where he had obviously tucked the door-opening letter. "Maybe I can find some inspiration on Roumain's small island, despite the U.S. Occupation."

"Don't go maudlin on me, Lang. I think you've had too much mulled wine. Promise me you won't go to Haiti looking to rabble-rouse. You're a poet not a politician."

Lang was no longer playful. He looked around the half-full café. His eyes then dropped down to the closed writing tablet in front of him. He looked pained, staring at that emptiness. Maybe Haiti was what he needed.

"My art has always been political, Brick. Now you need to watch yourself with this Pippa Nelson intrigue." The sternness in his voice returned. "Sure we need those pictures, but I don't want you getting yourself killed over them."

I smiled back at my old friend. "I'll be careful. And really, there is no chance that Changchang will let anything happen to me. Though I'd prefer that she stick with the culinary arts. She makes a mean chop suey and a variation of egg fu yung that she picked up from a jazzman from St. Louis called the St. Paul Sandwich. Authentic egg fu yung, plus mayonnaise, dill pickle, tomato, and lettuce on white bread. Come by and try it before you leave. It's become our signature sandwich. People get tired of the French croque-madame and -monsieur."

"I'll plan on stopping by. Just watch yourself. Sometimes it's best to leave dead white folks where they be, Brick."

"Understood."

"Here," said Lang, handing me a book. "Take this. You'll need a cover at Natalie's. There are only a hundred copies. That one has my autograph. Might be worth something one day," he guffawed.

"Thanks, baby. And you take this." I reached into my purse and gave him almost all the greenbacks and French francs I had. With Godmother obviously gone and Harlem out of vogue, he was but a poor, struggling artist again. I was sure he'd eventually remember that that's when he wrote best. His smile was all the gratitude I needed, as I watched him greedily stuff the bills into his well-used wallet. I blew him a kiss and headed out. The rain had stopped, thank goodness. As I passed beneath a streetlamp, the orange cover of Langston's book caught my eye: *Dear Lovely Death*. I hoped it wasn't an omen of what was to come.

THE WOMEN'S ACADEMY

IV.

Since the book was to be my entrée, I began skimming Lang's verses on the taxi ride over. I had read his jazz and blues verses before. He'd sent me a copy of *The Weary Blues* for the Bricktop Lending Library Collection back in 1928. Some of our kind of people only came to Bricktop's in the mornings to catch up on the latest news and reading from America.

I exited the taxi in front of Natalie Barney's two-story pavilion. Even at nightfall, its grandeur was evident. I hastily walked by the Temple of Friendship in the courtyard. *To be rich and bohemian,* I sighed. Most colored folks could only strive for the latter in Paris. Natalie Barney was an heiress. Money oozed from every delicate strand of her Ohio honey-blond head of hair to the tips of her pink, pedicured toes. Railway car manufacturing loot financed her intellectual and queer fancies, as she called them, in Paris, two pursuits that—as a woman—would have been impossible for her to practice openly in America.

I rang, but no one answered the door. So I summoned my moxie and pushed. There were about twenty women in the salon, listening intently to a reading by some woman poet I'd never heard of, going on about unrequited love and death. The Mother Goose of Montparnasse, Gertrude Stein, was seated, rolling her eyes in the direction of her dearest Alice Toklas. Neither obviously found the poetry worth much. On an impractically silk-upholstered settee, the exotic, pale-skinned Anaïs Nin was delicately kissing the fingertips of Henry Miller's June. June's blond head arched back, exposing her neck. Here Anaïs stroked her gently. I wondered when that affair had begun and how Henry felt about this *ménage à trois.*

Only Natalie looked up from the glum assembly. She walked over just as the poet finished her recitation. The group splintered. Some surrounded the reader, asking questions about technique and style, while others headed to a table stocked with wine, whiskey, chocolate cake, and an assortment of pungent French cheeses.

"Why Brick, it's been ages. What brings you to the Académie des femmes?" Natalie's lithe body seemed to tower over me. No wonder some people called her "The Amazon." As she reached down to hug me, I noticed the spider-veins in her bony hands.

"You haven't visited Bricktop's in so long I figured I'd just bring the mountain to Mohammed."

I knew Nat's story without being told. Once she'd had her fill of the "American Negroes under glass" exoticism of Montmartre, she'd sought new adventures. And her pet project of late was this Académie des femmes where women could socialize and share their artistic bric-a-brac, literary odes, prose, and cerebral passions, among more scandalous pursuits if the rumors held an ounce of truth.

"I haven't come empty-handed." I passed Lang's book to her when she released me.

"The title certainly befits our mood tonight," she said, shaking her head as she leafed through the pages. "We are mourning the death of one of our own. Have you heard?" She lifted her head to reveal moist eyes.

I debated whether to play dumb or smart. I went for smart. "Yes. That's why I'm here."

"Josie sent you, did she? That Sicilian Bluebeard of hers forbade her to socialize with us." Natalie's face with its fragile beauty screwed up when she mentioned Pepito Abatino.

We Negroes obviously weren't the only group Pepito had pushed Josie away from.

"She did," I lied.

"Well, good then. At least she is honoring Pippa. Wherever did you get Langston Hughes's book of verses in Paris? It looks fresh off the press."

I didn't think Natalie would be much impressed if I said I received it from the writer himself. She probably hadn't even read Lang before. So I offered up a name she would know and couldn't ignore.

"Carlo sent it to me from New York."

"Carlo? Carl Van Vechten. Why I still haven't gotten around to reading," she hesitated for a second or two, "his *Nigger Heaven*." A smile crossed her thin lips as she gauged my reaction.

"Umm hmm." *Why you stringy-headed heifer*, I seethed.

Natalie could be downright vexing sometimes. You would have thought her being queer, as she called it, and a woman, would have tempered her bouts of whiteness. But like Mama said, whiteness is a terminal disease. It just goes into remission sometimes. And she would know firsthand; two years before the Emancipation Proclamation was issued, my Scotch-Irish granddaddy gave in to a burst of whiteness when he took up with Big Mama Thompson, a blonde, blue-gray-eyed house slave.

Despite her misfires, I liked Natalie Barney. She and I were more alike than either one of us cared to openly acknowledge. She was generous with her time and true to herself in a way few people could claim to be. She pursued her desires openly and honestly. The Women's Academy was an example of her selflessness for a cause. Since women had yet to be inducted as *immortels* into France's prestigious Académie française, Natalie had decided to fill the void with her own Académie des femmes.

And there were a lot of things I liked about Carlo, but *Nigger Heaven* wasn't one of them.

"Would you care to read a few passages for us? I'd like that."

"That's why I'm here."

"Might I have your attention again," she announced to the Academy. "It is a rare opportunity indeed to have Bricktop among our company. Brick is here to read a verse on behalf of Josie Baker, who, as you all know, was very close friends with Pippa. We should be very grateful to have her join us this evening, even if the occasion is a solemn one."

I tried my mightiest to emulate their forlorn mood as I took the salon floor. Though I didn't know Pippa Nelson in the least, I reached for human empathy:

> Dear lovely death
> That taketh all things under wing—
> Never to kill—
> Only to change
> Into some other thing
> This suffering flesh,
> To make it either more or less,
> Yet not again the same—
> Dear lovely Death,
> Change is thy other name.

Tell that to Pippa. That poor woman had definitely suffered in flesh and was thoroughly changed with that pulverized face, broken neck, and a bullet to the head, if the newspapers were to be believed. Bleats of "oh" and "ah," and a few tears followed. Even Mother Goose touched my hand in appreciation, as she and Alice hastily gathered their things to depart. Gertrude never cared much for Natalie even though she was a member of the Academy. Each woman had staked their claim as the premier salonist of Saint-Germain.

I strolled across the room, trying to catch snatches of conversation, picking up a piece of chocolate cake my waistline didn't need and a shot a whiskey my gumption did. Tomorrow, I told myself, I'd fast-walk up the hill to Sacre Coeur Basilica, pray for forgiveness for my gluttony, and run back down to the Place du Tertre.

"Thank you, Brick. It's still hard to believe she's gone and in such a terrible way," Natalie offered after I positioned myself next to her, intentionally closer to the strong cheeses rather than that scrumptious cake.

"She seems to have meant a lot to Josie. It couldn't have been all hearts and roses, seeing as how Josie stayed with No Account." I was bait-casting.

Natalie smiled. Everyone in our American enclave knew the name I had given Pepito. "They were in love. They met here last June. It could get stormy between the two of them. Pippa came crying to me on several occasions. Finally, Pepito forbade Josie to come to the salon again, and she dutifully agreed. Pippa was miffed. She swore she would convince Josie to leave him."

"Really? How so?"

"That was love talking, dear Brick. Pippa seemed desperate about it. We all have our unmended heartbreaks."

"I thought time healed all wounds."

"There is always that *one*." Natalie's pale-blue eyes took on a faraway look. I felt a long, romantic story coming on, so I quickly switched the subject. "Have the police been by to question you and Academy members? They contacted Josie."

"As a matter of fact, I'm to meet with an Inspector Gravois on Monday. They probably think we're a queer sex cult that engages in the ritual sacrifice of our members."

"It does make you wonder. Who would have been so brutal? And why?"

"She liked to live a little on the edge, frequenting *boîtes* like Zelli's." She spat the name of that dive out of her small mouth. "We're an insular group of intellectuals. Pippa enjoyed more diverse company."

"So she liked slumming?"

"You could say that. But without all the mean race overtones it would carry back home."

"When's the last time you saw Josie?"

"Last month."

"At the Temple of Friendship?"

"Goodness no," she chucked softly. "It's winter outside. Don't believe everything you read about us in the papers."

My mind braced against the tsunami of bad press awaiting us Negroes if I didn't find those photographs. "Was her visit social?"

"No, though she acted as if it was. I hadn't seen her since June. She wanted something I didn't have. And even if I'd had what she wanted, I wouldn't have given it to her. I was annoyed with her, Brick. For ditching the Women's Academy like we were nothing but twaddle."

It raised my spirits to see that I wasn't the only one Josie had left in the dust. "Josie looks out for Josie," I blurted out before I could pull it back. Natalie's eyes narrowed and I could tell she was dying to dish about our mutual friend—which would only pull me further away from my mission that night. To put us back on track, I said, "So what'd she ask you for?"

Natalie played coy. "Brick, I'm not that easy. Like yours, my stock in trade is discretion. I've learned, over the years, to keep my own counsel."

I acknowledged our similarities with a nod. And following her eyes across the room, I pushed off in pursuit of new quarry. I spied a too-thin woman with hair that was more orange than red, pulled tight into a low hanging bun. Her skin was deathly pale. She was more ghostly than ghastly, striking rather than pretty. She hadn't been there when I'd first arrived. She had just finished scolding a meek-looking blonde, who scampered away like a rabbit newly released from its pen.

The orange-headed woman pursed her lips, which were fuller than most white women's I had known, and accentuated with a garish orange lipstick, crookedly applied. She said, "It's rude to stare."

"I'm sorry," I replied. "It's a habit I've developed in my business so I won't forget a face."

"Is that right? I know you. I go to Montmartre all the time to paint in Place du Tertre. I've even been to Bricktop's a few times with my friend Jonny Dumont."

That statement alone told me plenty about Miss Matching Lips and Hair. It explained her emaciated frame and paleness. *Dope fiend.* I wondered what her poisons were. Absinthe and cocaine? Hashish and wine? Or maybe heroin. I forced my mouth into a friendly smile. "You know Jonny?"

"Quite well. I like to sketch the jazz musicians while they perform in the clubs. He's my escort sometimes." She sipped from a glass of wine and then mumbled something about a cheap grape.

"I beg your pardon?"

"The grape. It's cheap. The wine is not very good. Neither is the company." She surveyed the room with a sour look on her face.

I decided not to take offense at her comment, since I had no interest in impressing her. "Why'd you come, then?"

"For Pippa. If I could have avoided coming here to pay my respects, I most certainly would have."

I understood then that all was not well at the Women's Academy, and it went beyond Pippa's murder. Just then, the doyenne herself sauntered over.

"Renata. It's good to see you."

"Don't push it, Natalie."

Carrot-Top Renata lit up a cigarette and glared at Natalie as she took a pull, leaving a bright orange ring on the Zig-Zag cigarette paper.

"There's no need to be rude. You'll have other occasions, but not this one. For Pippa's sake."

"We all know why she's dead," she jeered.

"I don't," I piped up.

Renata smiled, taking another pull on her cigarette. "Ambition."

"That's enough," Natalie shrieked.

Renata glanced spitefully at Natalie and stubbed the cigarette out, right on a mahogany table, inches away from a cut-glass ashtray. If we'd been at my house, that move right there would have made me pound Carrot-Top

Renata straight into the marble floor. But Nat stood stock still. Oh, these two women had some kind of tortured history—that much was obvious.

Renata turned to leave the room. "Nice meeting you, Bricktop. I'm in need of the toilette. Your face-remembering habit needs some work, I gather, since you didn't remember me."

You weren't worth remembering then. I won't forget you now. I twisted my lips into a frown. She was probably heading to the powder room for a fix. I didn't know what to make of Renata's gruff style. She seemed to have no use at all for Nat and a bizarre sense of irony about Pippa's death.

"I'm sorry, Brick. Renata's our bitterest pill."

"She's something," I replied, helping myself to another glass of whiskey. These Academy women were working on my last nerve. If tonight's digging didn't turn up any leads on those photographs, I'd have a look-see on Place du Tertre for another go at Renata.

⌒

"It's terrible," moaned the wispy blonde woman with painted-on eyebrows and an upswept hairdo. "Not the poem you read, but Pippa. I'm Ollie Knolton."

I could smell the wine oozing out of Ollie's skin as soon as I'd sidled up to her. She was the fast rabbit that I had observed earlier, scampering away from Renata. "Yes, baby," I responded, "it is a terrible thing. Did you know Pippa well?"

"We were friends, you know."

"You and Pippa?"

"Me and Josie," she confided. "We were all three good friends. At least, until Pippa and I fell all the way out."

"But now, here you are, forgiving all that. What did you two have a falling out about?"

"She wanted something from me that I wasn't willing to share."

This sounded suspiciously similar to Natalie's story. *What exactly was this thing that nobody was willing to share?* I said, "Give and take is the key to any friendship, Miss Knolton."

"Ollie. Please call me Ollie. I share. I'm very generous. I'd like to share with you."

"What's that?"

"Do you like women, Miss Bricktop?"

I thought about Peter. "It's Missus, baby. I like 'em alright. Just not that way."

Unlike Nat, clearly this Miss Anne dealt in Queens of Spade.

"Having an M-R-S in front of your name is hardly a stumbling block. Are you sure? I was thinking we could catch a drink at Le Boeuf sur le Toit and then head over to my place."

"Even if I did like women like that, I wouldn't take advantage of you in your present state." I gave her a wistful smile.

"You're beautiful, Missssssus Bricktop," she shamelessly stressed out the syllables. "What are you anyway? White, colored, both? I'd love to take some pictures of you." She leaned back clumsily and made the motions of a photographer behind a camera. Her hands were gloved.

Ollie Knolton now had my undivided attention. It was half past one Saturday morning, and the whiskey was muddling my thinking just when I needed to be nimble.

"I'm a Negro. I'd like to see some of your work when you have the time," I suggested, almost too quickly.

Ollie moved back awkwardly and retreated to the table topped with liquor and eats. She clutched the table for balance. The tightly woven scarf around her neck stayed dutifully in place. She reached for a leather satchel on a nearby chair. She pulled out an envelope and handed it to me. "They're artistic." The salacious grin on her face morphed into a wan smile, which only emphasized the scratches that ran along the creases on the left side of her mouth.

I took the bait and opened the flap. *Sacre bleu!* There was Josie. She was doing the huck-a-buck, hoochie coochie, and a six-leg frolic. The photographs were not the run-of-the-mill porn that you could purchase on the banks of the Seine; they were very creative—almost staged. Some were of Josie, Pippa, and Ollie, and others, of a higher quality, showed Josie and Pippa with more women I didn't recognize. The quality of the photographs without Ollie was much finer, which told me that whoever had been behind the camera when Ollie was in front of it wasn't nearly as good.

"Highly artistic," I nodded, frantically wondering how I might get my hands on the negatives. Visions of my prim, West Virginia Mama with her upright sensibilities stomped across my mind. She would have slapped me down for calling those photographs anything but smut. *But when in Paris . . .*

"Those are what Pippa wanted. We were supposed to meet about them yesterday," she slurred.

My, my, Pippa was quite busy.

Mixed in with the risqué photographs were several images of streets and clubs. Some I recognized from Harlem; one place in particular where I had performed. It was owned by that gangster Owney Madden. There were also some pictures of buildings in East Harlem and Little Italy. I wondered about Ollie's interest in these buildings.

As for the incriminating Josie photographs, Pippa obviously hadn't gotten her hands on them. Ollie had kept them for herself. I could have taken the pictures right then—but what I really needed were the negatives. Until I had those, I couldn't afford to frighten or enrage Miss Ollie Knolton. Oh, my fingers were itching to confiscate those photographs. But when Ollie tugged on them, I had to let go.

"Those are interesting photographs as well." I pointed to one of the New York street scenes. "You ever been to the Cotton Club? I worked there for a spell."

Ollie Knolton sobered up real quick, becoming dour in the process. "Those were for Pippa," she explained stuffing them quickly into the envelope.

I thought about what Natalie said about Pippa's keeping diverse company and Renata and Langston calling her ambitious. "Pippa had a thing for gangsters?"

"It's art," said Ollie. "Layouts for the magazine. Pippa didn't get involved with men. No gangsters. Nothing like that." She was speaking in short spurts, almost mechanically.

No gangsters? That's not what I heard. Ollie Knolton was lying to me for some reason.

Flirtatious Ollie had been replaced by a fiddle-footed shadow of herself. Ollie surveyed the room like an owl, eyes wide, moving all around, as if she was trying to see who might have overheard us. She was suddenly skittish, and I was desperate to reel her back in.

"Let's go to Bricktop's and have a champagne toast to celebrate Pippa's life," I proposed. It was a way to keep Ollie and those pictures in my sight for a little while longer.

"Delightful!" Ollie clapped like a small child, mangling the photographs. She was holding the reputation of my race in her tiny hands. She repeated my proposition to the downbeat room. "Hey," she gurgled, "let's go to Bricktop's . . ." At least Ollie would have some Women's Academy members to escort her home once the club closed for the night. I didn't want her accidentally on purpose needing to sleep off her drunken memorial to Pippa Nelson's life at my place, even if I did have an extra bedroom and Peter was on tour in Budapest. I gave some excuses for leaving ahead of them.

The women from the Academy arrived at my club in a fleet of taxis shortly after I'd parked myself at my barstool office. When they entered, Mabel was singing Cole's "Love for Sale" in her inimitable sweet soprano.

Old love, new love, every love but true love

I watched Ollie swoon from side to side with her eyes closed, like she was floating on Mabel's high and low notes.

"Mabel Mercer, everybody, singing Cole Porter," I announced at the end of the song. Though no one could sing Cole like Mabel, I was glad he was in Italy for the weekend. He hated for people to sing his songs in his presence, unless it was at the theater or he was accompanying them on piano. He was prickly like that.

I moved center stage and offered everyone at Bricktop's a glass of champagne on the house, in memory of someone they had loved and lost.

"To dear friends and family," I said, raising a champagne flute to the crowd. "Death, as painful as it is, is Change's other name." I added a silent toast to Lang and took a nice sip of bubbly.

That offering would cost me a pretty penny, but it was worth every top-quality glass to get my hands on Ollie's envelope and those negatives. *For the race.* I gulped down the champagne in two quick chugs.

As today seeped into tomorrow, we transitioned to our regular early breakfast at Bricktop's. The kitchen would start offering up eggs, bacon and ham, toast, and coffee and cocktails from six in the morning until eight thirty. And Negro musicians who had been playing at clubs all around town were filtering in to start off their weekends with a good meal.

In her sloshed condition, I had managed to earn Ollie Knolton's amity and the address of her abode. I was just short of giddy, thinking of how she'd agreed to meet for lunch like proper ladies at twelve thirty at Ladurée, a tea salon at rue Royale. That poor Ollie's nose was still open wide for Josie went without saying. Baiting my hook, I promised her that Josie would be there, too. If anyone could get those photographs and negatives from Ollie, Josie could.

I left Changchang at six thirty that morning at Bricktop's. But instead of going home directly to take my morning nap, I changed into comfortable shoes in order to fulfill that promise I'd made myself after my gluttony at Nat's salon. It was an odd get-up I was wearing for this long haul: a sparkling blue Chanel dress and lace-up walking shoes. '

Trudging briskly up to Sacre Coeur, I saw how plain rue Pigalle was during the daylight hours. It was much more attractive at night, dolled up in lights, and chock-a-block with colorful signage, promising a good time to all. It lacked the quaintness of rue Mouffetard, which also sat on a hill and was home to the lively open-air markets. Rue Pigalle gave succor to vim and vigor, and vice. It reminded me of Chicago's Black Belt, which is where I got my start in the entertaining business. So I felt right at home. Gritty in the daytime, we sure put the gay in Gay Paree by night.

As I huffed toward the entrance of the gleaming white portico of Sacre Coeur Basilica, images of Ollie's naughty pictures drifted through my head, crowding out the sights of Montmartre; the posed vignettes flashed across my mind like a crazy daydream. Suddenly I stopped—just short of Sacre Coeur's three grand archways. Gasping to catch my breath, I gazed up at the statue of Joan of Arc riding a horse.

Josie Baker had lied to me! She'd told me that she hadn't known about those group photographs. But they were clearly posed. What had possessed Josie to go along with such a thing? And why lie to me about it?

I was going to make her own up to it.

JOSIE, TEA, AND ME

V.

Later that Saturday, I woke up shortly before noon. My muscles were stiff from the vigorous walk and my head was pounding. A reminder to stick with champagne and leave the whiskey to my customers. I hurried to wash and primp for my rendezvous with Ollie and Josie at rue Royale.

I was halfway out the front door when Changchang appeared with a worried expression on her face. She didn't have far to go. Changchang had the apartment across the hall from me and Peter. I wanted to keep her near me in this foreign city so I could protect her.

"Don't tell me," I said. "Josie can't meet at Ladurée?"

"She'll be there. Mr. Langston came by this morning. He left this for you." She put an envelope on the salon table.

"I missed him?" That was a disappointment. I hadn't expected Lang's turnaround to be so quick. "How do you know it was him?"

"I recognized him from the photograph in the office that was taken when you both worked at Le Grand Duc."

Clearly, Changchang had already opened the envelope and digested some bad news. I wasn't angry at her. She was always in my business, just like I was always in hers. That's family. "What does it say?"

Changchang straightened the collar of my coat. "It's trouble. Like everything else involving Miss Josie."

I ripped opened the note penned in his looping, flamboyant script:

Brick,

Word on the Harlem streets, courtesy of Bumpy Johnson, is that Pippa was deep in the weeds working on some French-American mafia connection story. It was a hit piece on the mob. Imagine that! Nobody is happy about it here or there. It seems you were on to something. Word to the wise, my dearest Bricky: leave the dead white girl where she be. Focus on those pictures. For us. Wish me luck in Haiti.

Bises,

Lang

"Didn't you say that the Knolton woman froze when you asked her about those other photographs, Aunt Ada?"

Apparently I had. I'd been so tipsy when I returned to the club in the wee hours of the morn that I had little recollection of jabbering to Changchang in the back office. I had filled her in on what transpired at the Women's Academy, and then I'd had a big ole cry about my former friendship and fallout with Josie, while she force-fed me cups of hot tea until the breakfast revelers arrived and I had sobered up enough for my long walk.

"True," I said. "Ollie was jittery when I asked about those New York nightclub pictures. Maybe she was nervous that there might be a link between Pippa's death and this mafia story." I bent over to brush a piece of lint off my silk stockings.

"I think we should take Mr. Langston's advice."

"I helped raise you better than that," I huffed halfway up from the bend. "I don't like the police anymore than the average Negro, but I can't stand the gangsters even more. We can't just hold back information that could help solve the murder of an innocent woman."

Changchang rested a hand on her slim hip, all attitude. "Oh, yes we can! The mob leaves innocent, dead Negroes in Harlem's streets every day, and not a white person downtown cares a thing about it. It's not our problem. If it becomes our problem, that's different. Anyway, that letter didn't say the mob killed her, Aunt Ada. It seems to me that Miss Josie had more to lose than the mob. You're too close to her to see it, and you don't want to think the worst of her. But she's shown you nothing but her backside in the last four years, on account of a man."

Changchang sucked her straight, white teeth hard. "How do you know Miss Josie didn't kill that reporter while trying to get those pictures? She admitted that she and Pippa had a plan to meet. What if she beat that woman to a low gravy and shot her when she couldn't deliver those pictures? And don't talk to me about love. Since when did love ever stop a killing? We from Harlem, Aunt Ada. Love can turn to hate quicker than a cat licks its ass. Pardon my French."

༄

I arrived at Ladurée at exactly twelve thirty with Changchang's lecture ringing in my ears. Josie, dressed in a chic fitted black suit and an Elsa Schiaparelli scarf and hat, was already seated and had even signed a few autographs for tourists.

"*Voulez-vous prendre quelque chose, Madame?*"

"An *omelette*, please, and a *salade verte*."

My spoken French hadn't improved much in nearly seven years I'm ashamed to say. It worked to my advantage when I sang because audiences loved when I mixed my fractured French with English, but the waiter at Ladurée was not impressed.

"*La même chose*," Josie said.

As our server departed, nose in the air, I gazed over at what I had really wanted to order: an assortment of those macaroons Ladurée was famous for. But my girdle was already on the next to last notch. Shortness of breath was the price I paid for my full hourglass figure.

"Did you find the pictures?" Josie clasped her hands theatrically, in anticipation.

"Actually, I found out who has them. Why'd you lie to me, Josie?"

"What are you talking about, Bricky? Who has the pictures, and where are they?"

"Right about now, I wouldn't give you eye water to cry with. You know exactly what I'm talking about." I looked out the window, scanning for our missing lunch companion. "And Ollie Knolton's sloppy, hungover ass should've been here by now."

"Ollie?" Josie scanned the room. "How do you know about Ollie?"

"I'll ask the questions, Josie. You said you didn't pose for those pictures taken at Natalie's Temple of Friendship. But there you were, face out, ass up, looking right at the camera."

She was quiet for a few moments until she saw that I wasn't about to back down. "Okay, Bricky. I lied about those other photographs. I didn't want to admit how foolish I had been in front of Changchang. And maybe I knew you'd be disappointed in me. I didn't think twice about any of those pictures until after Pepito told me about the opera and movie possibilities last month. I don't want to spend the rest of my career taking my clothes off, and I don't want another boa of pink feathers between my legs either. I'm sick of wearing those erect bananas around my waist. Truth is, so is the French public. The novelty has worn off my *danse sauvage*. Reviews of my show at the Casino de Paris are just so-so. But I've been studying French and dance, and working with a vocal coach. Pepito says, "J'ai Deux Amours" is just the beginning.

"When I realized those pictures were floating around, I knew they could ruin all my hard work. I asked Pippa to find them and get them for me. I only went to Natalie's place twice. Pepito made me promise to stay away from that salon. He said there were bad rumors about Natalie when she lived in Neuilly. How she had to move because she'd put on a play about Sappho with some women in her garden. Naked as jack rabbits. He told me I'd only get myself into trouble—which is exactly what I did."

Josie smiled as our server returned and set down our plates. She put the napkin on her lap and took a sip of the fizzy water he had just splashed into our glasses. I looked over my salad of mâche and chicory and glanced back at the macaroons one more time before tucking into a leaf lightly coated with a mustardy vinaigrette.

As soon as the waiter was gone, Josie picked up where she'd left off. "When Pepito told me about those business deals, I went straight back to Nat's. I asked her about the photographs, but she laughed and said she didn't know what I was talking about."

"Natalie doesn't have them. Pippa didn't either. Ollie has them. I invited her here so you could talk her into giving them to you."

"Ollie has them? I should have guessed, since it was her camera that took the pictures. Oh, what a fool I am."

"You'll get no argument from me. So, who is this Ollie Knolton?"

"The American heiress. Knolton Railroads? Doesn't ring a bell?"

I shook my head.

"She's a photographer. She took the pictures of me and Pippa at Pippa's place after that night at Natalie's. But I had nothing to do with her after that one wild evening at Natalie's. That's the truth, Bricky."

I looked at my watch. Ollie Knolton was very late. It was already a quarter past one.

"Ollie and Pippa got into a row over those photographs, Josie. You did something with Ollie that she can't seem to forget. Since she took the pictures, that means she has the negatives, too. How much does Pepito know about all of this?"

"He knows I went to the salon, but he doesn't know about the pictures. He can't know. There are some things a woman has to keep to herself. He would be spitting mad. He knows I have other lovers. He has them, too. He's not jealous though. We're partners, sometimes lovers, and very good friends."

Josie was his meal ticket. So, of course, he could tolerate some of her on-the-side dalliances. She had bedded that wily Ernie Hemingway as an *amuse-bouche* and had Colette as a *digéstif*.

"Josie, you have to tell Pepito," I hissed. "Who cares if he's mad at first? I'm running all over town, calling in favors, when it was you who created this ugliness. You took chances to have your fun, but you don't want to take any now. And yet you've put us all at risk. Telling him is the right thing to do, in case things go sideways with Ollie. He's your manager. Maybe he can help."

"I can't. I won't do it. He didn't know about Pippa."

I could have slapped her down right then and there.

"But didn't you just tell me that he knew you had other lovers?" I was on the verge of screaming full out—something I hadn't done in a long time. Something I was trying hard to avoid. Instead, I reached in my purse for an H. Upmann cigar. Mama shipped boxes at a time to me. For a long time, she thought that I was handing them out to my elite customers at Bricktop's. Eventually, she figured out that I was smoking them myself. But that's not exactly right. I didn't really smoke them. I only needed to light one up and inhale two or three times before the quiet came. Something about the smell of sweet oak and spices in those leaves calmed my nerves. Mama said it was because of Daddy. My doctor concurred. The well-to-do white clientele at his barbershop back in West Virginia gave him cigars as gifts, and their earthy fragrance could have reminded me of him. I was too young to remember much about my Daddy. I was only four years old when he died. But maybe they were right.

I inhaled deeply from the smoldering end before stubbing the cigar out in the white porcelain ashtray. Josie watched quietly as I went through the ritual that I had become accustomed to performing since my own personal crash in 1929. Everybody, even Josie, knew about my little crack-up two years earlier, though no one would dare to mention it to my face.

"You lie like a rug, Josie Baker," I said calmly now. "And if it weren't for the fact that this could all come tumbling down on us, I'd leave you here and never look back." I pushed my chair back and set my napkin on the table.

Josie started scrambling. She couldn't make a scene because she was Josephine Baker after all. She whispered as loud as she dared, "Bricky, No! Please don't go. Please sit down."

I rose to my feet, making her strain her face upward to talk to me.

"She wasn't like the lovers I'd had in the past. You can't tell a man that you're deeply in love with someone else and expect him to understand. I cared about Pepito's feelings. Okay? I'd never leave him, but I couldn't give Pippa up either. Naturally, I don't want those pictures to be discovered by him or anyone else. And I can't be connected to Pippa's death in any way imaginable. It would ruin me. But I care. I do care. About all of us."

I took my seat again, and we stared at each other in silence.

"Josie, I've known you for six years, but I just don't know who you've become over the last four." I was channeling Changchang now and hissing like a snake. "Did you kill Pippa Nelson for those pictures?"

"No!"

"Did you have someone kill her?"

"No!"

"Do you know who would have wanted Pippa Nelson dead, Josie?"

"Of course not!"

"Think, Josie. Did you know she was writing a story on the mob?"

"We didn't talk about her work except for the Americans in Paris story. The mafia?"

I nodded. "Do you care at all about who killed Pippa? Or is this just about saving your career and stepping over her dead body in the process?"

"Of course I care! I loved her! But what can I do, Brick?!"

"Stop lying!"

"I lied to you because I want your respect. I lied to protect myself and those I love." She held my stare before putting her head down like a chastened child.

I didn't believe Josie had a hand in Pippa's murder. Maybe I was blind to it. Maybe I had willed myself not to believe it.

"I've got to rehearse, Bricky. It's one thirty. Pepito makes a fuss when I'm late for practice. Ollie's not coming."

"At least we know who has the pictures, which would explain why no one has tried to blackmail you about them. Why don't you call Ollie? She wants to see you—not me. I'm sure she'll give you the pictures. Make sure to get the negatives, too, will you?"

Josie fingered one of the waves flattened against her round head. "I'll call her this afternoon. Thanks, Bricky. If she won't give me the pictures, I promise I'll tell Pepito. About all of it."

"Josie, keep your clothes on, unless you're in a chorus on stage. And stay away from any cameras that ain't at the theater, rolling for a movie, or clicking for a newspaper."

She winked as she slid her chair back to rise. She dropped a few franc notes on the table to cover the bill and tip. Though tipping wasn't customary in France, everyone appreciated a few extra francs these days.

We both looked out the window to see a black Delage pull up at the front of Ladurée. Pepito emerged from the driver's side of the French luxury vehicle.

"That's a pretty car, Miss Baker," I said in a lighter tone.

"The secret of my hair is Bakerfix, I buy my shoes at Perugia, I enjoy music from around the world on my Bitus portable radio, and, of course, I drive a Delage," Josie repeated almost mechanically, smiling and giving me her signature eye roll. Pepito had trained her to say that line to any and every reporter who listened. It was part of the Baker brand.

The last time I'd seen him close up, Pepito had been on the big screen, starring opposite Josie in her first film, a silent one, *Siren of the Tropics*. Watching him get out of the Delage, I saw that he was still handsome in a pinched-face kind of way, with his dyed jet-black hair slicked back and his dark-brown eyes rimmed by glasses. He wore a well-tailored suit and polished shoes. He was leaning on a cane, which he must have thought made him look fashionable. He was no Rudolph Valentino. But he tried real hard. He looked more the part of an aging Casanova. And he was I-talian to boot.

I debated whether to get up from my seat to greet him. He hadn't bothered coming into the tea salon. I wondered whether Josie had even told him she was coming to meet me. I decided to see. When she jumped up and ran outside, straight into Pepito's waiting arms, I followed shortly on her heels.

"Hi, Pepito. It's been awhile."

They both looked stunned.

"It has, Brick. How've you been?" He changed emotional registers smoothly and looked genuinely pleased to see me. Like he used to be when we first met.

"Just fine. I happened to run into Josie here as I was waiting for a friend for lunch. We've been catching up, haven't we Jo?"

I could see the calm descend on Josie's tense shoulders. She nodded, still beaming up at him. He smiled back. I thought about how nice it must be to be protected from Josie's betrayals. How he'd need more than that cane to support himself if he ever came upon the truth.

"Maybe we can come by the club sometime. It could be like old times," he offered.

It could never be like old times because I still had hard feelings about No Account. He had encouraged Josie to snub us. On that score, I was more like Natalie than I cared to admit. I forced a smile. "The Duke will be there this Tuesday," I said. "Maybe then."

The street felt bitter cold with the wind slicing through my coat and stinging my cheeks. "I need to get back in here and wait for my friend." I turned my back to them, when I heard someone call my name.

"Madame Bricktop! Madame Bricktop!"

"Officer Bergeron! How are you?" I waved at the officer as he exited the passenger side of a police vehicle.

Jean Bergeron was a French police officer. He always made sure I was looked after in Montmartre, so for a cop, I found him quite likeable. He was a tall, whiskery man with a warm smile. He usually worked in the Montmartre district. He was the first French officer on the scene after the Baron had attempted to extort me in my own club on his first visit to Bricktop's. Bergeron had told me to shoot the Baron the next time he came to Bricktop's. I just assumed he was being colorful.

That same afternoon back in late January, Jean had escorted me to the station and assisted me in completing the paperwork to register Mister Speaker and file a formal complaint against the Baron. Americans were always smuggling firearms, alcohol, and other contraband into France. No one in customs bothered to check our belongings. I always packed heat. But Jean suggested that if I ever had to use Mister Speaker, it would be better to be a registered gun owner with the prefecture. Otherwise, I could suffer the fate of the jazzman Sidney Bechet and get kicked out of my beloved France. It made sense. Truthfully, it was probably the only time in my life that I listened to the police.

"What are you doing on this side of town?" I hugged myself to keep warm. "Please forgive my manners. This is Officer Jean Bergeron. And this is Pepito Abatino and . . ."

"Joséphine Bakair," the officer said with a degree of familiarity.

Josie pulled herself even closer to Pepito, if that was at all possible. Her nervousness seemed to be catching as they both fidgeted like two criminals on the lam.

"Bonjour, Monsieur," Pepito piped up finally after the awkward silence, offering the cop his hand while balancing his cane and Josie's arm with the other. Josie gave a half-smile and nodded her greeting.

I wondered if Jean Bergeron was one of the officers who had interviewed Josie on Friday morning. That would certainly explain her skittishness and his familiarity. Or perhaps he just knew her like everyone else did. As a star from afar.

"I am on my way to interview a landlord across town in Saint-Germain. There was a terrible murder there Thursday evening of an American. Our new inspector is pulling in the most experienced officers from all the districts. *Alors*, Madame Bricktop did you receive your license, as yet?"

"Just last week. I'm sure you had something to do with expediting it. Thank you for that." I touched my thigh through my coat where Mister Speaker was lodged. But my smile was now frozen in place and it wasn't because of the cold. Jean Bergeron had mentioned the murder that Josie was questioned about. Partially hidden behind Pepito's coat, Josie's eyes were as wide as saucers.

"You must protect yourself," he continued."Remember what I explained. If he bothers you again . . ."

"How about I let you get back to keeping us Americans safe? Indeed, I've got a meeting with a friend," I said, cutting him off before he instructed me in front of Josie and Pepito to kill a man. I looked down at my watch to signal I needed to push off.

"*Au revoir*, Madame Bricktop. He grinned hard at Josie like a star-struck kid and ambled back to the police sedan parked in the middle of rue Royale.

I pushed open the door to Ladurée and prayed that in these last few minutes maybe Ollie Knolton would show up. I watched Pepito and Josie from the window.

The tense moment had passed. I saw her explaining something to him—probably some version of the truth about how we Negroes had learned to never trust the police. He was in love, from the look of it. Nodding his head in agreement, he squeezed her tighter and rocked her like he was protecting her. It occurred to me that maybe it was possible to love two people at the same time. You just loved them differently. Josie and Pippa had been in the honeymoon phase—like Peter and me—when that white woman met her maker. And Josie and Pepito had been at it so long, it was probably a comfortable and comforting love. I watched them snuggle. He pulled her close by the fur-trimmed neck of her tweed coat, burrowing his face in her warmth like she had been gone so long or was intending to leave for a spell, and he needed to remember what she smelled like. She hugged him real tight for a long while. It was then that I understood her lying, even if I didn't like it. She did deeply care for him.

The world really was Josie Baker's oyster. When she gave Pepito a deep kiss that made him smile a mile wide, I knew that Josephine Baker had something under her skirts that could make a bulldog hug a hound. I was thinking that she'd have those pictures soon enough and I'd have peace of mind.

But I was mostly thinking about how I would be able to hit my sheets again a little after two o'clock that afternoon, since Ollie never arrived.

SHADOW BOXING IN BABYLON

VI.

It was Saturday night at Bricktop's and just shy of 11:00 p.m., our official opening time. I was behind the bar tallying up bottles of spirits when Leroy, who had been practicing at the piano, started yelling, "The Champ is here! The Champ is here!"

You wouldn't have known that Leroy was nearly blind in his right eye from a hard punch during his days as a journeyman boxer. He was the best piano player in Paris in 1931 next to Jonny Dumont—I'm talking about Jonny before the drugs got the best of him. And even half-blind, Leroy could still pick out the legendary Jack Johnson from way across the room.

Papa Jack hadn't been the World Champion since 1915, but he remained our hero. He towered over me like a heavy, dark shadow, carrying a cane with a gold-dipped handle and tip. Gray stubble pricked the top of his massive shaved dome.

"Come here, Brick," he said, reaching out a large hand for me. He smiled, flashing his gold-rimmed teeth.

"Well isn't this is a pleasant surprise? Come and have a seat, baby." I reached up to give him a hug.

Tonight, Papa Jack was with wife number three, Irene Pineau, a frump of a *femme d'un certain age*, draped in an exquisite, floor-length chinchilla coat. A lot of pelts went into covering her wide behind. That's what I was thinking as I escorted them to a table and had Leroy bring over a bottle of whiskey with two glasses. After my own recent bout with whiskey, I was sticking to champagne.

"So what brings you two to Paris in the middle of winter?" I asked.

"I'm doing some exhibition fights. Thinking about opening a boxing school in Berlin. I'm getting too old for much else, Brick." The champ rubbed his bald head in such a way that I could hear the stubble scratching.

"Ain't we all? I don't how much longer I can keep up these hours, and here in Paris, we're still feeling the effects of the Big Crash. But I'm having too much fun to slow down much. And I bet you are, too."

My staff threw open the doors right on time, and the crowd started trickling in. Chez Bricktop would be packed with tourists by midnight, and the regulars would arrive anywhere from one until dawn.

"It's show time," I said. "But I'm having a little something at my place in the country on Sunday. A nice meal. I got Rhode Island Reds running wild and a great French cook. My Peter'll be home just for the day before heading out on Monday for the Netherlands. So we're celebrating. Will you come? Leroy will give you the directions. Say around two o'clock?"

Papa Jack wrapped his big brown hands around that whiskey bottle and poured himself a glass. "Thanks, Brick. A home-cooked meal would be lovely on a Sunday afternoon. We'll be there. And anything by Verdi would be nice as well. After this evening, I'll be all jazzed out."

"Baby, I got some opera and drama for you," I teased.

I signaled for Leroy and the band to warm things up. Tonight we were featuring Alberta Hunter. The Bricktop regulars loved her, especially when she sang "Downhearted Blues." Alberta was versatile. She could do upbeat cabaret and down-home blues with ease. And you could feel her blues when she sang the first line of that song: "Gee but it's hard to love someone when that someone don't love you." She might have been singing about Lottie Tyler. But I think she was reliving the meanness of the music industry that had stolen her song and given it to Bessie Smith. That song had made Bessie a star.

I walked around the club, greeting my customers at their tables, as they all expected an audience with Bricktop. I never lingered long; familiarity would have ruined that *je ne sais quoi* that I was so careful to cultivate.

"Charlie Wales!" I planted a kiss on a lean, blond white man with green eyes. "I thought you were back stateside."

"I'm in Paris on a week-long stop over from Prague. Business is still going strong, I see, Brick."

"For how much longer, I don't know. You didn't lose a lot in the markets?"

"Oh, I lost some and made a good deal back since then. But don't count on me parting with as much money as I used to at Bricktop's," he laughed. "The crash taught me a hard lesson. I need a drink though. I haven't had one in almost two years; I'd like to celebrate my sobriety."

I hadn't seen Charlie Wales since he left in 1928 right before the year that reversed everyone's fortunes in America. He was a mess toward the end of his stay in Paris, and I'd heard he'd been committed to a sanitarium to dry out.

"Where's Scotty?"

"He's headed over to the Casino de Paris to catch Josephine Baker doing 'chocolate arabesques,' as he calls them. Josephine Baker is really something to look at. At least he can look unmolested over here in France without being called . . . Well you know what they would call us for that kind of eyeballing."

Josie again. I smiled tightly.

I gave a quick "Umm hmm" so he wouldn't be tempted to say the word that began with an "n" and ended in an "r," followed by "lover." "I'll have a fine glass of whiskey sent over to you to celebrate your return to Bricktop's. You don't mind drinking alone, do you?"

"No, you go ahead, Brick. I'll sip that drink real slow and take in Alberta's show. Scotty will be here soon enough."

I left Charlie Wales with his eyes glistening and plopped down at the bar with my book. I always kept my ciphering book nearby. Someone was always asking for credit or a loan, especially in 1931. Charlie Wales was my second on-the-house drink of the evening. But once Scotty Fitzgerald arrived, I'd more than recoup my losses. I'd heard he was writing again, which meant he was back in the black. And soon enough, he'd be back in the red again, from drinking and carousing. Those two were the epitome of dissipation. I pitied the women who loved them.

I wasn't at my barstool long before Changchang whispered in my ear that I was needed somewhere. She handed me an address on a slip of paper. I recognized it immediately: "4 rue Princesse, 4th floor." It was Ollie Knolton's place.

⌒

My stomach did a little flip. "Did she leave a number?"

Changchang shook her head, sending her long tresses flying. She was wearing a pretty hair pin made of multicolored crystals that caught the light. I wondered who had given it her. "Did she say what she wanted?"

"She said, 'Tell her to please come.' It wasn't Ollie Knolton who called Aunt Ada. It was Miss Josie."

That got my attention. "That's all Josie said?"

"Umm hmm. It's about those photographs?" Changchang asked me.

"I just don't know, baby. Josie was supposed to take care of it but we haven't heard a peep from her until now so—"

"I get the picture," said Changchang. "We'd better get over there and wrap this business up, once and for all."

"We? I hate to disappoint you, but I need you to stay here by the phone. Call Mabel in to cover things out front, and tell her no IOUs tonight."

Mabel Mercer and I had gone into the Bricktop's business together. With her singing and my special kind of meet-and-greet saloonkeeping, I knew we'd be an unbeatable team. I also knew how hard it was for Mabel to say "No." I'd just have to deal with any fallout from the customers when I returned. I was a stickler about the accounting, and Mabel couldn't count to save her life. Or maybe she was too gracious to keep track of who owed what.

"Brick, I need to talk to you for a minute," a man's voice interrupted my tête-à-tête with Changchang.

"What you need, Mr. Dumont?" Changchang glared at him for the interruption. She knew exactly what he needed. It was clear that Jonny Dumont was not high tonight. He was shaking again.

"I don't wanna talk to you. I wanna talk to Brick."

"What is it, Jonny? Get him a shot of strong bourbon, Changchang. That should help."

"Thank you, Brick." Jonny took a seat next to me as I folded up the scrap of paper with Ollie's address and tucked it into my purse.

"Do you really want to be supporting his habit, Aunt Ada? He needs to dry out."

Changchang had very little sympathy for addicts. She had fended off too many of them back in Harlem when they'd tried to rob her.

"Get the drink, Changchang," I repeated. "Now, what can Bricky do for you this evening, Jonny?"

"I was wondering if I could play here tonight?"

"Jonny, you're in no condition to play. Look at you shaking. You already spent the money you made last night on dope. No, Jonny," I said shaking my head. "You know I can't allow that. Besides, Leroy is my piano man now. If you want to play anyplace decent again, you've got to clean yourself up."

"I know that's what you want, Brick," he said, resting both hands on the stool to steady himself upright. "But maybe I don't wanna clean myself up. I like me just fine. It's just I can't take the lows, and without a regular income, I can't avoid them. I need a steady job."

"I really can't help you then, can I?" I hated the cold, firm tone of my own voice, but I knew it was necessary.

Changchang arrived with his bourbon just as he was making this last pitiful confession. "That's right. You can't help him. At all. You can't save the whole race, Aunt Ada. Not in this lifetime. You already cut him loose, and that's that."

I couldn't help thinking about Mama and poor Mr. Clovis, the soda pop king. It hadn't been easy for her to throw that nice man out of our rooming house, and it had been damn hard for me to fire Jonny. But there comes a time when you have to give up and let go—even when you admire someone's talent and who they used to be before the dope took over.

Jonny picked up the bourbon and gulped it down. I could have sworn I saw his pink tongue greedily lick the bottom of that glass. "You sure is a hardhearted young woman," he said to Changchang, who was paying him no mind.

Jonny gazed wistfully at Leroy at the piano and tried one more time. "Please, Brick. I need the work." The drink had started to have some effect. His shaking eased up. He was mellower than when he'd arrived. "You know how good I am."

"I know how good you were, Jonny. And it breaks my heart. But there's nothing I can do for you. Not until you get yourself straightened out. And then, only as a fill-in." I turned my back to him, just as Mama would have wanted. I was a businesswoman with a reputation to uphold, and a dope-taking Jonny Dumont was bad for my business.

"Time to go, Mr. Dumont," Changchang smiled. "You're upright enough now to find you some work banging on somebody else's piano. Try across town where nobody knows your habit."

Jonny rose from his chair. "One mean turn deserves another," he said, gruffly. And then he headed for the door.

The piano player's words gave me a chill, but I shook it off. Sometimes there's just no way to fix what's broke.

∾

"I've got your back, Aunt Ada. Don't you worry about the club tonight, we'll be just fine." Changchang tapped her chest to remind me where she kept her folding knife—right between her breasts. "You taking Mister Speaker?"

I got up from the barstool and smiled up at her. "Never go out without him."

"Good," said Changchang.

I felt a rush of affection for my feisty protégé. When I'd left New York for Paris seven years ago, I had promised my almost-niece that I would send for her as soon as I could manage it. There was nothing for a dreamy girl like her in Harlem but hard times, hard liquor, and hard men. It had taken me close to six years, and now here she was. And I loved her like she was my own.

∾

On a Saturday evening, the cafés and clubs in Saint-Germain were all lit up and lively. Brasserie Lipp, Café de Flore, and Les Deux Magots reigned supreme on the main boulevard. Ollie's apartment sat atop a bakery on a short, quaint side street that was filled with crêperies, restaurants, and apartments with barren flower boxes just waiting for spring to return so they could burst into color again. I tipped the taxi driver and found the main entry door to her walkup ajar. There was a car parked down the street toward rue du Four with a man seated on the driver's side, and smoke was billowing out the window.

I couldn't find the light in the corridor, which gave me a bad feeling. Now, I wished that I had let Changchang tag along for backup. But I shrugged off my anxiety. The sooner I made sure that those pictures and negatives were out of circulation, the sooner I could return to Bricktop's. I eased along the wall, holding onto the railing as I hauled myself up three flights of stairs, and then I squinted at the doors along the hallway, trying to decipher which one belonged to Ollie.

A sudden voice, hoarse and upset, said, "Shhh. It's me."

"Josie?" I shouted, nearly leaving my stockings in my shoes. I was still gasping for air, after that climb.

Hands reached for me in the dark. I had been so busy looking down and counting the never-ending steps that I'd missed the person hiding in the blackness between the two windows.

"Who else?! Now pipe down and stop that racket!"

All I could see was an outline of her shadow in the gloom. "Why the hell did you call me over here? Got me leaving my club and carrying on. Where is Ollie?" I put my hand to my chest to slow my fast-beating heart.

As I stepped further into the hallway, I could make out Josie's features from a streetlamp faintly streaming light through the windows. Her face was puffy and her eyes looked swollen from crying. I'd predicted wrong about Josephine Baker's unique powers of persuasion. She and Ollie had clearly had a knock-down-drag-out over those damned photographs.

"She's dead, Bricky." Josie started bawling quietly.

My voice caught in my chest. "Where is she?"

Josie led me to the entrance of Ollie's apartment. I groped around and found a light I could switch on. Ollie's place was compact and neat with expensive furniture and wall-hangings that were a blur to me as I rushed through the fair-sized salon, passing an image of Cole Porter's mirthful smile on the wall. I glanced into a tiny bathroom but didn't see a kitchen. Ollie was too busy to care to cook, and she'd clearly had the means to eat out. It felt surreal, thinking of her eating habits in the past tense.

The bedroom door was open and an odd smell rushed at me—a strange combination of cigarettes, wine, and something nasty.

"I can't be here, Bricky. I can't. You told me to see her. You told me . . ."

"Hush, fool." I made a motion with my hands to shut her up.

"You told me . . . I can't be here. I can't be here. No! No!" Josie sounded like a scratched record, repeating the same lines and blubbering in between.

"What?"

I quickly turned to look at Josephine, but she was gone. I heard her heels clickety-clacking down the steps, and the main entry door slammed with a bang before I could get a word out. I heard a car start up and peel off in the distance.

Ollie's bedroom was wrecked. The mattress had been ripped with something sharp. Bed stuffing was everywhere. Pillow feathers had wafted around her body. There were opened drawers, spilling over with expensive undergarments and hosiery. Clothes were strewn on the floor. Ollie was lying nude on the disheveled bed. The skin on her arms and legs looked mottled and bruised. There was a pillow where her face and neck should have been with two bullet holes in it. Blood had started to pool and dry on the mattress and floor. That was the rank odor I smelled. It was warm in that room from the heater, which contributed to the bedroom's fetid air.

I was a saloonkeeper and a cabaret singer. Guns, knives, blood, and death were part of the trade. I had seen it all in Chicago and Harlem and now Paris. I didn't bother removing the pillow, though. Why trouble my dreams? Ollie hadn't stood a chance. It looked like maybe she'd been sleeping when she was killed. Unlike Pippa, who had struggled and was battered and shot. Ollie's hands were stiff, covered in black and blue developing fluids. Her fingers, with chipped and jagged nails, were splayed and upright like she was trying to push back against a last death rattle.

I looked around the room, torn between looking for photographs and running out the door. My eyes fell on the bag that Ollie had carried at Natalie's the night I met her. The night she'd shown me the pictures. I peered into the satchel's gaping hole. There was no envelope this time. Josie had most likely collected what she came for.

I backed out of the room slowly as a dark thought entered my mind: Josie called me from Ollie's apartment. I started to dry heave, and sweat rolled down my armpits to my waist. Every one of Josie's hugs from the moment she'd walked into Bricktop's was a search mission for a soft place to stick the knife in and turn it. I ran out of Ollie's apartment, leaving the lights on. When I got to the sidewalk, I slowed my gait so as not to draw attention. Despite the cover of nightfall, my red hair would be a siren to passersby. Even the freckles on my nose felt like beacons of red light.

My mind was clicking over the possibilities. Two white women had been murdered. Could it really be about those scandalous photographs, or was something else going on? Pippa's death didn't make sense if Ollie had the photographs. And no one seemed to know Ollie had them, not even Josie until I told her. A voice in my head said, *Bricky, it's not about the photographs.* "No, it probably isn't," I said aloud, thinking about the missive Lang had left for me this morning

A dark-haired man smoking a cigar on the street near a bookshop/café looked up at the sound of my voice. I turned away quickly so he couldn't get a clear picture of my face.

"*Bonsoir, Madame,*" he said solicitously. "*Voulez-vous prendre un verre?*"

I probably looked like I needed a drink. But I didn't utter a word.

"*Putain!*"

I backtracked those few steps and hauled off and slapped him hard on the cheek. The cigar flew out of his mouth and bounced on the pavement. He stepped back rubbing his jaw. He gave me a sly grin like he thought I was a tease and reached out to grab at my breasts. I could smell vodka coming off his breath. This time I punched his nose. Hard. It was a blow that should have landed on Josie, but it felt damn good all the same.

"Merde!" he slurred. "Putain de merde!"

His nose sprayed blood, and I did my best to dodge the splatter. I then kicked him hard on the shin. "No, you didn't just call me a whore with your cheap-ass cigar," I muttered as he slumped down on the cold concrete, howling pathetically.

Trying to hail a taxi now would certainly jog memories later, especially with that bloody-nosed, drunken bastard screaming to the high heavens. So I walked, slowly at first and then picking up speed as I got further from Ollie's place. I turned off rue Princesse, moving across rue du Four with its upscale clothing stores and high-end art galleries. I slinked past a café where a smattering of well-heeled tourists had gathered to sip coffee under a brightly lit awning. When I finally reached Place Saint-Germain, I paused to steady my breathing, taking in the glowing lights that streamed off the façade of the stone church nestled on the square. And then I continued on to rue Jacob. I needed some information and a telephone.

I rang the bell this time and waited, hoping the hostess herself would answer. I didn't want to be seen going to Natalie's two nights in a row. I got lucky. She did, in fact, let me in, and I could hear a gaggle of women, their voices rising and falling in the next room. But when she smiled wide and turned to escort me into the salon, I balked.

"I came to see you. Alone." I looked down at my dress to see if the nose-bleeder had sprayed me. Red dots were sprinkled over my tawny satin shoes. I'd have to find a way to keep my feet hidden under my long dress. Under the circumstances, I didn't want to have to explain blood droplets to Natalie.

"What is this cloak and dagger about, Brick?" Her teeth were clenched. "I suppose you're too cat's meow to be seen around here with us queers?"

I thought about the mysterious devils out there doing these ofays in. Maybe I should draw a roadmap direct to Natalie's place and let them pop a cap in her mangy ass next. "Stop beating your gums, Nat. I don't have time right now for foolishness. You Miss Annes jump so salty when you think us colored ladies are snubbing you. You hear me?"

I was still shivering from the walk over in my thin shawl, and my dogs were hurting something awful in my high heels that were now ruined by my trek across town and that foul-mouthed Frenchman. A sick wave went through my body. It had now caught up to my head, which was pulsating with a red anger. Josie had left me holding the bag in a rich, dead white woman's apartment.

Damn you, Josephine Baker.

"It might interest you to know that somebody filled Ollie Knolton with daylight."

Natalie's eyes widened. She led me to a small alcove that served as a library and closed the door behind us. I took a seat on a cushioned bench tucked into a corner and reached into my bag for a handkerchief to wipe my brow. I was chilled but sweating. I draped my shawl over my lap and it formed a sort of silk throw at my feet. I kept my shoes tucked under it, as I began massaging my soles.

"Wh—What? Ollie? When? How do you know?"

It was the first time I had ever seen the cool Natalie Barney flummoxed—a priceless sight, though I would have preferred to discover it under less tragic circumstances.

I looked at my watch. It was now twenty past midnight. "It happened sometime between this morning when she left my club and this evening. I saw her, Nat. She was shot gangland style—just like what happened to Pippa. Did she go home alone?"

"Of course! Lily Simkins dropped her off by taxi. She was in no condition but to ride. Oh, my. First Pippa and now Ollie! Who would do this?" The Amazon looked calm, but her dainty fists were tightened to an ashen white.

"I was hoping you'd have some answers, Nat. I didn't know either one of them. At least not well. All I know is she tried to solicit my company after five minutes of chatting, so I wondered if she might have gotten unlucky with someone else. How well did Pippa and Ollie know one another?"

"They were both Midwesterners. Pippa was from Chicago. Ollie's family was from Minnesota. She was part of the Knolton Railroad family dynasty. Her brother is in the South of France. It'll be a circus in the newspaper society pages. Ollie and Pippa met here about two years ago. They became fast friends because of the Midwest connection. Ollie was doing some photography for Pippa, shooting scenes of the haunts of the French and American gangsters for a story. Pippa worked for *The International New York Review*. They wouldn't pay for a photographer to come to Paris—no resources in this terrible economy. So she asked Ollie. Ollie's rich, so she didn't need money and she had plenty of time. She liked adventure. Pippa, on the other hand, thought that this story with those pictures would catapult her into the major leagues like *The New Yorker*. Renata warned her it was too risky. The rest of us egged her on. Truth be told, we thought it would be great for Pippa's career. Do you think that's why they were killed?" Natalie's eyes burned with anguish.

I was glad she was so forthcoming. Death will do that to you. Jolt you into truth-telling.

"It could be," I responded. "That would make it simple. But to be honest, Nat, I don't really know."

I continued rubbing my feet. I could usually stand all night in high-heeled shoes, but tonight's escapades had required running, climbing, falling into doors, walking over cobblestones, and kicking a jackass. My slim-heeled shoes were ruined, and I groaned at the prospect of putting them back on my blistered feet when it was time to leave. I looked up to find Natalie eying me with suspicion. I checked to see that my shawl was still covering the blood droplets on my shoes.

"Why were you at Ollie's, Brick?"

For a moment, I was tempted to confide in Natalie about Josie's phone call, and how she'd run out on me, right after calling me to a murder scene. But the idea of criticizing a colored woman in front of a white woman—even a sympathetic one—was out of the question. So I stuck with the half-truth. I mentioned that Ollie and I had agreed to meet to discuss her wanting to photograph me. I didn't tell her our meeting was scheduled for lunch. I explained that, obviously, I had arrived well after Ollie and her pillow got better acquainted.

I couldn't resist asking, "Was Josie a Women's Academy member?" There I went again, hoping that not everything Josie said and did was a lie.

"No. What laurels would our little Académie des femmes bring to her? On the other hand, who would have refused *her* company?"

I still didn't know if Josie had retrieved those photographs from hell, so I couldn't help bringing them up to Nat. A voice in my pounding head was saying, *They could still destroy us all, Bricky. So keep digging.* "I heard Ollie and Pippa had a falling out over some pictures."

"Oh, not you too, Brick. Tell Josie her secret's safe with us. To the grave, at this rate. There *was* a to-do about the photographs. Pippa wanted all of them for some reason. Ollie offered her copies but that wasn't good enough for Pippa. Ollie was accustomed to having things her way. She wanted keepsakes of that evening. As far as I know, Ollie still has them. Or had them."

"Do you know if anyone else asked for copies? Any of the other Academy members?"

"There were eight women in the pictures, including Ollie and Pippa. If they did ask, Ollie wasn't sharing. She liked Pippa well enough and was absolutely enamored of Josie. As for the rest, there wasn't enough of that kind of love to go around. I was there when they took the photos. I sometimes like to watch. I've had them all at one time or another. Except Josie, to my everlasting regret. Lucky girls, they all were, especially Pippa. We all thought so."

I wasn't interested in Natalie's fantasies or her conquests. "I need to get myself home," I told Nat. "May I use your telephone?"

"Do you think we should call the police?" She fiddled with the pearl drop pendant necklace dangling from her swan-like neck.

I felt the heat rise to my face. I had been so interested in finding out more about Ollie and Pippa that it completely slipped my mind that Natalie Barney could now put me in the bedroom of the dead white woman. I had to tie off this loose end.

"Well, Nat I don't know. I mean there are now two dead women. Both of them belonged to your little academy. That's a strong connection for the police. This might line up with the theory that the Women's Academy is "a queer sex cult that engages in the ritual sacrifice of your members." I quoted her line back at her.

She grimaced. The effect of which was to deepen the lines in her alabaster forehead. "Oh God." She began to twist the fragile gold chain of the necklace.

I knew the police would discover Josie's phone call soon enough. But I didn't need Natalie making any introductions before the moment of reckoning. Natalie was as fiercely protective of the Académie des femmes as I was of Chez Bricktop. With the sting of that glib comment—fresh from her very own mouth to my ears—she would only give this Inspector Gravois names, professions, and places of birth at her Monday interview. Self-interest was also a hell of a motivator to silence.

In my stocking feet and closely clutching my ripped footwear, I followed Nat into a bedroom to place my phone call, careful to avoid the gathering in the salon.

෴

When Changchang drove up in the Citroën at one that morning, I limped to the car, wincing as my feet made contact with the hard, cold pavement. I threw my ruined shoes onto the floor of the car, cursing at them. Changchang passed me the spare pair of shoes I had requested and I almost wept with relief.

"We got trouble, Aunt Ada?"

"We do. Part of it's ours, and part of it's not, baby."

"Miss Josie again?"

"Umm hmm. That low-down, backstabbing heifer. Ollie Knolton was already dead when Josie made that call. Murdered. Josie called me over to that apartment and then ran like some kind of crying banshee."

"I'm so sorry, Aunt Ada. She wasn't crying or anything when she left the message."

"Not your fault," I said. "Josie can be quite an actress when she's properly inspired."

Did anybody see you?"

"I don't think so. Not leaving the apartment, at least. And I wore gloves in the apartment. I did have to clock a foul-mouthed Frenchie on her street though. He got a good eyeful of me. I need to get rid of these shoes. His blood is on them. Hopefully, he's just a stray dog roaming the neighborhood."

"Aunt Ada! That should teach you to practice what you preach. You're always telling me to practice restraint. Act like a lady."

"So you've been listening? I hope you're learning."

"I listen real well."

"He called me a whore." I frowned.

"And you didn't shoot him!?" she shook her head incredulously.

"Exactly. He's still living to curse about the beating I gave him in return. Keep your hands on the steering wheel. Now you understand what I mean about restraint. He should've been dead as the snake who gave up his skin for these here shoes I'm wearing," I grumbled.

"So you think Miss Josie could've killed both those white women over those photographs?"

"Maybe. Or maybe the mafia killed them over Pippa's mafia story. I tell you, Changchang. I can't help worrying that they're working with Josie. They had common interests—to make certain things or people disappear. Looks like Josie grabbed those pictures from Ollie's tonight. What if she sacrificed Pippa and Ollie to the mafia, in exchange for the photographs?"

Changchang furrowed her eyebrows. "You think Miss Josie would stoop that low?"

"I don't know what to think. But it sure looks like she's involved. They killed the story, her lover, and the photographer along with it. Everything's suddenly copacetic. On the other hand, Josie seemed genuinely upset. She kept saying, 'I can't be here' and 'You told me to see her.' Which I had. She's not that great of an actress. I believe she really loved Pippa Nelson. I just have a sinking feeling I'm looking at this whole thing upside down."

"Do you want me to find her?"

"No!" I knew what that meant: Josie turning up with a Cheshire cat grin across her throat.

I wiped my brow again. "I need a Stanback." Removing my kid gloves, I searched my purse for the analgesic. Putting the white powder on my tongue, I swallowed hard, trying to make saliva to wash it down. I was running hot and cold with a headache and anger. I lowered the car window and gulped in fresh air. "Josie will get her comeuppance, if she's involved," I said. "And we'll leave those dead white women to rest where they lie."

"That way everybody's safe," Changchang nodded. "Even Miss Josie. Then you can serve your dish cold, Aunt Ada." She was driving the car toward Bougival. "We'll dump those shoes in the river toward the Marais district. Unless they're looking for a body, the police won't dredge the Seine in that part of town anytime soon."

"Umm hmm," I nodded.

Young folks were always thinking about revenge. Me? I preferred justice.

THE GAME OF INSPECTOR AND SALOONKEEPER

VII.

I woke up Sunday morning in the arms of my Peter. Oh, what a handsome man he was, tall and lean with deep-brown eyes and a fetching New Orleans drawl. It was his smile that first caught me. He was playing his saxophone when he looked up and saw me staring at him across the club. Josie had just pointed him out. I swore I saw him smile, even with that horn still in his mouth. His dark eyes danced over me and seemed to say, "I'm for you. You can stop looking now." When Josie introduced me as Bricktop, he studied me hard and made up his mind to call me Red. Peter and I were still newlyweds, and I couldn't get enough of him. I had arrived at two that morning and woken Peter out of a sound sleep. It was never too late or too early to make love to one another.

Even when he was fast asleep and snoring, I took him for a real prize. I rose to freshen up, leaving *mon mari*, Peter, sleeping. He was a jazzman from the New Orleans Ducongé family. I knew we shouldn't have married, but I got swept up in the romance of Paris and my success. I thought I could succeed at anything—even marriage, despite all my misgivings about love and men, and Mama's loveless luck after Daddy died. A traveling jazzman and a café grande dame living happily ever after was an impossible dream, but I was in love and willing to try. Peter was easygoing, not high strung and controlling. We gave each other leeway. He accepted me for who I was. A lot of men wanted Bricktop, the glamorous public figure. But they didn't actually like me. Peter didn't mind my strong will. He liked me and he loved me all the same. Most times you get one without the other.

Making my way downstairs, I ran into Claire, our French housekeeper and cook. She and Alain, the butler and gardener, stayed in the house in Bougival while I was in Paris, and they always had the place nice and toasty by the time Peter and I arrived. It was a good and restful homecoming after so many long nights and early mornings in Paris. I longed to spend more time out there, enjoying the simple and clean countryside.

Claire greeted me with a smile. "Madame, would the Monsieur like some *café?*"

"He's still sleeping. But I'll have my tea by the fireplace in the salon. We're having guests over for an early Sunday supper at two o'clock this afternoon. Sorry I didn't tell you earlier this morning when I arrived. I just wanted my bed." *And my man in it.*

"I'll go into town to the *marché.*" Claire was humming the popular French tune by Lucienne Boyer, *"Parlez-moi d'amour."*

I found myself humming along. Lucienne had auditioned at Bricktop's before she became a household name. She had a nice set of pipes, but I'd heard she was a terror to work with. I didn't tolerate prima donnas at Bricktop's, so she'd found her own way to the big time without my help.

"Will you drive?" I asked Claire.

"*Non.* I prefer to walk, Madame. *Il fait beau, aujourd'hui.*"

"It's lovely weather, today" was one of the few French phrases I quickly picked up. The French appreciate a beautiful day, even if the air is *un peu frais* this time of year, so they can take a stroll outdoors. All that strolling explained why Claire, a grandmother, had the energy and legs of a thirty-six-year-old like me.

I stepped outside for a moment. The sun was out and it was unusually warm. It was a day for heavy sweaters rather than winter coats. Claire pulled out her little shopping wagon and headed into town.

Watching Claire march down the drive with the clear blue sky above, a warm yellow light filtering down through the naked trees, and morning dew atop the grass, I thought of impressionist paintings. I had been drawn to Bougival because it was fashionable. But it was fashionable because it was the cradle of impressionism. I couldn't paint worth a lick, but I did appreciate art. Enough artists frequented Bricktop's—Picasso, Matisse, Man Ray and Kiki. I considered myself an artist—a performance one.

I felt at home in Bougival.

When Claire returned, it was late morning. I could hear the wheels of the shopping carriage turning over the rock-strewn driveway. When she opened the door, she had a scowl on her face as though all the fruit at the market had been rotten, and the butter rancid. "Madame, the police are here to see you."

"The police?" I repeated, my eyebrows shooting up to my hairline.

"*Oui,*" Claire said as she put away her sweater in the hall closet.

"Give me a moment before you have Alain answer the door."

Had something gone wrong at the club? Surely, if anything catastrophic had occurred, Changchang or Mabel would have telephoned me.

"Madame Smith Ducongé *sera là dans un instant, Messieurs.*"

I was startled when Alain said "Madame Smith Ducongé," forgetting for a second that he was referring to me.

"Good morning," I greeted the three policemen. "How can I help you all on this beautiful Sunday morning?"

One of the officers was Jean Bergeron. "*Tout à fait, tout à fait. Il fait beau,*" said Bergeron. "Madame Bricktop," he continued with nervous formality, "my superior, Inspector Gilles Gravois, would like to speak with you."

I did a running tally in my mind of licenses and important papers. I had a current liquor license, an up-to-date club license. My taxes were paid. My passport had not expired. I stayed clear of the protection rackets and had even allowed a French singer and band to try out for the club per the French quota system. I didn't hire them. They were terrible. But that wasn't my fault.

I was on good terms with the law-upholding French police, but clearly I was on the hot seat for something. I thought about the Baron. I put a neutral expression on my face. "What's this about?"

Inspector Gravois stepped forward. "Good morning, Madame Ducongé, we have some questions to ask you."

"Smith Duongé," I corrected him.

He hesitated, rubbing his moustache before delivering the unpleasantness.

"An American, Mademoiselle Olive Knolton, was found murdered early this morning."

I almost dropped my cup of tea. I put it down quietly before they could see my hands shaking. "Olive Knolton. Should I know her? And if I did, it certainly wasn't very well," I hedged.

"*Non?* She was at your establishment in the twilight hours of Saturday morning with a group of women called, let's see," he reached into a pocket and pulled out a notepad, "Académie des femmes. She's a photographer."

I stared at him blankly. "*Et bien?*"

"*Et bien?* Madame Duongé, we are investigating a death, a murder."

"Yes, I've understood that. It's Smith Duongé, please."

"Did you speak with Miss Knolton?" Gravois was ignoring my correction and refusing to apologize for calling me out of my name.

"I might have. I try to chat with all my guests. That's what makes Bricktop's Bricktop's, Inspector Gravois."

"*Si, si, si,*" Officer Jean Bergeron intervened, "Madame Bricktop, we have been given information that leads us to believe that you knew Mademoiselle Knolton well."

Inspector Gravois stamped his foot and put his hand up to silence the younger officer. Bergeron had given up too much information. And he had done it intentionally, to help me. Inspector Gravois wanted to catch me in a lie. Even without Bergeron's help, I understood how to lie to the police without lying. I had practiced it for years—growing up in Chicago, and then making my way in New York City. Lucky for me, it seemed that I hadn't lost my edge in France.

"You've been misled. I'm sorry to say."

"I don't think so, Madame. Our sources are fairly reputable," Bergeron chimed in again.

"Officer Bergeron," Gravois interrupted with a hot glare. "Why not wait in the car outside while I finish up here?"

Bergeron looked confused and, for a moment, hurt, but then he collected himself, ready to follow orders. "*Mais oui*, good day Madame."

"I promise we have only a few more questions," said the Inspector. He waited until Bergeron had left the room. Then he nodded to the other officer who abruptly followed Bergeron, out to the black sedan.

Inspector Gravois made himself comfortable on the chair across from me.

"Do you mind if I have a seat?" he asked, after he had already planted his rear end on my cushions.

I didn't care for this police inspector—probably because he seemed to think I'd murdered Olive Knolton. He reminded me of the sleazy New York policemen who took kickbacks up in Harlem and still rousted numbers runners on general principle, even after they had received their payments. He was just more refined with his fancy trench coat, handmade shoes, French accent, and graying mane of hair. As he leaned forward, I could smell the coffee and cigarettes on his breath and see the tobacco stains on his bottom front teeth. I turned my face to catch my breath.

"I am French, Madame. I like French things," he whispered. "I don't particularly care for all you Americans in Paris with your vulgar music, vile dancing, and violent gangster movies. All your so-called artists rushing to France to escape whatever ails you at home in America. I am a tolerant man though. I have come to accept this American," he waved his hand dismissively, "cultural invasion."

The Frenchman sniffed. "After all, you did stem the bloodletting around Verdun in 1918. I lost a son there, but you helped save another at Argonne. Whatever my gratitude, I can assure you Madame, I will not tolerate murder. And there have been two murders of American women in Paris over the past three evenings."

Inspector Gravois thought of us expatriates as nothing more than a bunch of rabble-rousing Americans, making no distinction about color or class. That alone would have made a heap of colored and white Americans back home and here in Paris fit to be tied. I almost admired his colorblind prejudice against Americans. If nothing else, it was refreshing.

"I am a business owner, Inspector Gravois. I pay my taxes and cause no trouble. I can assure you that I am not involved in any messy murders of white American women."

"I did not say the women were, as you call them in America, white, Madame Ducongé." Inspector Gravois's eyes twinkled as he readied himself to pounce on me again with evidence of my untruths.

"You didn't have to. You said Olive Knolton was with the Académie des femmes. Every American in Paris knows that their membership is as white as bleached cotton."

"*D'accord*," he conceded, ruefully. "You also visited the residence of Natalie Barney, where you were seen speaking at length with Miss Knolton."

I didn't respond. At first, I thought he was referring to the tête-à-tête Natalie and I had just after midnight. I shook off that temporary panic. My mind was playing all the angles. At least twenty people saw me talking to Ollie Knolton.

Sensing an opening, he continued. "*Vous voyez*, Madame Ducongé, *mon dilemme* is that I have two witnesses that put you in the company of the deceased woman on two separate occasions and at two different places— on the same night before Mademoiselle Knowlton was murdered. Are you certain you want to stand by your original answer to my question that you didn't know her very well? Miss Knolton even gave you her private address, according to one source."

Two sources. Josie and Natalie? Women's Academy members? Had to be someone at the club. Natalie and Josie were not at the club. Who saw her give me that slip of paper? Keep it simple.

"As I said, Inspector Gravois, I try to speak to all my guests at Bricktop's. If she gave me her address, she might have wanted to pay for Charleston or Black Bottom lessons. I give those as well. I have references here in Paris, quite reputable ones like Lady Mendl or Mr. Cole Porter, should you care to follow up. I really don't recall this Miss Knolton. People give me their cards all the time, hoping to become fast friends. They sometimes interpret my hostessing efforts as an opening for a personal friendship. But I'm just a businesswoman who believes in catering to her clientele.

"As for Miss Barney's residence, I may have spoken to Olive Knolton there. I mingled, as is my nature. I was also a guest who happens to know the owner fairly well. All her guests came to my club that morning, as I recall."

"Did you know a Mademoiselle Pippa Nelson?"

My pounding heart accelerated. "No I didn't. Was she at Miss Barney's home that evening?"

He didn't respond to my question. Inspector Gravois wasn't buying any of it, but he couldn't contradict it either. He didn't have enough to haul my behind in. But this was just his first run. That's how the French police worked. They didn't kick your ass and take names later. They interrogated you, went back to check for inconsistencies, and then hounded you until you were cornered.

"Why were you visiting Miss Barney? You've said that their group is made up of white American women. To my eyes, Madame, you look as white as they do, but you call yourself a Negro."

I nodded my head, silently thanking Lang for the cover. I was cautious nonetheless, because we were veering back into Pippa Nelson territory. "I'm a Negro, Inspector Gravois. In the past, Miss Barney was a frequent guest at Bricktop's. I went to her place to deliver a book. I thought she would enjoy it at her literary salon. On Fridays, they do readings. Bricktop's is also a lending library. We expatriates like to share ideas." I didn't tell him that I took Lang's book right back from Nat's spidery-veined hands. I wasn't about to part with a gift Lang had personally given to me.

"A book?" he repeated incredulously, swallowing hard.

"Of poetry. Yes."

"The title, Madame?"

"*Dear Lovely Death*, by Mr. Langston Hughes."

Inspector Gravois smirked and pulled at his moustache. He had not spoken to Natalie, or else he would have known these facts. He probably remembered that he was to meet with her on the following day—Monday. Natalie wouldn't be of much help to him anyway. She'd be covering her own flank. That left Josie. I had never told her about Ollie coming to Bricktop's. She had given Changchang Ollie's address over the telephone so she didn't know I already had it, and I had never mentioned it. *The telephone call . . .*

"Is there a problem?" Peter's voice called out.

"No, baby. Inspector Gravois was just about to leave, weren't you?"

I stood up, as my husband approached us both.

Gravois sighed and rose, nodding toward Peter. "Bonjour, Monsieur. I shall not continue to disturb you any longer on this lovely morning."

I called toward the kitchen, "Claire, could you see the Inspector to the door?" The house was so still that I could hear Alain scraping pottery against wood in the hothouse herb garden outside.

She pushed open the heavy oak kitchen door, a dead chicken swinging by its neck from one hand. "Oui, Madame."

"Good day, Inspector Gravois," I said, turning my back to him and stepping into Peter's outstretched arms. I reached up to peck him on those soft lips and run my hand over his closely cropped brown curls. He smelled fresh, like sandalwood and toothpaste.

"If I may inquire, Madame Ducongé. Do you own a revolver?"

I was the one swallowing this time. Hard. "I own a peacemaker. In my line of work, you need one for the rowdy customers, conmen, gangsters, and police on the take."

Inspector Gravois stroked his moustache and grinned, again giving me an eyeball full of those stained teeth. "Ah, yes. There was one other detail I forgot to mention. Early this morning on rue Princesse, a gentleman was pummeled by a woman fitting your description. It seems quite a coincidence with all of this. You having Miss Knolton's address, there is her murder, and then an uninvolved stranger arrives at the Saint-Germain precinct to file a report about an assault by a well-dressed redhead in a hurry around the time of Miss Knolton's death."

I turned slowly from Peter's embrace. My eyes darted around the salon to the solid walnut rolltop desk. I walked casually over to the desk as I contemplated my response. "Was this 'redhead in a hurry' colored or white?"

"American," he responded coolly. "She insulted him in English just before she slapped and punched the poor fellow. She even kicked him."

"He might have deserved it. Lots of well-heeled Americans live in Saint-Germain. Redheads, too."

"*Oui, c'est vrai*," he gawked at me nonetheless.

"It's quite true," I translated while digging around the drawers, searching for my cedar box. I felt a pricking of my nerves.

"Perhaps you would consider coming into the station so that I may at least solve one mystery this afternoon?"

"Thank you for the kind invitation. I'll have to pass. I don't do any kind of work on a Sunday. Another time perhaps."

Someone had moved my humidor. I was running my hands up and down my bathrobe trying to dry my sweating palms. Gravois had asked me politely to volunteer to come down to his precinct. He might not be so considerate the next time.

"Another time then, Madame Ducongé. I'll be in touch. *Au revoir*."

"If you must," I said. "But I hope it won't be necessary." I didn't want to ever see Inspector Gravois again so I refused to say "au revoir" in return.

∾

Peter and I sat at the kitchen table over Claire's coffee and pastries.

"What was that about, Ada?" My husband wanted to know. "You were looking for that box of cigars. They're in the pantry. You can't get yourself worked up again. Tell me what you've gotten yourself into."

I was going over the loose ends in my mind. Inspector Gravois would soon discover that the last phone call made from Ollie's apartment was to me at Bricktop's. And that fool Frenchman. I couldn't believe he went to the police. What kind of a man would tell the police that a woman beat his ass? *The kind who would call a woman a whore*, I thought to myself. I was in some hot water, and the temperature was rising fast. I had to figure out who told the police about me and Ollie. That information didn't have Natalie's or Josie's fingerprints on it. I also had to avoid Inspector Gravois and his station until I did.

"Two white American women have been killed," I said as I retrieved the cedar box from the pantry and hugged it to my chest. "One of them visited the club the morning she was murdered," I explained to Peter. And then I filled him in on the rest of story about Josephine and those pictures, as he watched me light up a cigar and lose myself in the scent of it.

"I never cared much for Josie Baker and that fake Count, Ada. I owe her something for introducing us, but that's where my gratitude ends. You need to be careful and stay clear of that woman and her trail of dead bodies."

"That had been my plan. I can't leave it alone now. You heard that Inspector."

Peter kissed me on top of my head and sighed. "I won't be around here to help, and I feel mighty bad about that. But I've got to work, to take care of my baby and this house." He then kissed my cheek and began rubbing my back in a circular motion, something that always calmed me down. "Will you be alright? You know what I'm talking about, Red."

Tears sprung to my eyes, as I put the cigar out. Peter had seen me at my worst, and a piece of him always worried that I'd go back to that terrible place I'd landed in, a couple of years ago. "I'm not upset yet," I said, responding to his back rubbing. I could smell the *karité* butter he used on his hands to keep them from getting calloused from the saxophone playing. I liked the sweet, nutty smell. It reminded me of the nutmeg in my favorite dessert: sweet potato pie.

"You were looking for those cigars like they were something good to eat, Ada. I'm no fool. I know you think you've got it under control. But that's just the beginning of it. Why don't you come with me to the Netherlands so you can relax for a few days. We can drive to Bruges like we did for our honeymoon. We can eat at your favorite *pannekoken* house and walk along the canals. It'll do you good."

I was surely tempted. Recalling those glorious, carefree days with Peter was helping me to push from my mind the ugliness that Inspector Gravois had left in our foyer. I looked at the cigar again. We took our honeymoon back in August, even though we had been married in the dead of winter. This was February, and our everything, including my freedom, was on the line. "I'll be fine, baby. You know I can't go now. Not after everything I've just told you."

He did know it. But he thought he'd try to persuade me anyway. "You've got Mister Speaker?"

"Umm hmm," I replied distractedly. "You and Changchang ask the same questions."

Peter smiled. "With that tough gal around, I guess you'll be alright. I'm glad Claire woke me up. I know you wouldn't have said a word. You say you're not upset, but are you worried?"

"No," I lied.

Of course, I was worried. Someone was trying to play me for a patsy. Inspector Gravois was aiming to put me in the frame for Ollie's unseemly demise, and he was also trying to link me with Pippa Nelson. Why else would he have mentioned that he had "two murders of American women in Paris over the past three evenings"? Why else would he have asked me about Mister Speaker? And here I was stumbling blind. Who on earth were his sources?

Damn you, Josie Baker.

THE FEAST FOR NO SAINT

VIII.

Papa Jack was cleaning the meat off another whole chicken, and Claire was just about through with his gluttony. He didn't look like he was even near full.

She leaned over and whispered in my ear, "Madame, we have cooked four *poulets* for Monsieur Jack. Has he not well eaten by now?"

"Let's start with the cheeses and dessert then," I told her.

"*Eh bien,*" she muttered. "And what I am I to do about Madame Johnson? She is in my kitchen, demanding my family recipe for the *coq au vin.*"

I had to laugh. "Sorry Claire, you'll have to figure that one out for yourself." As Claire returned to the kitchen, I put my full attention back on Papa Jack and finished telling him about the murders. He looked completely absorbed in his meal—especially when Claire returned with a plate of assorted French cheeses and upside down apple tart. *Tarte tatin.* And coffee. I knew that he had heard every word I said. And so did Peter and Changchang, who had finished their meals and were eager to help me work out what to do.

Finally, Papa Jack wiped his mouth with his cloth napkin and sat back in his chair. "Doesn't sound good to me at all. And I know me a thing or two about the law. Shiiiiiiit," he emphasized the word. "Between the U.S. government, the police, the white press, and Chicago and New York gangsters, I been on the lam more times than I can count. You remember, Brick, back in Chicago when I first met you. You were on the chitlin' circuit singing and dancing with the Tough on Black Asses booking agency before I hired you at Café de Champion. The coppers hated me for marrying Etta with her snowy white complexion. The gangsters hated me even more because they couldn't get a piece of my purse."

"That was a fairly nice-sized purse in those days," Peter said.

Papa Jack was talking about his first wife, Etta Duryea. He'd served a year and a day in jail because of the Mann Act. He'd been convicted of transporting white women across state lines for immoral purposes; but he was mostly guilty of flouting the social taboos against race mixing. The haunted look in the Champ's dark eyes told me that despite his bravado, the constant hunt for him in America had taken a toll. Like Lang, he'd come to Europe for a reprieve. I wondered if he, too, would change his course and head for the Caribbean. He'd had a good run in the islands.

Peter cleared his throat. "These murders remind me of the syndicates."

"Could be," Papa Jack said. "Except reporters write stories on organized crime every other day in the papers. This doesn't seem big enough for them."

"They've murdered for less and more," I added.

"True." Papa Jack cut a sliver of Camembert cheese. "Let's say they killed that Pippa woman because of the story and Ollie for helping her. The killing will probably stop now, Brick. But somebody's trying to put you on the hook for two murders. The syndicates don't usually go to the trouble of setting up a fall guy; they just let the murder go unsolved, leaving the police to speculate. This seems entirely personal."

"That's what I was thinking, too," said Changchang.

Papa Jack threw her an appreciative look. If Irene Pineau had been at the table, instead of in the kitchen pestering Claire for secret French recipes, her husband would not have gotten away with that hungry look. Irene may have been frumpy, but she was no milksop, as I had discovered over the course of Sunday's dinner. She had given Papa Jack a few icy stares and sharp-tongued jabs that straightened him right out whenever his reminisces went too far afield.

"Let me give you some advice from the ring," he offered, quickly returning to the subject at hand as if he could feel Irene's glare burning a hole through the pantry door. "See, at first, you were just shadowboxing. But now you've got a real opponent. Have you thought about who your enemies are, in the local mafia?"

"Red," said Peter. "I don't like this one little bit. You're coming with me to the Netherlands."

"Hush, Peter. You know I'm not leaving Paris."

My husband frowned.

"You've got to think about the "why" of it," Papa Jack continued. "Convenience? Money? Wrong Place, Wrong Time? Revenge? Your enemies have drawn a bead on you, and they're still invisible. You got to play defense; wait for them to slip up, and then take them down."

The champ stood up. He started weaving and shuffling his feet with his fists up in a boxing stance. "Tread carefully now, but come out swinging when the time is right. Punish 'em good." He threw a few punches as if he had waited for just the right moment to take his invisible opponent out. "They've got you on the ropes, Brick. But they'll slip up soon enough, because they've underestimated you. Use your resources. You've got to find someone to point the finger at." He sat back down at the table to sip his coffee.

"What about Miss Josie?" Changchang asked.

"I sure do love the smell of chicory in French coffee." Papa Jack stuck his broken nose into his cup and inhaled deeply. "Josie didn't murder those women. She's put herself out there too much for her to be involved. Who's to say Bricky here couldn't just turn around and go to the police on her? Bricky's got standing here in France, too. Josie just wanted those pictures.

Calling Brick from that woman's apartment and then running, that's an example of foolish emotion, not smarts. You said so yourself, Brick. She was crying and carrying on blaming you for her going over to that white woman's apartment in the first place. Brick's enemies are more cold-hearted, more calculating. They'd be fools to bring Josie into their schemes. Brick's not dealing with fools. Were there any marks, scratches, or bruises on Josie?"

I shook my head. "None that I could see."

Changchang nodded in agreement.

"Well, there you go. Take it from me. The way the papers described that beat-down that first woman got, our beloved Josephine would have been bruised to the high heavens from giving her fists some exercise. That Pippa woman fought back. Trust me, Brick, when flesh hits flesh, the one who comes out on top may walk away, but they'll have bruises or scratches to show for it."

He reached greedily for the Roquefort.

Papa Jack's hypothesis about Josie was probably correct. I'd assumed as much. But he had brought a sharper perspective to things. And he agreed with my suspicions that those killings were going to be pinned on me. I hadn't worked out how the first one could be blamed on me, but something told me that whoever was setting me up had it all figured out. I had read enough Dashiell Hammett to smell a setup when it came flying at me.

The last time Mama had come to Paris, she'd brought a trunk full of American whiskey, bourbon, cornbread mix, hair straightener, cigarettes, the latest records by Duke Ellington, *The Crisis* and *Opportunity* magazines, and Hammett's *The Maltese Falcon*. I couldn't let those dead white women rest where they lay. They were now leading right back to me. My happily-ever-after was at stake. And someone had deliberately made it so.

Papa Jack looked over at Changchang and winked for the third or fourth time that afternoon. He was maybe thinking that he should have held out for something more exotic than this third plain Jane he had wed.

Jack Johnson had publicly sworn off colored women after he'd been publicly shamed by so many of them, during his Texas sportin' life days. Privately, however, he continued to dabble in dark meat.

Changchang threw him a shy smile just as Irene took her place beside him at the table. She looked from Jack to Changchang. She smiled at Changchang, whom she knew wasn't hardly entertaining any romantic ideas about her old-as-dirt husband. But she knew Papa Jack had been thinking something this side of dirty about Changchang. With his fork midair, she decided it was high time to help Claire immediately remove the cheeses and desserts to the kitchen.

Only the three of us, Papa Jack, Irene, and me, understood what she had done. I nearly snickered aloud. Papa Jack had chosen the right Frau. His boxing reach wouldn't have done him an ounce of good with Changchang. Child that she was, she would have deboned him like a duck with all his whorin' around. Irene Pineau was a woman, calm and steady. She knew just how to outmaneuver him. The Champ sat pouting for a good minute at the loss of his bounty. And he didn't so much as look or wink at Changchang again for the rest of the afternoon.

We rose from the table to listen to some opera on Peter's phonograph machine, but my mind was elsewhere. I was plotting my next moves. Sunday was the Sabbath, not to mention my only full day with Peter. I was going to keep it holy—or at least romantic. But Monday was a working day, and I would be ready for a new sun to rise.

∽

Peter was speaking in low tones into the telephone in our bedroom. "I want you to keep an eye out on Ada and the club until I return. I don't want to get into the particulars with you. I just need a few of you to post up there for a coupla nights."

I couldn't make out the voice on the other end, and I didn't dare ask, as I was pretending to be asleep.

"If you really want to know, I'm thinking about not going at all; but she wouldn't have me sitting around here waiting for trouble."

Peter had obviously seen through my threadbare confidence. I was worried and well on the road to upset.

"No, she can't know, fool!" he almost bellowed out before catching his voice. "She'd be fairly mad. Just try to be inconspicuous. I know that's hard for y'all to do. And don't bring those floozy-looking French women you meet in those stab-and-jab hangouts. You know Ada won't let your triflin' asses into her club." Peter chuckled softly into the receiver. "I'll take care of you and your boys in a few days."

He quietly eased the phone back into its place by the bedside nightstand and slipped under the bedcovers. He searched for my body and pulled me closer to him to make love one more time before he left in the early morning. I hadn't planned on sleeping that night. I intended to lie still and rest my body while my mind was in overdrive. Even as Peter drifted into a deep sleep, he continued to pursue me throughout the night and early morning: a hand on my thigh, a foot touching my foot. It was like our movements were choreographed. Now who could be peeved at a man like that?

Peter left early Monday morning, proffering a goodbye kiss on my forehead and some very sweet words as I still pretended to be asleep in bed. When I finally arose, I found a letter beside our bed.

Dear Ada,

You know I'm not one for writing letters. I prefer to write you love songs to a blues or jazz tempo. I remember the evening I first saw you at Parisi's. It was morning really. Your smile lit up the dark room. I remember thinking, "Who is that redbone?" You were wearing your hair longer then. I followed those red curls down the curve of your back when you turned to whisper something to Josie. I could smell the orchid in your hair. It scented the air. It was over for any other woman then. What's her name again? Whatshername? That's what I was thinking about the woman I was about to leave right then and there and step to you. Forever, my darling.

Then Josie brought you over. You said your name was Bricktop. I called you Ada, then Red. You looked at me and asked could I play Sippie Wallace. "Which one?" I said to your challenge. You needed to know what kind of man I was by the music I knew. You hummed it and then took the microphone. Me and the band followed. You were singing for me, love. You were telling me you were a "Mighty Tight Woman." That you were and are.

You sang,

> I come to you, sweet man
> And I'm, I'm fallin' on my knees
> Won't you kindly take me please

I said, "Yes," with my saxophone blaring loud. Then you sang,

> Cause I'm a mighty tight woman
> What I need is a good man
> And I will make him happy too

And my eyes said, "Ada. I want to be happy. I'm that good, good man. I want you to make me happy. Let me make you happy. Before you, I couldn't possibly have known a thing about it."

I love you, Red.

Your Peter

I was some kind of fool in love. I reread that letter and then tucked it in my drawer for safekeeping. With that kind of love, I knew I could face anything down. That's why my man wrote it.

So an hour later, Changchang and I arrived at Bricktop's to help serve breakfast to the musicians who came from all parts of Paris after their early morning gigs for a down-home meal. I was in the market for information, and the musicians were an ideal place to start. A belly full of good food and strong coffee would loosen some tongues. These musicians played all over town, and they knew about all kinds of things in Paris, including the organized crime scene.

"Falcon," I called out to a trumpet player who kept his ears to the ground.

Falcon was as high yellow as me but with hazel eyes. He was a very pretty boy and drove the French women wild with his French Creole ways. He was originally from Shreveport, Louisiana. Like my Peter, it seemed his entire family played jazz and blues in New Orleans. He was digging into a plate of slab bacon, polenta, and over-easy eggs. That polenta was the closest thing to hominy grits we could find in Europe.

"Falcon!" I yelled louder this time, to catch his attention. "What you know about them two American women killed here in Paris?" I asked loud enough for everyone to hear so they could offer their few cents. I needed facts and was willing to take all comers. Changchang came out of the kitchen to pick up the bits of conversation I might miss, moving from table to table.

"Why you axin' me, Brick? I don't know nothing about them women. They was white and American, and immune to my charms, if you know what I mean. Neither of them liked smoke, coal, or pipe."

He got a good laugh from the others.

I laughed along to get along. "You ain't quite that smoky, and there might be just a smidgen of coal in your wood pile." That got a chorus of loud guffaws. Everyone knew how sensitive Falcon was about his color. His daddy was a white Frenchman. I deliberately picked up the morning paper that had run the story of Ollie's death. "One of them came by here on Saturday morning. Now she's dead. The French police don't like dead Americans on their watch."

"She was rich and white, I know that," Falcon said. "That's what the French police don't like. They know they have to haul somebody's ass in for that crime."

"Yeah, see if it was you or me," said another musician as he bit into a baguette oozing with melted butter, "wouldn't nobody give a good got damn. But them families ain't about to let it go. And I can't hardly blame 'em."

"I heard they used to hang out over at that queer spot," Jonny Dumont, jumped in.

I followed up. "Le Boeuf sur le Toit?" I was remembering that Ollie had invited me there for a drink.

"Umm hmm," they said in unison.

I said, "It's nice to see you again, Jonny. You're not too mad at Bricky about Saturday night? Did you find some pickup work?"

"I'm doing fine, Brick. I followed Changchang's advice. I wish you could've kept me on, here at Bricktop's. But I got a little something at Le Boeuf. It's a three-week gig."

I wondered how long he'd last. Three weeks is a long time for a dope addict to stay clean. I gave him a week.

"I met one of your friends. A carrot-top named Renata. I wondered if you had a way I could contact her?"

"I 'on't know no Renata," he gulped.

"She said you and she were good friends."

"You know how those ofays are, Brick. They rattle off names so you'll think they okay." He laughed before he sipped his coffee, hands shaking.

"Yeah, Brick, ofays want to be okay," someone yelled out and they all tittered.

None of the men would make a liar out of Jonny. If he didn't want us colored women to know he was tied up with some white woman, they'd be silent as the grave about it. It was their players' creed.

I looked over at Changchang.

"That first one who got herself kilt—what's her name, Jonny?" Falcon asked.

"Pippy or something."

"Yeah, her. She switch-hit sometime. I saw her with the Baron one day when I was playing at Zelli's."

"Zelli's?" Changchang let out a squeal. "I can't believe you would be up in that jack-legged club, Falcon."

"I play where they pay, Changchang."

"If you got to use what they pay for bail money, makes me wonder about your sense," she said, grinning a little too much for my liking.

"Wasn't no raids the nights I was playing. Besides, I didn't know you cared," Falcon retorted, grinning just as wide as she was.

I felt some heat. I was too young to be menopausal. Something was going on between those two. That would be another mystery that needed solving. Nothing sweet could come of it. The minute she caught him with one of those Frenchies, smooth-talking Falcon would end up pipeless.

Changchang had rightly pegged Zelli's. I remembered Nat saying that Pippa Nelson liked to go there for the diverse company. It was low-rent and trashy. Sure, they had members' cards for entry. But it was a cathouse pretending to be a jazz club. The police had raided it more times than I cared to count.

"Is that the same Baron who tried to shake me down, Falcon?"

"There ain't but one, Brick."

I had a theory. I had to find the Baron to test it, but there was no way I was going to Zelli's.

"Where does the Baron do his business during the day when he's not pestering hardworking business owners?"

"You know, he funny like that," said Jonny Dumont. "He go to the same spot every day around five o'clock. Angelina's. They have the best hot chocolate. Makes you feel like a kid in a candy shop."

"Café Angelina on rue de Rivoli?"

"Yep. Try that *Chocolat l'Africain*. It's thick and rich, melted chocolate; and they serve it with heavy cream. I take the ladies there I want to impress," he peacocked.

I wondered if he took Renata there.

"That shit expensive, man? I need to up my game some," Falcon said, high-fiving Jonny and giving Changchang a knowing grin.

I couldn't resist asking, even as my hand was itching to slap Falcon down for leering at my niece, "What's a French gangster in the prostitution and protection rackets doing taking hot chocolate at five o'clock every day?"

"It's damn good hot chocolate for starters," Jonny chimed back after slurping up some more coffee. The musicians chortled like a backup chorus.

"Even gangsters have Mamas, Brick. The Baron's family is from the south, Nice or Monte Carlo, I heard. But they from some old family with a "de" something in their name. Baron something or the other *de* something. Old aristocratics with dirty money. His Mama moved north, hoping to get the Baron away from the family business. But that reach is long."

"How you know all of the Baron's business?" That was Changchang, looking upside Jonny's head real hard.

"I don't, really. But Gut Bucket does. The live-in maid is one of his Paris skirts. As soon as the Baron leaves with his Mama, Bucket shows up to tune her piano." Dumont sniggered, looking around the table for affirmation. He got it. His fellow musicians nodded in agreement, between shoveling food and scraping forks.

Gut Bucket was one of the best cornet players in Paris. To this day, I don't know how he got that name. He played for me sometimes at Bricktop's. He'd toured all over the continent and had a woman in every port. He and Jonny and some other musicians lived in a flophouse in MoMart. Because Bucket traveled all the time, he never bothered with a real apartment. And it was just that kind of closeness that produced casual information. I knew

I could count on the full-bellied musicians. I signaled for Changchang to join me in the back kitchen.

"I'm going to run an errand and then go home to rest. You close up here after they finish eating and come on back to the apartment to get some rest yourself."

My keen eye for things untoward had somehow failed me when it came to Changchang and Falcon. I couldn't figure out when that pretty boy had come courting my niece. She was a fully grown woman, but I still thought of her as the most precious little girl in long, dark pigtails—carrying a pearl and ivory-handle switchblade—in Harlem. She brought that Italian-made knife with her to Montmartre.

I had started thinking about her education here in Paris. She loved cooking in that kitchen, but she was too young to waste away back there. Plus, if I got her out of Bricktop's, I could keep Falcon away from her and safe, for his sake. She wasn't one to be trifled with. Most men didn't understand that.

Some women just cry their eyes out when a man hurts them; others tell you from the jump that they mean business if you do them wrong. I wasn't the killing or the crying kind. I was the leaving type. I had watched my widowed mother cry too many times over a man after my father's death. So much so, it made me scared to love. In fact, the best advice my Mama gave me about love was her poor example. I swore I'd never cry like that. I knew exactly when to cut them loose and walk away. Except for a man called Jed back in San Francisco and Peter, who had seen me through my darkest, lowest days of crying, cursing, and cutting the fool. He had disarmed me completely. I still don't know how he snuck in. I had taken a huge risk with Peter. But he was a rare, good man. Falcon, on the other hand, struck me as hardheaded, and Changchang was deadly. That was a recipe for a killing, or at the very least a whole lot of bleeding and crying on his part.

"Changchang, I've been thinking about you and Falcon."

"Aw, Aunt Ada, it's nothing. Just a little flirtation."

"Good." I wanted to add that I wanted better for her than some rag-tag musician. So what if I had married a jazzman. What I did or had didn't matter.

"I was also thinking about you going to school while you're here in Paris."

"It's funny you should bring that up, Aunt Ada. What I really want to do is open a *pâtisserie* with a small tearoom with jazz from noon to half past two and four to six. Like that fancy place Jonny Dumont described on rue de Rivoli. We could call it Brick's Tea and Jazz Room. You could come for the noon hour before you go back to bed. We'd offer Southern and French pastries and light lunches.

"We'd have a readymade clientele. It would be for lunching ladies and gentlemen who might not want to go out late at night but still want the flavor of jazz. We need to be in a real nice part of town so they can come dressed up during the day. MoMart won't do. I've got some money saved up from what you pay me for cooking. And Daddy and Mommy send me money that I don't ever spend since you and Uncle Peter pay my rent and take care of everything."

"You've really been thinking hard on this?"

She nodded her head emphatically.

"Okay, we'll start looking at that École de Boulangerie et de Pâtisserie and Le Cordon Bleu next week. They're supposed to be the best pastry schools in Paris. Don't worry about paying for this jazz tearoom. We'll take care of the rents. Just make sure you train that sous-chef to take your place at night. You can't go to school and keep up these hours."

"But I love it here. I don't know what I'd do without Bricktop's."

"You can work on Friday and Saturday nights. That's it."

My eyes started welling up. I wanted Changchang to do something with her life and to have something of her own. I was glad to hear she had dreams. Big dreams. But I would miss her nightly presence at Bricktop's.

I couldn't afford being sentimental these days, so I quickly straightened myself out. "We got business at four. You hear me? And no time for distractions." I glanced over in Falcon's direction.

"Really, Aunt Ada. It ain't nothing between me and him." She was fingering that shiny crystal hairpin again, and her bright eyes told a different story. I still wondered when it began, and how it had slipped by me.

A HELPMATE

IX.

I took a taxi to rue Chauchat and was deposited in front of a hulking stone building that flew the tricolor French flag. I needed help, and thus far, only one person had volunteered information without my asking. He had always behaved decently to me, so I never held his profession against him.

"*Monsieur Jean Bergeron, s'il vous plait?*" I inquired of the cop at the desk.

"*Et vous êtes, Madame?*"

"*Madame Smith Ducongé.*"

I took a seat on a beat-up chair in the badly lit entrance. I hadn't seen the policeman since his Sunday morning visit to Bougival with that hateful Inspector.

"Madame Bricktop, it is very good to see you. I am sorry about Sunday morning." He clamped my hand in his.

"It's fine, Officer Bergeron. You were just doing your job. I appreciated your trying to help."

His eyes swept through the busy station. "Please come back to the office."

I dutifully followed him into a cramped, dark space that held two metal chairs and a small wooden table. In this room, we could sit side by side and talk.

"I hate to impose on you," I said, softly. "But those so-called reliable witnesses—if I knew who they were, then perhaps I could help to clear up this misunderstanding." I was still working out who the second dime-dropper was. As for the vulgar Frenchman, there wasn't much I could do about him except play hide and seek. He could identify me; I had no doubt about that after Gravois's visit. And I intended to steer clear of police lineups for the time being.

"Madame Bricktop," he sighed, "you are a person of interest in two murders . . ."

He confirmed what I already knew. Gravois was looking at saddling me with both of those women's deaths. I felt palpitations in my heart. "I swear I didn't kill those women. I didn't even know them."

"Don't worry yourself. I don't believe it. But I cannot use my offices to identify police witnesses for you. Even as I believe you did not commit those murders. It is not ethical."

"Can you at least tell me what they think they saw? It's just so perplexing. I can't defend myself if I don't—"

The French officer looked very uncomfortable. He stood up and gestured for me to stop talking.

"How long do I have, then?"

"I am a family man, Madame Bricktop. I cannot lose *mon poste*. I have children and a wife to support. I shall try to look out for you when I can. You are a good American. I have already said too much perhaps."

I did my best to look as pitiful as I felt.

"Two days," he said. "Perhaps three."

"*Merci.*"

We stood up. He pressed my hands into his dry palms trying to comfort me. Dazed, I stepped back into the corridor.

"*Bonne journée, Madame Bricktop,*" he said loudly and waved goodbye.

I sped along toward the station's front doors. The cold air hit me like a bitter slap in the face.

∾

When four o'clock rolled around, Changchang and I headed to Angelina's. It was in a chic part of town on rue de Rivoli, across from the Tuileries and a stone's throw from the Hotel Meurice. I wanted to get there before the five-o'clock rush, so that I could have a bird's-eye view when the Baron arrived. Lately, English teas had become all the rage in Paris. Parisians sporting Coco Chanel daywear, as well as badly outfitted tourists, often formed a long queue outside of Angelina's. It was a place to be seen.

Changchang and I were both turned out elegantly in crepe wool suits. Getting all dolled up had lifted my spirits. My hair was pulled back in a bun with flaming red kiss curls on both sides, while Changchang wore a Chanel hat with matching gloves. She had angled her hat to cock to the side, and her long dark hair flowed out from beneath the brim.

We were seated at a table near the front where we could watch the patrons enter and exit. It was a prime location on the first floor of the fresco-adorned café. Chandeliers and delicate gold wall sconces threw off light in every direction of the room. White linens decorated the antique wood tables. Ladurée was elegant, but Angelina's was in a league of its own. The décor made you feel aristocratic and cozy all at once.

There was some commotion near the hostess's station. I saw a white woman about my age gesticulating wildly and pointing toward our table.

"I can't eat with them," she complained in an American accent.

"*Non*, Madame of course," said the hostess. "You will eat there."

She pointed to a table a few paces away.

The patron was still shaking her head like a spoiled child.

"Is there a problem?" Changchang reached for her purse on the chair. She wasn't reaching for the bag to leave. She was reaching to get into the purse's contents.

I shook my head, restraining her gently with one hand. "You can't cut her in broad daylight."

"Yes. There is a problem," the woman answered Changchang in her grating American English.

"What is it then?" Changchang called back. Her purse was on the table now.

"You."

"Do I know you?" Changchang was now genuinely scrutinizing the woman's face as if she were trying to place her at a club in Harlem or at her parents' chop suey spot.

"Heavens no. And I'd like to keep it that way. That's why you need to leave." She turned to face a group of women and began explaining loudly how she hadn't come to France to take tea with Negroes. She wouldn't entertain the notion in America, and she certainly couldn't be expected to do so in Paris.

Changchang pushed her seat back from the table.

I grabbed her arm firmly this time. "Let it go, baby. As good as it might feel, she's not worth it."

Changchang was still too fresh and young to believe that some battles were just not worth fighting. She was right to be angry and to defend herself against this uncouth cracker. I'd left America to get away from her type only to have them land in France with their poisonous tongues and pens.

But I wanted Changchang to understand that being so quick to violence was not always the best course of action. I only wished I had followed my own counsel on Saturday evening with that French derelict. I also wished that the crash could've kept this breed of ill-dressed American at home. It wouldn't have pained me a bit to tell her that her dress, a Paul Poiret to be sure, was *démodé*.

Josie had told me of an incident in the South of France where a white American patron had insisted she be removed from the hotel. She often had to move from hotel to hotel in Paris, with apologies from the French owners about overbooking, when the white Americans showed up. And I had read a story in the papers about an African prince who had been summarily jettisoned from a café in Paris at the insistence of white Americans.

In none of those stories was there an eager young woman with a switchblade ready to settle a score. I had to finesse the situation *and* tell this white woman to go to hell without Changchang taking that as a cue to open the woman's windpipe.

The French hostess took matters into her own hands. She said, "Madame, you may sit there or you may leave."

Everyone's shoulders dropped—some from relief and others from sheer embarrassment. But before I could savor the look of horror on Miss Anne's face, the Baron walked in with Mama Baron on his arm. Changchang and I both turned to stare at our new targets.

"Monsieur le Baron," I exclaimed, sidling up to the slender, aquiline-nosed Frenchman. "It's so nice to see you again."

A PIGEON IN OUR MIDST

X.

The Baron attempted to sidestep me as he was escorted to his table. He mumbled, "*Bonne soirée*, Madame Bricktop," as he tried to hurry his mother past our table.

"You're a wee bit too old to be hiding behind your Mama," Changchang said loud enough for the other patrons to hear.

He turned to glare at Changchang, whose perfect mouth, outlined in red lipstick, expanded to a double-dare smile. She stared him down with her father's dark-almond eyes. The gold flecks danced around her pupils like flames.

"I think you and my aunt need to talk," she said, holding her little purse primly. "I'll take Mama Baron to her table."

Mama Baron didn't understand a lick of English.

"*Qu'est-ce qui se passe?*" she inquired.

"*Rien, Madame*. Nothing happening at all," Changchang replied, while the Baron and I traded looks that were dirtier than dirt. Changchang was fluent in English, Mandarin, and French, her mother's side of the family being from Martinique.

The Baron quickly assured his mother that all was well, as Changchang held out her arm to escort Mama Baron to her table. I could hear Mama Baron pleasantly whispering to Changchang as they walked. Changchang winked back at me.

"This had better be important, Madame Bricktop. Have you reconsidered my offer?"

"I've told you that I don't need your kind of protection. But I do have some business with you. I was wondering, when was the last time you saw Pippa Nelson?"

"I don't know a *Pee-pa* Nelson." He said this a little too quickly.

"No?"

"*Non.*"

"Well, somebody saw you two real cozy at Le Boeuf sur le Toit and at Zelli's shortly before she was murdered."

The Baron pushed Changchang's abandoned lemon tart toward the center of the table and leaned in. "Your somebody is wrong. Now if that is all, my *maman* awaits me."

"Looks like she's doing just fine with Changchang." I waved to the table where Changchang and Mama Baron were sharing a pot of *Chocolat l'Africain*. They both smiled back at me and the Baron. Poor Mama Baron was as clueless as the night was short.

"She's probably better company than you anyway. Does Mama Baron know about your shakedown hobby, your running women, selling dope?"

"Shakedown? Running with the women? Dope? What is all of this?" Strands of the pretty Frenchman's gold locks shifted out of place with his insincere gestures.

"Are we going to play the language barrier game now? You rob innocent people of their hard-earned money. That's what we call shakedowns."

I said the last part so loud that Mama Baron and Changchang peered over at us.

The Baron squirmed, looking around nervously. It appeared my gamble had paid off, and Jonny Dumont's information about the Baron attempting to hide his extracurricular activities from his mother was spot on.

"You know Changchang's people are from the French West Indies. She can translate fairly well."

"Why are you doing this to me, *mon petit oiseau*? I merely wanted to offer you guidance and protection. Besides, what business is it of yours who I know or don't know? Unless you have other interests in me." He showed his perfect whites and placed that pale worm-fingered hand on the table.

I snorted at the implication of his words. "Somebody made it my business. Now you need to 'fess up about knowing Pippa Nelson or I'm going to tell Mama Baron over there about your involvement in the family business. She would be quite disappointed to know she moved north to escape the syndicate, only to have her son fall smack in the middle of it." I made a motion to stand up, bumping the table for exaggeration. A tea cup spilled a little of the Darjeeling I had ordered before the Baron had made his entrance.

"Please sit down, Madame Bricktop." He opened his jacket slightly so I could see his revolver.

I continued to stand, raising my skirt slightly to catch the Baron's attention and patting my thigh. He understood that I was packing a peacemaker, too. "Looks like we've reached an impasse, baby."

The Baron glowered at me. "Please sit down, Madame Bricktop." This time he didn't make any moves toward his gun. He said it real nice, so I sat down.

"Don't do that shit again," I said. "Changchang has a healthy respect for her elders. By the time you draw down on me, your mother will be drinking hot chocolate through a slit in her throat." I hated using rough language. It was so unladylike, so un-Bricktop like. But I was starting to unravel with this white woman murder mess. And this so-called Baron had made me so mad my red hair had started sweating back to its West Virginia roots.

"*Bien sûr.* I understand." He looked over at his mother, just to make sure her cup was meeting her lips. He said, "I knew Pippa Nelson." He said her name without all the French inflection now. "I was her lover. I have nothing to hide."

"You and a few others." I couldn't pass up this little dig. The Baron had threatened me with a gun. Again.

"I do not care about that sort of thing. I cared only for her. We French are liberal on that score."

"Did you care about her writing a story on French and American mob connections?"

He was silent, as if he was thinking hard about his response. "No I did not."

"Did you do a little too much pillow-talking?"

"Nothing serious was ever discussed. Entertaining stories. Easily found in newspapers. There was not much for her to write, *vous voyez?*"

"Yes, I see real clearly. Is that what you told your bosses to try to convince them? I'm not convinced. So I doubt they were." My theory was that the Baron murdered those white women to show his fealty for talking too much.

His slim hand flew up like a bird, like he was brushing away something bothersome. He then brought his hand down quickly on top of my forearm, pinning me to the table, as his other hand stroked my arm gently. "*Écoutez*, Madame Bricktop. I am my own boss. I would have never harmed a hair on Pippa's lovely head. It is also not acceptable to take advantage of a man's mother. Let me offer you some advice. Pay for my protection. *Tout sera bien.*"

"I want you to listen real close." I cocked Mister Speaker's hammer under the table. "You hear that? Now remove your fucked-up hand off me," I seethed. I yanked my arm from his firm grasp. The misshappen finger dragged across my forearm. I experienced a frisson. In my thirty-something years, I had never and would never stand to be manhandled.

"A woman doesn't like to have her livelihood taken advantage of either. What do you mean all will be well, *tout sera bien?*"

"It is quite simple. You are outmatched, *mon petit oiseau.*" He stood and walked over to his mother.

I sat rattled by the Baron's easy violence. My arm still tingled where he had grabbed it. I was also puzzling over what he had said. In my haze, I could see Changchang exchanging cheek-kisses with Mama Baron.

"Are you okay, Aunt Ada?"

I must have looked out of sorts. "No. Jean Bergeron said we have two, maybe three days before they roust my ass for those murders, and the Baron just dropped something on me."

"What'd the Baron say?"

"Something about my being outmatched. He wants me to pay up. He implied that all will be well with the world." I sighed.

"Humph." Changchang leaned over the table and picked over the lemon tart. "If you ask me, it sounds like he's got his hooks into that shady Inspector. We've got to find a way to get around Gravois. Do you think the Baron killed Pippa and Ollie and he's got his back?"

I rubbed my arm again, remembering his meanness. "It's very possible but not for the reason I thought at first. I believed he was just a low-level gangster who happened to fall in with Pippa and did too much pillow-talking like a lovesick puppy."

"And he killed those white women to make good with his bosses." Changchang sipped at her now-cold *Chocolat l'Africain.*

"Umm hmm." I absentmindedly rubbed my forearm again. "He got animated though when I implied that he had to answer to someone. He insisted he wouldn't have harmed a hair on pretty Pippa's head."

"So did Miss Josie. She didn't do it. He didn't do it. It's a word game, Aunt Ada. They could both be telling some version of the truth. He said Pippa, not Ollie. And that doesn't mean he doesn't know who did."

I nodded my head at Changchang's observation. "He knew Pippa had other lovers—which means he may have known all about Josie. He said he didn't care. I don't know if I believe that."

"Have you heard from Miss Josie?"

I shook my head no. I hadn't heard from Josie since that awful night at Ollie's, which made me pretty sure that she had lifted those photographs on the night of the murder. Otherwise, she'd still be pestering me about them. I imagined her laying low and focusing on her trade, feeling safe and ignoring the danger she'd put me in. "You finished?"

Changchang smiled down at the tart crumbs on her plate. "I think so."

"Come on then. We need to find Renata."

Renata was another piece of the puzzle. Her prescient warnings to Pippa and Ollie, and her cold response to Pippa's death gave me pause. Her words had been ringing in my head since I met her: "We all know why she's dead." *But only Renata seemed to know,* I thought. Only Renata could have told Gravois about my visit to Natalie's salon and my conversation, that night, with Ollie. She had even joined us at Bricktop's that morning for a toast to Pippa's life. She was also an addict, easily manipulated and disposable. I suspected she'd sell her own Mama for a hit.

We parked on rue Norvins and walked the short winding streets around the Butte—or the Hill, as we called that part of Montmartre—to the Place du Tertre, on the off chance that we might find Renata. The square's cobble-stoned pedestrian areas were bustling with tourists and artists. Tables for dining and drinks crowded the square. It was growing dark, but the area was well lit with street lamps, candles, and twinkling Christmas-like bulbs hanging from thick wires. With nothing to show for our efforts but red noses from the biting cold, I made my way home. Changchang went straight to the market and then to the club, where she would change from her tea suit to her cooking clothes. She planned to fry chicken, candy some yams, and make a pot of cabbage with smoked ham for our customers. I marveled at her youthful energy. Me? I couldn't wait to get home and put my feet up.

༄

I was still mulling over my meeting with the Baron when I left the apartment and headed to Bricktop's late that night.

The night air was arctic and the wind wasn't helping. I stuffed my hands into the long sleeves of my coat and quickened my pace. Bricktop's was a direct shot up rue Pigalle and a skip from my apartment. I decided to walk past the club and continue on, toward Place Blanche, despite the temperature. I needed to clear my head before stepping into the busy world of Bricktop's, and I liked the view of the Moulin Rouge from there, all lit up at night. Montmartre was sparkling as well.

The clubs were readying to open. I could smell the butter and thyme wafting out to the streets from the restaurants and club kitchens in the district. A man bundled up in a wool scarf and thick gloves was on the street selling hot-off-the-griddle butter and sugar crepes from a cart. When I shifted my nose in the opposite direction, the wine, garlic, Gruyère, and Emmental that made up the comforting cheese fondue scented the air. Despite the cold, tourists were out in force, probably walking from the beautiful church, Sacre Coeur, to the artists' square to enjoy a meal and shop for trinkets before moving on down to the Moulin Rouge or Montmartre for a night of French cabaret singing and dancing or American jazz. Some would probably hop from one hotspot to another until early in the morning. That's how nightlife was in our little quarter of Paris.

I was all caught up in that nighttime reverie until I noticed a black sedan creeping along the same road I was walking; its occupants were probably trying to decide which club to hit. But as soon as I stepped off the curb at rue Fontaine and rue Mansart, the car cut in front in me. I made my way around it, only to hear the window cranking down.

A familiar voice called my name. "Madame Bricktop?"

"Officer Bergeron?" I leaned down to see into the vehicle.

"Oui! Please." He opened the car door for me to enter, and I slid next to him in the front seat, relieved at the warmth inside.

"Madame Bricktop, I've come to warn you. Someone at your club is, how do they say in the American movies, a stool?"

"A stool pigeon?"

"*Oui, c'est ça, c'est ça.* The Inspector believes you are responsible for the deaths. He is relentless. I must tell you, he will prove his case. He will use whatever means are at his disposal. Madame Bricktop, we suspect he is not a good Inspector. He is not clean, clean." I didn't know if it was deliberate or a tic. But Jean Bergeron's penchant for repetition was, in this case, used to good effect.

"*Comprenez-vous?*"

"Umm hmm." I fully understood. Inspector Gilles Gravois was filthy dirty.

"He came to us from a little town near Ajaccio in Corsica about six months ago. Everyone knows how untrustworthy and brutal the Corsicans are, stabbing and shooting at the slightest insult. They have an Italian spirit, *vous voyez.*"

I dipped my head for him to continue on.

"He has a different way of doing things. He is very ambitious. This is how he got promoted to the Prefecture in Paris. I could not tell you this morning at the station. I must be careful. *Les oreilles* are everywhere," he said pointing to his large ears. "I am only telling you because I want to apologize. You have never caused problems for us."

"What are you apologizing for? Gravois?"

"I am sorry, that is all. You have made the gangsters very angry because you will not cooperate. You also insulted the Baron this evening."

"Are you saying the Inspector is in bed with the gangsters? And how do you know I insulted the Baron?"

"You must go now. Please be careful, Madame Bricktop."

He was motioning his hands like he was telling me to scoot. I opened the car door slowly, still thinking about what Jean Bergeron had just told me. The cold slapped me hard out my fog.

"Oh, I will, baby. Thank you, Officer Bergeron."

I don't think he heard me because he'd closed the door so quickly. He didn't want to be seen with me. Despite the cold, I was feeling very hot about the stoolie in my shop.

I made a list of my staff in my head. There were four waiters plus the head waiter. Then there was the doorman who made sure that only the reputable crossed Bricktop's threshold. There were two barkeeps. The dishwasher was hardly known to me. Changchang had hired him and the sous-chef. Then there was Clyde, our cleanup man. But none of them would have dropped a dime on me. I was their bread and butter in Paris where full-time, regular employment was scarce for Americans. I was still stumped about who had been singing an aria in falsetto to the police.

I made it to the club in a real funk. It was near midnight and Brick-top's was packed as usual, which was why I had begun my search for a larger club. I prayed for some time to myself, my bottom line be damned. I yearned for time to think without constantly catering to a relentless stream of guests, night after night.

I waved to Fred, Alphonso, and Joseph, the three musicians my Peter had sent to look out for me. They called themselves the Perry Brothers Trio, though they weren't the least bit kin. I had hired them now and then at Bricktop's. With an upright bassist, trumpet player, and drummer, they really got things going. It made sense that Peter had called in the Perry Brothers. They knew Bricktop's and my routine well.

And sure enough, they were sitting on a banquette with three hard-legged tarts that I had a mind to eject from my club. Those musicians couldn't tell nasty from classy. I decided to leave it be and just appreci-ate their efforts at keeping me safe. I was headed to the kitchen to tell Changchang about what Bergeron had said regarding the stool pigeon in our midst and to discuss how I intended to deal with it when I noticed an unfamiliar brutish man with a hulking body. I watched as he chugged down the last of whatever he had been drinking from his glass. The American socialite Wallis Simpson called my name from across the room. I waved and had a glass of champagne sent to her table. When my gaze returned to the oversized man's table, he was gone.

I scanned the club for him, and then I proceeded in the direction of the kitchen. But as soon as I took a few steps, chaos broke out. Lights were flashing outside, and the patent leather curtains to Bricktop's gave way to a stampede. We were being raided by the police. I could hear shrieks from the female customers. "No, get your hands off me, you brute." A policeman grabbed up Wallis. She splashed the flute of champagne I had just sent over in his face and made her fruitless getaway to the mobbed exit.

The police pushed tables and knocked over chairs in their mad rush to shackle up my patrons.

"*Qu'est-ce qui se passe?* What is this?" I cried out. My voice was swal-lowed up in swell of shrieks, curses, and screams. The band members made a beeline for the exit, freighted with their instruments, running headlong into coppers in the process. It was mayhem.

I rushed toward the kitchen but was caught up short when I saw the large man I'd spotted earlier blocking the doorway. His humongous back stretched the gray fine wool fabric of his pinstriped suit to breaking. I could see the outline of his muscles in the jacket's arms. The leviathan's hand-tailored suit was no match for his sculpted heft.

"Excuse me, may I help you? And why are you in my kitchen?" I squeezed underneath the space between one bulging arm and the doorway. The cuff of his left sleeve was missing a button.

"I came to talk with Changchang." The accent was French. I'd had clientele from all over the world so I could identify an accent. But he was no Parisian. He sounded like he'd come from the South of France.

His jawline was hard and angular, and his hands looked like pale, smooth catcher's mitts. Changchang and I looked at each other, sizing up our odds. Between the two of us we came in at about 240. He was over 300 pounds of hard muscle and at least six-foot-four with a larger peacemaker than Mister Speaker notched in the side of his belt. The way he stood in the doorway with one arm deliberately held up at an angle allowed an eyeful of the gun.

I glared up at his pockmarked face. "What business do you have with Changchang?"

"He had just asked me a question, Aunt Ada. I was at pains to answer it." Changchang's almond eyes narrowed. Her back was close to the stove where a pot of now-overcooked cabbage was boiling furiously. The ham perfumed the air. A cast-iron skillet was over a fire, readying for some lard.

"Is that right, Mr.?"

He didn't respond, as I had expected. Killers on a mission rarely leave calling cards.

"Perhaps I can answer the question. I don't much care for Changchang talking to strangers, or for that matter, strangers making their way into my kitchen uninvited." I could still hear the police sirens over the ruckus of shouting, pleading, and heavy footsteps toward the front of the club. There was a crash, and I prayed it wasn't my glass floors. I looked over the Frenchman's mammoth blockhead to the exit off the kitchen. There were stairs that led to a back alley.

His hard brown eyes followed mine. "Your question?"

"The question?" He eyed Changchang's body up and down. His gaze penetrating the starched white apron, taking in her curves where her waist was evident from the tiebacks and her buxom, youthful breast bulged from the top.

I was ready to pounce. I rubbed my temples hard. I could feel a line of sweat forming on my upper lip from the heat of the cabbage pot and searing skillet and from being just plain mad. He was looking at my baby like she was a two dollar ho whom he had already had his way with. I had decided then that I was going to make this man pony up good fashion for those foul-minded looks. I drew the line at anyone trying to pimp Chez Bricktop and disrespecting our womanhood. I had had enough of that in America and at the hands of so-called better white men than this French muscle for hire. I didn't take it then, and I wasn't about to take it now.

He restated the question for my benefit. "I *askt*," he said in clipped English, "*hur* if *iit* is sideways." He gave us a lewd, shark-toothed smile.

"Sideways, you say? You don't talk to ladies like that."

"If only you are." He lumbered forward into the kitchen.

There was a quick pop and then smoke from Mister Speaker's barrel.

"Beeetch." His wide-brimmed fedora fell forward, revealing a bald pate surrounded by a muss of chestnut curls.

The bullet grazed the Goliath's manly parts, causing him to groan loudly. It went through his pant leg and lodged itself into the floor. The casing bounced near my feet. He continued to stumble with a howl that blended in with the pandemonium in the next room. His arm went to his yonder parts. He then lunged at me.

My knee came up to meet Mr. Johnson and friends just as he locked on to my neck. Changchang came from behind him and whacked him with the searing hot cast-iron skillet.

"Ahhh! Ahhh!" The bald spot's flesh and curls sizzled from the heat. She hit him again. His knees buckled some and he released my neck. He still had a long way to go down before he hit the floor. My full height barely reached his chest. So I reared back and punched down hard in his manly parts between dry coughs where his fingers had pressed against my windpipe. He yelped like a pup.

Changchang was now moving like a silent angel of death. Her eyes were wild with anger and hurt. We both knew what this man would have done had we been less wily. He was on one knee, wobbly, but reaching for his gun. She straddled him, placing her leg between him and the gun.

"Ahh!! Ahh!!" Mr. Frenchie screamed again when she yanked back his now tender head by the singed curls. His thick neck revealed a large Adam's apple. You could hear the crunch of curls in her hand.

Changchang reached into her bosom and prepared to draw him a smiley face.

"No!! No!! You can't kill him, baby!!"

Distracted by my shouts, he reared up. Changchang stumbled back into the stove. The Frenchman was quick for such a large man. He was preparing a roundhouse. His large, pale mitt was midway to making contact with Changchang's face when she launched the cabbage pot into his face. I jumped back before the blistering hot liquid and its mushy, translucent leaves and pink fleshed contents splashed on me.

"Ahhh!! Pain! Pain!" The hit man was supremely wailing now. His hands burned as he tried to remove the hot cabbage and ham from where his eyes were. The flesh on his face began to blister. The palms of his hands were a pinkish-red from the task. He went back to his knees to stem the pain, where I then promptly kicked him hard in the chest. The heel of my pump dragged hard down his chest and stomach. He could barely see. His eyes burned from the pot's elixir. He fell back hard on the floor flailing under the remains of the hot facial mask.

I said to Changchang, "Pick up Mister Speaker's casing and the bullet. Now take him and go." I had never let anyone handle Mister Speaker. But I didn't want him found on me, especially where I was headed.

"Uhh uhh. Aunt Ada. I ain't leaving you here." She tugged, pulling out the banged up bullet.

"Listen to me, baby. I don't want you mixed up in this when the coppers come. Now go." I pointed toward the back door.

She slipped quickly out the door and down the steps without giving the Frenchman a second look.

The man was still breathing, but the pain from the skillet and scalding hotpot had obviously become unbearable. He had passed out. I could see the red and pink puckerings rising underneath the cabbage leaves. I retrieved his gun from his belt and aimed it in the exact same spot where Mister Speaker's bullet had been lodged. I placed the gun beside his now inert body.

Officer Jean Bergeron appeared at the kitchen door with two officers not less than ten minutes later. He looked down at the giant and then back at me.

"Madame Bricktop!" He ran his hand wildly through his bushy mane, perplexed at my handy work.

"I've been waiting for you all to come back here and save me from this brute."

BRACELETS AND COUTURE

XI.

I sat in front of Inspector Gravois in his drab, cavernous office, wondering whose payroll he was on and how he would go about pinning those murders on me. He would surely try to nail me for the attempted murder of this mysterious Frenchman. No doubt, he'd try to convince me that my troubles would be over just as soon as I let his cohorts start pimping and slinging out of my club.

I was proud to be a woman saloonkeeper. I'd never had a white boss, and having the gangsters and the police milking Bricktop's would be like having one. Mine was the only business in Montmartre that held out against the gangsters. They were going to make an example of me, for my stubbornness. It all seemed like a series of coincidences, but perhaps I had been played all along, starting with Josie's tearful arrival at my club four nights ago. Hard to believe how much had transpired in such a short amount of time.

Gravois preened in his chair like an old crow. He flicked an imaginary speck of dust off his shoulder, savoring his power to keep me waiting. I wondered if he had staged the raid just so he could put me in a lineup so that drunk from the other night could identify me. Did he know that the ratty chair I was sitting on had been poking me furiously through the soiled upholstery? I refused to let my discomfort show, and finally, he kicked things off.

"So we meet again, Madame Ducon_é. And sooner than I expected."

"You certainly made it so. Can you remove the bracelets? I'm afraid they do nothing for couture." I didn't even bother to correct him about my name this time. He was obviously an ill-bred jackass.

He walked around his wooden desk—a nicked and banged up piece that had seen better days—and removed the handcuffs.

Gravois's office was certainly not representative of the Paris to which I had become accustomed. I looked around at the assortment of unmatched and uncomfortable-looking chairs that had been crammed into the corners of the room. And then my eye traveled up the faded green walls. They hadn't spent more than a hardy nickel to decorate this shop. I wondered if this was even Gravois's office. Maybe this dingy storeroom was reserved for interrogations, making suspects feel as trapped as I was feeling right then. I wondered how many suspects he had broken down in this large, poorly lit space. Even though the walls were a cruddy color, the office was neat—a sign that the Inspector was meticulous.

"No Madame, you've made this meeting possible," he smiled. "You've broken the law. I am only pursuing the culprit. Have you had a chance to think about how well you knew Mademoiselle Olive Knolton?" He sat back, waiting patiently for my response.

"I haven't given our Sunday conversation much thought. I'm not going to start thinking about it now either. What law have I broken besides defending myself against an insane man in my club's kitchen?"

Inspector Gravois was like flypaper. He could afford to be all smiles and patient. He could hold me there all night in the hope of eventually breaking me down and making me sing. He said, "So you say. The facts are that there is an unidentified, unconscious man, at the Hotel-Dieu hospital with a concussion from being struck with a heavy object, a rather bruised groin from a gunshot and punches and kicks," the detective crossed his leg uncomfortably, continuing, "and third-degree burns on the top of his head, face, and neck. How do you account for so much damage to this gentleman?" He put down the file.

"He was no gentleman. He's a French thug. Sounded like he was from the south. Marseille somewhere, perhaps. He trespassed into my kitchen with a gun. He grabbed me by the neck as you see," I said pointing to bruises around my throat. "I kneed him several times in the groin. He continued to choke me, as I reached for his gun. We both struggled for his gun. It went off. He's a big, strong man. I'm a small woman. Just a hundred and sixty-two centimeters and fifty-four kilograms, give or take a few." I hedged on my weight like any lady would.

"He came after me again, and this time, I punched him in the groin, whacked him with a hot skillet, and poured the contents of a cabbage pot on him. All of this to stop him, you understand."

The Inspector looked at me incredulously. "Do you know this mysterious man from Marseille?" he sneered.

I gathered he cared as little for the rough and rundown port town and their breed of Frenchman as he did Americans. But he'd like them rather more, I suspected, if he could use him to send me to the clink or rattle some francs out of my pockets for the syndicates.

"I have never met him in my life." I shifted in my seat to avoid the annoying coil poking in my backside.

"You are certain you did all of this by yourself?"

"I was right scared for my life."

"Where was your chef and sous-chef?"

"They were caught up in the raid, as you well know."

"But not your niece. She's your chef, is she not? She is not on our list of those arrested."

My eyes widened some. "I sent her home." And I had, just not before we put a beating on that French hit man.

"A strange man walks into you club and decides to assault you, and instead you nearly kill him? *C'est la folie!* This is madness. You're a mad woman, Madame Ducongé. I don't like madness in my city," he said flatly. "I will get this Monsieur's version of events once he is conscious, I suspect in a day or two."

I needed about that much time. I swallowed hard, and it hurt. I hoped the Frenchman would stay under—forever—and not make a liar out of me. I touched my throat where the brute's hands had been.

"You also accosted a Monsieur Baron de Boulainvilliers with a revolver at, let's see," he said, opening another police report, "Café Angelina on rue de Rivoli. You cannot go around threatening French citizens with guns." He threw his hands up wildly. "*C'est la folie. Complètement, Madame.* This is not America." He pounded his rawboned hands on the desk.

"What?" I jerked to attention in my chair. "I was merely speaking to him. In fact, he accosted me at my establishment just this past Friday evening as well as last Friday morning. Do you have the police report for that? I had witnesses, too. I sure filed a complaint about a week ago."

I ignored that part about America. Gravois was a Francophile through and through, bordering, it seemed to me, on xenophobia. I wanted to protest that the Baron was a gangster like Monsieur Marseille laying up at the Hotel-Dieu, but Gravois knew that already. He was probably one, too. I was old enough to keep some things to myself, playing defense now, just as Papa Jack had counseled me to.

Gravois look at me suspiciously. "A police report?"

"Yes. When I came to the station to register my revolver, I completed one. Officer Bergeron took my statement."

"Please forgive me, Madame. I am only just settling into this office. I have not had a chance to review all the prior case reports."

Gravois pulled at his salt-and-pepper moustache in silence, annoyed by this oversight but fully intending to pursue his interrogation. He behaved like he had an ace he was waiting to slap down hard on the table. "There is some history here, I see."

"If you'd like to call it that. A history of the Baron trying to intimidate me, and then me, trying to smooth things over. History of his filing a scurrilous complaint on me because of the legitimate one I filed against him."

"There is another problem with this history."

"What's that?"

"Monsieur le Baron says you questioned him at length about his late fiancée, Mademoiselle Pippa Nelson. Does that name ring a bell?"

The Baron had upgraded himself to Pippa Nelson's fiancée, and my mind raced along, trying to determine where this conversation was going.

Gravois was turning up the heat, and I was feeling it under my collar. The flames were now hot enough to singe my hair. I had to choose my next words carefully. If I admitted to inquiring about Pippa, he'd asked why I denied knowing her when he questioned me at Bougival on Sunday. If I denied it, it would be my word against the Baron's, and I could see which one of us Gravois would side with, in order to hang Pippa's murder on me.

Lie without lying. How I lied could mean the difference between me leaving this place tonight a free woman for a little while or rotting in the French equivalent of Sing Sing for a double homicide.

"Isn't that the woman you asked me about Sunday morning?"

Gravois didn't respond.

I felt him willing me to start babbling and over-explaining like a fool. "I had no idea that this Pippa Nelson was the Baron's fiancée." That was all true. I left it at that.

"Are saying that you did not inquire about Miss Nelson, Madame?"

"I am saying that I did not inquire about his fiancée," I replied. Because that lying bastard never had one. "Perhaps you should be questioning the Baron about his fiancée's death. He's a nasty, small-minded man for filing a bogus police complaint."

The air was filled with silence for a good while.

"You are clever, Madame Ducongé. But not as clever as you think."

"I am still not clear on why you raided my cabaret and arrested me. Had I known that being cordial to the Baron was an illegal offense, I would never have engaged him."

Gravois smiled again. "You are doing some illegal business in Bricktop's."

"Bricktop's is an upscale club. I don't do anything illegal. I have paid all my taxes and have all my licenses in order. Whom I won't pay are your bosses."

I rubbed my wrists where the cuffs had been. They were so tight they had left red welts on my skin.

"My bosses are the people of this great Republic. You are doing France a grave disservice. I would have never taken you for a Madame."

"I most certainly am and I have a husband to prove it."

"*Non!* A purveyor of women. *Les prostituées, les filles, les putes!*"

He was spitting and some of the spittle landed on my hand.

"Prostitution!! I don't even let single women in Bricktop's without an escort. You've got the wrong doll, Frenchie. Zelli's is where the chippies are."

"So you deny this as well? The police would not have pursued you if they were not *absolument certain.*"

My Irish-trigger temper flared and without thinking, I was up on my feet and yelling. "I don't give a damn who told you what. The only thing Bricktop's sells are champagne, food, and fine liquors. Not women!"

"*Calmez-vous*, Madame Ducongé. *Asseyez*."

I knew it was best to obey the Inspector and sit back down, but when I glanced down at the ratty chair I had been perched on, I recoiled. My expensive Schiap Shop dress did *not* belong on that stained upholstery. *It's just a dress*, I told myself, resting my bottom on the edge of the seat.

All I could think about was the club, all my hard work, my reputation, and Mama. She would surely cry a pond of tears if she got a whiff of this "ho" business. I could have cried right then.

"I shall double-check to make sure no mistake has been made. You will have to pay a fine before you can reopen the club."

"Sure you will. A fine? Is that what they call payoffs now?"

"I have no idea what you are speaking of."

"Of course you don't. All this French double-speak. Another Frenchman I ran into claimed he didn't know what a shakedown was, though that was exactly what he specialized in. How much is it?"

"I do not know. You will need to see the clerk."

"Well, where is this clerk? Under a bridge along the Seine? I'll need to use your telephone so I can have the monies delivered. You prefer small bills in a paper sack?"

"*Alors*," he stared at me, exasperated. "The clerk will be here in eight hours. *Patientez*," he said as he looked at his watch. It was one o'clock Tuesday morning.

"I'll return in the morning then."

"*Non*, Madame. You must stay here."

"Here? You mean in the jug?"

"*Mais oui*. Where else? You are being detained, you understand. I've just had an idea. While we are waiting, I shall try to locate the gentleman who filed a complaint for assault against the crazy redheaded American woman on rue Princesse," he taunted.

"You do that; but I'm not your doll." I was looking around for an open window to jump out of.

There was a knock at his door. Gravois's knees creaked as he stood up to answer it. "*Excusez-moi*," he said. "I must speak with someone." He stepped out in the hallway and closed the door behind him.

"Sure, I've got all morning," I yawned as nonchalantly as I could. I was running hot all over again, thinking about how I was going to have to lawyer up if Gravois located Monsieur rue Princesse before the clerk arrived. He surely knew just where to find that nasty-mouthed drunkard.

He returned around twenty minutes later. I had lost track of the time I was so deep in my own thoughts. He didn't look so bee's-knees either. The engine had lost a little steam.

"It appears that you are free to go, Madame Duongé."

I wasn't going to let Gravois set me free only to snatch me up again on some trumped up charge of fleeing police custody. "What about the fine? What about keeping me in the can all night?",

"The fine will be taken care of, shall we say, by your benefactor."

"My benefactor?"

"An officer will escort you out of the building. Your staff and clientele have already been released. Goodbye for now, Madame Ducongé."

I quickly rose to go, without so much as a backward glance at Inspector Gravois. When I arrived outside, Changchang was leaning coolly against a dark car, wiping one of her switchblades down with a cloth. Beside her were Peter's three musician-watchdogs.

"Aunt Ada, are you okay? Did they hurt you in there?"

"No, baby, Aunt Ada is just fine," I gave her a kiss on the forehead. "How are you, baby?"

I reached out to touch her cheek. My hands trembled some when I thought about that hit man's plans for Changchang. I wanted to kill him. Kill him dead. But there were already too many dead bodies in Paris with my name attached to them. Hurting him real bad would have to do.

"Just fine. There's nothing like a pot of hot cabbage to lift the spirits." She was smiling like her old self. I had to remember that Changchang had faced worse in Harlem. This was catnip.

"So they nabbed you three up in the net?" I turned my attention to the Perry Brothers.

"It's alright, Brick," Alphonso said. "That's what we call short time. I've done more and harder time in a North Carolina holdover cell for trying to use a whites-only bathroom."

They all guffawed. I pretended not to know why they were hanging around waiting for me. Since Peter had gone through all the trouble of getting them involved and they had dutifully agreed, I saw no reason to reveal what I knew about their covert mission. It was a matter of pride with them, I could tell.

"I'm real sorry about the raid. But the Baron or some other mob shop is gunning after Bricktop's. I won't pay to play. They've got booby traps laying in the cut for me at every turn—beginning with the Baron and ending with that slack-kneed Inspector Gilles Gravois."

"Don't pay 'em nothing, Brick," Fred hollered.

"You got to stand your ground," Joseph followed up.

"Where are those women you were with this evening?" I asked pointedly.

"I swear we didn't know they was hos, Brick. They let them go a long time ago. Seems like the po-lice knew them real good. A history, you could say." That was Alphonso, chuckling softly.

"I knew what they were when you walked in with them," Changchang said as she kept cleaning that blade. "Mabel let them in with those women, Aunt Ada. You know she wasn't going to flat out ask if they were trading on their bottoms."

"It's okay. I appreciate you boys sticking around, though, to make sure I was alright. I'll be fine. Come on by the club anytime. Without those skirts though."

"It's still early. We going on up to Zelli's for the evening. Goodnight, Brick. Goodnight, Changchang," Joseph said as he made his way toward the taxi stand.

"Joseph!" Changchang called after him, "Zelli's is exactly where you pick up a certain kind of woman."

"Leave them be, Changchang. Those kind of women and those kind of men are equally yoked. I just don't want them yoked together in Bricktop's."

"Bricky."

There was that voice again, coming from the passenger side of the black Delage that Changchang had been leaning against, the voice that had started all of this. The car's driver, a tempting-looking young blond thing, had been sitting stiffly in his seat. Now that I was focusing on the car, I recognized it from Ladurée and the night at Ollie's apartment. There were no smoke clouds swirling out of the window this dark morning. Josie couldn't stand cigarette smoke.

"What are you doing here, Josie? And who's the blond youngster you got driving you?"

"My driver is Matthieu," said Josie. "He is nice on the eyes. But I don't do the help. As to what brought me here, your little moll here fetched me out of La Coupole. But not before she slapped the daylights out of Pepito's cousin Luca. There was blood everywhere because he bit his tongue and he lost a tooth."

"Aunt Ada, you would've been proud of me. He kept trying to put his hand on my rear end but I exercised restraint. I didn't even cut him." Changchang folded her switchblade into her bosom.

I was mighty proud of my Changchang. She was really trying to turn a corner. And after our run-in with that Goliath, little Luca should have been pleased that she hadn't taken out her predilection for slicing and dicing on him. She had moved on from cutting to slapping.

"Don't be mad," my niece added. "Everything started with Miss Josie, so I just went to get her for you. And I'm no moll, either."

Josie rolled her eyes, aiming for indifference—but I could tell she was a little afraid of Changchang, and maybe impressed with her, too.

I said to Josie, "Are you supposed to be my benefactor?"

"I know the Inspector quite well. I'll take care of the fine too, Bricky."

"That's the very least you could do. They're putting the squeeze on me, trying to pinch me for those white stiffs of yours. They raided Bricktop's!"

I didn't feel the need to tell her that Changchang and I had to damn near kill a white man during the raid, or about the attempted murder rap that is sure to follow.

Josie nodded, solemnly. "I know, and I'm sorry about that. I know what your club means to you."

I wasn't finished complaining. "Josie, my capon will be cooked when they get Ollie's phone records and find that sneaky call you made to Bricktop's. But what do you care? You've got your photographs."

Josie's eyes bulged in surprise. "What? I don't have those pictures, Bricky."

"I saw you run out of the apartment with them on Saturday. Ollie's leather satchel was picked clean of them." I hadn't actually seen the pictures in her hands, but it did seem obvious.

"No you didn't. And you know you didn't. I ran because I was upset. It was like someone was trying to pin those murders on *me*. She emphasized that last part. "You know me. I saw her dead body and called you because I was scared and didn't know what else to do. You told me to call her. You did, Bricky. So I did. She was groggy with a hangover and missed our lunch. She apologized and I agreed to come by there before my one o'clock show."

"You spoke to Ollie? Around what time? Where did you call her from?"

"Of course I spoke to her. She was alive at three in the afternoon when I talked to her. I called her from the Casino de Paris where I was in rehearsals.

So Ollie Knolton had been killed after three and before Josie's call to me at around eleven. Josie kept on blabbering in her squeaky soprano.

"The front door was wide open when I got there, and I went looking for Ollie, calling out like a fool. I didn't even step into the bedroom. I just pushed the door open and saw her lying there. Bricky, it was your suggestion that I meet up with her in the first place. So naturally, I called you when I found her body." Her lips were quivering again.

I hadn't thought about it that way. Still and all, she had left me holding. And those blasted pictures were still out there somewhere, just waiting to destroy us. I was so frustrated I could barely speak. "You helped set me up for murder all the same," I barked. "I should have run you out of my place when you first showed up."

"I'm sorry, Bricky. I didn't mean to cause you any trouble with the police. If I was out to try to hurt you, I could have called you and then called the police, and told them they could find you at Ollie's. But instead, I only called you, and I waited for you to get there."

Josie's waterworks had started.

I wanted to ask why she didn't call Pepito that night. He was the fix-it man. "You really don't have them? Have you told Pepito yet?"

"No. I haven't been able to sleep a wink because of those photographs and Pippa and Ollie's murders. I haven't said anything to him."

I was about to start kicking off in her lean behind. "Josie, we agreed you would tell Pepito if things went sideways with Ollie," I said.

"I know what I agreed to," she wailed. "But there is sideways and there is sideways. This was another murder. Not just some disagreement with Ollie over photographs."

I paused for a moment. Not even Pepito could wave his magic wand and make it all go away. So again, without wanting to, I saw her point. "How well do you know Gravois? I hear he's dirty."

"He likes my show at the Casino de Paris. *Paris qui remue*. That's all."

Me and Changchang looked at each other. Changchang started snickering.

"He likes your show alright. He likes that beautiful, tan, naked hide."

We all started laughing. For a moment, it felt like old times plus one. We could have all been the best of friends. We should have been—though I know it would never be possible as long as Josie was with Pepito Abatino.

We were a contrast of colors and ages. Josie looked rich and beautiful in her fur coat and jewels. Changchang glowed with youth under the streetlamp. Her shapely frame was accentuated by the tight-fitting gown she had worn to be presentable when retrieving Josie from La Coupole. And despite my hours in the clink, I wasn't anybody's chopped liver.

I pulled the three of us back down to reality. "Well, somebody has those pictures, and the negatives are somewhere, too. Right now, I'm thinking that Pippa was probably killed over the story she was writing. And maybe Ollie was killed over the pictures she took for that story, since they're now missing. Josie, those photographs of you are probably an accidental part of the package—which means we Negroes are still in limbo. And whoever has those pictures committed the murders and is trying to give me an extended vacation at the Château d'If."

"Aunt Ada, Miss Josie and I were talking. We can't let you go back to Montmartre and sulk about the raid all night. Clyde was hiding in the back alley of the club when you made me fly the coop during the raid. He said he was going straight back to Bricktop's after the police left to clean up the mess. We have got to open tomorrow evening. We've got to think about your reputation," said Changchang.

"Indeed!" I snapped. "And what about it?"

"We think you need to go out and show yourself," Changchang continued, ignoring the fire in my tone. "Everyone knows about the raid, and they saw you getting hauled in. You've got to hold your head up tonight. Let yourself be seen."

"I just spent hours in the can," I said. "I'm hardly at my best."

Josie stepped forward with a big smile. "We've got everything you need in my car. A fresh dress, stockings, shoes. It ain't roomy back there, but you've had small dressing rooms before. Matthieu won't look. He's a gentleman."

Changchang and Josie were right. With no time to lose, I had to shore up my reputation. I needed to be seen here, there, and everywhere throughout Paris to let folks know that Chez Bricktop was neither down nor out. Bricktop's was my baby. I had birthed her, nurtured her, and raised her until she was full grown. I wasn't about to let anyone tear me or her down.

"I'd do crazier things to save my club," I muttered. Then I wiggled into the back seat of Josie's car and began to strip off my clothes. Changchang tapped on the window, discreetly handing me Mister Speaker as I rolled it down.

"You'll surely feel naked without him."

THE PIGEON'S SWAN SONG

XII.

The Boulevard Montparnasse was still teeming with people and cars as we pulled up in front of La Coupole with its eye-popping red awning. This large café-club was one of Josie's favorite Parisian haunts. She danced, sang, and ate there with regularity. And the club owner loved her for it, as she brought in the crowd—the looky-loos, the eager beaver tourists, and even local city folks who aspired to be trendsetters.

We were promptly escorted to Josie's special table. Pepito and his behind-grabbing cousin Luca had already moved on. Luca had probably needed to pay an emergency visit to a dentist, thanks to Changchang. The café society began milling about our table; some even stopped to say hello to Josie and me.

"We represent half the colored women's population in Paris this morning," Josie cackled facetiously.

We all nodded our heads because what she said was just about right, thanks to the recent American exodus from Paris after the stock market took such a dive and the French tightened up on work permits for foreigners to offset French unemployment.

"What you drinking?" Josie flagged down a waiter from across the room. The man practically flew over to our table, clearly smitten with us since our arrival.

"Remy-Martin," I decided.

Josie turned to Changchang. "Given your steely constitution, I gather you'd like vodka straight up?"

"Actually Miss Josie, I'll take some nice warm milk on this cold night."

"Milk?" Josie rolled her eyes.

"Leave the child be, Josie. You're lucky she didn't ask for hot chocolate."

"Child? That's a full grown tiger you got there, Bricky. Here she is requesting milk like a kitten after bloodying mouths and loosening teeth!"

"Luca deserved more than a hard slap and a lost tooth," I interjected. "Damn I-talians. You know how they are, pinching on you and carrying on. My ass was raw when I left Italy." I didn't want anybody, especially Josie, trying to ruin all my hard work with Changchang. The girl had made good progress. I had abandoned my "no bad language" rule since all this Josie drama began. I was surely in hell and I didn't know when—or even if—I was coming back. I was deeply concerned about that half-dead Frenchman. I didn't want him to finger Changchang. I was wondering if I could get into that hospital across town and pillow-smother him. I almost laughed aloud, as I banished the murderous thought to a corner in my mind.

"Miss Josie," Changchang started up.

"Stop calling me, Miss Josie!"

"I was raised to respect my elders, Miss Josie."

"I ain't that much older than you!"

Changchang was being devilish. She knew she was scratching at Josie's age-obsessed soul. Every woman in her line of work knew they had an expiration date. Josie and Pepito's attempt to restart her career was a testament to her jitters.

"Here's how I look at it, Josie." When she dropped the Miss in front of Josie, Changchang gave a little smile that was more like a warning. "Everything outside of my person belonged to Luca. Everything on my person belonged to me. Wouldn't I have been a frightful sight with a hand sprouting from my rear end? It simply had to be removed and in such a way that it would never return. Now we three know what troubles you. You left my Aunt Ada of your own free will and never looked back until you needed something. I've chosen to stay."

Before Josie could respond to that last salvo, a commotion at the entrance of La Coupole distracted us all. There was pushing and shoving by a throng of reporters and light bulbs were flashing. Josie sat upright to see who could possibly have dimmed her spotlight.

It was Mistinguett, queen of the Paris Cabaret, who always found her way to Bricktop's after a show. "Hello there, Bricky. I went by Bricktop's and everything was pitch. *Je suis tellment triste.* Just too, too sad about it. It's good to see you on this side of town, even in present company," she nodded dismissively in Josie's direction, and Josie, in turn, chose to ignore her rival.

"Mistinguett." I wanted to tell her that I was the one sadder than blue about Bricktop's being shuttered. I got up from the table to give her a hug and a round of light cheek-kisses. Cameras continued clicking. I wasn't about to turn my back on her for Josie. When Josie had shown me her back, Mistinguett had remained supportive of my fledgling dream. She'd helped to give my place cachet, honoring us with her popular version of "Mon Homme," which was infinitely better than Fanny Brice's Americanized "My Man."

Over my shoulder, Mistinguett threw a comment to Josie. "If it isn't banana tits. And still following in my footsteps, too: first the Folies Bergère, now the Casino de Paris."

"Not quite, old battle-axe," Josie finally returned the favor of an insult.

The press corps giggled appreciatively. Celebrity catfights made for good copy. Josie and Mistinguett had been engaged in a fierce ongoing battle for the title of Paris's Queen of the Music Hall for the past five years. While Josie was an exotic import, Mistinguett had the advantage of being a homegrown native. But while the French seemed to care more about aesthetics than youthful beauty, Mistinguett had the disadvantage of being a tad long in the tooth. Given the attention span of the French public, the two stars frequently attempted to outshine one another, calling each other out to keep the public interested. When Mistinguett's Moulin Rouge show received glowing reviews, Josie, not to be outdone, had purchased her pet leopard, Chiquita. She'd put a diamond-studded collar on her and paraded her up and down the Champs-Élysées for effect. She even brought her exotic pet to her shows, pulling her out on the stage to create a stir.

"*Quelle belle fille!* And just who are you, my dear?" Mistinguett had just discovered Changchang.

Josie's expression tightened.

Changchang didn't take "the enemy of my enemy is my friend" route.

"Madame Bricktop is my aunt. And Josie Baker here? Well, she's like the sister you could have never imagined having."

She grinned mischievously at Josie, whose face was now gladdened with relief and amusement.

"Brick and I were just going to the stage, weren't we, Bricky?" Josie tugged at my hand.

Mistinguett was now moving toward a seat at a table quite near our own.

"Fine," I said, following Josie out to the dance floor. She instructed the band to play the song "Charleston." They weren't as good as my orchestra, but the music was *passable*, as the French say. We began with the Charleston and then went through a repertoire of all the American dances: the Shimmy, the Black Bottom, and the Cake Walk from our days on the vaudeville circuit. We had the place jumping. Cameras whirred and clicked as we laughed and danced like old times. Mistinguett, with a glass of some clear liquid, sat placidly in her chair, her face squarely turned toward the windows, gazing out at the boulevard.

"You needed that, Bricky." Josie squeezed my hand tight as we left the floor to applause.

"I really, really did," I let out a deep sigh. "I'm glad you weren't just trying to reclaim the spotlight from Mistinguett."

"Can't a woman want more than one thing?" Josie laughed, and I did, too. But that little burst of happiness wouldn't last long.

❧

Changchang and I left Josie at her Delage with Matthieu.

"Let's go over to Le Boeuf," I said.

"For Jonny Dumont?" Changchang's pretty mouth turned down at the corners. "He's the stool pigeon, isn't he? Leave it to a drug addict to come up with some crazy story about prostitution at Bricktop's."

The more I thought about it, the more Jonny Dumont seemed a likely candidate for a dime-dropper. He'd denied knowing Renata right to my face, and it occurred to me that he'd been hanging over my shoulder on Friday night, right when Changchang handed me Ollie's address. And what was that nasty thing he'd said on his way out the door? *One mean turn deserves another.* That's the trouble with dope fiends, they lose any good sense they were born with. Was he taking revenge on me because I wouldn't lower my standards and give him a job? That kind of selfishness made me sick.

"What a world," I said to Changchang. "I feel bad, bringing you to Paris to escape the hoodlums in Harlem—only to put you smack in the thick of it, right at Bricktop's.

Changchang dismissed my apology. "This is nothing compared to Harlem and you know it. I'm actually enjoying myself. Everything, even the violence here, seems so glamorous."

"Maybe Josie was right about you, girl," I laughed. "You are a bit of a moll. But please be careful, baby. I only got one of you, and you're too, too precious to lose."

Changchang was driving us in the direction of rue Penthièvre. We were going to Le Boeuf sur le Toit. Le Boeuf was a chic gay hangout that even straights didn't mind being seen entering. It was designed with glamour in mind, with high-back booths for privacy, gilded chandeliers and mirrors, thick, brocaded draperies and carpets, and Haviland porcelain made in the Limoges region of France. Le Boeuf was more of a fine supper club than a rowdy jazz spot, and I liked to go there sometimes for a drink and the music.

Le Boeuf's owner, Louis Moyse, instantly recognized me and gave us a plum seat near the front. Jonny Dumont was tinkling on the piano. He was playing his heart out. We waved at him, all friendly like. Louis asked would I sing for the audience. Since I had just danced at La Coupole, why not sing at Le Boeuf? I launched into "Manhattan." Everything was so heavy around me, I wanted to sing something light. Jonny picked up the tune right away, and I slipped into my fractured French.

> We'll go to Coney
> And *mange* baloney on a roll
> In Central Park we'll stroll
> Where our first *bisous* we stole

The crowd went wild for the French twist I put on the song. I took my seat next to Changchang, and we waited for Jonny. Sure enough, when the band took a break, he waltzed directly to our table.

"Hey, Brick, Changchang. Good to see you out this morning."

"You heard about Bricktop's?" I quizzed him.

"Everybody's heard."

"Why, Jonny? I gave you a job when no one else would. Not a permanent one, but you know I would've brought you back whenever I could."

Jonny was quiet. His hands began to shake some. Jonny Dumont took off running. He pushed through the dancing throng, elbowed one woman in the ribs who yelped loudly, and clawed at his shirt as he whizzed by.

He was hollering the whole time, "I'm real sorry, Brick. I had no choice."

Changchang and I looked at one another. I moved toward the back exit on Jonny's tail with Changchang at my heels. We were fast-walking so as not to trip on our long dresses.

"Go get the car. He's headed toward the back street."

I continued out the back exit. Jonny was still in my view. He would occasionally look around and holler again about being real sorry. He had turned around, running backward, trying to explain something I could barely make out.

By the time he turned back around to launch into a full stride, he ran straight into the driver's door of my vanilla Citroën C6 with Changchang at the wheel. She slid out quickly, slamming his midsection again with the open door.

We were both standing over Jonny Dumont.

"Jonny," I said huffing a good deal, "there's always a choice. You chose to set the cops on me. And you told them Ollie Knolton was at my club and gave me her address. You said I had prostitutes up in Bricktop's. What else did you tell them?"

Even in the dark, I could see that Jonny's face was filled with remorse, and some of it might have been genuine. He sputtered from exhaustion, "What was I going to do? They made me. The truth don't make no difference in this. See what they did to me, Brick?" He pulled at the buttons on his shirt and revealed bandaged ribs. "They told me what to say, and then they told me to get creative."

"Who's they?" I demanded, but Jonny shook his head.

Changchang twisted a satin shoe into a bandaged rib.

He groaned loudly. "Okay. Okay. Bricky make her stop, please!!"

I looked over at Changchang. She lifted her foot but then came back down hard on his ribs to a squealing Jonny. She then eased up. Jonny's lips shivered. "They wanted your back against the wall, and if I hadn't gone along, I think they would've killed me."

"And you think I won't?" Changchang's red lips were turned up in an inscrutable smile.

Jonny looked from me to Changchang and back. "Bricky, you wouldn't wanna let her kill old Jonny, would you?"

It was cold outside. But we were all hot and high off adrenaline. Jonny had to have felt it the worst being pinned on his back on the frigid cobblestones.

"Get up, Jonny." I gave him my hand. "And you know damn well I don't run a ho house," I bellowed for good measure. To me, that was worse than being called a murderess. I could feel the hairs on my neck stand up like an aggravated dog. I raised my voice louder. "Who's 'they,' Jonny? Was it the Baron?"

"Naw, it wun't no Baron, Brick. That's all I can say," he whimpered as he came to a standing position. He was trembling but not from the cold. "I'm a weak man, Brick. I can't leave it alone. They hurt me, too. Real bad. Then they gave me something for my trouble. It was Renata who told them about that woman's address on Friday night. That wasn't me, Brick, I swear. She saw her give it to you at Bricktop's."

"I'll make him tell us, Aunt Ada." Changchang took hold of Jonny's opened shirt and pulled his face close to hers. "I'll hurt you worse than they did. We'll see how well you'll be playing tomorrow night on nubs. I already had a practice run on another man this morning."

"Naw. Naw, Brick, don't let her hurt me! Please! How can she be so pretty and so mean? It don't make no sense. Please, Brick?"

I gritted my teeth. I had a sour feeling in my stomach, knowing we shouldn't have made such a scene back at Le Boeuf. It was all Jonny Dumont's damn fault, running and carrying on. "I'm mad as hell at you, Jonny." It took all kinds of restraint for me not to kick Jonny in his ass right there on that dimly lit backstreet. "You need to come by Bricktop's in the morning so we can talk. Okay?"

"Okay, I will. I'm real sorry, real sorry, Brick."

"Wait," I said. "Tell me about that Renata woman. Where is she?"

"I saw her this evening before I left to come to the club. At my place. But I 'on't know where she is now. She comes and goes as she pleases, which is fine by me. She sometimes stays over with that queer woman over in Saint-Germain. She gives her drugs to stay with her."

"Natalie Barney?"

"Yeah, but Renata said she wan't going there no mo.'"

This was interesting—something to think about, later. There was something bizarre going on between Natalie and Renata. In some ways, I admired Natalie, but I sure didn't approve of her giving drugs to that strung-out Renata.

Changchang leaned close to Jonny and whispered real calm in his ear, "You'll be sorrier than sorry if you don't show up later this morning."

He looked from Changchang to me and then nodded his head in the affirmative. He reached into his pocket for a cigarette but was too jittery to light it. "I better get back to the piano," he muttered, as he strolled down the alley. He looked back cautiously several times to see if Changchang was trailing him.

We returned to Le Boeuf and watched Jonny nervously tinkle out a few more tunes. Changchang and I managed to show our faces at La Cave and Chez Florence, but my heart was no longer in it. I tried to put on a good show of being unruffled by the events since Friday night, but I couldn't stop thinking about Jonny and Renata.

It was five o'clock when we arrived back at Bricktop's. Changchang went to the kitchen to change and prepare breakfast for the musicians.

Falcon came in, followed by Gut Bucket, and he was shaking his head in disbelief. "Have you heard?

"Heard what?" I asked.

Gut Bucket jumped in to deliver the news. "Jonny Dumont was found outside Le Boeuf sur le Toit this morning. His fingers were chopped off and somebody cut a shit-eating grin across his throat. Damn shame."

"Where did you hear that?"

"It's all over Montmartre."

I knew exactly what was coming next. And no more than an hour later, didn't "Flypaper" Gravois whiten my door?

The French Inspector strolled into my club, cool as an icicle. He was taking in the club's décor.

I went up to greet him. "We've got to stop meeting like this, Inspector Gravois."

"I do not go in for these sorts of places. This one though, c'est agréable. The glass floors are elegant. This is a sophisticated little boîte you have here, Madame Ducongé."

"Thank you. Would you like something to eat, Inspector?"

"Non. I have had my café. I need to speak with you and your chef."

"What about?"

"Monsieur Jonny Dumont."

"What about him?"

"Surely you've heard. He was murdered this morning after you visited him. Or should I say chased him?"

"I didn't visit him," I pushed down a gulp of air filled with grief. It felt like a series of hiccups in my chest. I reached for a handkerchief. A solitary tear had reached my chin. "I visited Le Boeuf sur le Toit."

"So you admit you were at that establishment?" Flypaper pressed, ignoring what he probably thought was a feigned show of emotion. "I admire your precision, Madame Ducongé. But come now. He elbowed a patron trying to escape the club. You gave chase. His hands were dismembered, and he was cut from here to here." He moved his finger from one side of his neck to the other.

"Why wouldn't I admit to being at Le Boeuf? I can hardly chase anyone in high heels and a long evening gown. When I left Le Boeuf, Jonny Dumont was alive and well and playing the piano. I'd like to know what Jonny's dismembered hands and cut throat have to do with me and Changchang?"

"Everyone knows about your knife-wielding chef. She has quite the reputation."

This was why I had stopped Changchang from slicing that Frenchman's throat. "You shouldn't believe everything you hear. Besides, what would a chef be without a knife? And seriously, why on earth would we kill Jonny Dumont? And when would we have found the time to do it? We stopped at a number of clubs last night, and I'm sure there are plenty of witnesses who could tell you this. If you must know, we visited La Coupole, La Cave, and Chez Florence this morning, too. Give it a day. You'll probably see photos of us in the morning papers. If we'd gone on a killing spree, don't you think our clothing would have shown it?"

I was glad for the press taking pictures at La Coupole. We'd been wise to squire ourselves there this morning with Josie. And Mistinguett's appearance was the cherry on top.

What I said seemed to stump the Inspector. "Perhaps you are right. I am merely tracing the decedent's last hours, *vous voyez*." He fingered his moustache, pulling at it, really, as if he were weighing my words against his lack of evidence.

I didn't respond. I would not let him hang Jonny's death on me, or Changchang. I wouldn't even admit to talking to Jonny at all, unless I was pressed. Gravois was now missing a critical witness in his case against me; and though I knew it wouldn't stop him, something in the universe had shifted in my favor. It had come at Jonny's expense, which was too bad. I liked Jonny, and I had deeply admired his music. His bandaged ribs told me he had tried to do right by me. Drugs, addiction, and a beating can be powerful inducements to lie.

Changchang stayed back in the kitchen, though I knew she was listening hard to every word spoken. Despite the breakfast crowd, Bricktop's was so quiet you could hear cotton balls blowing in the wind. All eyes were on me and the Inspector.

"Perhaps I shall trouble you for a *café* after all."

"Why certainly."

The usual jovial banter was quieted that morning at Bricktop's. Every-one ate in silence, watching the Inspector slowly drink his coffee and stroke his moustache. The musicians cleared out of Bricktop's just as soon as they finished eating. Gilles Gravois was like an old hant pursuing me. Whether he ruined my business and sullied my reputation as a murderess or a madame, it seemed that Inspector Gravois was determined to put the squeeze on me unless I paid up.

There had to be some way to cut the net he was weaving all around me. All I had to do was find the right tool. It would have to be something sharp. Like the truth. And another thing. I still had to get Josie's damn pictures back.

THE GANG'S ALL HERE

XIII.

The telephone had been ringing all morning. I kept staring at it. None of us dared to answer it or use it while Flypaper was there. We didn't want him meddling in our business any further than he had already inserted himself. If he noticed it, he didn't say a word. That was the longest cup of coffee I had ever seen a French person drink. And their coffees come in tiny cups, not like our big, watery cups of *jus de chaussette*, as the French called American coffee. *Sock juice.*

Finally, Creaky Knees took his leave. And as soon as he'd reached the steps leading down to the club's main entrance, I grabbed the telephone on the first ring. I could hear the operator trying to connect the call.

"Bricktop's."

"Ada? Ada? Where have you been all morning?"

It was Mama on the telephone, and I could hear the worry in her voice, as well as some irritation. She hated when I answered the phone "Bricktop's." She disliked my nickname with a passion. That's because there was an Irish prostitute with red hair, back in Chicago, called Bricktop. She had a pimp named Jet. You can imagine what color Jet was.

It was Barron Wilkins of Barron's Exclusive in Harlem who had first called me Bricktop. I'd met him when I was seventeen years old and that nickname just stuck ever since. I liked the tough and sassy sound of it, but it sure drove Mama crazy. She hated the name even more when she visited France and heard everyone calling me Madame Bricktop. It was just too much for a self-respecting, upstanding Christian Negro woman to hear her daughter called a double ho. I was afraid to imagine the fits Mama would have if she found out what Gilles Gravois was accusing me of. This is why you sometimes have to protect your parents from the truth. They feel your pain, sometimes even more than you do.

"I've been here, Mama. It's been busy all morning."

"From what Peter told me, it's been too busy."

I should have known Peter would call Mama. They were thick.

"It's nothing I can't handle."

"Gangsters and dead white women? I hear you taking up cigars again. That's more than anyone can handle. You need to come on home for a spell."

"I can't, Mama. It's the busy season. I can't just close the club and run on home like a little girl. I have a business to run, and money to earn, so I can send you some more of those fancy couture dresses you like so much." I tried to play it light so Mama would leave it alone.

"I'd rather have you home and safe than me marching around in couture dresses, baby. Besides, Blonzetta's got enough money for us all. You need to come back to Chicago, Ada."

My sister's real name was Etta, but we called her blond Etta because of her hair and that name eventually became Blonzetta. She had made a lot of money in the real estate business in Chicago. Enough to keep Mama in high cotton. But I was not about to turn tail and run back to America. There was nothing there for me anymore. I loved America, even if it didn't always love me back. But I was happy where I was. I was remembering that old song, "How're you going to keep 'em down on the farm once they've seen Gay Paree?" Maybe one day I'd return to America, but for now, France was my home.

Besides I couldn't leave. If I tried, the French police would probably be waiting for me at boat docks to take my passport. I was tempted to point this out to Mama, but I didn't want to get her any more riled.

"Everything is alright, Mama. Peter shouldn't have bothered you. I'll call you on Sunday when the rates are lower."

I was going to have a word with that husband of mine as soon as he returned home. I was touched that he'd been so worried that he called Mama. But if I wasn't going to the Netherlands and Bruges with my beloved Peter, I sure wasn't going to run home to Mama, all the way back to America.

I disconnected Mama's call and had a call placed to Natalie Barney.

"Natalie, it's Brick." I said it calm, but my stomach was in knots after the Inspector's visit.

"I hope you aren't bringing more bad news, Bricky darling. I don't know if I could bear another death. As it stands, we've suspended our meetings until things quiet down in Paris."

"I'm actually calling you about an old friend of yours. Renata. I need to locate her." I figured I'd cut to the chase.

Natalie didn't respond. Instead she breathed hard into the phone.

"Renata Vian. She's been nothing but trouble from the day I met her. No one has heard from her."

So Vian was Renata's surname. "So she was one of your liaisons?" I wanted to hear it from Natalie. Jonny had lied on me, so why wouldn't he lie on Natalie.

"She was more than that, but we're talking about old news. We've been together, on and off, for over ten years. She's a fascinating creature with a bit of a habit, if you know what I mean. Laudanum. Chloral hydrate. And she can be so stubborn. Reckless and vulnerable, that's Renata. Why are you looking for Renata?" Jealousy crackled through the telephone wires.

I said, "Renata's habit isn't news either. I heard somewhere that she and Jonny Dumont were good friends. That's why I'm calling."

"Don't mention his name to me. I hope to never see him again."

"You won't. Jonny was murdered sometime this morning. And I'm afraid the same fate awaits Renata if I don't find her first. She and Jonny have poor taste in associates. What did Jonny do to you?"

"What do you think? He stole my girl. With Jonny, she got the drugs, the jazz, and the excitement. He had a kind of primitive charm. After he got her interested in that jazz sketching, she hardly ever came around anymore."

I ignored Nat's crack about primitive charm. This was no time to pick a fight. Still, it irked me.

She sighed loudly into the receiver. "I'm ashamed to admit it. She would only come over if I supplied her drugs. She wouldn't let me touch her otherwise. I could hear the catch in Natalie's voice. But I wasn't feeling overly sympathetic.

"So you loved her and she didn't love you back."

"Something like that. I wanted to be with her, but I was never a one-woman kind of a woman, Brick."

"So she loved you then hated you, and you kept on loving her anyway. That's a terrible kind of love when you have to buy it with drugs. You're a good woman, Nat. I hope you never again exploit someone's vulnerability to make them love you. Maybe you should have left her alone."

I had to tell Natalie what I thought. She had been honest with me about her frailties and we were becoming something more than casual acquaintances. I couldn't go on sharing her confidences if I hadn't spoken my mind. I had a mental picture of Renata burning a hole in Natalie's mahogany table and it made more sense now.

"I know," she sobbed into the telephone. I feel so awful. You just don't know, Brick. I should have helped her. I should have been a better friend."

"Even Amazons have their weaknesses," I offered in compromise. "So where do you think she might be?"

"An opium den."

"There are opium dens all over Paris. It's not like there is a directory for them."

"I know. I'm sorry I can't be of more help. She liked the more exclusive drug dens, if that narrows it down any. You know that awful Inspector asked the same thing about Renata. He also inquired after you too, Brick. But I told him I could be of no use to him, even if I wanted to, seeing as though he had prattled on terribly about us vile Americans invading France. Imagine that?"

"Is that so?" I wrinkled my forehead. Gilles Gravois was at least consistent with his storytelling about Americans. I couldn't help but think the inspector's overzealousness about *la mère patrie* had to do with his being Corsican. French but not quite.

I wasn't too happy to hear, though, that he too was searching high and low for Renata. I wondered if he was lining her up to be picked off by his partners in crime.

"Why yes!" Natalie breezed on. "Brick, I do hope you find her before whoever got to Jonny Dumont does."

I didn't mention to Natalie that I had my own reasons for wanting to track Renata down. Only Renata could tell me what Jonny hadn't been able to—who put them up to framing me—and by extension—who had those damn photographs of Josie. I might also be able to her keep alive for another day, despite the fact that she had left me twisting in the wind. Drug addicts rarely enjoy long lives.

"Mmmm hmmm. Me, too. Well, Nat, I have to close up here and get some breakfast."

"Bricky?"

I could now feel sugar oozing through the telephone wire.

"Yes?"

"Do think about sending Renata on to me for safekeeping, will you?"

I pressed the dial tone in Natalie Barney's ear without responding.

I made one other phone call to a Monsieur René Claudel, the owner of the apartment at 19 rue Fleurus. Monsieur Claudel told me a lot of things about himself. He said he had just returned late Sunday from chasing the sun's rays at Villefranche-sur-mer on the French Riviera, that I had been lucky to catch him and not his timid assistant, Manu. He even described the apartment as *charmant* and *bel*; but he never, ever mentioned murder or Pippa Nelson.

After that call, I did something that morning that I had never done in all my years as a saloonkeeper. I took a swig of Remy Martin champagne at nine in the morning. *Poor Jonny. Maybe I should have hired him to keep him safe. Maybe then, he'd still be alive.* If only he'd told me what was going on and who was behind it. Maybe I could've done something. Or maybe it was all hopeless. I was a strong woman, yes. But who exactly was I up against? Jonny said it wasn't the Baron. But that didn't sit right with me either. Whoever my invisible enemies were, they didn't like loose ends. And that's what Jonny had become. I could still see him with his nervous laugh and shaky hands, begging me for his job back.

I heard the swoosh of the parting and closing of the curtains and rose from my seat at the bar. "We're closed," I explained to the footsteps entering the club. I hadn't bothered to look up.

"Even for me?" said the man with an accent I recognized. As he approached, I swiveled around to see that four men followed him.

"You've got a lot nerve showing up here after you had my club raided, made a false report on me to the police, and sent a damn hit man after my Changchang." I was giving Monsieur Baron de Boulainvilliers the business and the nastiest stare I could muster.

"*Alors*, Madame Bricktop. I did in fact report you to the police. It was my duty as a good French citizen, *vous comprenez*. You menaced me." He puckered his lips churlishly.

He meant to say threatened but found the French word instead. I couldn't help thinking it made me sound like some sort of mad dog on the loose in Paris—which was exactly how Inspector Gravois thought of me.

I pursed my lips in kind. The Baron's voice was soothing, sweet even to listen to if you could just ignore his profession and the words.

"There is, as you well know, an open investigation into the murder of my beloved Pippa," he spoke softly now, "and you, *mon petit oiseau*, asked too many questions. As to these other charges, I am *un peu perturbé* to hear you think so little of me. A hit man? We prefer to keep things in the family, don't we Paul-Henri?"

"*Bah, oui*," the henchman blurted out in agreement.

I furrowed my brow at his denials. "So you are a reasonable gangster who prefers his own kind, is that it?" He joined me at the bar, making himself comfortable on one of my stools.

"You've refused my kindness of protection," he continued, ignoring the jab, "you've menaced my mother even. Yet, I have returned to speak with you in the gentlest way possible about that kindness. I am a persistent suitor. *Mon petit oiseau*, this spurning of my *gentillesse* makes me feel *terrible*," he added in a few French words for effect. "I cannot have this. The others," he turned his head toward the streets, "will suspect I have soft spot for you and follow your very bad example."

I thought about shooting the Baron dead. I did a quick once-over of the club. My odds didn't look too good. I was outnumbered and outgunned. My legs felt wobbly, so I perched back on my stool, trying to make it look casual. This was no time to be showing weakness.

When I'd first struck out on my own after Le Grand Duc and opened the short-lived Music Box, the coppers and the gangsters had swarmed like flies. I had a temporary license back then. A *provisoire*. My club was getting so much foot traffic the other club owners in Montmartre got jealous. So they'd sicced the cops and the mob on me, and I was shut down because of noise. Noise! It had never occurred to me until the Baron's visit that maybe the local gangsters and corrupt cops had simply been biding their time. They had let me open Bricktop's because they knew that they could have a go at me again and try to take a piece of the good action. I was still silent and mean-mugging the Baron with my best efforts.

"Gangster? I am not a gangster." He meandered back to my original charge when I hadn't responded. He said gangster the way French people do: *gong-stair*. "We are business people. You and I."

"You're in the hustling business. I'm in the entertaining business. It's different, you see?" I finally blurted out because I could no longer contain myself. "This ain't that kinda joint. You talking about me offending you. You people got me up to my neck with the police. You're killing friends of mine after you finished using them. Discarded poor Jonny like he was dirt." I almost took another hit of that bottle thinking about Jonny Dumont.

"I haven't killed any friend of yours. We don't murder people, do we, Paul-Henri?"

It must have been a rhetorical question because Paul-Henri did not cosign this time.

He showed that even set of pearly white teeth. "We are all hustling, as you say. Even you. You really don't have much of a choice. I've been very patient, and I've come here now to talk terms. You have had a rough night, I understand. That would never have happened with my protection." He said this as he did a gallant sweeping motion with his arm across the now cleaned-up club.

He seemed a man of grand gestures and elegant flourishes like his gabardine woven suit. The wormy finger gave him away everytime though. "We've given you plenty of leeway. It's time to get down to the important things at hand."

He had the litany of clichés down pat in English. *Talk terms. Not much of a choice. Time to get down to things.*

Gangster movies should be banned in France. That's what I was thinking when I shook my head. "The only thing I'm getting down to is the floor from this here barstool." I slid off.

"It is not beneath me to slap a broad." He hesitated and then laughed for a good while to himself. "Is that how you say it in English?" He nodded and his flunky henchman, Paul-Henri, came up from behind me, holding a knife to my throat.

That's when I saw a meat cleaver whizz by and someone—not me—was roaring in pain. The tips of three fingers went flying off on a table in front of me, and blood began spraying all over the table and floor.

I heard chairs turning over and an oomph sound. If I moved my head too far in one direction, Paul-Henri pressed the knife deeper into my throat. Another someone was on the floor whining like a newborn. The Baron fired a shot toward the kitchen, another toward the area where the chairs had been turned over, and a third toward the leather curtains at the entrance, where I heard what sounded like a bottle being smashed, a few thuds, and a "Take that motherfucker" from a voice that sounded remarkably like one of the Perry Brothers.

Distracted by the mewling, screams, shots, and flying cutlery, the Baron began playing his own version of dodge ball. He moved so wildly he couldn't aim straight.

To my right, I saw a dark fist connect with the French hoodlum holding me. I heard a hard snap. As Paul-Henri fell back from the blow, he had nicked me with his knife. I felt a trickle of blood down my neck. He had released his grip on my neck completely.

Paul-Henri now had a shocked look on his face. He doubled over low to the ground from another punch to his face. Between gasps for air, he started blubbering, "Mon Dieu, mon dieu."

"God can't help you now, baby. You should have thought about that before you eased up in here and cut me with that knife." I kicked him hard in the face. He fell back into Papa Jack's open-handed slap upside his head.

He was hiccupping up saliva and swallowing tears on the floor. I turned and pulled my revolver on the Baron. He had been keenly focusing on the knives slicing through the air from the kitchen. At the same time, he was now aiming his piece right at my chest.

Papa Jack Johnson, who was standing beside me, adjusted his tailored suit jacket. "We got the drop on you, Mr. Baron."

"Yeah, motherfucker. Up in here, bothering Brick and Changchang. What's up, Champ?" I immediately recognized Alphonso, and standing beside him was Fred.

Papa Jack nodded to Alphonso before fixing his gaze back on the Baron. "I think you need to be going along now, Mr. Baron, before you suffer what your boys here did. You don't want none of that there," Papa Jack pointed at the four downed men.

Changchang had two knives in her hand when she emerged from the corridor leading to the kitchen and back office.

It was time for me to make my stand. "I am going to make you an offer, talk some terms in the gentlest way I can," I told him. "We can fill you with lead, stainless steel, or glass, or we can pummel you good," I tossed my chin toward Changchang, Papa Jack, and two of the Perry Brothers, Alphonso and Fred, "or you and your colleagues can leave here now, while you still have some pieces intact—and don't come back again."

Paul-Henri let out a moan of relief. I guess he thought we were going to slaughter all five of them. I reached for a cloth napkin to press against the fresh cut on my neck and surveyed the damage. There were splashes of blood on my glass-panel floors, the bar, and tables.

Paul-Henri wailed loudly again when he tried to get up off the floor. Another bad character had a broken jaw and was holding his ribs. The hoodlum closest to the entrance had been hit with a champagne bottle and was still laid out on the floor, dabbing his injured head with a handkerchief. Mister Missing Digits in the corner was wrapping one of my good napkins around his wounded fingers to stop the bleeding. Every time he looked at his hand, he started upchucking his breakfast and calling out, "*Aidez-moi! Aidez-moi.*"

"Leave my damn napkins alone. You want help now, do you?" I tossed a freshly laundered bar-top rag toward the corner. He crawled on his knees through dark red spots of his own blood to get to it, his pant legs mopping up the droppings as he slid along the glass. "Now get to stepping so I can clean my place up."

The Baron moved out coolly. He tipped his hat at me. I knew it wasn't over. I had disgraced him. But I knew that I had also underestimated him. I wouldn't do that again. We were going to the mattresses with the French mob. The Baron had plenty of manpower. I had Papa Jack, but he was just passing through. And I couldn't hire the Perry Brothers permanently at Bricktop's as both entertainment and muscle; Bricktop's cabaret called for variety. As it was, I wondered what Peter was paying them already. No. The Baron would think I was easy pickings because I was a woman, and he would never tell the rest of his gangster compatriots about this bloodletting.

I turned toward the curtains as the hoodlums were departing in single file, hobbling and sniveling. Then, suddenly, I saw them backing up, into the cabaret.

"Madame Bricktop, are you okay?"

For the first time in my life, I was happy to see the police. Jean Bergeron had arrived with two of his officers.

"I'm fine. Just a little nick. These men were harassing us."

"We have been instructed to watch your establishment. I saw them go up. They did not look especially friendly."

"As you can see, they weren't." That was Papa Jack.

Jean's men began handcuffing the Baron and his gang.

Meanwhile, Jean was transfixed by the Champ. "Monsieur, you are . . . Monsieur Jack Johnson?"

"Why yes I am," he smiled, pleased to be recognized, though he was no longer revered in some quarters.

"Jean Bergeron. You came to France in 1913 when I was just a boy of fifteen. I begged my father to take me to that fight. We did not go. We were too poor. But I remember the posters. It is a pleasure to meet you finally."

After shaking hands with Papa Jack, whose squeeze was so hard it made the officer cringe, Bergeron watched his men prod the gangsters out of my club. As he departed, the officer called back cheerfully, "These men will not bother you again, Madame Bricktop."

No, not those men, I thought. But there will be others just like them.

The Baron was getting desperate to rein me in. There was obviously some truth to his concerns about other club owners thinking they could follow my example. He needed to get me in line and *tout de suite*. We were going into week two of our Battle Royale. In the last five days alone, he had run at me two times. Though he denied yesterday night's raid and the unseemly antics of the leviathan Frenchman, his sorties counted as three. The pressure was building to an explosive climax. I could feel it. The Baron would just be more careful in his next approach. This meant that I had to be more careful as well.

All of a sudden, everything was quiet and still. "Where did you come from?" I asked Papa Jack, giving him a hug and peck on the cheek.

"I called him, Aunt Ada, just as soon as those men whitened our door." Changchang walked over to retrieve her meat cleaver from the floor, as though she was picking up a soup ladle or a bunch of flowers. The gore didn't dismay her one bit. With Changchang, it didn't matter if it was meat cleavers, bottles, or hammers, it was all in her hand-eye coordination. Knives were just easier to tote around. That hit man really was lucky that I had been there to save his hide. I shook my head.

Papa Jack grinned. "Don't be mad, Brick. I slipped her my telephone number after dinner Sunday. Told her to call me anytime at the Grande Hotel Sacre Coeur. I was hoping she'd call me for something other than gangsters. Good thing the hotel is so close by. I got here in two shakes."

"I let him in through the kitchen back door, and he slipped in like a panther," said Changchang.

"The bar was a nice shield or else that Mr. Baron would have popped a few caps in my behind," he laughed heartily. "Those other boys didn't know what hit them. The chair or my fists."

"Oh I'm not mad. Mighty grateful's more like it. My Changchang's a smart girl." I looked proudly in her direction.

"Smart and so, so pretty. She's a little too dangerous for Old Jack, though." Papa Jack sighed. "Maybe when I was a younger man and could run a little faster than the speed of a knife."

I was still perplexed about how I got so lucky. I turned to Alphonso. "Did Changchang let you two in as well?"

"Naw, we were just leaving Zelli's, and we saw them making their way up here. Fred didn't like the shoes on one of them."

Fred interrupted to explain. "He was wearing two-toned oxfords. Daywear. If he'd been out on the town all night like us, he would've had on spectators, wingtips, or something dressy. So this ofay was either coming here from home or went home and changed. *Now why would he do that?* I asked myself. Everyone knows breakfast at Bricktop's closes by eight thirty. So what the hell is this little posse doing up here, closer to nine?" Fred asked no one in particular.

"My, my, my, Fred. You've got a keen eye for details. You know I don't care for Zelli's, but I'm glad you were just leaving there this morning. Thank you both. Where's Joseph?"

Alphonso shrugged his shoulders, looking in Changchang's direction. "He picked up one of those kind of women Changchang don't like at all and went back to our apartment around five this morning."

We all started laughing but stopped just as quickly when we heard a chair turn over.

"Who's there?" I called out, aiming the gun in the direction of the commotion.

"It's me, Brick. Clyde."

I forgot that Clyde had been at Chez Bricktop's since the wee hours of the morning to clean up after the raid. In his mid-sixties, Clyde was still strong, but he wasn't fast on his feet. I was relieved that he hadn't gotten caught in the crossfire.

"Clyde, you been hiding under these tables the entire time?" I asked.

"I was in the back when all hell broke out. Saw the whole thing. Damn, y'all put a whuppin' on them gangsters! It was like the picture shows."

"Yeah the picture shows. I suspect that's what those Frenchies were hopped up on. Hollywood. You got a lot to clean up again. I'm sorry about that," I said, pointing at all the blood.

"It ain't nothing that some bleach and soap water can't handle." Clyde's rheumy eyes suddenly took in Papa Jack. "Say, you're the Champ, ain't you? I saw you fight in 1926 in Oklahoma." Clyde was downright woozy about seeing Papa Jack and the damn-near killing theatrics he had just witnessed.

"Whoo hoo!" He hollered. Then he let out a long, deep belly laugh as he pumped Papa Jack's hand.

I said, "Make sure you really clean the glass floor panels."

"I'll take care of it. Just gone git cha breakfast. Gone now," he said, waving his ropy arms at me like I was interrupting the best dream he'd ever had. He started running hot water into a bucket and whistling Skip James's "Sickbed Blues."

I'd forgotten that Clyde was from the Mississippi Delta. He could sure pick a song. Those gangsters were definitely in "awful pain and deep misery."

I went to my back office to change into one of my "just in case of emergencies" dresses I kept stored there. My Lanvin dress was now streaked with blood, and I tossed it in the trash. It was the second one I had thrown away in five days thanks to that French gangster. I wondered if the Baron had something against his countrywoman, Jeanne, or just me wearing her clothes line. I left Changchang, Papa Jack, and Clyde at Bricktop's while Alphonso and Fred escorted me out safely to catch a taxi. I had an appointment on the other side of Paris to see an apartment.

GOOD EVENING, HEARTACHE,
AND MY NERVES ARE BAD BLUES

XIV.

When the taxi pulled up in front of the two grand doors to the apartment building, a balding Frenchman with a pronounced limp was pacing outside. He wore a scarf and gloves, and despite the chill in the air, he was carrying his cap.

"Monsieur Claudel?"

"*Oui.* Madame Bricktop?"

I nodded in the affirmative. I had told Monsieur René Claudel to just call me Bricktop over the telephone, but he insisted on Madame when he realized who I was.

"I hope you haven't been waiting long?" I asked, relieved that Monsieur Claudel understood English.

He had laughed at my faltering between bad French, jumbled Franglais, and finally English when I'd called him this morning. He'd told me he was a composer and part-time landlord and had spent some time traveling in America. He therefore spoke much better English than I did French. He preferred to rent to an American clientele, exclusive, monied, or well-connected in some way, if at all possible—which would explain how working-class Pippa ended up a client. His contact information had been easy enough to find, thanks to Josie. She had, on several occasions, paid the rent on this apartment. She said Monsieur Claudel was very discrete. He only filled vacancies by word of mouth and recommendations. Since he knew immediately who I was when I called, it had the effect of an open sesame to his rarified world. I knew his type well. I'd get no more information from Claudel than was absolutely necessary. So I hadn't intended to ask any more of him than that. His livelihood depended on it.

"*Non, Madame.* You are *à l'heure.* Would you like to see the apartment now?"

"Yes, please. I'm looking to relocate to the Saint-Germain area of Paris. I'm just glad that you could accommodate my request on such short notice."

"The apartment hasn't been available for long," he said as we climbed the stairs to the second floor. He had no trouble maneuvering with his bad leg. "This is a very chic arrondissement. Ah, we are here. Please forgive the untidiness. But the layout, *c'est parfait.*"

It was typical for French landlords to rent out recently vacated apartments "as is." It was up to the incoming tenants to clean up the place.

"The former tenant's family is coming to retrieve her personal belongings. The furnishings will be left behind, of course."

I had desperately hoped to find Pippa Nelson's place in an "as-is" state, so this was a stroke of luck. "Even in this state of disarray, I think I can I get a very good sense of the apartment."

Monsieur Claudel agreed to wait outside after he opened the door, instructing me to seek him out at the café across the street when I finished.

Pippa's apartment reflected the force of her personality. Or at least the personality I imagined her having from that newspaper photograph. It was a charming studio with a kitchenette. And unlike Ollie, Pippa cooked. There was a very small basin and toilet off in a side room. I spotted a drain in the washroom floor and a bright red hose hooked up to one of the basin's spigots, creating a makeshift shower.

Despite its small size, the apartment felt airy, thanks to the high ceilings. I imagined Pippa as a happy and light woman. Josie would have found this place enticing. They would have been like kindred souls there, hidden from the world. Pippa had decorated the windows with organdy curtains. The thinness of the fabric allowed the sun to shine brightly throughout the apartment.

The bed, a ball of white coverlets and pillows, took up most of the space. There was a book about Italy on the nightstand. I picked it up to skim its contents. The author, a professor of history, was writing about Italian unification and the rise of crime families along the Mediterranean. Next to the book sat an empty photo frame. Someone had removed the frame's contents.

Clearly, the landlord had had some sprucing-up done. I could still smell bleach from the cleanup of Pippa's blood on the walls and floor. The way the papers described the scene, Pippa had fought the good fight. But she was no match for a gun.

I didn't exactly know what I was looking for, since I had to assume that Pippa's attacker, as well as the landlord and the police, had already removed anything of value. But perhaps they'd missed something—for example, the photos and negatives that had gotten me into this mess in the first place.

So I started with the cabinets in her kitchenette, rifling through cooking implements and tableware. Next, I scooted the bed and box spring across the floor to see if anything was stashed underneath. There was nothing in the nightstand drawer, the shallow closet, or between the bed's mattress and box spring. Pippa's suitcases were lying open, as if they had been emptied out. There was a small table with a lace top covering, on top of which sat a typewriter. Nothing useful to be found.

Not quite ready to give up, I did another survey of the place, opening her breadbasket and the cupboards once more. My shawl snagged on the woven breadbasket. I pulled at it gently hoping not to cause the material to run. The basket was empty except for a dark gray button. I took it and put in my purse like a regular thief and scampered for the door in search of Monsieur Claudel.

"Did you find it to your liking, Madame Bricktop?" He smiled a smile that only a mother or a fellow tobacco aficionado and incessant coffee-drinker could appreciate.

"It has wonderful light, but I'm afraid it's too small for me."

"I understand. Americans are accustomed to more space, though it was an American who rented this place," he said.

"If you have something with more room. Something to accommodate a hobby of mine. You see I like to take pictures."

Paris was just that small for us Americans. I figured Monsieur Claudel might know who the landlord was for that newly vacated apartment. I had passed through so quickly that night I was now wondering if there was a darkroom in her place where I might happen upon the negatives of those photographs. If Pippa's apartment could find itself back on the market so quickly because French landlords needed flush tenants that badly, Ollie's spot might soon see the light of day as well. Murder was no disincentive to making a franc or greenback.

"But yes, Madame! There is another apartment I own that just came available this weekend as well. On rue Princesse. Would you like to see that one? I can have it readied by the end of this week."

Ollie's place? Claudel had really cornered the dead, white female American expat real estate market.

"I'm afraid I don't have that kind of time." And I didn't with the police two steps behind and in front of me.

He hesitated. He knew I could find a place today if I wanted. "The soonest it can be available for viewing is tomorrow."

"Wonderful! I'll see you tomorrow morning then. Around eight? The sooner the better, you know," I added, pressing him to accept the early morning appointment. I knew the French didn't like doing business that early. But *tant pis*, as the French say.

We parted company on 19 rue Fleurus with a promise I had every intention of keeping. I had already seen enough of Ollie's place to last several lifetimes, but I knew what I needed began with her.

When I arrived back at my apartment in Montmartre, I wasn't feeling quite myself. I still needed to scare up Renata Vian, so I placed a telephone call to Cole Porter. Cole knew where every high-class drug den in Paris was located. Natalie didn't dabble in recreational drugs, but on occasion, Cole certainly did. And I figured he knew Renata, at least a little. So I hoped he could point me toward her favorite knockout drop spot. Plus, I needed him to venture by Bricktop's over the next few days as part of my public relations strategy to offset last night's debacle. Cole's presence would say loudly without saying a word that we were still the place to be.

"Bricky! I am so glad you called," purred the familiar voice.

"Cole Porter! I certainly need to talk to you."

"Wonderful," said Cole, "because I want to invite you to my party at the Ritz. Just for an hour, starting at midnight. No one who's anyone shows up at Bricktop's before one. I've booked a suite. Everyone would be so delighted to have you there. No dancing, just singing. A few tunes and then you're back at Bricktop's before anyone misses you."

"Impossible," I told him. "The Duke's at Bricktop's tonight." I could feel the bile rising to my throat. Moreover, I had done enough gallivanting because of the raid. Traipsing all over town to various clubs like I didn't have a care in the world. Like that raid was some kind of police error. I needed to find Renata and get out from under these murders.

"Cole, I have a question for you. Where's Renata Vian's favorite drug den?"

Cole lived in Saint-Germain, which is where most of the Women's Academy members resided, and I knew that he had attended Natalie's salon on more than one occasion as a special guest.

Cole responded, perplexed. "What's the matter, Brick? Why are you interested in Renata and her laudanum habit? It's not even a chic drug. Take . . ."

"Cole!" I shrieked into the telephone to focus him. I didn't have time for a lesson on the latest drug fads befitting a woman of my stature. "Have you been following the murders of two American women in Paris?"

"Just a bit. I leave Paris for the weekend and a murderous fiend is on the rampage, and targeting American women to boot. I'm glad I had Dear Linda leave Paris back in December . . ."

"Cole," I spoke calmly this time. "The police are trying to figure out an angle to involve me somehow. Renata was a supposed witness. So was Jonny Dumont, before someone killed him. I'm asking you about drug dens because I need to find Renata and I can't go around inquiring about them myself. It wouldn't look good for Chez Bricktop's, seeing as though the police already raided the club just last night."

"Oh no! Brick! Of course. Of course, you can't go around asking about such things. Terrible, terrible," he tutted. "I didn't help you build your business only to see you lose it over some cheap drug. But why are police trying to implicate you?"

"If I knew why, I'd know who." I was on the verge of yelling at his simple ass. "I need to find Renata. And I need your help. She's the only one who can tell me who set me up and why. Right before Jonny was murdered, he told me they forced him and Renata to implicate me."

"Goodness!" he screeched. I pulled the receiver from my ear.

Cole muttered on. "I haven't been to a drug den with Renata in ages. But there will be people here tonight from the Place du Tertre. That's the company she keeps when she's not with the Women's Academy. So come to the party and I'll ask around for you. A trade for a trade. There'll be plenty of gossip. I'll even come by the club later in the morning to make a show of it. And I'll send a car for you tonight. Your fee plus tips, Brick. Pretty please?"

I was glad he understood my predicament with the club's reputation. My fee plus tips would also be a boon. With the customer credit crunch and my big plans for Changchang, I could use the spare change.

I felt myself giving in. "Is this a boy's party or mixed company?"

"Mostly boys. You're safe with us," he giggled. "You know us fairies love a princess. I just thought you'd be such a wonderful surprise. Besides, no one believes I'm your very best friend."

"Have the driver pick me up at Bricktop's at eleven thirty. That'll give me a chance to check in and get things going."

"Your chariot will be waiting," he squealed in delight before hanging the phone up in my ear. I could hear him yelling for Felicity, his maid, just before the dull hum of the dial tone.

The queasy, dizzy feeling I had made me take to my bed. I closed my eyes for what seemed like minutes, but hours had actually elapsed. I continued to toss and turn so, and the queasiness refused to fade. I finally sat up at seven and scrambled out of bed in search of something to calm my stomach. One look in the bathroom mirror stopped me in my tracks. I had sweated out every curl in my head to straight. My already pale skin was even paler, making the red freckles on my face stand out even more. I was too far gone for cigars. As I was running cool water in the basin to revive my skin, I heard a racket coming from the kitchen.

What now? After this morning's botched shakedown, I didn't think that devious Baron would come after me again so soon. But maybe he was more malicious and impatient than I gave him credit for. I turned the water off and tiptoed back to the bedroom. Reaching under the bed for my bat, I walked toward the sound, which was coming from the kitchen. Before I got to my intended destination, I heard pans rattling.

This is just too rich. These gangsters don't have an ounce of decency. The bastards are fixing themselves something to eat in my kitchen before putting me down for a dirt nap.

I leaped out from the parlor, swinging my bat hard and wild, aiming for knees and skulls.

"Damn, Ada, what you doing with that bat?"

"Peter! Peter!" I rushed to my husband.

"Put that bat down, baby." He stepped aside as the bat swung past his knees. "What's the matter? Oh baby, why you crying so? What's happened since I left? I told you to be careful. I came back early to see about you. I scared you, Ada? I'm so sorry. You were sleeping when I came in. You were moaning so. I thought I'd heat some water for tea when you woke up. I'm sorry, darling, really I am."

"No. No. Peter." I collapsed in his arms while we were still standing. I couldn't talk for the tears. "It's my nerves."

He took one look at me and said, "Ada, I wish you'd come with me. Sit down. I'll make you some dinner. You know what you need to do, right?" He was gently stroking my back and making those calming, rubbing motions again.

"Yeah," I nodded and brushed my lips against his warm cheek.

I turned to go to the bedroom in search of my bathrobe and slippers.

Two years ago, in 1929, I'd had a nervous breakdown. My doctor told me it was from the stress of running the club, that I was always trying to please everybody. She said I was saying yes too much. But what was I supposed to do? I'm the hostess of the club. I am Bricktop's. I'm supposed to make everyone happy. So the doctor told me I should try some scream therapy, shouting at the top of my lungs to get things out that I couldn't express at the club. She was what they call a psychotherapist. A perky French woman who wore scuffed shoes and cat-eyed spectacles, Madame Dr. Babel claimed she had had plenty of success with this treatment with World War I veterans and their families. Goodness knows I couldn't have been any more stressed than those mangled soldiers returning home from the battlefront and their starved and sundered families.

In the weeks that followed, right after the club closed in the morning and right before the breakfast crowd arrived, I went home and changed into my nightgown, bathrobe, and house slippers—an outfit so different from those fancy clothes I always wore at the club. I took to the streets of Montmartre, walking up and down, from Place Pigalle across rue Victor Massé and rue Fontaine and back up rue Pigalle. It started out as low muttering until I finally succumbed to screaming like a she-devil and looking like an unkempt mass of dowdiness.

I used the worst language, things I would never say under ordinary circumstances. My neighbors at first thought I was crazy. I was shouting, "No, motherfucker, you can't have that gin," or "That's one tired ass song. I ain't singing that shit no more. You sing it," or "I wish your raggedy ass would pay your damn overdue tab." That last remark became one of my favorites because the market had just crashed, Americans were leaving in droves, and a lot of folks had started asking for credit.

After a while, my neighbors would just shrug their shoulders with understanding and say, "Madame Bricktop is relaxing her nerves this morning."

It worked. Two months later, I felt stronger again. And then, all I needed every now and then was a whiff of a cigar to pull me off the ledge. And I had been feeling just fine until Josie Baker showed up last Friday night. So I was going to try this screaming business again. I had a night-club to run in spite of the gangsters, police, worrisome customers, a missing laudanum addict, a murdered jazz musician, and two dead white women.

Peter, who had told me he would always be mine, understood how my mind worked, and his generous caring kept me sane. I didn't know how long our love would last, but during those dark days, the way he stood by me was as necessary to me as breathing. Sometimes love doesn't have to last a lifetime. You take it when it comes to you, and for as long as it will stay.

"I'll be back," I sighed as I closed the door behind me.

LES MISÉRABLES, OR JAVERT AND JEAN(NE) VALJEAN

XV.

I heard men's voices coming from the salon as the door clicked behind me. I took a deep breath. My hollering walk had done me some good after all. It had certainly helped me prepare for this moment, one that I'd been dreading since Sunday morning.

I had to figure out how to buy me some time before they framed me up for the murders of Pippa, Ollie, and Jonny. Peter had the good bourbon on the coffee table and Gilles Gravois had helped himself to a glass. He was settled in quite nicely, as far as I could see, with one creaking knee crossed over the other. I went in cautious but calm.

"Well isn't this some kind of Southern hospitality?" I fixed a stare at Peter and then at my good bottle of bourbon that had escaped Prohibition America's customs officers to arrive safely in Paris, courtesy of Mama. "And Inspector Gravois, I am beginning to think I'm playing Jeanne Valjean to your Javert."

Gravois was at first taken aback by my appearance, accustomed as he was to seeing me in a more fashionable state of dress. Then, realizing what I had just said, he chortled in appreciation. "Les Misérables. I'd like to think that I won't hurl myself into the Seine because of some moral dilemma."

"I'm sure you won't suffer from any crise de conscience where morality and justice are concerned."

I did a great deal of reading at Bricktop's. People always brought me their novels and such for the library and sometimes just for my opinions. There was nothing too shocking or beyond the pale for me. Except that time Henry Miller gave me a copy of his Tropic of Cancer. Now, I had done a lot of what he described—in many and varied positions—but I would never have put it on paper. When he came by to ask what I thought, I told him exactly that.

I kicked off my house slippers and took a seat near Peter, who was calmly absorbing the conversation. Peter was more a musician than a reader of dead French writers like Victor Hugo. He reached out to hold my hand. He wanted to listen real close so we could talk about it later. I knew Peter wouldn't be able to help me untie this knot. I didn't need money. I didn't need muscle. I needed time.

To find a murderer.

"I don't underestimate you," the Inspector smiled. "This is, in fact, why I am here. Ollie Knolton called you the night she was murdered. We have a way of uncovering these things, and the connecting operator remembers putting the call through to your club."

He took a sip of my good bourbon from my clean glass in my nice apartment. I pursed my lips, thinking about how refreshing my hollering walk had felt. About how I might just go back out again this same night and call Gilles Gravois a few "French motherfuckers" for good measure.

But there it was. I had been waiting for Josie's phone call to be discovered. In fact, it had been haunting me. I had desperately wanted Inspector Gravois to discover it and lay it on the table so we could get to dealing. I knew he would try to use that phone call to tie me to Ollie's murder.

"I didn't speak to Ollie Knolton." I was so calm when I said this, I surprised myself.

"Mais, mais oui. She called your nightclub, Madame Ducongé."

"I can't dispute that now can I? I don't sit by the phone at my club. I sing, dance, talk to my customers. She could have called to ask when we opened. Or when we closed. But she wouldn't have got that information from me. She didn't speak to me." I hated lying and this was one of those times that I didn't have to.

"Oui, that is what you say, Madame. But let us review the situation. I have a witness who saw you speaking to Mademoiselle Olive Knolton at the Académie des femmes' gathering. This same witness says you inquired about Pippa Nelson. You own a revolver. Both victims were shot. There were no casings, of course, to be recovered. That speaks to a certain cleverness on your part. I have a different witness who saw Mademoiselle Knolton at Chez Bricktop. One of my sources tells me that on this occasion, you acquired her address. Another witness reported an assault by a woman fitting your description right near Mademoiselle Knolton's apartment on the night of her death. He has since disappeared. I don't suppose you know of his whereabouts?"

It was a rhetorical question, so I didn't bother answering.

"You also accosted a well-respected French citizen, using your revolver to threaten him and his elderly mother, only to inquire about his fiancée, Pippa Nelson. Next, I have a telephone call placed from Mademoiselle Knolton's apartment to your establishment on the night she was murdered. Even the timing of events is suspicious, where you are concerned. That same witness who saw you speaking with Mademoiselle Knolton early Saturday morning also saw you leaving your club shortly after this new piece of evidence—the telephone call—late Saturday evening. Unfortunately, your chef saw to it that he wouldn't be around to testify to this fact. And my other witness has also mysteriously disappeared. Then there is the matter of the near murder of this unknown Frenchman, for which you claim self-defense. He is still unconscious thanks to your unimaginable brutality."

"It was self-defense," I piped up, angry, touching my neck again where his hands had been firmly placed. But I had cringed as he went down his list. It was all damning, to be sure. Yet, he no longer had his witnesses to prove much of it. At least for now. One, as he noted, was still under the weather and hopefully never to recover. Jonny would never talk again, and he hadn't mentioned Renata Vian by name. I wanted to confirm that she had also spoken against me. "Who are these so-called witnesses?" I demanded.

"I will not name them," said the Inspector. "Because anyone who reports your suspicious behavior to the police ends up murdered, disappeared, or unconscious."

I had a lump in my throat. I poured myself a glass of bourbon and quaffed it so I could feel the burning all at once, warming my insides. As that tingling sensation coursed through my limbs it occurred to me that the most junior defense lawyer could pick Inspector Gravois's so-called evidence apart. This was probably the only reason he didn't already have me shackled and on my way to the clink. No matter how many fingers were pointing at me, it was all still circumstantial and explainable, except for that odious French drunk on rue Princesse. But since he'd done a disappearing act for the moment, I couldn't be concerned. The hit man would need to explain why he was in my kitchen, choking me. But I was terribly afraid for Changchang. I didn't want her accused of Jonny's murder or that assassin's flogging in any way. She had a future ahead of her that I was helping to prepare. I intended to protect her in the same way I would my club. I understood enough though to realize that even the most crooked cop needed to establish a plausible case that included a motive. And if the inspector had come up with one, he would not have been sipping bourbon with my husband like they were old poker buddies.

"I know your witness list included Jonny Dumont," I said. "But it would have been awful hard for him to see me leaving for Ollie Knolton's apartment, or whatever else he claimed to have seen, Inspector. He wasn't playing at Bricktop's Saturday. Why, Jonny hasn't played regularly at Bricktop's in months. Furthermore, Inspector, I don't recall telling you that I never spoke to Miss Knolton. I said I didn't know her well, if I knew her at all. And Changchang had nothing to do with Jonny's murder, as I've told you before. Don't you think it's more than a coincidence that Jonny was sliced five ways to Sunday and then a little birdie tells you that my Changchang is adept with knives? As I said, she's a chef. Humph. And we will just have to wait and see about that trifling assassin I had to put out like the mad dog he is. You saw my bruises."

Peter was mumbling under his breath, about to explode. Instead I damn near squashed his hand. I know he didn't like hearing about any man putting a hand on me.

"When you were interviewing your so-called witnesses, you should have gone back to verify their stories." I sniffed in the Inspector's direction, as I traced around the rim of my glass with my left hand.

Inspector Gravois puzzled over what I had said. I saw the doubt in his eyes. Perhaps he was trying to decide who he believed more: dead, lying Jonny, who had also said I ran a club of ill-repute; Renata Vian, the missing dope fiend; or me. He tugged at his moustache. A habit I had come to realize he had when he was frustrated. He stroked it when he thought he had the upper hand.

Watching his uncertainty, I saw a little daylight. If Gravois was aiming to frame me, he could have done a much better job of it. He could've planted evidence at one of my two homes, or the club, and then had his officers "discover" it. The fact that he hadn't done this made me think that he might be shady but he wasn't completely corrupt. Sure, he was looking for a scapegoat to blame—he couldn't afford an unsolved case like this on his blotter. He was, as he and Bergeron said, "new" to the Paris Prefecture. But maybe he'd be just as happy if I could find the real killer to bring to justice. It was a theory worth testing.

"Give me a few days, Inspector Gravois. Someone is trying to turn my world upside down, and I want to know why. You got murders to solve. Rich Americans and government officials breathing down your neck to find a killer. I can't let you cuff me for something I didn't do." I figured I would just keep talking, hoping he would listen and cut me a break. "I've got important friends too. Just give me until Thursday. I'll help you find the criminals who are responsible for this mess."

"Jeudi?"

"Yes, Thursday. I have some ideas I've been looking into and I'm sure I'm getting closer to the truth. If that's what you're really after."

Peter looked at me with wide eyes. He couldn't believe I was rambling on so much. He squeezed my hand to make me shut up this time. It was like his squeeze opened up another floodgate. I kept right on talking about murder, white women, a dirty-dog French assailant at my club, the time I needed, and folks being framed until, finally, Gravois held up his hand to silence me.

"Thursday, Madame Ducongé. Not a day more." Creaky rose from the salon's sofa. He took one last sip of the bourbon. "Un très fin goût, Monsieur," he complimented Peter on the bourbon's age before stroking his moustache. "À bientôt, Madame."

Peter's mouth was still open when the door closed behind the Inspector. He finally found some words after clearing his throat for a few minutes. "Woman, who the hell put his hands on you? I'll kill him dead. Where is he? And what you know about finding murderers and such?" He jumped up, pacing the floor. "You getting on the next ship or train out of here, Ada. I don't care where it goes. First thing tomorrow morning. And you gone tell me where this hit man is."

"Calm down, Peter. I'm not going anywhere. Changchang and I handled the hit man fairly well, I must say. I'd rather have that Inspector believe it was just me and that Frenchman fighting like wild cocks than Changchang."

I gave Peter a quick rundown of the events and my suspicion that the Baron had staged the raid in cahoots with the police somehow, and how he had sicced that French gun for hire on Changchang because she had his mother hemmed up over a hot chocolate at Angelina's. I didn't believe for one minute the Baron's claim of innocence. There was no honor among thieves. To my mind, he was a thief through and through, trying to steal my hard-earned money from Chez Bricktop. As I stretched out on the chaise in the parlor, I also told him that whoever was framing me up for Ollie and Pippa's untimely demises had also had Jonny killed.

"Was it the Baron? We can kill him tonight."

"Peter Ducongé, you will not do any such thing. The last thing we need is a dead gangster up in MoMart. Jonny said the Baron wasn't involved in shaking him down to rat me out. But Jonny said a lot of things. So I'm still twisting in wind, you see." I put my glass down and reached out to catch my husband's brown hand. It was warm. He had stopped pacing by now.

"This is our home, baby. No one is going to run us out of here. I don't know much about murderers and such, but I have to find out who killed those women and Jonny Dumont. Besides, that there Inspector is as crooked as a barrel of crab legs. He wants money. He's in with the syndicates. He's just hanging those murders over my head until I break down and pay up. If they threw me in jail, my club would close and they'd never get a penny out of Bricktop's."

"You're in something way over a saloonkeeper's head, Ada. And I'll be damned if I can figure out how to help you. It's all Josie's fault. But that man don't act like no crooked cop, Red. He's like a damn hound dog, relentless, and he's got the scent of you right up his nose."

Now it was Peter who needed some reassurance. "This could all be fine in a couple of days," I said. "I'm like cream, baby. I'll rise to the top." I gave my Peter a long kiss when I stood up from the reclining chaise, hoping it would make him feel surer than I was feeling at that moment. "Now where's my dinner, baby?"

PIN PIN'S PALACE

XVI.

I dressed carefully that evening because the Duke himself would be playing at Bricktop's that night. After hoarding his records like contraband for
years, the great Duke Ellington was finally coming to perform at my club.

I chose a red floor-length dress with a long train across one shoulder
and a slit up the front to show off my dancing legs. It had a ruched and
tailored bodice. Since my hair was now a flat mass of red strands, I slicked
it back into a chignon. I couldn't have conjured a kiss curl if I prayed.

I had red lips, red nails, a red silk purse, and matching silk dress heels
by Greco, decorated with colored semi-precious stones.

Peter watched me clip a white crystal flower to the back of my chignon. "You look good, Red."

"Not too much?"

"Naw. Just right. Especially that part there," he said, running his fin-
gertip down my cleavage. I giggled like a little girl.

We were in a funny mood that evening. We refused to look back or
forward, preferring to concentrate on the sweet here and now.

"I need to check on Changchang. I'll be right back." I opened my
front door and there was Falcon.

"Hey, Brick. I'm here to see that Changchang gets to the club okay."
He smiled sincerely. I thought it was a mighty nice gesture, not enough to
change my mind but sweet nonetheless.

I looked at my watch. "I'll see you two at the club then." I closed the
door to my apartment slowly.

A few minutes later, I could hear Changchang in the hallway telling
Falcon they had to hurry. She hadn't let him in. That was a good sign.
She was chattering on about how Claire and Alain were driving in from
Bougival with eggs, herbs from the greenhouse garden, and freshly plucked
chickens. She liked to be there for the deliveries. I could hear Falcon's deep
voice interjecting an occasional "umm hmm." He didn't even try to get a
word in edgewise.

"Falcon's come a courting," I said to Peter. "He's walking her over."

Peter, who had every intention of having a jam session with the Duke,
picked up our coats and his saxophone. "A man can change. I did, for you.
He knows what the stakes are with Changchang."

We walked silently to the club. It was cold and dark. "It's gonna
be alright, Red," he whispered in my ear as he opened the door to Chez
Bricktop.

I went straight back to the kitchen to see Changchang. "What's on the menu tonight?"

"Roasted chicken, seasoned up real good, cornbread, black-eyed peas, and French green beans. Maybe I'll make a Mississippi caramel cake. I'd like to start doing some desserts."

I touched my waistline and groaned out loud. We laughed. "As soon as you're finished cooking, I'll need you out front to keep an eye on things. Mabel's performing at the Diga Diga Do club tonight since we've got the Duke coming through.

Changchang had been rubbing garlic and butter on a whole chicken and stuffing its cavity with fresh tarragon leaves. Now, her hands froze and she looked up at my face with concern. "I don't get it. Where will you be?"

"At Cole's party to get some information about Renata. It was a fair trade, I suppose. An hour of my time for a life line."

"But you can't miss the Duke playing here at Bricktop's. I know how much you and Uncle Peter have been looking forward to it."

"No choice, baby. I'll only be gone a couple of hours. I just have to find Renata and get to the bottom of the mess Josie started. Not even the Duke can distract me. If I don't help Gravois crack this case by Thursday, he'll throw me in jail."

Changchang wiped her hands on a kitchen cloth. "You want me to go along with you and make sure . . . ?"

I shook my head. "I need you here. The Duke will be here shortly. If I'm out chasing Renata, he'll need a sitter. You're as good as me."

Changchang blushed at the comparison. "I love you, Aunt Ada," she said.

"I love you too, baby." I blew her a kiss like I used to when she was a little girl. She caught it and blew one back. I dabbed my eyes with a napkin and turned on my heels to leave, heading toward the music.

I found Peter at my office at the bar. I glanced down at my crystal watch and saw that it was time for me to leave. Sure enough, Cole Porter's driver was waiting for me at the club's curtained entrance. "It's show time," I whispered to my husband. "Help Changchang to make sure the Duke has everything he needs. I'll see you later, baby." I kissed Peter on the mouth before leaving.

He squeezed me hard before releasing me. He knew I was more than handful when he met me.

I arrived at the Ritz at midnight. Everyone was tipsy over this part of town. The fashionable Place Vendôme was all that, and then some. It was the exclusive domain of those in the know, and in the dough. I sailed past the doorman, Émile, with a nod and smile. Cole's decision to host his party here and not at 13 rue Monsieur—his home—was not lost on me. It meant that this was going to be a very naughty party. I hoped to be long gone before it got too wild.

Cole always rented the same suite on the sixth floor. It offered panoramic views over the roof of the Palais Garnier—an appropriate choice, since there was always some drama at his parties.

"Bricktop is here," Cole announced with a showman's flair as he led me into the party. His skin glowed a ghoulish white in the suite's dim lighting. Cole was not a handsome man; his eyes were too large for his face, his hair was mousy, and his hands were small and thin. I guess my taste ran more along the lines of Alberta's song about a "two-fisted, double-jointed, rough and ready man." But I loved Cole so much he always looked good to me.

He was a very fine composer, but even at the top of his game, he didn't bring in a boatload of cash. His musical successes alone could not have afforded him the kind of luxuries to which he was accustomed. Instead, his lavish lifestyle was funded by family money and his wife Linda's giant nest egg. I guess it's true that it pays to marry well. I had known Cole since 1926 when he saw me at Le Grand Duc dancing the Charleston. Soon after that, he'd invited me to a party in Venice, Italy. Next thing I knew, I was teaching his friends the Charleston and spending my summers with Cole and Linda Porter at a beautiful palazzo called Rezzonico. He and "Dear Linda" (as he liked to call her) had an arrangement in matters of love. He would be discreet, and she would look the other way.

In the suite at the Ritz, I greeted the boys with a smile, ignoring their various states of undress. I tried to repress my annoyance at the over-enthusiasm being displayed by Cole's guests. Cocaine and liquor had been distributed and consumed handily.

Cole took his place at the piano, and we went through a few numbers, starting with his own, "Paris—Let's Do It, Let's Fall in Love" and concluding with "Begin the Beguine."

When I was finally released to mingle, I sat with Leslie "Hutch" Hutchinson for a minute or two. It was hard not to suck my teeth at his washed-up prospects for playing piano professionally. I had counseled and pleaded with him long and hard just as I had Paul Robeson; he went and ruined his career anyway by taking up with that socialite Englishwoman. Love. Hutch was in his cups. But at least he was a merry drunk. And he was still very easy on the eyes.

The coco was all over the piano's black top where the boys rubbed it across their gums, licked at it, and snorted it happily.

Cole buzzed over to me. "I've got a secret."

"What is it?" I looked at my watch. *12:45 a.m.*

"It's about Renata."

"Is she dead?"

"Oh no, darling, nothing that perverse. She's at Pin Pin's Palace. It's a high-class opium den off rue de Montpensier."

"Umm" was the only utterance I could manage. So Renata Vian was high and not dead. She was tucked away in the confines of a dope house with a pipe attached to her lips or a medicine dropper at her side. I felt a slow rumble starting in my stomach. "I need your driver to take me there."

"You sure? It's rather a scene. Safe but steamy."

"Couldn't be any steamier than here," I replied, giving him a sarcastic smirk and looking over the assortment of male bodies. "I'm still a woman, you know."

Cole was right; Pin Pin's Palace was a scene. It wasn't so much that it was crowded (though it was). It was that visiting this place was like stepping into the most intimate boudoirs of complete strangers. Men and women were reclining on divans; legs and arms peeked out from heavy curtains. Some of the dopers were fully nude. It wasn't a raucous crowd. They looked contented, sedated even. The opium den was decked out like an Oriental despot's hideaway with red and gold splashes, velvet and silk, lanterns, and the like. The palace occupied one of the beautiful *hôtels particuliers* on this rarefied block in the Palais-Royal quarter. No expense had been spared in the furnishings or the dope. The hefty entrance fee of two hundred francs, about ten greenbacks, kept the riffraff out. I paid but declined a taste of the product.

I had no idea if Renata Vian was still here. And it wasn't as though I could go to the management and ask for her by name. The clientele here paid a premium for anonymity. I certainly wasn't going to start tapping shoulders and turning over bodies. I didn't want to blow anybody's high. Goodness gracious knows how junkies act when you bring them down before the drug does. Wandering slowly around the establishment with a dreamy look on my face, I secretly scrutinized any female clients I could find, in search of Renata's eye-popping hair.

Only two women were not partnered up. One of them was dancing slowly to a rhythm only she could hear. She was dressed for the evening in a long, mulberry-colored gown. Her dark brown hair was pulled up in a rather orderly fashion, showing off her slight, bare shoulders and a pair of handcrafted earrings. Cartier, if I had to guess. I turned my attention to the woman reclined quietly on a red divan.

Renata's eyes were closed. Her carrot-orange hair fanned out against the divan, contrasting vividly with the crimson fabric. It was clear she had no intention of staying all night. She was dressed in the same well-made overcoat and boots she had worn on the first night I met her at Natalie's. It was cool inside the Palace but not cold. It was like she had planned to swoop in for a brief respite and had gotten stuck there, frozen in time. She would have been pretty with her pouty lips had she not been so gaunt and pale.

"Renata. Renata Vian," I leaned over the divan, whispering real low.

She didn't move. Her eyes didn't flicker in recognition of the name. She was in some sort of dream sleep.

"Renata," I said louder, whacking my purse against her boot.

"Whaaat? Whaaat?" she groaned, slicing the air with an emaciated hand.

"I need to talk to you. Not only are you in danger, but you put me in harm's way." I thought I'd keep it quick and simple.

"Bricktop?" she almost sang my name. She sat upright and looked past me before turning her focus squarely on me. "What are you doing here? How did you find me?" she asked in a tiny voice.

"That doesn't matter. You need to get to talking, and fast. None of that sass like at the Women's Academy. Who put you up to fingering me for Pippa and Ollie's murders? Do you know that Jonny's been murdered too?"

I wanted to yank her up by just a lock of her ginger mane.

I heard a low grumbling that all of sudden bubbled up into hissing. "Yes, I know Jonny's dead. That's why I'm here. Mourning."

"Well?

"Do you have something for me? I was paid handsomely the last time I provided information about you."

"Sure. I got an ass-whupping and a half for you. Like Jonny got. You're high enough. Don't play with me. Who paid you and for what information?"

"Oh hell. His name was the Wolf. I never saw him. That's all I know. Jonny said that's what he was called. On Sunday morning, two men approached Jonny at Le Boeuf during his break; being curious, I went to check on him. They had him pinned against the wall, punching him, slapping him around. Asking him did he understand what he needed to do and saying that the Wolf would be real pleased with him if he cooperated. When they saw me, one of them grabbed my arm. Asked Jonny who was I and what I knew." She lay back down and closed her eyes like she was going to sleep.

"Oh no, Miss Anne, we're not done here." This time I did yank her up by her arm like a rag doll.

"Leave me be!"

"Hell if I will. What else?"

She pouted, trying to figure out how best to get me on my way so she could enjoy her dope sanctuary. "They offered us an incentive to talk. Something to ease Jonny's pain and my come-down. I'd never tried cocaine. I told them what I saw. I didn't see any harm in it. It was the truth. You asked about Pippa. You took Ollie's address. I saw you with my own eyes. Later that morning, I told the same thing to an Inspector Gilles Gravois. He seemed very pleased. Afterward, the Wolf arranged for Jonny and me to have some more candy for our trouble."

"How did you know where Gilles Gravois's office was?"

"Jonny knew where to go. He had instructions."

"Did they tell you why they wanted you and Jonny to implicate me?"

"Why would they? And I didn't ask. You must have pissed some tough guys off pretty bad, just like Pippa did. I told them what they wanted to know. They made me practice my story in front of them. They knew cop-speak well. I had no trouble remembering exactly how to say what I needed to that Gravois fellow."

"You sure you never saw the Wolf?"

"I don't think he was there. But Jonny told me he's the muscle in Montmartre and he's trying to organize the drug trade and dabbling in the *filles* as well."

Jonny would have made it a priority to be *au courant* about the drug trade. Drug rings had slowly begun to infiltrate Montmartre. Most folks used recreationally and usually copped from a generous friend. But the gangsters realized that the prostitution and protection rackets could be supplemented by dope dealing. Given the concentration of tourists, musicians, and good-time girls in Montmartre, a handy profit was there for the taking. The legitimate coppers were more than a few steps behind on these new developments.

I wondered if the Wolf was actually the Baron, despite Jonny insisting he wasn't involved. He simply may not have known the Baron's other street name. So I asked Renata about this. She was lucid enough to keep up with my questions, even between nodding off.

"No," she said. "The only names that were mentioned were yours, Pippa, Ollie, the Wolf, and Gilles Gravois."

"Did they talk about those photographs?"

"The ones Pippa made Ollie take of gangster hangouts? No, they did not. But that was a foolish undertaking. I warned Ollie to be more careful."

"Kind of like you warned Pippa?"

"Exactly. She's the reason Ollie's dead. Ollie was terrified and very angry with Pippa after she was up to her eyeballs in it, you know. Pippa was too ambitious for her own good. That was a function of her station. I always thought she was NOCD. She liked courting danger."

"Her station? . . . Are you speculating or are you just smart like that?"

"Yes, her class. She was not of ours, dear. As I said, NOCD . . . I don't go in for gangsters and hooligans, if that's what you're implying. But it's only logical. Plus, I see and hear a lot, due to my own predilections."

"Some friend you are to Pippa. I half expected you to rat me out. But goodness, have you no scruple?"

"Pippa. Pippa," she sang out, mimicking me. "That idiot. If she'd listened to me, she'd still be alive. I had no scruple about saving my and Jonny's asses. I didn't know you or love you enough to protect you. But I stuck to the truth when I spoke to Gravois. Little good the truth did me and Jonny anyway." She pouted and crossed her arms.

Jazzmen and drugs. I pursed my lips in disgust, thinking about her predilections. I guess I had seen much of the same in my line of work. "Do you think those men and the Wolf are gangsters or cops?"

"Is there a difference? If they're gangsters, they've got a direct line to that Inspector. Convenient isn't it? If they're cops, they're as corrupt as gangsters." She started cackling.

"This isn't a laughing matter. You need a safe house, fool. I'm taking you to Natalie's. I don't need another dead white woman on my conscience." I held my hand out to assist Renata up from the divan.

She waved me away, laughing. "Really, Bricktop, I'm not going anywhere near Natalie. I'm not servicing her white ass anymore. We had our time. Tell her we're done and to leave it be."

"I'm just the messenger. You tell her the rest of that spiel yourself when you get to Saint-Germain."

"Didn't you hear me?!" Renata's voice got louder as she tried to stand up.

Her arms were flailing every which-a-way; her legs were watery, and next thing I knew, her thin body buckled under. She hit the side of divan like the sky-high addict she was, overturning a small, red-lacquered Chinese table. "I don't give a damn! You tell her I can take care of myself. Now she cares? Now she fucking cares?"

And then she gasped. "Look what you made me do!!" She had accidentally turned over a small bottle with all her flailing and flopping. Its contents had spilled on the rug. She was on her knees now, trying to recapture the contents by shoveling it back into the bottle with her fingers before it seeped into the thick carpet. She put her mouth on the rug and began making a sucking noise.

I backed away slowly. I knew a hopeless cause when I saw one. Pistol-whipping Renata Vian with Mister Speaker had crossed my mind, especially with her so rudely cursing and carrying on at me. But even drug dens had decorum. The way she was licking at that carpet let me know she wasn't going anywhere but to junkie's paradise in her dreams.

"You've been told," I yelled back at Renata.

"Tell her to stay the fuck away from me!" She licked at her fingers wildly.

I could still hear her hollering as I made my way back to the car where Cole's chauffer sat patiently waiting. Love had clearly cut the wrong way. Natalie may have still been stuck on Renata, but Renata wanted nothing to do with her. Natalie had obviously hurt her real bad, and Renata had left her, trying to keep a semblance of her dignity intact. And now she was slumming in drug dens. Pin Pin's was more luxurious than the cheap human wastelands I knew about in Montmartre. But it consumed its clients just the same. It would be awhile before I'd be able to shake the image of her desperate face in that lush carpet.

I eased back into the sedan's backseat, sweeping the train of my red dress in so it wouldn't get caught as the driver closed the door behind me. In my dash out of Pin Pin's to the car, I had figured out a thing or two. Jonny Dumont knew all about the drug trade in Montmartre, so he had to know who the Wolf was—which was why he was as dead as Pippa and Ollie. Renata had no idea about the Wolf's identity. Yet, the Wolf and his thugs couldn't be sure what Jonny had told his erstwhile lover. Her days were as good as numbered. But she wasn't my problem anymore.

Damn dope fiends.

BIG RED RIDING HOOD AND THE WOLF

XVII.

Cole's driver dropped me off in Montmartre just shy of two in the morning. The Duke and his band were warming up the crowd with "Mood Indigo," which meant that I hadn't missed much of his show. Relief poured through me. The Duke's music cut through my dark mood and coursed through my veins, reminding me that life was bigger than gangsters and drug addicts. Next, he played a more upbeat number that I had never heard before. Mama hadn't sent it to me yet, anyway. He kept singing, "It don't mean a thing."

"This is swing ya'll," he announced, gleefully.

It was a crowd pleaser. Everyone was on the dance floor doing the Charleston and the Lindy Hop—a dance we created in Harlem and named after Charles Lindbergh's trans-Atlantic crossing. Dresses were flying up, legs were going every which-a-way, and folks were having a good time. Peter started playing, trying to catch the tune. I went to the microphone to join in with a few "Doo-wat, doo-wats." I was on needles, waiting to make another exit to search for a howling wolf in Montmartre. But I had to hang around Bricktop's for a spell. I had a business to run, even if my troubles kept haunting me. I looked down at the glass floor panels for signs of blood, but Clyde had done a real fine cleaning job. I left the microphone to meet and greet my guests. There were some folks who came to Chez Bricktop just to see if Bricktop the woman really existed.

The Duke bowed and left the stage, and our house orchestra took over. I escorted him to a banquette and ordered up some champagne for his table.

"It sure is good to see you again, Brick. I'll never forget how you helped give me my first big break when no one else would. Who would have thought I'd be here playing for you in your own place. It's mighty nice. Mighty nice," he said with his signature toothy smile. He reached over and patted my shoulder like he used to do back in Harlem. There was nothing more to it than how he showed his approval.

"It's been a while, hasn't it? Barron's, Cotton Club, and Connie's Inn days. How are things back in Harlem?"

"Not so good. The bad markets have taken a toll on nightlife. That's why me and the band decided to hit the road and tour until we got tired." He straightened out his white bowtie and put his top hat down on the table.

"Well it's good to see you, baby. I'm glad you thought about little old Bricktop."

"You kidding me? Everybody thinks about Brick and Bricktop's," he said flirting.

I gave him a kiss on the cheek and went to my office at the bar. He was the Duke, but all my customers were treated the same. I couldn't linger at his table any longer than the others.

I felt a gentle tap on my shoulder and when I turned around, I saw No-Account Count Pepito Abatino. Josie was with him, cheesing from ear to ear. I was tongue-tied at first, not knowing quite what to say, even though I had just seen them on Saturday. I hadn't expected them to take me up on the invite.

"Brick," said Pepito, by way of a greeting.

"Well, look at what the cat dragged into Bricktop's. Hello, Pepito. Glad you took me up on my offer."

He really did look like something the cat had pulled in from the yard. His dark suit seemed ill-fitting. Managing every aspect of Josie's career was taking a toll. Up close, he looked a little gaunt, not like the spiffy Pepito I had seen on Saturday afternoon. He had aged noticeably over the last four days.

He reached for my hand. "It's good to see you again, too."

He was smooth. Much more polished than his days at Le Grand Duc. Back then, he was just slick. It really wasn't good to see him, but I couldn't say that, as I was still trying to figure out what I felt about Guiseppe Pepito Abatino.

I had sometimes marveled at his ingenuity with respect to Josie; other times, I resented how possessive he was of her, how he had squired her away from our kind of people. He used to lock Josie in the bedroom until she agreed to practice. He was training her to make her a star, trying to instill discipline in the wild child. It had paid off.

I just smiled my hostess smile. I looked over at Josie. Her eyes were pleading with me. She wanted us all to make up and make nice. She had obviously convinced him to come. I made the effort as well. After all, he'd met me more than halfway by coming to Bricktop's.

"Can I offer you a drink?" I had my barkeep pour a round of Remy for everyone.

"*Grazie*, Brick."

I had grown so used to hearing French that Pepito threw me for a minute.

"*Prego*," I offered back about the free champagne.

"I couldn't help but overhear your conversation with that French officer you introduced us to on Saturday. You've been having trouble at the club?"

"Nothing I can't handle," I smiled. "Montmartre is overrun with gangsters. Everybody wants their cut."

Pepito shook his head. "They're not just in Montmartre. They have their hands in everything. The picture shows. Theater. I've had to pay my share in order to open doors for Josie. It's like highway robbery in America. But Josie needs to return to the United States and make some waves there. I think of it as overhead. The cost of doing business. Otherwise, it would eat at me. You should pay up, Brick. It's easier that way. You can't shoot every gangster who approaches you. One goes down and another one rises to take his place. It's just too dangerous to take them on."

I didn't know why I was having this conversation with Pepito, but there we were. He was a sensible and shrewd businessman, and I couldn't deny that there was some sense in what he said. But it wasn't his money he was forking over either. It was Josie's.

"I can't. I won't. It's a matter of principle with me."

"We've had our differences over Josie. But I don't want your principles to get you hurt. That's all, Brick." He leaned over and kissed me on the cheek this time. He was good. He had nearly won me over because I believed he was sincere. I wondered then if Pepito knew more about Josie's affairs than he let on. I wondered if he would murder to keep Josie. The thought passed through my mind just as quickly as it had entered.

Josie cut in. She was bouncing with excitement. "Bricky, I was hoping you could introduce us to the Duke." She smoothed her skin-tight pink dress and adjusted the feathers in her hat like she was some kind of duck.

"Of course." I walked them over to the table and left them there to mingle. The Duke offered them a seat.

I watched them for a few minutes. Josie was animated talking to the Duke. Pepito had his hand clamped solidly around her waist even as they sat side by side. She was leaning into him, occasionally kissing his cheek and forehead between talking. He smiled wide, just like he did in front of Ladurée.

Peter put his hand on the hip of my red dress, still flushed from the pleasure of playing alongside the Duke. "Maybe some good could come out of all of this after all, huh? I mean if it means you and Josie being friends again. Even if she is trouble."

"Umm hmm. I need to run another errand, baby. Could you keep an eye on the Duke for me? Make sure he has what he needs?"

"Where're you going?"

"This little red riding hood is going to find her a Wolf."

Peter looked puzzled. "Now you're chasing wolves. Next it'll be coyotes. Hell, Ada, this is too dangerous. I'm coming with you."

I put my finger up to his lips. "I'm only going two doors down. I have to do this alone."

"It's come to that? I never thought you'd make that walk again. Well, if I can't come, I intend to watch you from the door." The love of my life stood his ground firm.

There was no arguing with Peter. Things were just that bad and I was just that desperate.

~

I did something I hadn't done since my first naïve days in Paris. I dropped into Zelli's. I didn't have a member's card, but I was Bricktop and that was still worth something—at least until Inspector Gravois had his way. I was ushered in without a hitch. It was smoky and dimly lit—intentionally so. The club was surprisingly nicely decorated with dark and durable fabrics on its few benches. The cabaret was small, and the relative elegance of the décor was compromised by the *filles* sitting around the bar, waiting for some mark they could pick off. They were dressed the part of respectable ladies, but Zelli's was a pickup joint. Some women were giving private dances in the corners, easily covering their activities with dark, heavy coats and the muted lighting.

I sat down at the bar next to a buxom brunette and greeted the tall bartender whose face reminded me of a guppy. "Hey Zachary."

Zachary's bulbous eyes seem to run smack dab into his cheeks when he grinned. "Brick! It's good to see you. Trying to check out the competition? Whatever you're drinking is on the house."

"You know I can't compete," I smiled. *There's no business like the ho business* is what I was really thinking; it would always be more profitable. "I'll take a Remy. I'm looking for someone."

"Who might that be?" Zachary asked. For years, he'd been floating from cheap nightclub to cheaper nightclub. I knew him from my youthful days at Connie's Inn in Harlem.

"The Wolf."

Zachary winced. "Some names you don't call out loud. Some people don't like to be looked for either. I don't know nobody by that name, Brick." He splashed some of the Remy on the bar top, missing my glass entirely. He quickly mopped it up with a thin, tattered rag that could have used a tablespoonful or two of bleach in its next washing.

"Is that right? That's too bad." I sipped from my glass. You sure you don't know him?"

"Uh-uh," he responded, wiping that same spill over and over again though it had long been wiped clean.

I continued working the club, asking about the Wolf, sometimes calling him the Fox, "or something like that," I would say casually. I repeated my inquiries at Parisi's, Chez Florence, and the Diga Diga Do, where Mabel's heavenly soprano poured out sweetly into every corner of that drab club. And the whole time, Peter watched from Chez Bricktop's doorway as I walked up and down rue Pigalle. Each time I asked for the Wolf, I was met with shoulder shrugs or dropped their eyes. It was like watching a classroom full of children kicking the floor and refusing to own up to some transgression like busting a window. I did that until four. All I learned for sure was that everyone was terrified of the Wolf. Going hunting for a predator was surely a dangerous prospect. But five mornings ago, I had added "Dangerous" as my sixth middle name.

"Any luck finding that Wolf?" Peter asked as soon as we were through the heavy curtains at Chez Bricktop.

"Seems he likes to play hide-and-seek. Let's talk about it later."

We bid a warm farewell to the Duke, saw the last guests out, and finally, we closed up. We told everyone that there would be no breakfast this morning at Bricktop's. I was on the clock. I didn't have a second of a minute of an hour to spare. It was Wednesday morning. I had a day.

At five, the streets of Montmartre were clear and dark. Changchang, Peter, Falcon, and I were making our way back to the apartment.

"After you see her to the door, you need to be on your way," Peter told Falcon.

"I know, Peter. Changchang never lets me come in."

"Of course not. We raised her better than that," I said.

We all laughed. Though I was hankering to know how many times he had visited and how long he had been trying to get in.

A car was driving slowly toward us. It sped up suddenly and began barreling down the small, curvy street. The vehicle veered onto the sidewalk, gunning its engine. Nearly blinded by the headlights, we scattered like blackbirds in all directions, shouting and screaming into the still night, our caws carrying down the small street. We were running fast toward the apartment for cover.

"Shit! What was that about?" Falcon asked.

The three of us looked at each other. We were panting hard. My garter had unattached itself from my stockings, which were now hanging loosely around my ankles and shoes. I was trembling because my legs were bare. We were in front of our light ochre-colored stone building with its large dark wooden door. There were six units in the building, two per floor, with floor-to-ceiling street-facing windows framed by white shutters. The windows had tiny wrought-iron balconies. Except for flowering baskets, they were unusable. We entered the vestibule and quickly ascended three flights of stairs.

"Wait," said Peter as he opened the door to the apartment, entering its foyer. A cold breeze swept over us all with the door's opening. "Something's wrong. Falcon, come on in with me. Changchang and Ada, you wait here in the hallway."

We waited, as requested, but I pulled out Mister Speaker, and I could tell that Changchang was ready to pull out her blade at the first sign of trouble.

Peter left the door open. He turned on the lights, and then he and Falcon slowly went through Changchang's apartment and then ours. "Red, come on in."

It was freezing cold inside. We hadn't left any windows open but someone else had. With gunshots. There was glass all over the apartment floor in the bedroom, bath, and salon.

"We can't stay here," I said. The Wolf had returned my call. I packed as much as I could in a suitcase; Changchang gathered a few things from her apartment with Falcon standing guard.

I called Cole at the Ritz, and he arranged for a suite for the three of us. We arrived in a foul but determined mood around six. There was no sleep to be had. I had one day left to hunt the Wolf before he mauled me.

THE DARK ROOM, OR A PICTORIAL HYMN TO APHRODITE

XVIII.

Changchang and I left Peter at the Ritz around seven thirty that morning, drinking a strong dark coffee and eating a flaky croissant. He had insisted on checking on our apartment before a nine thirty gathering with his band members at the Flea Pit, a hangout across town in Montmartre. They had a series of shows they needed to practice for before their debut at the Diga Diga Do this weekend.

We paced back and forth in front of Ollie's apartment trying to stave off the glacial temperatures as we waited for Monsieur Claudel. When I finally spotted the plodding man in his rumpled suit, I nearly shouted at him to put some pep in his step. Then I remembered his limp. My anxiety had made me thoughtless. I swore I was going to make it up to him, and to Cole, and Peter, and anyone else I was railroading over, just as soon as I got this big mess sorted out.

"I see Madame is again à l'heure and it is me who is en retard."

"I haven't been waiting very long. I just appreciate your arranging to have the viewing so quickly and at this uncivilized hour." I tried to tamp down my agitation as I looked down at my watch. 8:05.

"Bonjour, Mademoiselle." Claudel smiled in Changchang's direction. I had brought her along to distract him, and she was already doing a fine job.

"Bonjour Monsieur." She smiled back at him.

She towered over the rumpled man. She was wearing a Marlene Dietrich–style slack suit with a black cloche hat that Mama had sent over. Changchang had adorned the hat with a red and black silk flower. She looked richer than rich in the fur swing coat I had loaned her.

"Quel bel accent," Claudel continued admiring her exotic looks. All one had to do was utter a few words in French and some Frenchies fell all over themselves with compliments. All she did was say "Hello," damn man. I was ready to pounce on him. I needed to get into the apartment quick fast and here he was ogling and making pretty French small talk on a hard concrete sidewalk on a frigid, squally morning.

"I think you will like this apartment. It is bigger than the other. Nice windows. Separate sleeping quarters," he said, returning to business.

Again, I was following Monsieur Claudel into a murdered white woman's apartment building.

"And my hobby?"

"Si si si, Madame. The previous client rented the apartment across the hall. Apartment B. She and you shared a fondness for photography. It is open for you as well. I did not have time to clean it. It is smaller and the chemicals smell awful. Since Madame does this hobby, it should not bother you, *non?*"

"Not at all." I rubbed my gloved hands together in quiet content. I could feel a gurgling deep in my stomach from excitement. I looked to Changchang.

"Will the Mademoiselle be looking at the apartment as well?"

"No. She will wait at the café down the street for me."

"*Très bien,*" he nearly clapped. The gimp-legged geezer could barely contain his glee. We were both ready to be done with one another.

"I shall accompany her then. I have already been up to the apartment once this morning to tidy things up for you Madame. My leg, you understand." He pointed to his bad leg with a frown.

Lying ass, Frenchman.

"I shall leave you here to look around, then?"

"Please," I said turning toward the staircase.

I winked at Changchang as she followed Claudel out into the street. Then I made my way up the long flight of stairs. But I wasn't huffing and puffing this morning. My anticipation had me almost skip two steps at a time.

I found the familiar door. The salon was as I remembered it—neat as a pin. But in the daytime, it no longer looked sinister. Light poured in from the windows, and it was a very nice apartment—if you could ignore the fact that someone had recently been murdered in it. Monsieur Claudel had wasted no time in having the bedroom cleaned and painted. There were no remnants of the sheared mattress stuffing or the pillow feathers. The smells of bleach and fresh paint were muted by the aroma of fresh-baked bread that poured in through a slightly opened window.

It must have been nice, early in the morning, to awaken to the smell of freshly baked baguettes, *pains perdus, pains chocolats,* and other butter-filled pastries and breads from the *boulangerie* on the first level.

Ollie's personal belongings were still in the drawers. Her family had yet to arrive to claim them. I looked through them. Nothing.

I didn't find any spare photographs in Ollie's drawers, which was suspicious, given her profession. But she did have some impressive photographs of Paris on her walls. Blown up large, they showed café scenes and portraits of people I knew from Bricktop's. I glanced at Ollie's beautifully framed photograph of Cole and Linda Porter. I was struck by Ollie's talent. Even the way she hung the photography was artistic. Some of it was sepia-toned. Other prints were hand-tinted. It told me a lot about who she had been— her potential—and I shuddered to think about how she had died. My jaws went tight.

I walked across the hall to Apartment B and opened the door. On one table sat three cameras, by my quick count, photographic printing paper, several easels, small bottles filled with liquids, a number of tongs tossed everywhere, and, more importantly, the pungent chemical smell.

The smell was indeed nasty. But I had smelled worse, including the stench from Ollie's apartment the night she was murdered. I got used to the chemicals after a couple of deep inhalations. Ollie had all sorts of photographs hanging to dry. I studied them. Doorways with addresses and street names in Paris and New York. There were some highly stylized pictures of Natalie with several women fully clothed. Also, the interior of the Women's Academy courtyard on an overcast day.

I picked up a photograph of a dark-haired woman waving from a market scene. She looked familiar. I reached in my purse to compare it to a newspaper clipping. It was Pippa Nelson. I stared at the photograph of the young woman. She really was pretty with dark eyes and shoulder-length wavy hair. She was laughing. I wondered what had made her laugh so. Was she happy to be in love with Josie? To be with a friend? Was her work going that well?

Her white teeth showed brightly and her arms were up in the air, straining against a dark, heavy coat, like she was dancing. It was an almost childlike pose, all innocence and happiness. I turned the photograph over. Ollie had noted the month and year. *New York, December 1930.*

Her work. I looked at the pictures of doorways and street addresses again. The *same ones from the night I met her.* I thought about how I had been trying that same December to get Dutch Schulz out of my house in Bougival. We were all preoccupied with gangsters in December 1930. I wasn't intrigued by them, tracking them like Pippa and Ollie had. I didn't truck with gangsters.

I took two steps in the tight little space to the only other table of photographs. These were studies in nudes. I flipped quickly through the pictures. And there they were, the erotic scenes with Josie and the Women's Academy members, including Ollie and Pippa.

Though Natalie had told me she only watched, I was certain that it was her French manicured hand resting on the bottom of one of the women. I went back to Ollie's stylized photograph of Natalie. Same hands. Same dates, I noticed, when I turned the photographs over. *June 1930.* Natalie's and Josie's recollections all pinpointed June 1930.

I squatted slightly to take a look at the two shallow shelves beneath the table. On the one, I found a thick envelope. A red leather-bound journal, emblazoned with gold lettering on its cover: *The Paris Journal.* Its pages were trimmed in gold. An autographed picture by Jacques Viven of Josie in her banana skirt sat atop the journal. And a gun. Ollie Knolton must have been as terrified as the sage Renata had said she was.

There on the second shelf sat a thin, brown appointment book. I glanced through it quickly, taking in particularly the last few months. There were dates about Natalie's Women's Academy meetings. Lunches and such. A meeting with Pippa on Thursday evening. I lifted the appointment book just in case there was something else to be discovered.

Obviously the killers didn't know about her darkroom. Neither had the coppers. During Monsieur Claudel's sun-chasing adventure in the South of France, his assistant Manu was in charge. Given Claudel's penchant for discretion, either Manu didn't know about the darkroom or he had only given the police access to what they asked for. *The crime scene.*

I turned to search for a light switch. I shook the envelope. Out fell the series of pictures that Ollie had shown me the night at Natalie's salon. These were duplicates of the ones hanging. Ollie Knolton must have taken the envelope full of photographs out of her purse and put them in her darkroom for safekeeping before she was murdered on Saturday. Clearly, she was scared and careful.

I opened the journal, skimming its pages. The name Pippa Nelson was inscribed in the front in looping, ornate dark ink. Out flew several pieces of paper and another set of photographs.

I picked up the photos and papers from the dark floor. These pictures were of Josie and Pippa. This time, I studied and counted them carefully. There were nine in all. The photographs were very different from the staged group shots that were taken at Natalie's Temple of Friendship.

The intimacy and tenderness between the two women leapt off the photographic paper. In the first five images, Josie and Pippa were holding hands, facing each other in ceremonial poses, dancing and laughing like two gamines, kissing each other lightly on the lips. In the last four, they were lying down and taking turns lightly caressing one another. *Lovers in repose.* Their stillness gave them a statue-like quality. These intimate portraits were taken at Pippa's apartment with all that white and lightness. They were Ollie's masterpieces.

REVELATIONS

XIX.

I gathered up all the photographs and negatives in sight, putting them in my purse. I was jittery. My hands shook a little and my stomach was roiling. I'd just hit pay dirt. At the moment, all I could think was how terrified both Ollie and Pippa must have been. Enough to hide this treasure trove in the darkroom for safekeeping.

Then I went back to the first table and began opening up the cameras to pull out their contents, hoping to damage the film. I poured the chemical solution in the small bottles over everything I didn't take, including the film. If I could have set fire to that little studio, I would have. So no one else would happen upon a compromising photo of Josephine Baker.

I then opened the journal. Pippa had apparently been writing in this little book since her arrival in Paris in 1927, though most of the entries were short and cryptic. I skipped through her scrawl until I reached the most recent pages.

15 May 1930

I stopped by Natalie's for tea this afternoon. Renata was there. She stayed in the bedroom, but I could hear her crying and swearing terribly. She told Natalie she would never come back again. That this was her last visit. We both knew that was a lie. She can't stay away. It's not just the laudanum and knockout drops. Despite her pushy ways, Natalie is a dedicated lover. We pretended not to hear Renata's curses, and I confided to Natalie about my Very Important article and meeting my brand-new lead who can help me flesh things out. The Amazon's face turned glacial when I mentioned meeting him at Zelli's. She can't stand that place. Calls it trashy and told me to be careful about slumming. She's a snob, our Natalie. But I suppose you can afford to be, when you're independently wealthy. If I'd been born a man, I think my parents would've been proud to send me a little bit of cash they'd saved over the years until I'd found my own footing. Instead, they're hoping I give up my "unwomanly" pursuits and crawl back home to marry one of the bland, forgettable men who work with Daddy at the pork-packing factory. It's a good living, they said. Look at us. We are buying our home. Look at it!! Not even a tick above the slums. I want more. I hadn't scrimped and saved by working at a local Chicago rag as a secretary to get to New York and then Paris as a low-level reporter to turn around and go back home. No! No! No! I jumped at the first assignment overseas to Paris in 1927, even paying my own freight, for a chance to follow my dreams and my mentor, JF. Our weekly meetings in the Village had opened up a new world to me. They are too shortsighted to realize that their lack of support has given me a strong backbone. I'm more determined than ever to prove myself as a real journalist.

I told Natalie that in my line of work, I can't be choosy about leads and where they might be found. You go where the story takes you. That's why male reporters always get the scoop. No places are too ruinous to their reputations. It's high time we women reporters are allowed to court danger too!

My, my. Reading Pippa's optimistic words got me all choked up. She had no idea how much danger she was heading into. I wondered if Pippa and I might have been friends, under different circumstances. I admired her determination. Her Chicago, no nonsense spirit. I reached in my large handbag for a handkerchief to dab my eyes. I kept reading.

28 May 1930

I spoke to Janet Flanner today at Brasserie Lipp about my Big Idea. We leaned so close, so as not to be overheard, that at one point, our heads knocked together! We discussed how I could make it stand out from all the earlier stories on the subject, all written by men. Readers want drama and substance, not just the fluff that's delegated to women reporters. This is why I wanted to write this story in the first place. I plan to follow JF's advice—to cast a wide net and connect the dots. If I do it well, my career will be golden. It could blow the doors open for women in the profession. I could be a trailblazer. I worry a little about the danger—these are not people to mess with. But I have to admit, I'm more worried about someone scooping me, which is why I have to stay cagey about specifics until I've got all the pieces in place. What if someone found my notes and scooped me? I would just die. But I trust JF. No reservations there. She doesn't have the brass to do this story.

30 May 1930

We did it. Nothing like horrible John Fitzwilliams back in Chicago when I was nineteen and was over before it began and hurt like hell in his crummy little backseat.

With BB, I wouldn't mind doing it again, and again, and probably will. He's very taken with me. Don't know what I feel about him though. He's a swell guy. Handsome. Well dressed. Always smells so good. I like how he makes me feel. Not to mention, he's saving me a fortune. I don't have to pay for dinners or nice dresses or nights on the town. I've developed a taste for champagne and escargot. A welcome relief from the camembert and tomato baguette sandwiches I've become accustomed to here in Paris. I've been to places I could never afford on the Champs-Élysées. Mother surely wouldn't approve of me acting like Mata Hari. But damn it! A female reporter has to use all of her resources. To heck with morality. It never paid a goddamn bill.

I sat up from the table I was leaning on, mouth wide open. *BB. The Baron de Boulainvilliers?* I wouldn't touch him to slap him, but maybe he knew his way around the bedroom. And maybe his claim that Pippa was his fiancée wasn't as ridiculous as I'd first thought. Maybe he'd really fallen for her, and maybe she'd given him good reason to.

15 June 1930

I'm in love. It's real this time. JF introduced us at Natalie's. I'm still in shock that it was really her. I first saw her at the Théatre des Champs-Élysées as Fatou with BB. She's the toast of Paris. I invited her back to my place after the salon. We spent a day together last week in Versailles. She had never been. She'd been too busy. We toured the Hall of Mirrors. Acted like Marie Antoinette and giggled, "Let them eat cake." I explained to my new beloved that the Queen never really said those words. We walked in the gardens and finally kissed on the steps of Versailles. Story #2: Americans in Paris. A fluffy piece more than suitable for a female reporter. I can be with her all the time. Have to figure out what to do with BB. He insists he wants me to move to another apartment he'll pay for. Thinking about Independence. Possessive? I like it.

Josie. I rubbed my eyes from fatigue. Pippa's handwriting was deliberately small and nearly illegible. I felt a little guilty poring over her private thoughts, but I decided that Pippa wouldn't mind my nosiness; she would want me to find out who was to blame for snuffing out her life. And if Josie minded, too damn bad. As for the Baron, I never believed he didn't mind sharing. French or not, he was a man after all.

For the next few pages, Pippa doodled the initials J. B. plus P. N. with hearts. She was like a young girl experiencing her first love. By August, she was moving between BB and JB with regularity, and Ollie had been brought in by September to take photographs for the unnamed story that would make her golden. Finally, a reference to the photographs! I began to read faster.

10 December 1930

Renata with her matted orange hair is a bitch. Everyone else was so happy for me. But not Renata. She sat in the corner spewing venom about how idiotic my venture was and how I was endangering Ollie. She is scaring Ollie, who is only helping me because she wants to see JB. Nag. Nag. Nag. I should have drawn the line at my place that second time. I wonder what Natalie sees in Renata. I wouldn't put it past Renata to give my story to another reporter. She's insane. A skinny, washed-up poet with a habit is what she is. No more sharing or readings when Renata's around. What a pill. Maybe she will never come back like she keeps promising. She'd be doing all of us a favor.

4 January 1931

We had such a nasty row, fucking, fussing, and fighting. Heavens, I have a terrible mouth. JB refuses to visit the Women's Academy. It's his fault, of course. This can't go on forever. She says she wants us to be together. And I'll hold my breath, Miss JB. BB is my refuge. J'ai deux amours.

18 January 1931

I told him everything. We met at his office in Paris. He laughed at first. He was dreadfully dismissive. Then he became furious when he realized I was serious. I showed him. He called me a snotty bitch. He escorted me to the door and slammed it behind me.

I nearly bounded out of the darkroom except I now had a raging headache. I dug around my purse for a Stanback and a flask of water. I took a swig while thinking about Peter and his love letter to me. I would have beat the dickens out of any chippie for running after my man and coming to tell me about it. Alberta's "Downhearted Blues" was running through my head, all about the cost of unrequited love, half-assed love, and borrowed love.

There are lovers and there are lovers. The entries ended. I turned my attention to the loose folded pages that were in the journal. My head was swirling and pounding, but I had to focus. The pages were typed notes, unlike the journal entries. There was also an outline for Pippa's multipart story for *The International New York Review*. Lang was right. She was a thorough reporter. It was a hit job on the mob. She had been able to trace members and lieutenants of some of the *arrivistes* New York families like the Pozzallos, the Naros, the Milazzos, and the Gaggis. The number of names was staggering.

According to Pippa's notes, these families ran the syndicate in the Mediterranean, from southern Italy to parts of southern France. Some families had immigrated to America via New York and were directly involved in the Castellammarese War, a power struggle that had been raging between various factions of these families in New York since 1929. They were now making their way back over the Atlantic, moving north and rousting the good citizens of Paris. The number of gangsters coming into Bricktop's again made sense to me. With their numbers and businesses still expanding, these crime families were looking for new markets for their illegal activities.

Some of the names—Luciano, Siegel, Costello, Lansky, Schultz, Anastasia, and Genovese—were familiar to me from my days in Chicago and New York. Harlem was overrun with gangsters—colored, Jewish, Irish, and I-talian. I never dealt much with Bumpy Johnson, but there was his name, along with Jack "Legs" Diamond, who had been cut down that past December. I mopped my brow with my handkerchief, reflecting on how he had just been to Bricktop's.

Pippa's story was written like an epic for the cinema houses. This was no fluff piece. She had deftly followed Janet Flanner's advice. It had high drama, murder, revenge plots, generational rifts, and double-crosses. The journal and papers disappeared into my handbag. The story was bad enough. Like Papa Jack said, everyone was writing stories on the syndicates. She had had an assist from the Baron, which probably added some color, but this masterpiece went far beyond anything he could have helped her write. *And those photographs.* Before I knew it I was shaking my head and making a tutting sound. Those pictures identified where the gangsters holed up; they could be used in the worst of ways by rival gangsters and good and bad coppers. How Pippa Nelson slept at night I would never know. And I guess that didn't matter now anyway.

I went back to Ollie's apartment and placed three phone calls. It was now a respectable nine in the morning. It didn't matter to me now who would later discover where I was calling from. I called Josie. One good turn deserves another. Then I called Officer Jean Bergeron to ask him to accompany me to a meeting with Inspector Gilles Gravois. I needed a good cop to trap a bad one. Then I called Gilles Gravois himself to set up a meeting for two that afternoon. He was, as I had planned, surprised. I was a day early.

"Monsieur Claudel, what a cozy darkroom. This would be a perfect *pied-à-terre* for me if the kitchenette was already in place," I announced to him as I opened the door to the Café Princesse.

His reed-thin lips turned downward. "But Madame . . ."

"No. I can't be convinced about this one either." I had another idea though. I wanted to throw him a bone for his time and trouble. He was an honest man trying to earn an honest living, even if he hadn't bothered to mention that the apartments he was showing me had belonged to murdered women.

I wanted a new place for Changchang, someplace out of Montmartre where she could meet a different sort of people than nightclub carousers and merrymakers. Montmartre was fine for me. I was at the top of the game. But Changchang wasn't me. I wanted her to inhabit a world that was as pretty, sweet, and textured as the hand-pulled sugar flowers she would learn to make at *patisserie* school.

"I've decided I don't much want to move. My niece here, though, she'll be starting pastry school. A studio with a kitchenette would do nicely. We won't be needing it right away. Probably in a few weeks. March, I'm thinking."

"I ain't hardly moving, Aunt Ada. I like it just fine where I am." Changchang fluffed her hair before putting her cloche hat back on. She fiddled with the flowered hatpin.

"If you are going to open that new café and go to school, you need to live on this side of town to keep an eye on things, don't you think, baby?" I said, trying to convince her. I wanted her with people her age who were doing things and going places. I mostly wanted her away from Falcon.

"Humph." Changchang nodded like what I said made some sense, even if she didn't care to admit it aloud.

"*Alors*, there is the first apartment I showed you. *C'est sympa*."

"Yes, it's nice." I wanted to slap the taste out of Monsieur Claudel's vapid mouth with my leather shoe. My earlier guilt about his limp was evaporating fast as he tried to pawn Pippa's apartment off on Changchang. *Squirrely little Frenchman.* I didn't want my precious baby living in some dead woman's apartment. "Do you have anything near Boul'Miche?"

"There is one. My last, Madame Bricktop, *et je vous jure*, it is lovelier than the first and second one. The views are over the Seine. It is near Place Saint-Michel. Plenty of restaurants and shops. *C'est tout à fait agréable*."

"You swear, *non?* Expect a call from me and Changchang next week, then, Monsieur Claudel, to set something up. We'd like to take a ride by the area as well. Can you provide me the address?"

"*Oui, Madame. Pas de problème.* He scribbled out the address.

"He don't care a lick about bad juju." Changchang wrinkled her nose, thinking about Monsieur Claudel. She tucked herself behind the wheel. She looked like a modern woman, easily handling that car.

I could drive myself. Like many women in 1931, I loved cars as much as I had loved getting the vote in 1920. But the novelty of driving had worn off when I left America. These days, I preferred to be driven.

"Hell no, he don't. That man there has cornered the market on endangered clientele. But I'm going to make sure no murdered white women have been found in this new place."

PUTTING ON THE RITZ

XX.

The Stanback had finally kicked in and so had some understanding of the web I'd been caught up in.

"You found those dirty pictures, Aunt Ada?"

"Those and then some."

We drove silently down Haussmann's Grand Boulevard, heading toward the Champs-Élysées and the Place Vendôme. Today was the day of toting up wrongs, rights, and evens.

Changchang smiled as she closed the driver-side door and handed the keys to the valet at the Ritz. "*Nous en aurons besoin plus tard. Laissez-la voiture ici, s'il vous plaît,*" she instructed the valet. He looked her up and down appreciatively. He took the keys but allowed the car to remain parked at the front of the Ritz, as she had requested.

Changchang winked at him. I could hear him calling, "Mademoiselle, mademoiselle," as we approached Émile the doorman.

If I didn't want her ending up with some rag-tag musician from MoMart, I certainly didn't want her stuck with a French valet, so I took Changchang's arm and called out. "*Allez-vous-en.*"

We rushed through the lobby of the Ritz in the direction of our suite. I wanted to safely stow my newly found discoveries. They were burning a hole through my purse. These were my insurance policies. I tucked them into the nightstand drawer under my undergarments. Then the telephone jangled. I looked up at Changchang, who was standing in her stockinged feet.

"Who could that be?"

I shrugged my shoulders and spoke into the receiver, "*Allô oui? J'écoute.*"

"*Oui, Madame Bricktop*, you have a visitor in the lobby bar."

"I'll be right down."

I placed the telephone in its cradle. I slid my shoes on and stood up by the nightstand. Changchang raced across to her bedroom door and grabbed her shoes.

"I'm coming with you, Aunt Ada." She was hopping on one leg, trying to place a shoe on her foot.

I considered. "This could be dangerous. I need you for backup. I need you to wait by the telephone."

"Uhh uhh. This is a nice place. I won't kill anybody in it, I swear. But Uncle Peter would never forgive me if I let you go down there by yourself."

"Really? So why do you have your knife in your bosom?"

"Old habits die hard. Even in nice places." She finally got a shoe on. "Besides, you've got Mister Speaker."

"Well then that should be good enough for you."

She pouted and plopped her lean frame into a Louis XIV chair. "What if you need me and you can't get to a phone?"

She was right. How was I going to get to a phone if I was in danger?

"What if I sneak down behind you? Watch from a distance?"

Reluctantly, I agreed. "Just remember what we agreed about the killing part."

No sooner had I passed through the Ritz's lobby in the direction of the bar then I heard a familiar voice.

"Bricky, Bricky," the handsome white man called out from a barstool.

I didn't have time for Charlie Wales's drink-besotted antics this afternoon. The Ritz was still obviously his favorite American hangout in these worst of times. He was on a nostalgia trip, I was certain. First Bricktop's, now the Ritz.

"Hey, baby," I said calmly though my legs were shaking with nervous energy. "Bricky has an important meeting with," I searched around the bar, "that man over there." I pointed to the handsome man sitting comfortably in a dark winged-back chair. He was tucked deep into a secluded corner far from the bar. A glass filled with brown liquid dangled from his pasty hand. I glanced down at my watch. *11 am. Too early for these white men to be drinking.*

I could see from Charlie's pupils that he was not that far gone in his cups. He was probably on his second martini. My mind started clicking away. I walked over to the bar where Charlie's third drink sat awaiting him.

"Once I finish up this business with him over there, I'll have the waiter bring your next drink over to my table." I was smiling my sweetest smile.

"But Bricky . . ." Charlie looked dejected, like a child who didn't believe his mother would keep her promise.

I held firm. "Can you be patient for me, okay, baby?"

He smiled faintly.

The Baron de Boulainvilliers was all by his lonesome this time. I sat down in the deep chair across from him. The soft leather and winged design swallowed me up. I had half expected Gravois to send the Baron my way soon after my telephone call this morning from Ollie's apartment.

"I see you have come alone. That was wise." He crossed and then uncrossed his legs. I could hear the rustle of his wool slacks.

"Likewise. You just don't know when to quit do you?"

"I told you I am a persistent suitor. A drink?"

"It's too early for drinking."

"*S'il te plaît?*" He had a smirk on his princely face. "I do not like drinking alone. You do not mind if I *tutoyer* you? I feel like we've become such intimate acquaintances in such a short time."

"*Vousvoyer, tutoyer. Cela m'est égale.* It's all the same to me under the circumstances. We're neither intimates nor acquaintances. You aren't too nice to those who've flown too close to your flame. Like Pippa Nelson," I hedged. "Now what is it exactly you want? I think I've made it clear I'm not paying you a franc."

His manicured hand lightly shook the glass. The solitary ice cube clinked against the sides before he took the bourbon up to his lips. I watched the liquid flow between his polished white teeth, his pink tongue playfully flicking at the remaining alcohol.

He sighed before he began to speak softly. "I am not a killer. Pippa Nelson was special to me. I intend to find her killer. As for you, I have something that might assist you to, *comment dit uh, uh,*" he said, resorting to the national French tic of searching for the right word with a few "uh, uhs." "How do you say, change your mind." He raised his dark blond eyebrows. "Now let us conduct ourselves in a way that befits the environment." His hand made a theatrical gesture toward the room and its Old World décor. "This is not Montmartre. No scenes, Bricky."

I deeply resented the swipe at MoMart even more than his being familiar. As if folks on this side of town didn't indulge in all sorts of skullduggery. My last few days alone in Paris's well-heeled ramparts confirmed that. And he knew it, too.

"You've got nothing I want." I tried to sit up, but the depth of the chair seemed to pull me back down.

"*Oui, oui, ma chère,* I do. Something. *Non. Je m'excuse,* someone quite dear."

I saw all kinds of red then. I fumbled around for my purse and realized I had left it in the room. I started cursing under my breath. *To hell with the cigars.* Like an alley cat, I begin clawing instead at the inside pocket of my slack suit jacket, where Mister Speaker was snugly tucked. I decided I was going to put a cap in the Baron's ass right then and there. And then I thought about the audience I had at the Ritz. Setting an example for Changchang went through my head. I ached for Peter.

"You're ransoming my husband? Where is he?" I asked, taking a few deep breaths and cutting through the silly talk.

"He is being well looked after at my newest club. *T'inquiètes pas.* Don't worry your beautiful red head, *mon petit oiseau.*" The Baron then put his hand on my knee.

Fucking forward Frenchman. That was the oldest move on the European continent. I swung my crossed leg to the other side.

"You're a dirty, lower-than low garden-variety bastard." My voice quivered. "You've been quite improvisational in the past. Why should I believe you now?"

I stood up, leaving my peacemaker in its place for now. My knees buckled for a second as I drew in another deep breath. I had to sit back down. I was experiencing vertigo. "I should have shot you after the police told me to," I divulged rather deliberately.

The Baron looked stunned. His matte gray eyes moved around the room in displeasure, then he grimaced. "*Eh bien.* Honorable, corrupt help is difficult to find."

"I bet it is in your line of work."

He reached into his jacket and pulled out a timepiece. He placed it on the table. "Your evidence, *Madame.*" He winked.

I could see that it was Peter's from where I sat. Cartier notched four-digit reference codes on their watches. I knew that code by heart because I had purchased the timepiece. I felt tears well up before I could blink them back down. "What's the trade for my husband's life?" I steadied my voice. I wanted to rip his eyelashes out one by one for that wink he gave me.

He drew down the remaining bourbon from the glass. A diamond in his cufflink caught the light from the colored glass lamp on the table when he tipped the drink forward. "Twenty percent of Chez Bricktop's profit. You will continue on as hostess. We will add a few dancing girls to the place—like Zelli's. It's too *sophistiqué chez* Bricktop. We need to, *comment ça va dire?*—how do you say?—jazz things up." His eyes were laughing as he sat back in his chair. He was a cool customer, but his demeanor had grown increasingly agitated.

"I told you I'm not in the hustling business." I smiled back, though I wanted to kick this French spasm's thin ass for even thinking about dragging Bricktop's down to Zelli's two pumps for a franc ho level. I also wondered why he hadn't inquired about Ollie's pictures and Pippa's sensational story. I guessed his task was to focus on the business end of things. The real dirty work he'd leave for my two o'clock appointment with Gravois.

"You will be soon enough, Bricky. You'll be doing a lot of things you've refused before."

I opened my jacket slightly, wondering if anyone had ever been shot dead at the Ritz. They had done just about everything else up in those rooms I knew.

My hands were faintly shaking. I was struggling for self-control. "I think I'll take that drink."

"Let's hurry things along. The sooner I get what I want, the sooner you can see that husband of yours." The Baron motioned for the barkeep.

"Hell no!" I yelped wildly to let him know I was deadly serious. "I'll order it myself. I wouldn't touch you to claw your eyes out, let alone allow you to buy me a drink." I hissed with the conviction of a desperate woman.

He shooed me toward the bar in a way that spoke his agitation. Like he couldn't wait to get on with this business so as to attend to something more pressing. I followed his hands to the bar, looking out of the corners of my eyes for Changchang, hoping she'd see what was happening.

She moved in my wake like a shadow.

I knew Peter's going to our apartment this morning had been a bad idea. I should have been more insistent. They had snapped him up somewhere between staking out our apartment and his run to the Flea Pit. The Baron had found my weak, sweet spot. He'd also sent me to the well of "come hell or high water."

Having reached the bar, I signaled for the barkeep, buying time. "*Un martini pour le Monsieur.*"

Charlie ambled over quickly with the martini in hand. He took up a seat in the last of the three wing-backed chairs surrounding the ebony four-squared table.

"*Qu'est-ce qui se passe?*" An irritated Baron snapped about Charlie the interloper.

"Nothing happening at all. In a moment we'll be going. Just as soon as we can get to the car." As I said these last phrases, I raised my voice and cut my eyes toward Changchang. Silently, she left the lobby. I hoped she'd correctly read my mind.

"Charlie's just an old friend. But you've made me a wee bit desperate, Mr. Baron, threatening my husband, my club, and just plain carrying on something terribly awful." I was saying this while I was reaching in my jacket pocket for Mister Speaker. "And for working my nerves like you have, I'm not giving you shit."

"You threatened, Bricky? Who the hell do you think you are, buddy?" Charlie said loudly, placing the martini on the table.

Charlie Wales stood up and began rolling up his sleeves. As I recalled from his days at Bricktop's, he wasn't much of a fighter. He didn't have the muscle or bullying chops of Ernie Hemingway. But he was quite a blowhard.

The Baron smiled at Charlie's pathetic show of manliness. "I have business with Bricky. Perhaps you want to take your leave?"

"I'll do no such thing," Charlie brayed. Drops of spittle landed on the Baron's chin.

Baron de Boulainvilliers dabbed his chin with a silk kerchief he withdrew from his pocket and stood up. So did I with some difficulty on account of that damn chair. I snatched up Peter's timepiece on my way up to standing and dropped it in my pocket. It clinked lightly against Mister Speaker, which I now had by the handle. In my three-inch high heels, I was just two inches shorter than the Baron. I delivered a quick whack to his head.

He was stunned. He reached for me in that tight space, bumping his knee against the table, spilling the martini when Charlie stepped in to take a wild swing that got them both tangled up. Charlie leaped back swearing and threatening as I delivered three more dollops of Mister Speaker's handle upside the Baron's head. His knees finally collapsed. He landed yowling in the winged-back chair. Charlie was back on him, throwing punches and hollering like it was the Baron who had him by the hair.

"We must call the police at once, Brick!" He shrieked in excitement between strikes to the Baron's body. The French gangster was weakly pawing back.

"You do that! And then send them over to Bricktop's."

I flew quickly through the Ritz's front door, leaving Charlie to revel in his gallantry. Émile sprung the hotel's door wide open to reveal Changchang waiting eagerly in the C6. The passenger door was already open and the engine was turned over.

"We're going to Bricktop's." I inhaled deeply and exhaled slowly to focus. I was on my way to meet the Wolf. And for some reason, I didn't even feel the urge for a cigar or a session of screaming.

RENDEZVOUS IN THE NINTH

XXI.

Changchang was busily sharpening a knife's blade. She shifted the car into gear. I stared hard at that knife, thinking about the she-devil I was about set loose in Paris.

"Aunt Ada, you were beating the mess out of the white man. Now don't deny it. I saw you when I came back into the lobby to make sure you were alright . . . And you told me not to make a scene. What's going on?"

I filled her in on the kidnapping and the plans to trick out Chez Bricktop, and then told her to drive to my club.

"How do you know Uncle Peter is at Bricktop's, Aunt Ada? They may have him hidden some place less obvious." She was nervously tapped the steering wheel now, as she changed lanes and accelerated quickly toward the Butte.

"He's there alright. That presumptuous dandy said as much when he told me he was being looked after at *his* newest club." I said this as she pulled up to the curb a good half block from Chez Bricktop.

"Can I kill him, Aunt Ada? It's only fair."

I looked at my sweet but lethal niece affectionately, dark, thick hair in shiny waves down her back. I reached over and stroked a curl. "We're still visitors in France. We'll do whatever is just short of that."

Changchang looked at me and smiled wide. "Now that's what I'm talking about, Aunt Ada." She bobbed her pretty little head up and down with approval. She folded back part of her suit jacket sleeve to show me a set of six pointed dart knives. As she slid her long legs off the car seat onto the street, I could see part of the folding knife handle nestled in her bosom.

"Now you've come over to my way of handling business."

"Umm hmm." I nodded in approval. I was a woman who preferred justice to revenge. And if I had to take it, I'd always preferred it cold. But today, I'd take it piping red hot. Gravois had put two of my family members in harm's way, tried to frame me for murder, destroy my reputation, and hustle me out of my club. As far as I was concerned, he was a feral Wolf who needed to be put down. I was just the woman to lay him among the sweet peas. But first I had to rescue my husband from his goon squad.

WOLF TRAP

XXII.

"Do you see him?" I asked Changchang, pointing to the lookout man in a dark overcoat in the distance. He was standing in front of Chez Bricktop.

"Yeah, I got him."

"No killing. Just disable him."

She frowned. I shrugged, as I reached in the backseat for a champagne bottle.

She reluctantly nodded her head and then sauntered provocatively up the block. I walked slowly behind her on the sidewalk on the other side of the street.

"*Monsieur, cette boîte, Chez Bricktop, c'est agréable?*" She was facing the man, as he leaned against a black-on-gray sedan, smoking.

He stared at her for a minute, taking a last puff of his rolled cigarette. "*Oui, c'est agréable, je crois,*" he said disinterestedly, looking down to stub the cigarette on the bottom of his shoe.

Changchang hit him hard in the windpipe. His hands went up to his throat. He couldn't shout or scream. In two shakes I was on him. I laid the champagne bottle hard across his head. His head bounced lightly against the car's hood. I hit him again for good measure on the knees. The bottle's contents and glass exploded on his pant legs. The lookout's knees buckled. He slid abruptly to the curb. He'd have one hell of a headache when he woke up.

Changchang and I walked quickly toward the club's back entrance. As we got close, we began to tiptoe and press ourselves against the wall across from the entrance where a small, bird-faced thing of a man was posted up. I heard a faint sound like a mosquito buzzing by my ear. I saw the spare man tip over in slow motion. I heard him gasp. I ran to catch him, before his fall made a loud thud into a trash can. As I laid him down, Changchang smoothly pulled one of the dart knives from his throat and wiped it clean with the dark cloth. The blood oozed steadily from his wound.

His eyes were wide. He flailed about, clawing at his throat.

"I told you not to kill him."

"Yes, you said not to kill *him*." She pointed toward Chez Bricktop's entrance on rue Pigalle. "Besides, he ain't dying, Aunt Ada. He's just disabled. I bet he won't be doing no screaming, though." She bent down and pulled his pistol from his jacket.

I looked down at the man. I pressed his hand to the small hole at his throat. I took his other hand to help lift him up. "Get out of here unless you want to get dead. *Allez.*" I pointed down the alley.

He stumbled forward. He half-walked and half-ran like a man reeling from an all-night bender.

We entered the club. Changchang headed for the kitchen. I followed quietly, as we listened to the rumble of voices out front. The men were speaking French.

"There's at least four of them," I concluded.

"We're going to play a game called 'smash the bad man's windpipe,' Aunt Ada. My daddy taught me this game back in Harlem. He learned it in Chinatown working with the associations." Changchang removed four plates from the cupboard. The small pistol was notched in her bosom along with her folding knife. I had Mister Speaker drawn from my jacket. I didn't want to shoot wildly though for fear of hitting Peter.

"No killing." I was beginning to sound like a broken record. I grimaced. And not because of the bloodbath that was about to begin but because of my Haviland china plates she was going to use to start the bloodletting.

"They'll wish they were dead anyways." She seemed to have read my mind and put the porcelain back in the cupboard. She grabbed instead a few cheap white plates.

As soon as we passed my back office where all of this mess had begun, we rushed forward at once. The chandelier lights and crystal wall sconces lit up Bricktop's like Christmas. Changchang quickly pitched two plates. They crashed loudly to the glass floors, after making contact with two hooligans. I could hear gasping. The panic in their eyes was palpable even from across the room. I heard the click of a gun. Changchang dropped the other two plates.

And finally I saw Peter. With a gun to his head. But the man holding it was the one person I'd trusted in the whole corrupt system—Jean Bergeron, whom I'd called myself when I found the pictures. God, how could I have been so blind? Suddenly, in one of those odd avalanches of realization, it seemed so clear: Bergeron was the Wolf! He'd had me register Mr. Speaker, so the cops would know I had a firearm. He'd set Jonny and Renata on me. He wanted me to kill the Baron, because he intended to take over his territory. He'd even taken my statement *and* the Baron's complaint against me. But mine was disappeared.

Damn, I was an idiot!

My husband's hands and feet were bound in intricate knots of rope; his mouth was taped shut. I saw the surprise in Peter's eyes.

"*Assez!* Enough!" Jean Bergeron yelled.

"Let him go!" I aimed Mister Speaker at Bergeron.

"Did you bring those pictures and that story with you?"

One of Bergeron's sidekicks had his gun trained on Changchang. If I shot Bergeron, he'd shoot Changchang.

"I'm quite surprised to see you, Officer Bergeron. But I'm afraid those are my insurance policy. You shouldn't have promised them to your colleagues."

He licked his dry lips greedily. "I am a dealmaker, Madame Bricktop." He was still so respectful. He ran one large hand through his thick mane.

"There is a war brewing in Montmartre, in New York, Chicago, the South of France, Italy, Madame. *Vous voyez, vous voyez,* I chose a side. I have a family to support and a mistress who likes Hermès." He smiled slickly, revealing his yellowing canines. "Besides I have practically run Montmartre for the Baron. I saw no reason why I should not run things for myself. I provided you with ample opportunities to assist me in this endeavor and yet you refused. I could not do so directly without great cost to myself and my *family.*" He moved the gun's barrel closer to Peter's temple when he emphasized the last word.

"So you're scared of the Baron's connections and you wanted me to do your nasty work? Well, I'm not a killer. And killing my husband certainly won't get you any closer to getting what you need."

I kept Mister Speaker aimed dead at him.

"I really liked you, Madame Bricktop. *Mais les affaires sont les affaires. Le* business is *le* business. You should have killed the Baron and paid for protection. The trail would have led to a dead Monsieur Dumont. A drug addict killing for money. *Oui, oui, oui.* That was my plan, my intentions. Noble, you see?"

Jean Bergeron was speaking of liking me in the past tense. I didn't like the sound of that at all. I began to shake my head thinking about my last run-in with Jonny Dumont.

"It's business to you. Not to me, you see. Jonny Dumont was my friend. And those women have families who love them. You sent that brute to kill Changchang." I stomped my foot on the glass panel.

"*Les affaires, les affaires.* He nodded his head as if to will me to accept his way of thinking. "Kill Changchang? *Non! Jamais!* Never! Just hurt her a *lee-ttle. Et les Américaines?* The women knew too much. The Baron understood this. He is not a sentimental man, Madame Bricktop."

I never believed he was despite Pippa's diary entries. Though I wish he had been where she was concerned.

All of our ears pricked up at the police sirens approaching.

His wingman fidgeted. "Jean, Jean. *La police!*"

Bergeron glanced quickly over at him, "*Tais-toi, Didier.* Shut up!"

I could see Changchang fidgeting slightly after hearing what Bergeron had said about having her tightened up a little bit.

"Take him."

Didier did a slight two-step backward when the dart knife penetrated his left cheek. Changchang scampered closer, hurtling three more to his chest before she dislodged the small pistol from her bosom and shot him in the hand clasping his gun. He tumbled down the stairs of Bricktop's entryway, screaming with each strike against those twelve steps.

Bergeron got a shot off in Changchang's direction. It missed, shattering a glass panel in the flooring. Using the patent leather entry curtain as a shield against the flying glass chips, she slipped down the stairs to finish slapping Didier around. I could hear him mewling loudly. She was going to make sure he would remain incapacitated.

By the time Bergeron returned his attention to me, I had already landed a blow with Mister Speaker across his jaw. He was dazed for a second when I then planted my Roger Vivier–encased foot in his scrawny French ass. He shook his head wildly, trying to shake off the whupping from Mister Speaker. His bushy mane was now every which-a-way. He was on all fours with his gun still cupped under his hands.

"You bastard! You backstabbing French jackass!" I got three kicks off to his ribs. I was heated and happy to find the source of all my discontent.

With each kick, he howled loudly. With each kick and howl, I felt a terribly thrilling sensation rush through my body. I kicked his gun across the dance floor to a corner.

On my fifth kick, a little harder and with a bit too much enthusiasm, he caught my leg. I went up and crashed down against the glass paneling. Mister Speaker shot off in the air. A bullet sliced through a crystal wall sconce. The glass floor was thick enough. It took the blow of my body without splintering into shards. I lost my grip on Mister Speaker though. He slid just out of my reach.

I was on my back near the bar. I looked up to meet Peter's fierce eyes. He was wiggling and whimpering on the barstool—his limbs tied tight and mouth taped shut. I looked back toward the charging Bergeron who had recovered his gun. Breathless and bruised from my kicks, he was unsteady but still ready to pounce. My arm was outstretched toward Mister Speaker, fingertips barely clawing the handle. Bergeron waved his gun toward me. Peter tipped over the barstool. His body thudded dully when it hit the glass floor. His heavy coat acted as a sound barrier. Yet it was enough of a distraction for me to scoot the required inch.

"*Salaupe! Comme vous êtes si désagréable!*" Bergeron fired wildly. The shot struck the bar top and ricocheted into a few bottles of high-priced liquor. I could hear the liquid splashing.

Damn, this French motherfucker!

I couldn't imagine why he thought I should be agreeable after all he had done, not to mention just calling me a bitch.

"Fuck you, Bergeron." I squeezed off a shot.

His body recoiled in shock as the bullet entered his thigh. He grunted loudly. He hadn't seen it coming in his mad charge toward me. A second shot caught his pistol-holding arm; the gun smashed against the floor. He charged again, a little slower.

"*Salaupe! Salaupe!*" He barked his schoolyard taunt again. I was still on my back. He was within two feet of my feet when his body convulsed and jerked slightly backward. He never turned around to see who had delivered such discomfort. He didn't have time. Blood rushed from a slit on the side of his neck. I scooted backward across the glass floor to avoid the blood splatter. The panels were slick enough from my nervous sweat to easily accommodate my slip and slide floor work.

Jean Bergeron fell sideways into the bar, awkwardly holding his neck to seal the wound. He knocked over a couple of barstools as he slid slowly down to the floor.

I heard the clickety-clack of shoes. "Are you okay, Aunt Ada?" Changchang held out her hand to help me up.

"Help your uncle, baby. I'll be just fine." Tears streamed down my face.

We were all silently listening to the rustle of Changchang's knife against the ropes binding my husband when the police arrived.

∾

"What a fine mess they have made of your elegant little place, Madame," Gilles Gravois said as he took in the mayhem at Chez Bricktop.

"Yes, they did," I responded while holding tight to Peter's now freed hand. "I don't much appreciate the agony you put me through when the trail leads right back to you and yours."

Beads of sweat began to form in my armpits, my cleavage, and even my hairline. I was almost glad, because I had read stories about people who got so angry that they spontaneously combusted—but the way I was sweating, I was too damp to catch on fire.

"*Évidemment.*" He glanced down at Jean Bergeron and the two other officers flailing around on the floor, gasping for air and weeping. "*C'est regrettable. Alors,* we have the Baron de Boulainvilliers in custody for assaulting you and that American fellow named Charles Wales. Monsieur Boulainvilliers has informed us that Jean Bergeron was extorting him. He is hoping for leniency."

So the Baron flipped on Bergeron. He knew immediately whom I was referring to when I let it drop that the police told me to shoot him dead. He hadn't liked it one bit, as I now vividly recalled. He understood Bergeron had had it in for him.

"Leniency? He's been shaking down all of Montmartre with the help of the Paris police." I narrowed my eyes.

Gravois sighed, and then he pulled at his moustache. "I can assure you, Madame Smith Ducongé, it pains me greatly that the Paris police force is involved in something so unsavory. We will need a statement from you about Monsieur Boulainvilliers and Officer Bergeron."

Inspector Gilles Gravois had somehow happened upon my correct address. Gone was the ill-bred calling me out of my name. *Humph.* As far as I was concerned, his pursuit of justice involved creating a personal hell for me. He would need a large helping of crow to go along with his croissants and coffee for a good long while.

When I didn't respond immediately to his request, he continued, "As luck would have it for you, the Frenchman who reported an assault by a woman fitting your description near Mademoiselle Knolton's apartment was drunk when he filed the complaint. *Un fou!*"

I saw no need to press the issue of the assault on the crazy Frenchman, as Gravois had called him. Since he believed he was crazy, I was more than willing to play dumb and crazy, too.

"And the mystery hit man at the Hotel Dieu?" I asked casually.

"He was found dead this morning. Asphyxiation. He was under police protection." Gravois glanced sidelong at the pale, limp Bergeron lying on the floor.

I raised my freshly tweezed eyebrows.

"You can come by the Ritz tomorrow for a statement and a few interesting artifacts. I gather this statement won't disappear into the police archives?"

He winced visibly at that remark. I understood him better, I thought. Gravois despised dirty coppers even more than he despised Americans in Paris. We weren't necessarily playing for the same team, but we were no longer sworn enemies.

I turned from Gilles Gravois then. "Changchang, we need to leave baby so the police can do their job." I squeezed Peter's arm. He brushed a red curl that had plastered itself with the help of sweat to my forehead.

"I'll meet you at the car. I can't leave my good knives."

"This is going to hurt a *lee-ttle*, Officer Bergeron," I heard Changchang whisper to the moaning dirty copper as she plucked, pulled, and wiped down each dart knife in his back and neck.

I collapsed in the backseat. I was wound up and exhausted all at once.

"It's okay, Red. It's okay. I knew you'd come. I knew I'd be alright," Peter repeated in soft tones as he wiped my tears and kissed me gently. My husband was holding me tight and rubbing my back in that soothing circular motion.

I was shaking something awful.

J'AI PLUS AMOURS

XXIII.

It was already four o'clock when we all arrived back at the Ritz. Exiting the car, I spied Josie Baker at the entrance of the hotel. She looked grand in a white, ermine waist-length coat with bell-shaped sleeves. The coat hugged her figure, showing off her lean curves. We had all given up the boyish flapper style for something more feminine and curvy. Changchang and Peter greeted Josie, kissed me, and proceeded to our suite.

We headed into the hotel lobby. "I need to go to my room. I'll be right back."

Josie took a seat in the tearoom.

"Here's your damn fool pictures. You should have told me you had been with Ollie a second time after you took those pictures." I pushed the envelope across the table as I sat down across from her. I needed that seat. I was wobbly after my narrow escape from Jean Bergeron.

"I want to explain some things to you, Bricky."

"Umm umm. Josie. You need to hear me out first. Pepito knows about you and Pippa. She confronted him."

"Pepito knows?!!" Her eyes were wide in disbelief. She started to weep.

"He's known since January, Jo. She showed him the pictures."

"Did he kill her? Please tell me, Brick. Please tell me he didn't do this."

"No, Josie. I never liked Pepito. But I feel fairly bad for him. Ollie Knolton killed Pippa. They got into a fight about those photographs and probably over you. At least Pippa read things that way. I honestly think Ollie was just plain scared and got mad at Pippa for bringing her into this gangster business. I thought a French gangster had killed Pippa. I found a button from his jacket sleeve in her breadbasket. Pippa was already dead by the time he got to her apartment. He would have surely killed her. He didn't have a scratch on him though.

Pippa fought hard. Ollie had bruises and scratches on her hands, face, and neck the night I met her at Nat's salon. She tried to cover them up with developing fluids and a scarf. I suspect they argued, fought, and Pippa may have fallen and broken her neck. Ollie panicked and shot her to make it look like the syndicates. They both had done enough reading to know what to do. I found Ollie's gun and Pippa's journal in her darkroom. And an autographed picture of you that should have been in a frame at Pippa's apartment." I handed the journal and picture to Josie. I figured she should be the one to have Pippa's private thoughts.

Josie's face grew earnest and soft. She took the journal and fingered the pages. "I have to explain everything to you. I was like a child when

Pepito and I first met. I looked up to him. I still do. I guess I want to be a star too, just not as much as he wants me to be one. The more I rebelled, the more stifling he became. He eventually accepted the affairs. But Pippa? It was different with her. She wanted me to leave him. For us to go back to the United States together. She just didn't understand. I couldn't make her understand that I can't go back. Leaving Pepito would have ruined everything. She thought I had created it all on my own, Bricky. She didn't understand how it would be, how it was for a colored woman. How I would have had to rejoin the Negro circuits. It's harder on the chitlin' circuit. There's not a lick of glamour in it. I'd be a washed-up chorine, if that. That's all they'd let me do in America, despite my success in Europe. It's always that damn color bar. You know what it was like. I lived it every day in those Negro revues, *Chocolate Dandies* and *Shuffle Along*. I couldn't trade what I had built with Pepito for those moments of happiness with her. I just couldn't."

I couldn't bear to look at Josie—her hunger was so raw, it was like studying a person whose skin had been peeled away. I gazed out the window and concentrated on her words. I wasn't ready to abandon her.

"I know what my limitations are, Brick. I've got a small voice. What Negro in Harlem can't dance? And I'm no Fredi Washington in the looks department. But here, my limitations don't matter. They think I'm beautiful. Life is gay and glamorous in Paris. I've been so unfair to Pepito. We've worked hard, Bricky, so hard that we forgot why we fell in love. He must think he's lost me, but I do still love him. I need him. I do."

I forced myself to meet my old friend's gaze. "I know you do, Josie. You should try to do right by him then." I couldn't believe I was rooting for Pepito Abatino. Times had surely changed.

"Brick. There's another reason I can't leave him. Pepito is sick. He has cancer. And I want to be there for him, as he's been there for me."

I had noticed Pepito's changed appearance at Bricktop's the evening before. It was like he was being eaten up slowly. I nodded silently.

Maybe Pepito would have a few more tricks up his sleeve to help Josie's career before he'd be forced to step aside. She was right. I was light and bright and she was brown. Traveling with the Negro revues taught me that there was a clear hierarchy around color, and some of our greatest bandleaders and show composers like Sissle and Blake enforced it. When I first met beautiful, brown Josie she was using lemons on her skin as a lightener. I suspected she was still using them. Old habits die hard.

Josie took my hands and squeezed them. "I'm not here to explain me and Pepito. Or me and Pippa, really. I'm here to say thank you, Bricky. I have four loves. Paris, America, Pepito, and you. *J'ai plus amours*," she sang laughing through tears.

I found my own eyes tearing up. "Josie," I said, "I didn't like you drag-ging me into such a mess. But if you hadn't, I would have gone on being mad at you forever, for leaving like you did. So believe it or not, you've helped me too."

It occurred to me that I had learned a thing or two from Josie—things that I could use with Changchang. Like knowing when to let someone go whom you loved more than a man. Josie had needed more than I could give her as a friend and sister, and she had every right to pursue her dreams. Changchang, too, deserved to stand on her own two feet. Pushing my niece out on her own, to her own apartment, her own career, would only keep her closer to me in the long run.

Josie and I exchanged a hug like good women friends do. She was crying hard because she knew we would probably never be this close again, even if we were in the same room. We'd see each other socially. But that's an altogether different thing than what we were sharing now. We moved in different social circles and Pepito wanted it that way. Josie would go along because she hadn't quite believed that she could do it on her own. I knew she could. Even Pippa thought so. But Josie needed to believe it herself.

I'd never tell a soul about the secret we now shared.

The race was safe now.

So was Josie Baker.

∾

I found my husband relaxing atop the large bed in our suite. "I'll call the but-ler to have him bring up tea and sweets," he said with his arms outstretched.

I walked over to the bed to give him a hug and kiss. I kicked off my shoes.

"Where's Changchang?"

"She's on the telephone with Falcon. That boy has left a dozen or so messages. He's in love, Ada."

All I could muster was an "Ummph."

The butler brought the tea, some napoleons and petits fours, and two sets of newspapers, one from the morning and evening editions of *Paris jour* and *Paris soir*, in French and English.

Peter and I sat at the tea table; the sunlight streamed in through a stained-glass window.

I took a sip from the delicate tea cup and bit into a napoleon. The sweet cream oozed out the sides of my mouth.

Peter looked up from reading and gave me a soft kiss on the mouth, licking the cream.

"Warm," he teased, as he sat back down in his chair.

I began skimming the afternoon edition of the French paper. I caught a headline about a woman found dead in the Bois de Boulogne at seven this morning. The Bois was a park on the edges of the sixteenth arrondissement. She had been pronounced dead at the scene from an apparent overdose. I shook my head, thinking about Natalie. It was Renata Vian. Renata had never made her way to Natalie's as I had advised her. She must have left Pin Pin's Palace and made her way instead to the Bois.

In the Bois, you could find any and everything. All kinds of love for sale and drugs I'd never even heard of. But something told me that Bergeron had tracked Renata down after I saw her at Pin Pin's—just as he had tracked us down in Montmartre—overdosed her and dumped her wasted body in the park. *Dear Lovely Death.*

For an instant, I thought about telephoning Natalie. I hadn't had time to tell her about seeing Renata at Pin Pin's Palace. I hadn't any intention to, really. In a strange way, I felt I was respecting Renata's wishes. Renata Vian was now on ice in some Paris morgue. She was beyond saving. I had a feeling that Natalie would want to claim her remains and have them properly buried. What she couldn't have in life, she would at least have in death.

I reached for the telephone receiver, only to put it back down. My call to Natalie could wait until tomorrow morning. I needed a moment's break with my husband after all this intrigue. I touched his hand across the table.

He pointed to bed. I followed. We fell on the bed together, smiling into each other's eyes.

"Bruges?" He pulled me closer. "First thing tomorrow morning, my mighty tight woman?"

"Bruges, it is, my love."

GLOSSARY (BOOK II)

In the spirit of Harlem Renaissance authors Carl Van Vechten and Zora Neale Hurston's glossaries found in his *Nigger Heaven* and her research notes on 1920s Harlem slang, respectively, *The Autobiography of Ada "Bricktop" Smith, or Miss Baker Regrets* offers the modern reader a glossary of 1930s slang common from Harlem to Paris and in American *noir* fiction.

Bee's knees—the ultimate; describing an extraordinary person, thing, event, or state of mind
Bracelets—handcuffs
Cat's meow—similar to bee's knees; something or someone that is great, extraordinary
Chippy or Chippies—a loose woman or women, prostitutes
Doll—an attractive woman
Don't deal in coal—doesn't associate with Negroes, particularly Negro women
Dropping a dime—passing on information
Fill someone full of daylight—shoot someone full of bullet holes
Gum beating, beating one's gums—talking about nothing
High-toned—light skinned
Jook and juice joint—low-class nightclub or lounge
Jug—prison, jail, holdover cell
Kitchen mechanic—domestic
Moll—a gangster's girlfriend
Miss Anne—a slang for a white woman
Negro dispatch—informal network among Negroes for disseminating information or gossip; word on the street; word of mouth
Negrostocracy—upper crust of Negro society; the Negro aristocracy
On the lam—fleeing from the police or some authority figure
Pinch, to get pinched—to be arrested by law enforcement
Schiap Shop—refers to Italian designer Elsa Schiaparelli's dress shop in Paris's Place Vendôme
Skirt—a woman
Smoke—reference to blackness

Sportin' life—running women; a life among pimps and prostitutes
Studying—paying attention to someone or something; usually meant in a
    negative way, as in "not paying attention"
Switch hit—bisexuality

NOTES TO BOOK I

INTRODUCTION: THE OTHER AMERICANS, 1919–1939

1. Laura Andrews, "Lois Mailou Jones: Invisible, Black and very successful against all odds," *New York Amsterdam News*, November 9, 1996, 25.

2. Charles H. Rowell, "An Interview with Lois Mailou Jones," *Callaloo* 39 (Spring 1989): 359.

3. Marita O. Bonner, "On Being Young—a Woman—and Colored," *The Crisis* 31:1 (1925): 63.

4. The town of La Négresse is two and a half miles outside the seaside resort of Biarritz. The woman for whom it is named allegedly opened an inn (*auberge*) that Napoleon used as a stopover to Spain. I use the words "oddly enough" because the woman's name has been lost to history and *négresse* is not necessarily an honorific. There are currently online protests and petitions regarding the derogatory implications of the town's name. Those protesting want to raise funds to employ a historian to uncover the woman's name and identity so that the town can be appropriately named after her. See T. Denean Sharpley-Whiting, *Black Venus: Sexualized Savages, Primal Fears and Primitive Narratives in French*, for a critical reading of Maupassant's short story.

5. See Mary Church Terrell Papers in the Library of Congress, Washington, DC. See also Jennifer M. Wilks's introduction to and translation of Terrell's diary from that time period in *Palimpsest* 2:2 (Spring/Summer 2014).

6. There has been a good deal of debate about the maternity and paternity of the Black Nun of Moret, whose small portrait hangs in the Bibliothèque Sainte Geneviève in Paris. Some speculate that her parents were the Queen Maria-Theresa of Spain, wife of King Louis XIV, and her favorite black servant, Nabo. Others conclude that she is the daughter of the Sun King of himself. I will take up this debate in chapter 2, "The Gotham-Montparnasse Exchange," where Anita Thompson mentions this enduring tale of sex and royal court intrigue. See also a photograph of the portrait and discussion of the nun's royal blood in *D'un regard l'autre: Histoires des regards européens sur l'Afrique, l'Amérique et l'Océanie* (Paris: Musée Quai Branly, 2006), 92–93.

7. See Tyler Stovall's *Paris Noir: African Americans in the City of Light* (New York: Houghton-Mifflin, 1996); Tyler Stovall, "The Color Line behind the Lines: Racial Violence in France During the Great War," *American Historical Review* 103:3 (1998): 737–69; Harvey Levenstein, *Seductive Journey: American Tourists in France from Jefferson to the Jazz Age* (Chicago: University of Chicago Press, 1998); T. Denean

Sharpley-Whiting, *Black Venus: Sexualized Savages, Primal Fears, and Primitive Narratives in French* (Durham, NC: Duke University Press, 1999); Petrine Archer-Straw, *Negrophilia: Avant-Garde Paris and Black Culture in the 1920s* (London, UK: Thames & Hudson, 2000); Jeffery Jackson, *Making Jazz French: Music and Modern Life in Interwar Paris* (Durham, NC: Duke University Press, 2003).

8. See Stovall's *Paris Noir*, particularly chapter 1, and William Shack's *Harlem in Montmartre: A Paris Jazz Story between the Great Wars* (Berkeley, CA: University of California Press, 2001); also see T. Denean Sharpley-Whiting's *Negritude Women* (Minneapolis: University of Minnesota Press, 2002) for discussion of blacks in the military and France. For more on novels of writers like Pierre Loti and Paul Morand, see Sharpley-Whiting's *Negritude Women* and *Black Venus*.

9. Morrill Cody with Hugh Ford, *The Women of Montparnasse: The Americans in Paris* (New York: Cornwall, 1984); Shari Benstock, *Women of the Left Bank: Paris, 1900–1940* (Austin: University of Texas Press, 1986); Nancy Milford's *Zelda: A Biography* (New York: Perennial, 2001); Andrea Weiss, *Paris Was a Woman: Portraits from the Left Bank* (San Francisco: Harper, 1995).

10. Michel Fabre, *From Harlem to Paris: Black American Writers in France, 1840–1980* (Champaign-Urbana: University of Illinois Press, 1980), 114.

11. Morrill Cody does nonetheless provide a chapter on Josephine Baker; see Cody with Ford, *The Women of Montparnasse*.

12. "Famous Artists Draw Color Line against Student," *New World*, April 5, 1923, 3.

13. *Paris Tribune*, February 1, 1923, n.p.

14. I have selected post-1880s as my cutoff date, as many of the women would not have traveled on their own before the age of eighteen. Equally, it allows me to differentiate between a generation of women who were adults and more particularly situated in the nineteenth century—like Church Terrell, Mary McCleod Bethune, Anna Julia Cooper, Ida Gibbs-Hunt, Addie Hunton, and Kathryn Johnson—and who had also arrived in Paris during the interwar period for political talks, tours, and conferences but were not necessarily peers of the Jazz Age set or part of the literary and cultural flourishing associated with the New Negro movement.

15. Weiss, *Paris Was a Woman*, 23.

16. Tyler Stovall, "Harlem-sur-Seine: Building an African American Community in Paris," *Stanford Electronic Humanities Review* 5:2 (1997): n.p.

17. Bricktop and James Haskins, *Bricktop: Prohibition Harlem, Café Society Paris, Movie-Mad Rome—The Queen of the Nightclubs Tells the Exuberant Story of a Fabulous Life* (New York: Welcome Rain Publishers, 2000), 125.

18. Joan DeJean, *The Essence of Style: How the French Invented High Fashion, Fine Food, Chic Cafés, Style, Sophistication, and Glamour* (New York: Free Press, 2005), 2–5. DeJean's work represents an excellent history of the rise of French style. Its primary shortcoming is a glossing over of how Louis XIV and Jean-Baptiste Colbert, his right hand in matters of finance, were able to generate the revenue that allowed for this dominance, namely, subsidies from the Third Estate *and* the free-wage labor and global exports of sugar and sugared delicacies derived from New World slavery.

19. Bricktop's husband, Peter Ducongé, was from New Orleans. His family name was spelled varyingly as DuConge, Duconge, Ducongé, and DuCongé. As with

her first name Ada, which she sometimes spelled Adah, Bricktop played with her last name—when she occasionally used it. In the end, for consistency, I selected Ducongé.

CHAPTER ONE: *LES DAMES*, GRAND AND SMALL, OF MONTMARTRE: THE PARIS OF BRICKTOP

1. Langston Hughes, "Adelaide Hall New Star of Paris Night Life: Her 'Big Apple' Glows Over Rue Pigalle," 1937, 2, unpublished essay in the Langston Hughes Papers (LHP), JWJ Collection, Yale Collection of American Literature, Beinecke Rare Books and Manuscript Library, Yale University.

2. Biographical information on Bricktop has been culled from a memoir she cowrote with James Haskins, *Bricktop: Prohibition Harlem, Café Society Paris, Movie-Mad Rome—The Queen of the Nightclubs Tells the Exuberant Story of a Fabulous Life* (New York: Welcome Rain Books, 2000); archival documents in the Manuscript, Archives, and Rare Books Library (MARBL) at Emory University (Bricktop MSS 831 and Delilah Jackson MSS 923); the JWJ Collection, which contains the papers of Carl Van Vechten and Langston Hughes, among others, at the Yale Collection of American Literature, Beinecke Rare Books and Manuscript Library; and the Ada Bricktop Smith Papers at Schomburg Center for Research in Black Culture, New York Public Library.

3. Douglas W. Bristol, *Knights of the Razor: Black Barbers in Slavery and Freedom* (Baltimore: Johns Hopkins University Press, 2009), 1–4.

4. Bricktop and Haskins, *Bricktop*, 18.

5. See Edward A. Robinson, "The Pekin: The Genesis of American Black Theater," *Black American Literature Forum* 16:4 (Winter 1982): 136.

6. Bricktop and Haskins, *Bricktop*, 19.

7. See correspondences in the Ada Bricktop Smith and Carl Van Vechten Papers at BEIN.

8. Delilah Jackson audio interviews with Bricktop, MARBL; and Bricktop and Haskins, *Bricktop*, 34.

9. Bricktop and Haskins, *Bricktop*, 81–82.

10. Frank C. Taylor with Gerald Cook, *Alberta Hunter: A Celebration in Blues* (New York: McGraw-Hill, 1987), 69–70.

11. Bricktop and Haskins, *Bricktop*, 81.

12. Tim Brooks and Richard Spottswood, *Lost Sounds: Blacks and the Recording, 1890–1919* (Urbana-Champaign: University of Illinois Press, 2004), 360.

13. Delilah Jackson Collection, MARBL, Series 8.

14. Taylor with Cook, *Alberta Hunter*, 96.

15. Eugene Bullard, "Shooting at Us," *Chicago Defender*, April 4, 1925, col.1, 7.

16. Hughes, "Adelaide Hall," 1.

17. For more on Florence Jones, see Barbara Lewis, "Florence Embry Jones: When Paris Adored Flo-Jo Jazz Goddesses," *New York Amsterdam News*, Saturday, May 18, 1996, 24.

18. There has been some back and forth among jazz aficionados and scholars on this point.

19. "Foreign News: Chez Florence," *Time*, Monday, June 20, 1927, n.p.

20. Henry Hurford Janes, unpublished account of Josephine Baker's arrival in Paris in the 1920s, Hurford Janes–Josephine Baker Papers, JWJ, Manuscript 2, Box 4, Folder 163, 17–18, BEIN.

21. Hughes, "Adelaide Hall," 1.

22. Bricktop and Haskins, *Bricktop*, 92.

23. "'Bricktop's Happy," *Chicago Defender*, March 21, 1925, col. 5, 8.

24. Langston Hughes to Countee Cullen, March 11, 1924, Countee Cullen Papers, Amistad Research Center, Tulane University.

25. Langston Hughes to Harold Jackman, May 25, 1924, LHP, Box 1, Folder 9, BEIN.

26. William McBrien, *Cole Porter: A Biography* (New York: Vintage, 2000), 108.

27. Hughes, "Adelaide Hall," 2.

28. *New York Times*, January 1931; *Le Figaro*, "L'echec de la commission du chomage," February 1931, 3.

29. F. Scott Fitzgerald, "Babylon Revisited," *Saturday Evening Post*, February 21, 1931.

30. Bricktop and Haskins, *Bricktop*, 102.

31. See Ada Bricktop Smith Papers, Box 1, Folder 1, SCHOM. Bricktop kept a series of small appointment book journals in which she made notations about everything from dinner dates to salaries.

32. Telegram from Cole Porter to Bricktop, Bricktop Papers, MARBL, Box 1, Folder 2, 1920–1929.

33. See Bricktop Papers, Box 4, Folder 2, MARBL. Handwritten notes by Bricktop.

34. McBrien, *Cole Porter*, 108.

35. Bricktop and Haskins, *Bricktop*, 128–29; see also Martin Duberman's biography *Paul Robeson: A Biography* (New York: New Press, 1995).

36. Cartier jewelry receipts, Bricktop Papers, Box 1, Folder 2, 1920–1929, MARBL.

37. McBrien, *Cole Porter*, 367–68.

38. Bricktop and Haskins, *Bricktop*, 93.

39. James Haskins, *Mabel Mercer: A Life* (New York: Atheneum, 1987), 11.

40. Bricktop Papers, handwritten notes by Bricktop, Box 4, Folder, 2, MARBL.

41. Robert McAlmon, *Being Geniuses Together: A Binocular View of Paris in the '20s*, revised, with supplementary chapters and an afterword by Kay Boyle (New York: Doubleday, 1968), 316–17.

42. Ada "Bricktop" Smith Duconge's journal in Ada Bricktop Smith Papers, 1920–1929, SCHOM.

43. Ibid., Friday, September 16, 1938, and Wednesday, May 3, 1939, SCHOM.

44. See Eric Ledell Smith, "Lillian Evanti: Washington's African American Diva," *Washington History* 11:1 (Spring–Summer 1999): 24–43. He is completing Evanti's autobiography. See also *Madame Evanti*, documentary video, Imani Productions for WETA Public Television, Washington, DC, 1987, for interviews with her only son as well as secondary biographical information.

45. "The Horizon," *The Crisis* 28 (September 1924): 215.

46. Madame Evanti composed two memoirs. Citation from this autobiography, Lillian Evanti, "The Negro in Grand Opera," unpublished manuscript, Evans-Tibbs Collection, Anacostia Museum, Smithsonian, Washington, DC, 55, 59.

47. Jessie Fauset to Langston Hughes, October 8, 1924, LHP, BEIN.

48. Lillian Evans-Tibbs, "Where My Caravan Has Rested," unpublished manuscript in the Center for Black Music Research Archives, Columbia College, Chicago, Illinois (CBMR). Evans-Tibbs replaced the French *égalité* with the anglicized *equalité* for equality. Since the manuscript was typewritten, she did not use the acute accent on the "e."

49. *Le Figaro*, "Spectacles & Concerts," Friday, October 2, 1925, 6. The original announcement is in French. Translation by author.

50. The memoir amounted to eight pages. See the Henry Hurford Janes–Josephine Baker Papers, BEIN.

51. Josephine Baker and Jo Bouillon, *Josephine*, trans. Mariana Fitzpatrick (New York: Marlowe & Company, 1988), 48.

52. Hurford Janes, unpublished account, 1, BEIN.

53. Janet Flanner, *Paris Was Yesterday* (New York: Viking, 1972), xx.

54. Ibid., xx.

55. As quoted in Baker and Bouillon, *Josephine*, 51.

56. In *Paris Noir*, Tyler Stovall discusses the relationship between the two women during the early years in Paris, mostly drawn from Bricktop's memoir with Haskins.

57. Baker and Bouillon, *Josephine*, 276.

58. Bricktop and Haskins, *Bricktop*, 108.

59. See the Josephine Baker Papers, Gene Lerner Collection, Stanford University, Palo Alto, California.

60. Ibid.

61. Ibid.

62. Delilah Jackson Papers, audio interviews, MARBL.

63. Baker scholar Bennetta Jules-Rosette graciously discussed the rumored relationship with Bricktop as well as the mystery woman with me in spring 2010 at the Black France Film Festival. Jules-Rosette was disinclined to believe that there was a romantic liaison between the two. Unlike other performance artists during the era (Hunter, Waters, et al.) whose relationships eventually come to light, there is no physical evidence (letters, diaries, etc.) or testimony by others on either side, outside of Jean-Claude Baker, to confirm the intimacy—which of course doesn't mean an amorous relationship didn't exist.

64. Bricktop and Haskins, *Bricktop*, 106, 131.

65. Bricktop and Haskins, *Bricktop*, 156.

66. In Baker and Bouillon's *Josephine*, Baker denies this charge, arguing that she and Pepito purchased assets jointly. The papers in the Lerner Collection at Stanford would seem to confirm this still-extraordinary fifty-fifty split. In Montmartre, nonetheless, the rumors swirled and Bricktop clucked on in concern. Baker did, in fact, have to go to court to divest her property from Pepito's estate upon his death. Whatever wrangling she had with Pepito's family over those monies did not seem

to impact her relationship with his mother and older sister. Moreover, the ill will Baker and Abatino may have had in life clearly ended when she buried him next to her mother at the Castelnaud-Fayrac cemetery in Dordogne after she purchased Les Milandes.

67. Bricktop Papers, "Letter to Blonzetta," Box 1, Folder 4, 1940–1949, MARBL.

68. Florence Mills Papers, "Contracts," Box 1, Folder 7, SCHOM.

69. Ibid.

70. Claude McKay, *A Long Way from Home* (New Brunswick, NJ: Rutgers University Press, 2007), 112–13.

71. Florence Mills Papers, "Contracts," Box 1, Folder 7, SCHOM. McKay executed this agreement on March 3, 1922.

72. Ethel Waters with Charles Samuels, *His Eye Is on the Sparrow* (New York: Pyramid Books, 1967), 185.

73. Florence Mills Papers, "Lyrics," Folder 8, Box 1, SCHOM.

74. Bill Egan, *Florence Mills: Harlem Queen of Jazz* (Lanham, MD: Scarecrow Press, 2004), 60.

75. Florence Mills Papers, Box 1, Folder 1, SCHOM.

76. Egan, *Florence Mills*, 4.

77. Mills biographer Bill Egan notes (95) that she and her husband, U.S. Kid Thompson, took a quick honeymoon jaunt to Paris after the success of the *Dover Street to Dixie* production in 1923 where they toured and met up with the Black Montmartre crowd. Bricktop was not in Paris until May 1924.

78. See Smithsonian National Portrait Gallery, *Le Tumulte Noir: Paul Colin's Jazz Age Portfolio*, http://www.npg.si.edu/exh/noir.

79. Mills Papers, "Telegrams," Box 1, Folder 4, SCHOM.

80. Mills Papers, Clippings file, Folder 9, SCHOM. The article appears on page 22, however, the magazine title is not provided. The article title is: "Les 'Black Birds' Aux Ambassadeurs."

81. Ibid. The article begins with lines from "I'm a Little Blackbird" in French and then inquires, "Qu'est que ce libre poeme? Tout simplement les premiers vers dans notre langue qu'ait appris Florence Mills"/"What is this free verse? Quite simply it is the first verses in our language that Florence Mills has learned." The article goes on to call her "la reine de la danse du jazz."

82. In a "talking heads" preview clip to *La Sirène des Tropiques*, Jean-Claude Baker discusses the blowback Baker received from the French critics when she attempted to refine her image, leaving the erect bananas at the music hall.

83. Bricktop's journal, 1920–1929, SCHOM. Notations for July 2, 1926, Friday, "dinner with flo, kid," and July 24, "Sat dinner for flo, kid."

84. Bricktop's journal, 1920–1929, SCHOM. Brick writes on June 6, 1926: "dinner Florence, kid mitchell Nora."

85. "Raid on Rooming House 'Love Nest' Reveals Double Life of Married Pair," *New York Amsterdam News*, January 20, 1926, 1–2.

86. More on Nora Holt can be found at the Kansas Historical Society (KHS); also see Bill Reed, *Hot from Harlem: Profiles in Classic African-American Entertainment*

(Riverside, CA: Cellar Door Books, 1998), and Eileen Southern, *The Music of Black Americans: A History* (New York: W. W. Norton, 1997).

87. Carl Van Vechten, *Nigger Heaven* (Urbana-Champaign: University of Illinois Press, 2000), 163, 179.

88. Nora Holt to Carl Van Vechten, September 20, 1927, CVV, BEIN.

89. Holt to Van Vechten, October 26, 1926, CVV, BEIN.

90. Holt to Van Vechten, October 27, 1926, CVV, BEIN.

91. Holt to Van Vechten, November 14, 1926, CVV, BEIN.

92. Ibid.

93. Waters with Samuels, *His Eye*, 186.

94. From Bobby Short's 1971 autobiography, as quoted in Reed, *Hot from Harlem*, 60.

95. Or 1900, 1903, or 1909. Snow gave multiple dates for her birth as well as her place of birth—Washington, DC, and Chattanooga, Tennessee. See Dorothy C. Salem, *African American Women: A Biographical Dictionary* (New York: Garland, 1993).

96. Mark Miller, *High Hat, Trumpet and Rhythm: The Life and Music of Valaida Snow* (Ontario, Canada: Mercury Press, 2007), 11, 52–53.

97. Bricktop and Haskins, *Bricktop*, 183.

98. Baker and Bouillon, *Josephine*, 40.

99. Stephen Bourne, *Elisabeth Welch: Soft Lights and Sweet Music* (Lanham, MD: Scarecrow Press, 2005), 9.

100. Ibid., 17.

101. See "Gold Star Mothers' Reception in France: As Seen by a Performer," *New York Amsterdam News*, August 6, 1930, 8.

102. Bourne, *Elisabeth Welch*, 15. See also Bourne's *Ethel Waters: Stormy Weather* (Lanham, MD: Scarecrow Press, 2007) and Donald Bogle's *Heat Wave: The Life and Career of Ethel Waters* (New York: Harper Collins, 2011).

103. Taylor with Cook, *Alberta Hunter*, 147.

104. Waters with Samuels, *His Eye*, 208.

105. Bourne, *Elisabeth Welch*, 20.

106. Waters with Samuels, *His Eye*, 208.

107. Ethel Waters to Carl Van Vechten, October 9, 1929, CVV, BEIN.

108. Bricktop to Carl Van Vechten, October 5, 1929, CVV, BEIN.

109. For more details on Alberta's European travels, see Taylor with Cook, *Alberta Hunter*.

110. Ibid., 130.

111. Bricktop to Carl Van Vechten, October 5, 1929, CVV, BEIN.

112. Bricktop and Haskins, *Bricktop*, 140–41, 143–44.

113. Taylor with Cook, *Alberta Hunter*, 90.

114. Ibid., 70.

115. See the *My Castle Rockin'* video, Studio: V.I.E.W. Video, 2001.

116. Taylor with Cook, *Alberta Hunter*, 124, 165.

117. I am drawing this urban definition from R&B artist Michel'le Toussaint's "Nicety."

118. *New York Amsterdam News*, November 16, 1927, 9.

119. *New York Amsterdam News*, January 11, 1928, 11.

120. "Billy Rowe's Out of Harlem Notebook," *Pittsburgh Courier*, July 23, 1939, 11. See also Rowe's June 18, 1938, column. Also see Edgar Wiggins, "Across the Pond," *Chicago Defender*, February 12, 1938, 12.

121. *New York Amsterdam News*, February 9, 1935, 1.

122. *Pittsburgh Courier*, December 30, 1930, 3.

123. Ibid.

124. Alberta Hunter Papers, Hunter to Mr. Hull at the U.S. Department of State, May 1, 1940, Box 3, Folder 4, SCHOM.

125. Hughes, "Adelaide Hall," 2.

126. Iain Cameron Williams, *Underneath a Harlem Moon: The Harlem to Paris Years of Adelaide Hall* (New York: Continuum, 2002), 78.

127. Bricktop and Haskins, *Bricktop*, 134.

128. Williams, *Underneath*, 179.

129. Ibid., 191–92.

130. Bricktop to Carl Van Vechten, April 1936, CVV, BEIN.

131. Bricktop Journal, 1930–1939, SCHOM.

132. Bricktop Papers, Letter from Cole Porter to Bricktop, July 14, 1936, MARBL.

133. "Adelaide Hall Café Tops in Paris," *Chicago Defender*, January 29, 1938, col. 5, 19.

134. *Chicago Defender*, December 10, 1938, col. 4, 18.

135. "Paris 'Big Apple' Closes Its Doors," *Chicago Defender*, January 7, 1939, col. 1,18.

CHAPTER TWO. THE GOTHAM-MONTPARNASSE EXCHANGE

1. Jessie Fauset to Langston Hughes, January 6, 1925, LHP, Yale Collection of American Literature, Beinecke Rare Book and Manuscript Library, Yale University.

2. Ibid.

3. Ibid.

4. See Ann duCille, "Blues Notes on Black Sexuality: Sex and the Texts of Jessie Fauset and Nella Larsen," *Journal of the History of Sexuality* 3:3 (1993): 418–44, and Ann duCille, *The Coupling Convention: Sex, Text, and Tradition in Black Women's Fiction* (New York: Oxford University Press, 1993).

5. Fauset to Hughes, May 6, 1924, LHP, BEIN.

6. Fauset to Hughes, January 6, 1925, LHP, BEIN.

7. See David Levering Lewis's *W. E. B. Du Bois: Biography of Race* (New York: Henry Holt, 1993) for more on Du Bois's philandering.

8. For more on Ida Gibbs-Hunt, see Adele Logan Alexander's *Parallel Lives: The Remarkable Gibbs-Hunt and the Enduring (In)Significance of Melanin* (Charlottesville: University of Virginia Press, 2012).

9. See Elizabeth Hadley Freydberg's pioneering study on Coleman, *Bessie Coleman: The Brownskin Lady Bird* (New York: Garland, 1994). I borrow the moniker "brown-skinned ladybird" from Hadley; also, see "Negress Pilots Airplane: Bessie

Coleman Makes Three Flights for Fifteenth Infantry," *New York Times*, September 4, 1922, 9.

10. Jessie Fauset, "What Europe Thought of the Pan-African Congress," *The Crisis* 23:2 (December 1921): 63; Fauset also excluded Gibbs-Hunt; see Alexander's *Parallel Lives*.

11. Carolyn Wedin Sylvander, *Jessie Fauset, Black American Writer* (Troy: The Whitson Publishing Company, 1981), 23–24.

12. See Sylvander, *Jessie Fauset*; Deborah McDowell's *"The Changing Same"* (Bloomington: Indiana University Press, 1995), Cheryl Wall's *Women of the Harlem Renaissance* (Bloomington: Indiana University Press, 1995), and Ann duCille's writings on Fauset previously cited for more discussion about how Fauset has been dismissed by literary critics.

13. *Paris Tribune*, February 1, 1923, n.p.

14. Jessie Fauset, *Plum Bun* (Boston: Beacon Press, 1990), 239.

15. McDowell, *"The Changing Same,"* 66. Carolyn Wedin Sylvander, Thadious M. Davis, and Ann DuCille also address the issues of the marriage plot and nursery rhymes in Fauset's writing. For more on Fauset and Bennett in France, see also Michel Fabre's *From Harlem to Paris: Black American Writers in France, 1840–1980* (Urbana-Champaign: University of Illinois Press, 1993).

16. Fauset to Hughes, April 20, 1924, LHP, BEIN.

17. Fauset to Hughes, October 8, 1924, LHP, BEIN.

18. Fauset to Mr. and Mrs. A. B. Spingarn, February 10, 1925, Manuscript Division, Arthur B. Spingarn Papers, Box 94-4, Folder 75, Moorland-Spingarn Research Center (MSRC), Howard University, Washington, DC.

19. Fauset, *Plum Bun*, 374–76.

20. Fauset to Harold Jackman, December 21, 1924, James Weldon Johnson Collection (JWJ), BEIN.

21. Fauset to Hughes, December 21, 1924, LHP, BEIN.

22. Fauset to Mr. and Mrs. A. B. Spingarn, February 10, 1925, ABS, MSRC.

23. Fauset to Jackman, December 21, 1924, JWJ, BEIN.

24. Fauset to Hughes, October 8, 1924, LHP, BEIN.

25. Fauset to Hughes, January 6, 1925, LHP, BEIN.

26. Fauset to Jackman, December 21, 1924, JWJ, BEIN.

27. Ibid.

28. Ibid.

29. Langston Hughes to Countee Cullen, March 11, 1924, Countee Cullen Papers (CCP), AMIS.

30. Fauset to Hughes, January 6, 1925, LHP, BEIN.

31. Fauset, *Plum Bun*, 375.

32. Laura Wheeler Waring Papers, Box 180-1, Folder 13, MRSC.

33. Laura Wheeler Waring Personal Statement for Harmon Foundation, 1928, Harmon Foundation Papers (HFP), Library of Congress, Washington, DC.

34. Ibid.

35. Ibid.

36. See David McCullough on Mary Cassatt in *The Greater Journey: Americans in Paris* (New York: Simon & Schuster, 2012).

37. Present-day Cheyney University. The school was originally named the African Institute. It was founded with funds from the philanthropist Quaker Richard Humphries.

38. Laura Wheeler Waring to William E. Harmon, January 15, 1928, HFP, LOC.

39. Wheeler Waring Personal Statement, HFP, LOC. In "'A Constant Stimulus and Inspiration': Laura Wheeler Waring in Paris in the 1910s and 1920s," *Source: Notes in the History of Art* 4:24 (Summer 2005): 13–23, Theresa Leininger-Miller states that Wheeler was in Europe for fifteen months rather than the eighteen months the artist indicated in her statement to Harmon. Her essay draws from scant sources as well as a private collection.

40. James Porter, "The Work of Laura Waring," in James V. Herring and James Porter's *In Memoriam, Laura Wheeler Waring, 1887–1948: An Exhibition of Paintings*, May and June 1949, Howard University Gallery of Art, Washington, DC, n.p.

41. Gwendolyn Bennett diary, Sunday, June 28, 1925, Gwendolyn Bennett Papers, Reel 1, Schomburg Center for Research on Black Culture (SCHOM), New York Public Library, New York, NY.

42. Wheeler Waring Personal Statement, HFP, LOC.

43. Porter, "The Work of Laura Wheeler Waring," n.p.

44. Ibid.

45. Gwendolyn Bennett to Harold Jackman, January 11, 1926, JWJ, BEIN. Bennett writes of receiving "Jessie's lovely cable for Christmas which makes me very happy."

46. See A'Lelia Bundles, *On Her Own Ground: The Life and Times of Madam C. J. Walker* (New York: Scribner, 2001).

47. Carl Van Vechten, *Nigger Heaven* (Urbana-Champaign: University of Illinois Press, 1999), 21.

48. Carole Marks and Diana Edkins, *The Power of Pride: Stylemakers and Rulebreakers of the Harlem Renaissance* (New York: Crown, 1999), 75.

49. See Bundles, *On Her Own Ground*, and Joan DeJean's *The Essence of Style*, cited in the introduction.

50. Harold Josephson, "Outlawing War: Internationalism and the Pact of Paris," *Diplomatic History* 3:4 (1979): 377–90.

51. Bundles, *On Her Own Ground*, 279. I have been unable to locate the favorable references in *La Liberté*.

52. See, for instance, *L'Intransigeant's* December 2, 1921, headline, "M. Briand n'a pas telephoné: Le Paris est encore trop loin de Paris," and "M. Briand est rentré," December 3, 1921, 1.

53. See Dena Goodman, *The Republic of Letters: A Cultural History of the French Enlightenment* (Ithaca: Cornell University Press, 1994) and "Enlightenment Salons: The Convergence of Female and Philosophic Ambitions," *Eighteenth-Century Studies* 22:3 (Spring 1989): 329–50.

54. Alain Locke to Charlotte Osgood Mason, February 26, 1929, Alain Locke Papers, MSRC.

55. See George Hutchinson, *In Search of Nella Larsen: A Biography of the Line* (Cambridge: Harvard University Press, 2006).

56. George Schuyler, "The Curse of My Aching Heart," in "Shafts and Darts," *The Messenger*, August 1926, 239.

57. Wallace Thurman to Langston Hughes, undated letter, JWJ, BEIN.

58. Gwendolyn Bennett, "Tokens," in Charles Johnson, ed., *Ebony and Topaz* (New York: *Journal of Negro Life*/National Urban League, 1927), 149, 150.

59. Gwendolyn Bennett, "Wedding Day," *Fire!!* (November 1926): 25.

60. For more on Joe Gans, see William Gildea's *The Longest Fight: In the Ring with Joe Gans, Boxing's First African American Champion* (New York: Farrar, Straus and Giroux, 2012).

61. Bennett, "Wedding Day," 27.

62. Ibid., 28.

63. Ibid.

64. Bennett diary, September 29, 1925, SCHOM.

65. Bennett diary, Sunday, June 28, 1925, SCHOM.

66. See Sandra Govan's "Gwendolyn Bennett: Portrait of an Artist Lost" (PhD dissertation, Emory University, 1980) as well as Govan's "A Blend of Voices: Composite Narrative Strategies in Biographical Reconstruction," in Dolan Hubbard, ed., *Recovered Writers/Recovered Texts* (Knoxville: University of Tennessee Press, 1997), 90–104, and "Kindred Spirits and Sympathetic Souls: Langston Hughes and Gwendolyn Bennett in the Renaissance," in C. James Trotman, ed., *Langston Hughes: The Man, His Art and His Continuing Influence* (New York: Garland, 1995), 75–85; and Darlene Clark Hine, ed., *Black Women in America* (New York: Carlson Press, 1993).

67. "The Horizon," *The Crisis* 31:5 (March 1926): 243.

68. Bennett to Hughes, August 28, 1925, LHP, BEIN.

69. Travel guide portion of Bennett's diary, n.p., n.d., SCHOM.

70. Bennett diary, Sunday, September 27, 1925, SCHOM.

71. Travel guide portion of Bennett's diary, n.p., n.d., SCHOM.

72. Bennett to Hughes, August 28, 1925, LHP, BEIN. None of Bennett's art from this period survived. A fire at her stepmother's home destroyed her artwork.

73. Marcia Mathews, *Henry Ossawa Tanner: American Artist* (Chicago: University of Chicago Press, 1995); David McCullough, *The Greater Journey: Americans in Paris* (New York: Simon & Schuster, 2012), 427–28.

74. Bennett diary, Sunday, August 2, 1925, SCHOM.

75. Bennett to Jackman, February 23, 1926, JWJ, BEIN.

76. Bennett to Countee Cullen, August 28, 1925, CCP, AMIS.

77. Bennett diary, August 8, 1925, SCHOM.

78. Bennett to Jackman, February 28, 1926, JWJ, BEIN.

79. Bennett diary, June 30, 1925, SCHOM.

80. Bennett diary, Sunday, August 2, 1925, SCHOM.

81. Bennett diary, October 1, 1925, SCHOM.

82. Ibid.

83. Bennett to Jackman, February 25, 1926, JWJ, BEIN.

84. Bennett travel guide portion of Bennett's diary, n.p., n.d., SCHOM.

85. Ibid.

86. See Kenneth R. Janken, *Rayford W. Logan and the Dilemma of the African-American Intellectual* (Amherst: University of Massachusetts Press, 1993); Lauren Sklaroff, *Black Culture and the New Deal: The Quest for Civil Rights in the Roosevelt Era* (Chapel Hill: University of North Carolina Press, 2009).

87. Collectif, *Alexandre Dumas ou les aventures d'un romancier* (Paris: Gallimard, 1986), 75.

88. For more on Gurdjieff, see *Beelzebub's Tales to His Grandson (All and Everything/First)*; P. D. Ouspensky, *In Search of the Miraculous* (New York: Harcourt, Brace and Company, 1949) and *The Fourth Way: An Arrangement by Subject of Verbatim Extracts from the Records of Ouspensky's Meetings in London and New York, 1921–46* (New York: Knopf, 1957).

89. For more on Peterson, see Thadious Davis's excellent biography, *Nella Larsen, Novelist of the Harlem Renaissance: A Woman's Life Unveiled* (Baton Rouge: Louisiana State University Press, 1996); see also Dorothy Peterson Papers in JWJ, BEIN as well as Van Vechten and Larsen Papers in BEIN.

90. See H. Pearce, "Mrs. Adis & Sanctuary," *The Gleam: Journal of the Sheila Kaye-Smith Society* (2003): 16.

91. See Davis, *Nella Larsen*, as well as George Hutchinson's updated biography, *In Search of Nella Larsen* (Cambridge, MA: Belknap Press, 2006).

92. Nella Larsen to Carl Van Vechten, March 22, 1931, CVV, BEIN.

93. Ibid.

94. Davis, *Nella Larsen*, 368.

95. See Patricia A. Morton, *Hybrid Modernities: Architecture and Representation at the 1931 Colonial Exposition, Paris* (Boston: MIT Press, 2000).

96. Larsen to Van Vechten, May 11, 1931, CVV, BEIN.

97. Peterson to Van Vechten, July 19, 1931, JWJ, BEIN.

98. Ibid.

99. Larsen to Van Vechten, May 11, 1931, CVV, BEIN.

100. Anita Thompson to Beatrice Thompson, February 10, 1931, Anita Thompson Reynolds Papers, Manuscript Division, Box 2, Folders 24–25, MSRC. See also George Hutchinson, *In Search of Nella Larsen*, where he also mentions Thompson's time in Paris.

101. See Thompson's unpublished memoir, "American Cocktail," Box 4, Folder 1, MSRC.

102. Anita Thompson, "A Story from Paris," *Flash* (June 29, 1929): 10.

103. *D'un regard l'autre: Histoire des regards européens sur l'Afrique, l'Amérique et l'Océanie* (Paris: Musée du Quai Branly, 2006), 92.

104. Joëlle Chevé, *Marie-Thérèse d'Autriche: Épouse de Louis XIV* (Paris: Pygmalion, 2008), 253.

105. *The Memoirs of the Marquise of Montespan, Written by Herself Being the Historic Memoirs of the Court of Louis XIV* (Boston: 1899), chap. 40. Gutenberg Project.

106. Duchess Anne-Marie-Louise d'Orléans, *Memoirs of Mademoiselle de Montpensier*, vol. 2, chap. 8, June 1664–1666, digitized version.

107. Chevé, *Marie-Thérèse*, 252.

108. Thompson to Thompson, February 10, 1931, MSRC.

109. Ibid.

110. George Hutchinson has recently edited with notes and an introduction one of the many drafts of Thompson's memoir as *American Cocktail: A "Colored Girl" in the World* (Cambridge, MA: Harvard University Press, 2014).

111. See the foreword with a dedication to Andrew Young to "American Cocktail: The Tan Experience," 2–3, MSRC.

CHAPTER THREE. WOMEN OF THE PETIT BOULEVARD: THE ARTIST'S HAVEN

1. Nomination blanks for Lois Mailou Jones, Harmon Foundation Papers (HFP), Library of Congress (LOC).

2. Charles Rowell, "An Interview with Lois Mailou Jones," *Callaloo* 39 (Spring 1989): 358.

3. A good deal of scholarship exists on Jones as opposed to the other artists covered in *Bricktop's Paris*. I will point the reader, then, to just a few important works on Jones's life and work. Laura Andrews, "Lois Mailou Jones: Invisible, Black, and Very Successful against All Odds," *New York Amsterdam News*, November 9, 1996, 25; Paul Gardner, "When France was Home to African-American Artists," *Smithsonian* 26:12 (March 1996): 106; "African Culture Inspires American Artist and Teacher," in *Lois Mailou Jones: Imagining Africa* at the National Museum of Women in the Arts, Press Release, February 15–May 12, 2002; Tritobia Hayes Benjamin, *The Life and Art of Lois Mailou Jones* (San Francisco: Pomegranate, 1994).

4. Rowell, "Interview," 361.

5. Lois Mailou Jones Papers, "Selma Burke," Box 215, Folder 40, MSRC. See Jacqueline Trescott's article, "Selma Burke: The Story behind the FDR Dime," *Milwaukee Journal*, Thursday, April 17, 1975,10. In this article, Trescott mentions the close friendship between Burke and Jones. The original article was published in the *Washington Post* on Monday, March 17, 1975.

6. Martha Severens, *Greenville County Museum of Art: The Southern Collection* (New York: Hudson Hills Press, 1995); Leslie King-Hammond, Tritobia H. Benjamin, Carolyn Shuttlesworth, *Three Generations of African American Women Sculptors: A Study in Paradox* (Philadelphia: Afro-American Historical and Cultural Museum, 1996).

7. Trescott, "Selma Burke," 10.

8. Ibid.

9. Ibid.

10. Burke's most famous perhaps but least known—at least in terms of attribution to her—is her bas-relief of Franklin Roosevelt's profile, originally cast in bronze and made public at the Washington Recorder of Deeds Building in 1945, which strongly resembles the profile on the U.S. dime. Controversy ensued in 1946 when John Sinnock, the designer whose initials are on the dime, was accused of lifting Burke's design for the coin.

11. Bricktop and James Haskins, *Bricktop: Prohibition Harlem, Café Society Paris, Movie-Mad Rome—The Queen of the Nightclubs Tells the Exuberant Story of a Fabulous Life* (New York: Welcome Rain Publishers, 2000), 200.

12. "'Bricktop,' Café Owner, Is Broke," *Chicago Defender*, January13, 1934, 5.

13. *Vincent's Choice: The Musée Imaginaire of Van Gogh* (Amsterdam, Holland: Exhibition Guide, Van Gogh Museum, 2003), 87.

14. Nancy Elizabeth Prophet diary, August 11, 1922. Nancy E. Prophet Paris diary, 1922–1934, John Hay Library Manuscripts, Brown University (JHL).

15. *Liber Brunensis*, 1907, 107, JHL.

16. Prophet diary, April 10, 1929 and May 30, 1929, JHL.

17. Blossom Kirschenbaum, "Nancy Elizabeth Prophet, Sculptor," *Sage: A Scholarly Journal on Black Women* 4:1 (Spring 1987): 45–52.

18. Prophet diary, August 11, 1922, JHL.

19. Prophet diary, JHL; the entry date is unclear as Prophet did not write daily. Her first entry is dated August 11, 1922, but that period goes on for pages, covering events in 1924 to 1925 until a November 11, 1925, entry is made.

20. Prophet diary, April 30, 1926, JHL.

21. Prophet diary, September 19, 1926, JHL.

22. Prophet diary, June 27, 1927, JHL.

23. Ibid.

24. Nancy E. Prophet to W. E. B. Du Bois, November 14, 1931, W. E. B. Du Bois Papers (DBP), Library of Congress, Washington, DC (LOC).

25. Prophet diary, May 2, 1932, JHL.

26. Prophet diary, January 1928 (day not entered) and January 15, 1928, JHL.

27. See Countee Cullen, "Elizabeth Prophet: Sculptress," *Opportunity* (July 1930): 204–05; Kirschenbaum, "Nancy Elizabeth Prophet, Sculptor"; Theresa Leininger-Miller also provides a splendid study of Prophet in *New Negro Artists in Paris, African American Painters and Sculptors in the City of Light, 1922–1934* (New Brunswick, NJ: Rutgers University Press, 2001).

28. Most of Prophet's work was either destroyed by the artist herself; by the elements, as she could not afford proper storage; or left behind, as it was expensive to ship to the United States. The majority of the works are only available via photographs in the Nancy Elizabeth Prophet Collection at the John P. Adams Library, Rhode Island College (JPA). *Head of a Negro* (1926–1927), *Silence* (1930), and *Discontent* are at the Museum of Art, Rhode Island School of Design; *Congolais* (1931) is in the Whitney Museum of American Art.

29. EP to DB, August 20, 1931, DBP, LOC.

30. Prophet to Georges Haynes, December 30, 1930, HFP, LOC.

31. EP to DB, August 20, 1931, DBP, LOC.

32. Again, see Patricia A. Morton, *Hybrid Modernities: Architecture and Representation at the 1931 Colonial Exposition, Paris* (Boston, MA: MIT Press, 2003).

33. Du Bois telegram to Prophet, September 12, 1929, DBP, LOC.

34. "Negress Demands Entry to French Art School," *New York Times*, April 24, 1923.

35. Fauset, *Plum Bun*, 115, 345, 95, 109–10, 337.

36. Ibid., 344–45.

37. "Miss Savage Tells Story at Lyceum: Has Not Yet Told Her Mother in Florida," *New York Amsterdam News*, May 16, 1923, 7.

38. I have culled information on Savage from various sources. See Romare Bearden and Harry Henderson, *A History of African-American Artists from 1792 to*

the Present (New York: Pantheon Books, 1993); Jessie Carney Smith, ed., "Augusta Savage," in *Notable Black American Women* (Detroit: Gale Publishers, 1992); Deirdre L. Bibby, *Augusta Savage and the Art Schools of Harlem* (New York: Schomburg Center for Research in Black Culture, 1988); Leininger-Miller, *New Negro Artists in Paris*, 162–201; Augusta Savage, "An Autobiography," *The Crisis* 36 (August 1929): 269, as well as various articles in the *New York Amsterdam News* and other newspapers cited throughout this chapter.

39. Savage, "Autobiography," 269.

40. Ernestine Rose reference for Augusta Savage, August 31, 1927, HFP, LOC.

41. David Levering Lewis, *W. E. B. Du Bois, 1919–1963: The Fight for Equality and the American Century* (New York: Henry Holt/Macmillan, 2001), 82

42. Ibid., 81.

43. W. E. B. Du Bois, "A Lunatic or a Traitor," *The Crisis* (May 1924): 8.

44. Claude Clegg, *The Price of Liberty: African Americans and the Making of Liberia* (Chapel Hill: University of North Carolina Press, 2004); Tony Martin's *Race First: The Ideological and Organizational Struggles of Marcus Garvey and the Universal Negro Improvement Association* (Dover, MA: Majority Press, 1976), *Marcus Garvey, Hero: A First Biography* (Dover, MA: Majority Press, 1983), *Literary Garveyism: Garvey, Black Arts and the Harlem* (Dover, MA: Majority Press, 1983), and *Amy Ashwood Garvey: Pan-Africanist, Feminist, and Mrs. Marcus Garvey No. 1, Or, A Tale of Two Armies* (Dover, MA: Majority Press, 2007).

45. Lester Walton, "Negro Girl Gets Fund to Study Art Abroad," clipping in Julius Rosenwald Archives, Box 445, Folder 12, Fisk University, Nashville, TN; "Miss Augusta Savage," November 11, 1928, Box 445, Folder 12, JRA/FISK, unpublished manuscript.

46. See correspondences between Jones and Arthur, Jones and Edwin R. Embree (who took over as president of the Rosenwald Fund in 1928), and Jones and Frederick Keppel, president of the Carnegie Corporation, JRA/FISK.

47. Augusta Savage application blank for Julius Rosenwald Fund, 3, Box 445, Folder 12, JRA/FISK.

48. George Arthur to George Haynes, January 8, 1930, HFP, LOC.

49. Nina Mjagkij, "A Peculiar Alliance: Julius Rosenwald, the YMCA, and African Americans, 1910–1933," *Journal of American Jewish Archives* 42:2 (1992): 587.

50. Ibid., 587–89.

51. Walton, "Negro Girl Gets Fund," JRA/FISK.

52. Du Bois to Augusta Savage, August 27, 1929, DBP, LOC.

53. EP to DB, September 12, 1929, DBP, LOC.

54. AS to DB, September 22, 1929, DBP, LOC.

55. EP to DB, September 14, 1929, DBP, LOC.

56. AS to DB, September 22, 1929, DBP, LOC.

57. Ibid.

58. Felix Benneteau-Desgrois's progress letter to the Rosenwald Fund, November 1, 1929, JRA/FISK.

59. Savage to Arthur, June 15, 1930, JRA/FISK.

60. Arthur to Savage, May 28, 1930, JRA/FISK.

61. Like Prophet, it is difficult to date Savage's work. Savage's letters and those of her correspondents offer some timeline. That she was in France for two years, unlike Prophet's twelve, helps narrow the time frame.

62. Archives at Bibliothèque Musée de l'Opéra, Bibliothèque nationale de France (Place de l'Opéra) (BNF).

63. Savage to Dorothy Eldridge, September 30, 1930, JRA/FISK.

64. Savage to Edwin Embree, May 1, 1931, JRA/FISK. See also an article written up in *The Metropolitan* by T. R. Post, "Augusta Savage" (January 1935): 28, 51, 66.

65. Savage to Eldridge, September 30, 1930, JRA/FISK.

66. Archives d'Outre Mer, Slotfoms III, 81, no. 595 and V, 2, "La Dépêche africaine et reports policiers," May 30, 1930, Aix-en-Provence, France.

67. Paulette Nardal, "Une femme sculpteur noire," *La Dépêche africaine* (August–September 30, 1930): 5.

68. Nardal, "Une femme sculpteur noire," 5.

69. Ibid.

70. Ibid.

71. I refer the reader to the photograph of *La Divinité nègre* in *La Dépêche africaine*. It is to date the only one that I could find available and does not reproduce clearly.

72. Savage to Embree, May 1, 1931, JRA/FISK.

73. "Miss Augusta Savage Finds No Bread Line in Gay Paris: Sculptress Back," *New York Amsterdam News*, September 2, 1931, 3.

74. Ibid.

75. Augusta Savage, Julius Rosenwald Fund Negro Fellowship review form, March 18, 1936, JRA/FISK.

CHAPTER FOUR. BLACK PARIS: CULTURAL POLITICS AND PROSE

1. For more on Essie and Paul's early years, see Martin Duberman's definitive study, *Paul Robeson: A Biography* (New York: New Press, 1995), 31–46.

2. Paul and Eslanda Robeson Papers, Eslanda Robeson's diary, Box 1, MSRC.

3. University College of London copy of coursework transcript from 1933–35. Eslanda Robeson Papers, Box 1, MSRC.

4. Eslanda Robeson Papers, Box 4, MSRC.

5. For more on West, see Cherene M. Sherrard-Johnson, *Dorothy West's Paradise: A Biography of Class and Color* (New Brunswick, NJ: Rutgers University Press, 2012).

6. Dorothy Peterson to Carl Van Vechten, October 22, 1928, CVV, BEIN.

7. Eleonore Van Notten's *Wallace Thurman's Harlem Renaissance* (New York and Amsterdam, The Netherlands: Editions Rodopi, 1994) provides a wonderful analysis of Thurman's life and contribution to the Harlem Renaissance.

8. ER to CVV, August 28, 1925, CVV, BEIN.

9. ER diary, August 25, 1925, MSRC.

10. ER diary, August 27–28, 1925, MSRC.

11. ER to CVV, September 7, 1925, CVV, BEIN.

12. For more on the Robesons' visit to Paris in 1925, see Duberman, *Paul Robeson*, 87–108.

13. ER to CVV, November 16, 1925, CVV, BEIN.

14. Ibid.

15. Ibid.

16. Ibid.

17. See Duberman, *Paul Robeson*; also see Barbara Ransby's *Eslanda: The Large and Unconventional Life of Mrs. Paul Robeson* (New Haven, CT: Yale University Press, 2013). Although much of this early material can be found in Duberman's definitive study on Paul Robeson, Ransby's work offers us more details about Eslanda Robeson's interior life and evolving political dynamism. Many have suggested that Duberman was too enamored of Paul to treat Essie fairly. Ransby then offers an excellent corrective. The France interactions are also covered in both Duberman and Ransby, while the *Challenge* series with Nardal has been previously taken up in Sharpley-Whiting, *Negritude Women* (Minneapolis: University of Minnesota Press, 2002).

18. See Duberman, *Paul Robeson*, chaps. 8–9, and Ransby, *Eslanda*, chaps. 3–4.

19. While I have used Tovalou in other publications, namely, *Negritude Women*, I will use Houénou here since Essie Robeson uses it in her published work. She refers to him as Kojo in her diary entries.

20. See Philippe Dewitte, *Les mouvements nègres en France, 1919–1939* (Paris: L'Harmattan, 1985); Christopher L. Miller, *Nationalists and Nomads: Essays on Francophone African Literature and Culture* (Chicago: University of Chicago Press, 1998); Harvey Levenstein, *Seductive Journey: American Tourists in France from Jefferson to the Jazz Age* (Chicago: University of Chicago Press, 1998); Babacar M'Baye, "Marcus Garvey and African Francophone Political Leaders of the Early Twentieth Century: Prince Kojo Touvalou Houénou Reconsidered," *Journal of Pan-African Studies* 1:5 (September 2006): 2–19; Emile Derlin Zinsou and Luc Zouménou, *Kojo Touvalou Houénou, Précurseur, 1887–1936: Pannégrisme et Modernité* (Paris: Maisonneuve & Larose, 2004).

21. See Zinsou and Zouménou, *Kojo Touvalou Houénou, Précurseur, 1887–1936*, and Miller, *Nationalists and Nomads*.

22. Kojo Tovalou, "Paris coeur de la race noires," *Les Continents* (October 1, 1924): 1.

23. "Black France" went after a troubling article published in *The Freeman* in January 1922 by Norman Angell, "The Negro Conquest of France." Angell argues that France is a utopia for the Negro that sets a bad example for the white, Western world because of its appearance of granting social equality; he further argues that black Frenchmen prefer to be recognized as French versus the American Negro, who is adamant about his/her blackness. Angell then dovetails into a discussion about black American GIs frequenting white prostitutes in France. Du Bois, for his part, continues his taking apart of Angell's argument in the "Looking Glass" section of the same *Crisis* issue.

24. Eslanda Robeson, "Black Paris," *Challenge* 1:4 (January 1936): 12.

25. Ibid., 12.

26. Ibid., 13.

27. A good deal of discussion on Nardal and *The Review of the Black World* is taken up in Sharpley-Whiting, *Negritude Women*. See also Paulette Nardal, *Beyond Negritude: Essays from "Woman in the City,"* ed. T. Denean Sharpley-Whiting (Albany: State University of New York Press, 2009) for more on Nardal's writing and activism once she left France for Martinique at the beginning of World War II.

28. ER diary, June 16, 1932, MSRC.

29. For more on Nardal, *The Review of the Black World*, and the Robeson interview, see Sharpley-Whiting, *Negritude Women*.

30. Clara Shepard, "L'institut normal et industriel de Tuskegee/Tuskegee Normal and Industrial Institute," *La Revue du monde noir/The Review of the Black World* (December 1931): 15–16.

31. Shepard, "Les Noirs américains et les langues étrangères"/"The Utility of Foreign Languages for American Negros," *La Revue du monde noir/The Review of the Black World* (February 1932): 30–01.

32. ER diary, June 17, 1932, MSRC.

33. Robeson, "Black Paris," *Challenge* (June 1936): 9–12.

34. Ibid., 14.

35. ER to CVV, November 16, 1925, CVV, BEIN.

36. Robeson, "Black Paris, 14.

37. Duberman, *Robeson*, 130–32.

38. ER diary, June 13, 18, 1932, MSRC.

39. ER diary, June 13, 1932, MSRC.

40. ER to Harold Jackman, August 30, 1932, JWJ Robeson, BEIN.

41. See both Duberman, *Paul Robeson*, and Ransby, *Eslanda*, for more on Eslanda Robeson's journalistic ambitions.

CHAPTER FIVE. EPILOGUE: "HOMEWARD TUG AT A POET'S HEART"—THE RETURN

1. Both Florences—Jones and Mills—had left Paris and died well before the war; A'Lelia Walker's trip to Paris was her one and only. She, too, died before the war in 1931. Ethel Waters preferred America to France. She did not return to Paris during the heyday of Bricktop; hence, she, too, had come and gone before the outbreak of World War II.

2. Frank C. Taylor with Gerald Cook, *Alberta Hunter: A Celebration in Blues* (New York: McGraw-Hill, 1987), 151.

3. Mark Miller, *High Hat, Trumpet and Rhythm: The Life and Music of Valaida Snow* (Ontario, Canada: Mercury Press, 2007), 110–11. Snow has given contradictory accounts of her time and treatment in Copenhagen. See also "Valaida Faces Annulment Suit," *New York Amsterdam Star-News*, June 20, 1942, 2; Julius J. Adams, "Swap 2 Nazis for Valaida Snow," *New York Amsterdam Star-News*, June 13, 1942, 1, 5; Alfred Duckett, "Life in a Nazi Prison Camp, *Washington Afro American*, April 24, 1943, 1, 9. The Danish National Archives in Copenhagen has several police reports regarding Snow's confinement. Translation was provided for me by a curator. Mark Miller also draws from Danish newspaper accounts. The Simon Wiesenthal Center in Los Angeles also has some interesting materials on Snow.

4. Miller, *High Hat*, 111–12.

5. Adams, "Swap 2 Nazis for Valaida Snow," 5.

6. *Chicago Defender*, April 2, 1939, col. 5, 18; "Menaced by European War Rumbles," *New York Amsterdam News*, September 2, 1939, 16; that war was imminent was announced in fall 1938, "Actors Flee War Zone: Foreign News Fails to Alter Singer's Plan," *New York Amsterdam News*, October 1, 1938, 1.

7. Ada Bricktop Smith Papers, Letter to Blonzetta, October 1, 1939, MARBL.

ARCHIVES AND LIBRARIES

ACM/SI	Anacostia Community Museum, Smithsonian Institute, Washington, DC
ADOM	Archives d'Outre Mer, Aix-en-Provence, France
AMIS	Amistad Research Center, Tulane University, New Orleans, Louisiana
ASA/SI	National Air and Space Museum Archives, Smithsonian Institute, Washington, DC
BEIN	Yale Collection of American Literature, Beinecke Rare Book and Manuscript Library, Yale University, New Haven, Connecticut
BHV	Bibliothèque historique de la Ville de Paris, Paris, France
BNF	Bibliothèque nationale de France (Richelieu and Mitterand), Paris, France
BMO	Bibliothèque Musée de l'Opéra (Place de l'Opéra), Paris, France
CBMR	Center for Black Music Research, Chicago, Illinois
CHM	Chicago History Museum, Chicago, Illinois
DNA	Danish National Archives/Rigsarkivet, Copenhagen, Denmark
JHL	John Hay Library, Special Collections and Archives, Brown University, Providence, Rhode Island
JPA	John P. Adams Library, Special Collections, Rhode Island College, Providence, Rhode Island
JRA/FISK	Julius Rosenwald Archives, Special Collections, Fisk University, Nashville, Tennessee

KHS   Kansas Historical Society, Topeka, Kansas

LC/STAN   Eugene Lerner Collection, Stanford University, Stanford, California

LOC   Library of Congress, Washington, DC

MARBL   Manuscript, Archives, and Rare Book Library, Emory University, Atlanta, Georgia

MSRC   Moorland-Spingarn Research Center, Howard University, Washington, DC

SCHOM   Arthur B. Schomburg Center for Research in Black Culture, New York Public Library, New York, New York

SWC   Simon Wiesenthal Center, Los Angeles, California

SELECTED BIBLIOGRAPHY*

Allan, Tony. *Americans in Paris*. Chicago, IL: Contemporary Books, 1977.

Bearden, Romare, and Harry Henderson. *A History of African-American Artists from 1792 to the Present*. New York, NY: Pantheon Books, 1993.

Benjamin, Tritobia Hayes. *The Life and Art of Lois Mailou Jones*. San Francisco, CA: Pomegranate, 1994.

Benstock, Shari. *Women of the Left Bank*. Austin: University of Texas Press, 1986.

Bernard, Catherine. *Afro-American Artists in Paris: 1919–1939*. New York, NY: Hunter College Art Galleries, 1989.

Bibby, Deirdre. *Augusta Savage and the Art Schools of Harlem*. New York, NY: Arthur B. Schomburg Center for Research in Black Culture, New York Public Library, 1988.

Chadwick, Whitney, and Tirza True Latimer. *The Modern Woman Revisited: Paris between the Wars*. New Brunswick, NJ: Rutgers University Press, 2003.

Dewitte, Phillippe. *Les mouvements nègres en France pendant les entre-deux-guerre*. Paris: L'Harmattan, 1985.

Duval, Daphne Harrison. *Black Pearls: Blues Queens of the 1920s*. New Brunswick, NJ: Rutgers University Press, 1990.

Fabre, Michel. *Black American Writers in France, 1840–1980: From Harlem to Paris*. Urbana: University of Illinois Press, 1993.

Fabre, Michel, and John A. Williams. *Way B(l)ack Then and Now: A Street Guide to African-Americans in Paris*. Paris: Centre d'Etudes Afro-Americaines, Université de la Sorbonne-Nouvelle, 1992.

Finkelstein, Hope. "Augusta Savage: Sculpting the African American Identity." MA thesis, City University of New York, 1990.

Fitch, Noel Riley. *Sylvia Beach and the Lost Generation*. New York, NY: W. W. Norton, 1963.

Flanner, Janet. *Paris Journal*. New York, NY: Atheneum, 1965.

Jackson, Jeffrey. *Making Jazz French: Music and Modern Life in Interwar Paris*. Durham, NC: Duke University Press, 2003.

Jules-Rosette, Bennetta. *Josephine Baker in Art and Life: The Icon and the Image*. Urbana: University of Illinois Press, 2007.

---

*Sources cited throughout the volume appear in full at the first citation in each chapter in the endnotes.

Kellner, Bruce, ed. *Letters of Carl Van Vechten*. New Haven, CT: Yale University Press, 1987.

Kirschenbaum, Blossom S. "Nancy Elizabeth Prophet, Sculptor." *Sage: A Scholarly Journal on Black Women* 4:1 (Spring 1987): 45–52.

Levering Lewis, David. *When Harlem Was in Vogue*. New York, NY: Alfred A. Knopf, 1981.

Leininger-Miller, Theresa. *New Negro Artists in Paris: African American Painters and Sculptors in the City of Light, 1922–1934*. New Brunswick, NJ: Rutgers University Press, 2001.

Lottman, Herbert. *The Left Bank: Writers, Artists, and Politics from the Popular Front to the Cold War*. Chicago, IL: University of Chicago Press, 1982.

Rampersad, Arnold. *The Life of Langston Hughes, Volume 1: 1902–1941, I, Too, Sing America*. Oxford: Oxford University Press, 2002.

Rose, Phyllis. *Jazz Cleopatra*. New York, NY: Doubleday, 1989.

Shack, William. *Harlem in Montmartre: A Paris Jazz Story between the Great Wars*. Berkeley: University of California Press, 2001.

Smith, Jessie Carney, ed., *Notable Black American Women*. Detroit, MI: Gale Press, 1972.

Stovall, Tyler. *Paris Noir: African Americans in the City of Light*. New York, NY: Houghton Mifflin, 1996.

Wilkerson Freeman, Sarah, and Beverly Greene Bond. *Tennessee Women: Their Lives and Times, Volume 1*. Athens: University of Georgia Press, 2009.

Willis, Deborah. *Posing Beauty: African American Images from the 1890s to the Present*. New York, NY: W. W. Norton, 2009.

Wiser, William. *The Crazy Years: Paris in the Twenties*. New York, NY: Atheneum, 1983.

———. *The Great Good Place: American Expatriate Women in Paris*. New York, NY: W. W. Norton, 1991.

———. *The Twilight Years: Paris in the 1930s*. New York, NY: Carroll & Graf, 2000.

INDEX